Poetry, Politics and Culture

Poetry, Politics and Culture
Essays on Indian Texts and Contexts

Akshaya Kumar

First published 2009 by Routledge

2 Park Square, Milton Park, Abingdon, Oxfordshire OX14 4RN
711 Third Avenue, New York, NY 10017

Routledge is an imprint of the Taylor & Francis Group, an informa business

First issued in paperback 2018

Transferred to Digital Printing 2009

Typeset by
Star Compugraphics Private Limited
5–CSC, First Floor, Near City Apartments
Vasundhara Enclave
Delhi 110 096

British Library Cataloguing-in-Publication Data
A catalogue record of this book is available from the British Library

ISBN: 978-0-415-48005-5 (hbk)
ISBN: 978-1-138-38420-0 (pbk)

For Madhu, Nafeesa and Tathagat

Contents

Preface

The making of this book has its own little narrative. After my first book on the poetry of A. K. Ramanujan, I was advised by my friends and colleagues that it was time I switch over to something else—preferably writing on fiction or theory. Even my own pragmatic professional self informed me that poetry has hardly any market, and a critical book on it is the surest way to oblivion. I indeed started writing a book on literary theory after 'deconstruction'. I had done enough spade-work and had written about seventy pages as well. Suddenly, I realized that theory is at best my second choice, and that market or no-market, poetry continues to be my sole stay. I counselled myself and resolved that I cannot write a book on something I do not put my stakes on. Poetry files had to stage a comeback on my desktop.

Private passions do not necessarily translate into academic ventures. But what saw me through this predicament were my compulsive forays into poetry in various seminars straddling across issues as diverse as global terrorism, diaspora, female foeticide, morality in public life, the future of the family in India and even prison reforms. Instead of being an Arnoldian substitute for prayer, poetry has always been to me an exercise of participation in the secular domain. It is this interventionist capacity of poetry that the present book seeks to explore and espouse. The underlying endeavour is first, to retrieve poetry from the stranglehold of scriptural solemnity, and then to pitch it as an instrument of assertion, protest and participation in the arena of everyday culture. My embattled postcolonial situation demands a political reading of poetry, its appreciation in terms of its capacity to enfigure power and to negotiate history. Poetic subtlety does not obfuscate reality or postpone history; rather it brings it into prominence. Poetry, politics and culture constitute a continuum, where none precedes or supersedes the other; rather all the three co-appear as supplementary discourses, acting and countering on each other in a dialogic way.

For the purpose of precision and focus, I have relied on Indian texts and contexts that need to be explored beyond the oft-orientalized sanskritic past/poetry or much-globalized Indian English present. The book makes a critical shift towards the study of an immense variety of language-literatures (*bhasha sahitya*) that, despite the so-called postcolonial patronage, continue to suffer relative neglect. The present endeavour confines itself to the discussion of three streams of Indian poetry—Hindi, Punjabi and Indian English. The selection of the three languages is strategic; at present all the three languages are locked in a fierce battle of supremacy in India, and as such provide a compatible frame of comparative analysis. The selection is also determined by the fact that my own competence of Indian languages does not go beyond these three. Punjabi is my mother tongue; (Indian) English is the language of my profession and as such, a la A. K. Ramanujan, the father-tongue of my cultural make-up; and Hindi (in its dialectal form) has been the language of my everyday interaction with my friends and classmates of Haryana—the place of my naturalized belonging.

What, however, prompted me to undertake a book-length project on Indian poetry was the sudden proliferation of essays written and published over the last four–five years as part of my UGC-sponsored post-doctoral major research project on comparative Indian poetry. In the present book only four of these previously published essays are incorporated; the rest have been written exclusively for the book. The first chapter of the book was published in the *South Asian Review*. The first three chapters covered in Section II of the book were published in *Indian Literature*. Permission to include these essays in the book is gratefully acknowledged. The essays published before have been sufficiently modified and updated. Though written over a period, these essays are informed by a consistent vision according to which poetry not only re-writes 'reality', it even claims postcolonial agency to transform culture and society in tangible ways.

But the most fundamental impulse that nurtured my interest in poetry and a book on it, stems from my literary parentage. My father, Dr. O. P. Gupta, a Ph.D. on Walt Whitman, not only wrote poetry in three languages—Hindi, Punjabi and English—he wrote its criticism too. In moments of stalemate, he used to provide me the necessary break. What lends special poignancy to my book is that it comes in the backdrop of his prolonged illness which incapacitates him totally. Neither does he recognize, nor speak; yet I have written this book almost in a silent dialogue with him. During the process of the book I also lost my mother, Soma Gupta, an avid reader of literary fiction. The writing of the book sustained me during these bouts of trial and attrition.

During moments of self-doubt that surfaced quite often during the process of the book, reprieve came from Narendra Kumar Oberoi, a senior colleague and friend who hates to be addressed as 'professor'. An author of an infinite number of unwritten books, his animated telephonic conversations were no less than long classical recitals that charged my sagging spirits. His indirections directed my venture in ways that are too subtle to be verbalized. My friends—Ashutosh, Anup and Rajkumar, have co-travelled with me, everywhere and anywhere. The book is as much their journey as mine. I am fortunate enough to enjoy solid family-support in my academic pursuits. My wife Madhu and children Nafeesa and Tathagat have been my emotional bank all through. At a very intimate and informal level, I feel like extending them co-authorship of the book.

My activist friends Manjit Singh, Satyapal Sehgal and Sukhdev Singh deserve to be specially mentioned. They lent me easy access to their personal collections with a sense of camaraderie that I will always cherish and find hard to reciprocate. My colleagues in language departments, research scholars and students constitute my primary constituency that provides me both a necessary boundary and an engaging perspective. The book, thus, in a way, enjoys a much 'enlarged' authorship than is suggested by my name alone as its formal author. I finally thank the entire team of Routledge India, and Dr. Nilanjan Sarkar in particular, for approving and then processing my script for publication with professional finesse.

Akshaya Kumar
Chandigarh
July 2008

Introduction

Literary space is singularly monopolized by the aesthetics of prose —both fictional and non-fictional. Despite apocalyptic deaths and re-births, the novel, theory, autobiography and essay continue to occupy centre stage, pushing poetry to the literary margins, if not into a state of irretrievable extinction.[1] Its criticism is all the more scanty and sparse. This book attempts to remove the misgivings that have often been propagated about the potentialities of poetry in negotiating with the shifting dynamics of politics, history and culture. These misgivings could be summed up as: one, poetry is illusion; two, poetry is non-dialogic; three, poetry cannot make anything happen; and four, most polemically, poetry is dead.[2] The consensus is so unrelenting that any critical re-opening of each of these final truths amounts to challenging time. Championing poetry or even defending it, that too as the very discourse of politics, history and culture, in an environment that is so utterly sceptical about its potentialities could be dismissed as a mere atavistic lapse into some defunct romanticism. Advocating its popular revival amounts to an intellectual audacity, which perhaps the present book stops short of.[3]

This book is an extended endeavour to re-view the generic merits of Indian poetry in postcolonial contexts of political agency and participation. The effort is to underline and assert the role that poetry has played along with politics, ideology and culture in shaping not just our outlook, but innermost responses as well. Poetry is neither a secondary pursuit, nor a passive reflection of the so-called primary or basic discourses of life that vary from religion to economy-driven ideology.[4] It is neither just 'an exercise of persuasion, nor mere enunci-ation', nor even a simple 'commemoration' of something outside it.[5] The effort is not to assert a fundamental 'superiority of poetry' over other discourses; such an extreme stance would only distance it from the praxis of life, defeating the very purpose of its production.[6] Poetry is a competing as well as a complementary discourse of participation and mediation (if not of overt alignment and commitment), and it is in this sense that its position needs to be re-assessed and re-mapped. This book maps the evolution of Indian poetry from its quasi-spiritual nationalist longings to its present-day subalternist aspirations. It is in this sense that the book is not just an academic exercise; it is an intervention of a kind hitherto not imagined in the context of any critical study of Indian poetry as such.

Mere political poetry that borders on propaganda or sloganeering, or religious poetry that provokes originary battle cries does not explain the subtle negotiations that 'awakened poetry' in general enters into with the structures of power.[7] The interface of poetry with politics and culture is therefore multi-layered, and too intrinsic to be contained within any extended introduction. So, departing from the usual conventions, the present endeavour contains as many as three mini-introductions, each prefacing a distinct section of the book. These mini-introductions cover various facets of poetry such as its capability to imagine and re-write the home/nation along with its contesting and competing nativities and its spilling borders; its stakes in political and social activism; its implications in the processes of culture, religion and history. The introductions are deliberately short and precise, as the method of argumentation in the book is more illustrative, less theoretical. Besides this, each chapter contains its own theoretical premise and corollary that it subsequently consolidates through textual evidence.

The primary scope of the book is Indian poetry in its three 'prominent' language streams—Indian English, Hindi and Punjabi— with two minor exceptions.[8] A major part of chapter 10 in the final section pertains to the study of Marathi dalit poetry, and a Gujarati text available in Hindi translation has been used in the chapter on Meera. The time-span covered ranges from the early nationalist/ colonial period to the present-day post-nationalist era. Among the Indian English poets, while the thrust of the study remains on the post-independence poets such as Nissim Ezekiel, A. K. Ramanujan, Jayanta Mahapatra, Kamala Das, Keki Daruwalla, Arun Kolatkar and Agha Shahid Ali, the poets of the late 1990s—Rukmini Bhaya Nair, Sudeep Sen, Vikram Seth, Meena Alexander, Sujata Bhatt, Imtiaz Dharker and others—have also been discussed in the context of the expanding frontiers of Indian English poetry as a whole. Among the Hindi poets, the range is more inclusive. Kabir and Meera have been studied in terms of their latter-day manifestations in different language literatures/translations; Bhartendu, Maithilisharan Gupt, Dinkar, Muktibodh, Nirala, Mahadevi Verma, Bharati and Dhoomil and a host of contemporary poets such as Alokdhanva, Manglesh Dabral, Leeladhar Jagudi, Rajesh Joshi, Anamika, Katyayni, Gagan Gill, Ashok Vajpeyi et al. have been studied in the context of the ever-shifting configuration of India as a nation. Among the Punjabi poets, the 'iconic' poets of the earlier generation, namely, Amrita Pritam, 'Musafir', Shiv Kumar Batalavi and Pash have been discussed and analyzed with a number of other poets like Lal Singh 'Dil', Sant Ram Udasi, Manjit Tiwana, Shashi Samundra, Sukhvinder Amrit and others. A chapter is devoted to the study of dalit poets such as Omprakash Valmiki, Namdeo Dhasal, Gurmeet Kallarmajri and a number of dalit poets of the 1990s.

But since the study is not purely author-specific, the emphasis shifts from the poets to the poetry in general, its location and timing. More than the authors and their chosen texts, the different streams of poetry have been analyzed in terms of their stakes in the political and cultural processes of the nation. Despite the broad trajectory of the work, the so-called representative poetic texts from each of the three streams have been included for analysis and argument. The poets/texts that could not be accommodated in the main body of the chapters have been used in the Notes section to complement and buttress the arguments. In the scheme of the book, the notes at times become as good as parallel essays for they contain (counter-) comments/observations that do not otherwise fit in the running logic of the main text.

The methodology is comparative wherein each stream becomes a critical context for the other. Poetry becomes the text and the context both, suggestive of its self-reflexive, meta-critical character. Even in chapters that do not cover more than one stream of poetry, the implied methodology remains comparative and evolves as critical dialogue among the different streams of poetry. Within the overarching frame of comparative study, insights from recent cultural theories such as new historicism, subaltern historiography and postcolonialism have been deployed to understand the textual and the discursive formations of poetry. Critical theorists such as Stephen Greenblatt, Hayden White, Benedict Anderson, Bakhtin, Harold Bloom, Fredric Jameson, Partha Chatterjee, Ranjit Guha, Homi Bhabha, Edward Said, Ashis Nandy, Eric Hobsbawm and others have frequently been invoked to understand the operation as well as the implication of literary imagination in postcolonial power games and vice versa.

A comparative work that involves literatures in three languages entails a lot of translation. Most of the Hindi and Punjabi poets/texts included in the book have not been translated independently.

Despite the resurgence in translation of late, poetry continues to be the last choice of translators. The quotes inserted in the book have been translated for the first time by myself. These translations tend to retain the thematic and syntactic grids of the original, yet there is no such claim made about their quality. They remain of a working nature only and are at best functional translations. Some of the texts that are available in translation have, of course, been used as such, to avoid additional labour. If there is any inconsistency in the quality of translation, it is because of varying levels of linguistic competence in the three languages. The original quotes of Hindi and Punjabi poetry have not been retained. However, where it is absolutely essential, the originals appear in parenthesis in Roman script. But such instances are very rare.

Occasionally, non-poetic texts—such as plays and skits—have been used as complementary texts to extend the argument of the chapters. But most often these non-poetic texts are not so non-poetic because they contain a lot of poetry in the form of chorus, prologue/epilogue and even dialogues. These texts, often heralded as long poems, dramatic poems or poetical plays in their respective language-traditions, trudge along the fault line of poetry and prose. Texts like *Bharat Durdasha, Andha Yug* in Hindi, *Palang Panghure* in Punjabi and *The Golden Gate* in Indian English defy easy generic divisions and classifications.

The three sections of the book entitled 'Mapping "Nation/Post-nation"', 'Re-writing Culture' and 'Disseminating Dissent' are not mutually exclusive. The chapters contained in one section may as well belong to another without much thematic deviance. However, there is a definite trajectory covered through these sections; the first section maps out the macro-level matrices of Indian poetry, the subsequent two sections reveal the pressures of sub-/post-national imperatives and their articulation in poetry. These sections bring forth the inherent currents of re-writing and internal self-protest through which any dynamic postcolonial nation renews and revalidates itself. Far from the discourse of facile resolution and esoteric abstractions, Indian poetry, as each section unfolds, gravitates towards the articulation of the silenced subaltern. Each section is so structured that it includes as far as possible at least a chapter/text each on all the three streams of Indian poetry covered in the book.

Finally, a word needs to be spoken about the evolution of the book to account for the possible discontinuities and gaps in its execution.

The book as such is not a one-time event, for four essays (the details are provided in the Preface) collected here are written on different occasions and at various intervals of time. Of course, even these essays appear in the book in their revised and updated form. Written over the last four years, these essays may not ideally be taken as organic 'chapters' of a book, yet they are the building blocks of a sustained critical endeavour that seeks to assign political participation and agency to poetry, hitherto allowed little interventionist role in our practical life. Also, there are many poets and texts that could not be incorporated in the over-all scheme of the book. Since the book does not survey different streams of poetry with any encyclopaedic intention, such exclusions could not be helped. An imbalance in the book creeps in on account of the limited language-streams covered in it. Of the three Indian languages included for study in the book, two are predominantly North Indian, which in itself is a limiting factor. For lack of competence in Urdu, even the book's North Indian character could not be fully realized. Ghalib, Iqbal, Faiz, Ali Sardar Jafari, Firaq Gorakhpuri, Kaifi Azmi and other Urdu poets are of course available in multiple translations but their translated versions failed to register in the mind as such.

Notes

1. The novel stages comebacks after its so-called exhaustions. Steiner, commenting on the post-Joycean phase of the English/European novel made this pronouncement: 'We are getting tired of our novels . . . genres rise, genres fall, the epic, the verse epic, the formal verse tragedy. Great moments, then they ebb. Novels will continue to be written for quite a while but increasingly, the search is on for hybrid forms, what we will call rather crassly fact/fiction. . . . What novel can today quite compete with the very best of immediate narrative?' (quoted in Rushdie 2002: 54). Countering such 'imperial views', Rushdie defends the novel in the postcolonial context: 'a new novel is emerging, a post-colonial novel, a de-centred, transnational, inter-lingual, cross-cultural novel; and that in this new world order or disorder, we find a better explanation of the contemporary novel's health' (ibid.: 57). After a temporary eclipse, literary theory staged a comeback in the mid-1980s. At least in the metropolitan academia of the First World, theory has overtaken literature/creative writing. The following quote from Quentin Skinner's edited book *The Return of Grand Theory in the Human Sciences* explains theory's resurgence despite resistance from some quarters: 'We, next need to note that, during the past two decades, there has been an unashamed return to the deliberate construction of precisely those grand theories of human

nature and conduct which Wright Mills and his generation had hoped to outlaw from any central place in the human sciences' (Skinner 2000: 13). The autobiography has also staged a remarkable comeback. Now, instead of the elite, it becomes an instrument of assertion and self-presentation in the hands of the subaltern. A series of autobiographies by dalits and women has displaced literary preferences. Many fiction writers herald the arrival of non-fiction as the emerging form of the post-9/11 phase of history. V. S. Naipaul, in an interview, declares that non-fiction is more powerful than fiction and that the novel is dead as it is incompetent to take up pressing civilizational problems. He says, 'And the fictional form was going to force you to do things with the material, to dramatize it in a certain way. I thought non-fiction gave one a chance to explore the world, the other world, the world that one didn't know fully' (quoted in Donadio 2005).

2. Plato's distrust with regard to the very veracity of poetry, argued so eloquently in his *The Republic*, is evident in the following excerpt from the book: 'the imitative poet implants an evil constitution, for he indulges the irrational nature which has no discernment of greater and less, but thinks the same thing at one time great and at another small—he is a manufacturer of images and is very far removed from the truth' (Book X, see http://classics. mit.edu/Plato/republic). Bakhtin, the proponent of dialogism, also holds that poetry, as a genre, is 'authoritarian, dogmatic and conservative sealing itself off from the influence of extraliterary social dialects' (1998: 287). Ironically enough, the poets themselves have expressed reservations about the capacities of poetry. According to A. K. Ramanujan, 'Poems aren't even words/enough to rankle, infect,/or make smallest incisions' ('Any Cow's Horn Can Do It', 1995: 94). Jayanta Mahapatra also questions the convictions of a poet:

> This is a man who talks of pain
> as though it belonged to him alone.
> Maybe he has invented it himself
> and made a virtue of it.
> Maybe he is a poet.
> ('Of a Questionable Conviction', 1992: 36.)

Adorno makes the infamous apocalyptic pronouncement in the wake of the Holocaust: 'To write poetry after Auschwitz is barbaric. And this corrodes even the knowledge of why it has become impossible to write poetry today. Absolute reification, which pre-supposed intellectual progress as one of its elements, is now preparing to absorb mind entirely' (1981: 210).

3. In an essay published in *The Hudson Review* (2003), Dana Gioia, argues in favour of poetry's comeback in the new electronic age: 'verse has changed into a growth industry, though its rehabilitation has happened mostly off the printed page.' However, in the very next line, there is some scepticism about its quality: 'Whatever one thinks of the artistic quality of these new poetic

forms, one must concede that at the very least they reassuringly demonstrate the abiding human need for poetry' (ibid.: 25).

4. Here, the views of culture critics like Raymond Williams are very useful as they bring dynamism into the orthodox dialectical hierarchy of 'base versus superstructure'. Instead of 'reflection', his preferred paradigm is that of 'mediation' between the two: 'The simplest notions of a superstructure, which is still by no means entirely abandoned, had been the reflection, the imitation or the reproduction of the reality of the base in the superstructure in a more or less direct way . . . the modern notion of "mediation", in which something more than simple reflection or reproduction—actively occurs' (2001: 163–64).

5. Suvir Kaul, in his book *Poems of Nation, Anthems of Empire*, while maintaining that poetry is not 'an exercise of inwardness' (2000: 8), however, confines eighteenth-century British poetry to mere exercises in persuasion and enunciation: 'the important work performed by the eighteenth-century poems we have considered here, their persuasive dynamic, is their enunciation of both the energetic possibilities, and the limiting realities of the idea of a great and imperial nation' (ibid.: 272). Philippe Lacoue-Labarthe, while studying a poem by Paul Celan observes: 'the poem commemorates. Its experience is an experience of memory' (1999: 21).

6. Under the rubric of New Criticism, poetic truth was accorded greater sanctity and authenticity over any other form of truth.

7. Namvar Singh's observation on the 'awakened poet' in this regard is clinching: 'The awakened poet during the process of his poetic-act, keeps on defining the political contexts in a very cautious manner and thus while avoiding to write directly on political issues, gives every creative piece a definite political meaning' (Kavita aur Rajniti 2003: 216).

8. The three languages are prominent in the sense that English continues to be the language of metropolitan India, Hindi is officially the national language and is spoken by the vast majority of Indians, Punjabi is one of the major North Indian languages which is becoming global due to the widespread Punjabi diaspora.

Section 1
Mapping 'Nation'/'Post-nation'

Section 1: Introduction

What could be the genre of the 'nation' in the emerging scenario of displacement from within and without? If displacement, as is fiercely argued, is a space of negotiation and exchange, its genre should also be as much negotiated. But before the question is ever raised, it is settled in favour of fiction without much critical debate. In a sweeping critical estimate, we are told that fiction not only actually participates in the mapping of the nation; it continues to be its allegory/narrative even in the era of multinationalism/multiculturalism.[1] Thus, very conveniently and without much critical contestation, fiction becomes the genre of the home and homelessness as well. It is presumed that poetry is a discourse of un-negotiated rootedness and centripetal belonging. The implied distrust on poetry stems from two a priori notions—one, that poetry is hardly a discourse of negotiation and exchange that any multicultural situation entails, and two, that poetry is more a discourse of a cohesive and rooted vertical self, than of the horizontally proliferating selves. The spatial strengths of poetry have always been ignored in favour of its temporal depth.

Poetry is not a one-time invention/event that is complete and conclusive; it undergoes revisions and mutations as any other secular genre does. The ever-expanding corpus of Indian diaspora poetry— more so in native tongues than perhaps in Indian English—offers a range of responses to the condition of displacement right from a nostalgic invocation of a ghettoized self in the embattled multicultural situation to its intelligent negotiation. Within the new space of this poetry, cultures do meet, quarrel and negotiate with varying degrees of accommodation and assimilation. From a discourse of roots, it becomes a discourse of routes, of shifting destinations, of changing locations, and of many homes. Nation, post-nation and nativity—the possible addresses of the self-in-exile—enrich the texture of Indian diaspora poetry in ways that are unprecedented. Amitav Ghosh identifies 'epic without text' as the new genre of Indian diaspora.[2]

The first chapter of the section deals with the stakes that Hindi poetry has evinced in the making of India as a nation-state through a detailed textual analysis of eight seminal texts pertaining to the pre- and postcolonial period. Since the rise of Khari Boli as a medium of mainstream Hindi literary medium parallels the evolution of the Indian freedom struggle, the study of Hindi poetry as the preferred genre of Hindi writers has the potentiality to offer us a non-political perspective on the mapping of the nation-centric imagination of the people of the dominant Hindi heartland. The poets covered are Bhartendu, Maithilisharan Gupt, Subhadra Kumari Chauhan, Dinkar, Dharamveer Bharati, Muktibodh and Dhoomil. Most of these poets were in the vanguard of the Indian freedom struggle and post-independence social movements. While Gupt and Dinkar were hailed as national poets/poet-laureates (*rashtra kavis*), Bhartendu was a frontline Indian reformer during the nineteenth century; Nirala often had his encounters with the nationalist elite from Gandhi to Nehru. Subhadra Kumari Chauhan actually took part in the freedom struggle as a Gandhian *satyagrahi*. The participation of the poets in political meetings/programmes/rallies suggests that there was never a wedge between the political and the poetical.

If, in the pre-independence period, the modern statist imperatives collided and colluded with the traditional cultural nationalist moorings of Hindi imagination, in the post-independence period the post-statist aspects begin to surface and threaten any process of the consolidation of the state along elitist lines. The nature of binaries changes radically. In fact, the binaries fracture further into multi-directional fragments, generating a hybridity whose structure is no longer bicultural or bipolar. The erstwhile cultural encounter of the East versus the West or the colonized versus the colonial gives way to an ideological encounter of the elite versus the subaltern or capitalism versus socialism. The process of making the nation-state turns self-critical as Hindi poets take a society-centric approach. The opening of the political discourse from statist to society-centric paradigms in post-independence India is very much anticipated by the evolving Hindi poetic imagination.

The second chapter, a natural extension of the first, explores the configuration of home/homelessness in the Hindi poetry of the post-1990s—a period which has brought about fundamental changes in the course of human civilization. Most of the poets covered in the chapter happen to be *janvadis*, who, while protesting against the oppressive nature of the nation-state, are strongly sceptical about the liberating potentials of globalization. Much against the growing political consensus on the politics of privatization, poets like Leeladhar Jagudi, Alokdhanva, Rajesh Joshi, Arun Kamal, Manglesh Dabral, Prayag Shukla and Katyayni offer a sustained poetical protest that reveals its essentially counter-hegemonic character. Hindi poetry of this period steps out of the cultural nationalist hangovers as it clamours for a people-centric voice. The possessive centripetal tendencies do not give way to radical centrifugal ones, but the sense of displacement from within does generate possibilities of negotiated and critical belonging in the Hindi poetry of the post-1990s.

In the next chapter—entitled 'From Hyphen to High-fun: Towards a Topology of New Indian English Diaspora Poetry'—the cultural dynamics of the post-independence Indian diaspora have been mapped in terms of its shifting topologies of space and time. As the new diaspora gains greater mobility across cultures and civilizations, it becomes increasingly 'rootless' which it celebrates with the convictions of a postmodern nomad. The Indian English poets, of the post-1990s in particular, are at home in the global arena as they defy postcolonial identitarian politics in favour of a new, though seemingly, 'wishful' identity of global citizens. The chapter undertakes a close textual study of the poetry of Dom Moraes, A. K. Ramanujan and Agha Shahid Ali in terms of their distinct strategies of negotiation within the space of diaspora. The major part of the chapter is, however, devoted to the new breed of young poets such as Vikram Seth, Sujata Bhatt, Meena Alexander, Suniti Namjoshi, Sudeep Sen, Rukmini Bhaya Nair, Jeet Thayil et al. Due to constraints of space, only one anthology each of these poets has been focused upon for analysis.

The latter generation among the new diaspora poets actually seems to arrive at a post-diasporic state of consciousness wherein the binary between the native and diasporic no longer remains functional. The universality that these poets aim at is not the metaphysical unity/objectivity of the erstwhile epic poetry; it is rather 'a play of perspectives' or a discourse of 'epistemic cooperation'.[3] These post-diasporic poets evince some common characteristics that lend their poetry a radical distinctness. One, these poets clamour for a pre-lapsarian, pre-political past which militates against the division of humanity into parochial nationalist boundaries. Two, these poets do not evince centripetal tendencies; the erstwhile nostalgia for the homeland gives way to a ready recognition of the post-national, multicultural world order. The range and scope of inter-textuality becomes manifold, so much so that almost without exception these poets are compelled to give extended notes on the cross-cultural references they use in their poems.

Notes

1. In his *Nation and Narration*, Homi Bhabha rallies around the novel as the possible narrative of postcolonial 'ambivalences', 'temporalities', 'ruptures' both from within and without. Though he avoids zeroing in on a specific genre, yet the characteristic features of 'double time', 'transactional social reality', 'instability of knowledge', 'liminality' (1990: Introduction) etc., which he identifies for his kind of hybrid postcolonialism befit very much the realist fiction theorized by Lukacs, Bakhtin, Walter Benjamin, Benedict Anderson, and others. Though Fredric Jameson uses the term 'Third World literature' as the allegorical site of Third World nationalism, yet for purposes of illustration he too depends on fiction. For Jameson, Third World literature becomes 'national allegory' when it 'develops out of predominantly western machineries of representation, such as the novel' (2000a: 69).
2. 'The links between India and her diaspora are lived within the imagination. It is therefore an epic relationship: an epic without a text, which is all for the better perhaps, for if that text were ever written it would be a shabby, bedraggled, melancholy kind of epic—but still formally, an epic it would have to be. It is because this relationship is so much a relationship of the imagination that the specialists of the imaginations—writers—play so important a part within it' (Ghosh 2002b: 247–48).
3. R. Radhakrishnan describes the dynamics of new configurations of universality and objectivity in the multicultural context: 'universality has given way to radically heterogeneous locations and subject positions that refuse implication in relational macro-narratives. . . . The ontological status of objectivity is reconceptualized as an epistemological property of perspectives, which in turn are mandated to look for objectivity as a function of their never-ending negotiations among themselves' (2003: 36–38). Satya P. Mohanty spells out the contours of 'epistemic cooperation' in the emerging multicultural context thus: 'Difference and individuality are not opposed to a deeper communality, a community of purpose. Even in a world that is not fundamentally structured by (cultural) inequality, healthy pluralism is more likely than cultural homogeneity to lead to the fruitful coordination of our epistemic efforts. That is, I believe, the strongest argument that can be made for multiculturalism, and it is based not on moral or cultural relativism but rather on a realist account of the cognitive component of cultural practice and the objectivity of value' (1998: 247).

1

Negotiating Nationalism(s): Hindi Poetry During and After the Colonial Period

The evolution of modern Hindi as a medium of poetic expression from Khari Boli and other North Indian dialects provides a 'reliable' concurrent cultural frame to the dynamics of the politico-historical restructuring of India from the so-called Hegelian 'stateless society' into a modern nation-state during the colonial period and after.[1] This chapter maps out India's struggle to define itself as a nation-state through its poetry written in Hindi, its most dominant indigenous language. Instead of presenting an evolutionary account of the state-consciousness of Hindi poetry through a survey of a plethora of texts dwelling on the play of nationalism(s) during the colonial period and after, the present endeavour is limited to the study of some chosen texts that mark decisive shifts in the Hindi imagination of the nation.[2] The effort in this chapter is to contain and build the argument through only these texts. Each text is a site of multiple voices—conflicting as well as complementary—revealing the underlying tensions and anxieties of defining India as a nation-state.

The four poetic texts undertaken for re-historicizing India's struggle to nationhood during the colonial period include Bhartendu Harishchandra's *Bharat Durdasha* (1951a [1880]), Maithilisharan Gupt's *Bharat Bharati* (1989 [1912]), Subhadra Kumari Chauhan's 'Jhansi ki Rani' (1930, see www.manaskriti.com/kaavyaalaya/jhansi) and Suryakant Tripathi Nirala's 'Ram ki Shakti Pooja' (1988a [1936]).[3] The period after independence has also been remapped through four seminal texts—Ramdhari Singh Dinkar's *Rashmirathi* (1960 [1952]), Dharamveer Bharati's *Andha Yug* (2005 [1953]), Muktibodh's 'Andhere Mein' (1991 [1964]) and Dhoomil's 'Mochiram' (1980 [1972]). The texts are either long poems or poetic plays—the two forms that suited most of the poetics of transition that India as a cultural space was undergoing during and after the colonial period. Both forms (d)evolve from the non-negotiable as well as trans-historicized genre of the grand epic.[4] The imperatives of politics, existence and temporality collide and collude with those of religion, spiritualism and nationalism to yield long poetic narratives that re-write culture in ways never plainly linear or transcendental.

Each text mentioned here has its unique cultural context and a 'nationist' configuration, mapping a distinct stage in India's rather bumpy journey into statehood. Each one is evaluated primarily at three levels that are crucial to the understanding of the nation-centric imagination of the poet/poem concerned. The first level pertains to the particular variety of Hindi—dialectal, sanskritic, Hindustani or secular—that is employed in the poetic articulation. The second level pertains to the atlas of India that each text draws in terms of its geographical coordinates. Finally, each text is studied not only in terms of its allegorical (pre)tensions but also in terms of its interventionist capacities in the making of the nation.

I

Bhartendu's *Bharat Durdasha*, as a post-1857 poetic-play, is significant for its nationalist overtures as it dramatizes the destiny of Bharat as its protagonist.[5] As the growing Indian middle class clamours for a sustained form of nation-making (as against the localized, sporadic and non-official native nationalisms of pre-1857) either through the imitation of the modular forms of nationalism or through the audacious invocation of defunct sanskritic nationalism, Bhartendu's Bharat struggles for emancipation in the bewildering medley of nationalist discourses.[6] Before the configuration of the play of various nationalisms in the poetical-skit is worked out, it is pertinent to give more than a passing glance to its linguistic composition because language has always been one of the major sites of competing nationalisms. The invention of a national language is inevitably interlinked with any aspiration of modern nationhood.

In terms of its linguistic make-up, the skit incorporates different language registers that were at play in the latter half of the nineteenth century in northern India. While the songs in the skit have been conceived in the native dialects of Brij and Avadhi, the dialogues are largely in Khari Boli with a liberal sprinkling of Urdu and Sanskrit words with quotes in-between.[7] What makes this 'code-mixing' intriguing is Bhartendu's own strong advocacy of a standardized Hindi as an official national language.[8] Why should the poet-playwright then succumb to the non-official vernacular and Sanskrit-centred linguistic registers? Is it a sign of the confusion from which the new Indian elite suffered due to a lack of clarity of nationalist ideals/frames? Or is it a sign of the poet-playwright's mature negotiation with the pressures of print, oral and classical nationalisms?[9] Either way, the skit falls short of inaugurating in the domain of Hindi literature a formal Hindi-specific nationalism; it is more Hindustani than Hindi. Bhartendu, hitherto credited with the invention of Hindi nationalism, does not evince any such exclusive inventiveness in *Bharat Durdasha*.[10]

Does the heteroglossia of speech empower the protagonist of the skit? If the tragic ending of the skit is any indication, it proves to be utterly suicidal as it hardly lends stability to the character of Bharat. The linguistic confusion is symptomatic of a larger cultural confusion that India as a nation was undergoing in the 1880s—the incipient decade of its modernist nationalist struggle. Various forms of linguistic nationalisms—official, popular/native and sanskritic—collide and appear with their inherent contradictions, but the catastrophic ending suggests no easy resolution of the cultural confusion that early nationalists faced in imagining India. The poet-playwright is caught in a cultural quandary—whether to press for India's sanskritic past, or to petition for its institutional consolidation under the Raj tutelage, or even to forge a working everyday nationalism. The ideals of sanskritic nationalism, the imperatives of modern-day nationhood, and the 'assumptions, hopes, needs, longings and interests of ordinary people, which are not necessarily national and still less nationalist' (Hobsbawm 1990: 10), constitute the three-pronged dimension of Hindi nationalism during the latter half of the nineteenth century.

Sanskritic nationalism is cherished and derided in the same breath. In the prologue itself, there is a vehement nationalist assertion that proclaims India's Vedic past as originary and absolute:[11]

> Where god bequeathed richness and power first
> where civilization descended long ago
> where a sense for aesthetics came first
> where knowledge dawned first . . . (1951a: 469)

This is indeed an audacious act of mimicry and self-glorification. Before this brand of backward-looking nationalism becomes loud and celebratory, a strong sense of its critique sets in and the abstract notions of nation propagated through the high principles of *advait* invite sharp criticism from within:

> Maharaj Vedant did a great service. Every Hindu became a Brahma.
> None had a sense of duty. After having acquired knowledge, each
> one turned away from god, each became too conceited that there was
> no room for emotions. And when there are no emotions, where is the
> motivation for national emancipation? Only jai shankar ki! (ibid.: 475)

Keeping in view the high-pitched attempts of the reformers of the
pre- and post-1857 period, from Rammohun Roy to Vivekananda,
towards the revival of upnishadic ideals of Hinduism, Bhartendu's
spoof of Maharaj Vedant is bold and daring. Bhartendu goes on to
catalogue a series of brahmanical practices that have ruined India as
a civilization. The *satyanash fauj*—the army of destruction—stages a
spectacle through which it parades its achievements in undoing
nationalist India thus:

> Created many castes, invented hierarchies of low and high . . .
> Did not allow marriage without horoscope
> Marriage during childhood, destroyed scope for adult romance . . .
> prohibited widow-remarriage, which only promoted adultery
> prohibited going abroad, encouraged narrow-mindedness (ibid.)

The politics of revivalism runs into the politics of reform, forcing a
revision of stance. Bhartendu's protagonist Bharat, desperate as he is,
swings from one extreme to another to come out of his stupor. Unlike
fundamental nationalists, Bhartendu's Bharat has no reservations
about clinging on to British-sponsored nationalism, provided it
redeems him from his present state of wilderness.

The official nationalism as an alternative to sanskritic nationalism
and as propagated by the Raj also receives both approval and dis-
approval. Bharat pleads for the benign intervention of the British
Queen, addressed in the poem in divine terms as 'Bhagavti Raj
Rajeshveri', to facilitate his rescue. The last speech by Bharatbhagya
is virtually a salutary acceptance of the Raj:

> See the sun of education rises from the West. It is not the time to sleep.
> If you don't wake in this raj, when shall you redeem yourself! . . . The
> education has spread far and wide. Every one gets a right to speech
> and representation. New knowledge and technology comes from
> abroad. . . . Hey divine Imperial Queen hold my hand and redeem us!
> (ibid.: 496)

The colonial rule is hailed (if not cherished), but the fact that it diverts Indian capital to Great Britain pains the poet-playwright: 'The English rule does bring a lot of comfort/but what sours most is the drain of our money abroad' (ibid.: 470).

Thus, both types of nationalisms, indigenous and colonial, fail to revive the unconscious Bharat. Any other type of nationalism is not explored as much in the skit; however, Bhartendu's use of mixed language does suggest the possibility of an alternative working nationalism, which is fairly composite, if not assimilative, in character and scope. Bharatbhagya's suicide has more to do with his failure to tap this innate popular everyday nationalism rather than the inadequacies of other types of overarching nationalisms. Caught in the easy orientalist binaries of East versus West, Bharat fails to carve the in-between space between the modular and the sanskritic, despite Bhartendu's use of what Vasudha Dalmia terms 'the third idiom'.[12] Bharatbhagya's dramatic suicide only suggests the limitations of a much-theorized two-edged/ambivalent postcolonial nationalism of resistance and collaboration.[13]

II

As nationalistic discourse comes out of its supplication mould, the fundamental dichotomy between the cherished stateless glorious past and the mandatory statist future continues to beleaguer the Hindi imagination.[14] While celebrating India's civilizational past, Maithilisharan Gupt, in his *Bharat Bharati* (1989 [1912]), laments its de-cultured present.[15] The poet, very much like Bhartendu, seeks the Raj's intervention in ameliorating the civic condition of the people; yet both in intent and diction, the tilt is towards cultural nationalism.[16] The long poem, divided into three sections and written in a series of quatrains, 'Ateet Khand', 'Vartman Khand' and 'Bhavishyat Khand', lays down not only the futuristic blueprint of India along the lines of the modern West, but also celebrates its cultured past in a language that is overtly sanskritic, scriptural and sermonizing. The diction tends to be cumbersome and 'clumsy' (Rosenstein 2002: 4); the Urdu–Khari Boli mix later described by Gandhi and other nationalists as Hindustani, is abandoned in favour of a chaste and pure classical idiom. The effort is to approximate Vedic Sanskrit at least in diction and style. The poem opens with a conventional epic invocation:

> *manas-bhavan mein aryajan jiski utarein aarti—*
> *bhagwan! bharatvarsha mein goonje hamari bharati .*
> *ho bhadrabhavodbhavani vah bharati he bhagvate!*
> *sitapate! sitapate! geetamate! geetamate!!* (1989: 1)

> (in the edifice of humanity that Aryans worship—
> O god! let our prayer echo throughout India
> Let gentle emotions come forth from the goddess of knowledge!
> Sita's lord! Sita's lord! Mother-Geeta! Mother-Geeta!!)

The deployment of high-sounding multi-syllabic compounds and hyphenated words (*manas-bhavan, bhadrabhavodbhavani*) along with their distorted native forms (*bhagvate, sitapate*) points towards the inherent poetic/political compulsion of forging a classical image of native India. Throughout the poem, the poet strives to literally plant tedious sanskritic vocabulary into his otherwise prosaic poetic enterprise. The process of what may be termed as the Hinduization of Hindi begins with full gusto in the Dwivedi period.

In terms of its cartographic horizons, Gupt's *Bharat Bharati* orbits around the holy and sacred landmarks of the Hindi heartland. India is rather confined into a narrow sacred strip of landmass between the Himalayas and the Ganges, with hardly any reference to its eastern and southern regions and seacoasts: 'pride of earthly-world, where else is nature's sacred play-ground?/There it is, spread around splendid Himalayas and the water of Ganges' (ibid.: 4). Barring a passing reference to Shivaji's Maharashtra or Rana Pratap's Mewar, the location of the poem does not go beyond the Hindu *rashtra*, which in the words of the poet is 'rishi-bhoomi' (the land of seers). Namvar Singh's observation is no different: 'But in *Bharat Bharati*, there is no place for the south of India. The glorious image of the past that the poet draws has room neither for Madurai-Meenakshi nor for Thyagaraj. *Bharat Bharati*'s Hindu in the end remains confined to a region from Ganga to Doab' (2003: 364).

At times, Gupt rarefies his Hindu India so much that its definite geographical co-ordinates are almost entirely lost in the process; heralding India to be the mother-civilization, the poet contends: 'Even in America, tangible signs of our presence are found' (1989: 21) and also 'Japan was a disciple of old *Bharatvarsha*' (ibid.: 23). Even Greeks, as the poet claims, gained knowledge only after accepting Hindus as their gurus (ibid.: 22). India becomes the epicentre of enlightenment:

> Had we not seized darkness, not invented new things perennially
> The light that travelled from our east, couldn't have reached west,
> Even nature stands witness to the fact that till today everywhere
> The sun rises in the east, and not in the west. (ibid.: 25)

The homologous relationship that the poet establishes between the sun and India only underlines the overarching, non-cartographic nature of poetic imagination.

After having sung ancient India's golden glory in almost quasi-*mantric* terms, Gupt's *Bharat Bharati* descends to prosaic poetry marred by reformatory rhetoric. According to Orsini, if one were to take out rhyme from the 'Vartman Khand', it could as well be taken as 'one of the many articles on *Bharat Durdasha* coming straight from Dvivedi's pen' (2002: 201). In this section, the poet criticizes contemporary India for its cultural amnesia:

> What we have become from what we were, is simply forgotten
> Tell me, who really bothers about our esteem
> We don't know as to who our ancestors were,
> Quite a burden it is to offer in their name even handful of water.
> (1989: 145)

The tendencies of revivalism compete with the emergent discourse of reformism in a highly arbitrary manner. In the 'Bhavishyat Khand', instead of holding on to the glory of the ancient golden past as the possible plank of India's future recuperation, the poet switches over to the modular paradigms of nation-making of the West. The urge to establish Hindi formally as a national language is one clear instance of mimetic nationalism:

> There is no national language in this country as yet
> to make our ideas known to each other.
> Hindi is worth it, yet it has not received that status.
> Without language there cannot be emotional unity. (ibid.: 175)

The prosaic expression suggests the blandness of nationalist imagination during the 1920s. The swing from proto-nationalism to modern statism is charted out without a convincing poetics of transition and negotiation. Partha Chatterjee explains this kind of swing in terms of his theory of 'two domains'—the 'outer' material and the 'inner' spiritual—as unique to Indian nationalism during the colonial period.[17] However, the fact remains that such a formulaic nationalism lends quite a paradoxical and even opportunistic character to Indian nationalism as a whole.

III

Subhadra Kumari Chauhan's 'Jhansi ki Rani' (1930, see www. manaskriti.com/kaavyaalaya/jhansi) provides an example of patriotic poetry written during the Gandhian period of the freedom struggle for an understanding of what may be termed as the 'nationalist-feminist' perspective. Not only is the poet a woman, the subject matter of the poem is also the phenomenal bravery of a woman. How does the nation account for women in its making? Are women subsumed within the predominantly masculine discourse of cultural nationalism or are they allowed to participate in the enterprise of nationalism in their distinct ways? The questions assume special significance as Chauhan is an associate of Gandhi and a freedom fighter herself.[18]

In terms of its tone and tenor, Chauhan's poem is not very different from the mainstream (male) nationalist poetry of the Dwivedi period. Neither the female subject, nor the female authorship makes much difference to the poetics of nationalist poetry. The language of nationalism continues to be sanskritized Hindi as is evident from the high-sounding beginning: '*sinhasan hil uthe, rajvanshon ne bhrikuti taani thi*' (ibid.) ('the thrones were shaken, and the royal dynasties raised their eyebrows'). The belligerence is phallocentric, too: '*chamak utthi sun sattavan mein vah talwar purani thi*' (ibid.) ('the sword that blazed in the year 57 was old'). However, the reformatory self-critical streak of the early nationalists gives way to combative nationalism.

The absence of reformatory rhetoric reduces the poem to a purely retrogressive nationalist ballad allowing Chauhan to engender rare lyricism in its texture.[19] The poet, therefore, manages better acoustics than her prosaic predecessors could ever do; the classical idiom is combined deftly with native refrains and rhythms:

> *Bundele harbolon ke mukh se hamne sooni kahani thi*
> *Khoob ladi mardani vo to Jhansi wali rani thi . . .*

> From the mouth of Bundels and Harboles, we heard a story
> Like a man gallantly she fought, such was the queen of Jhansi . . .
> (ibid.)

The female folk sensibility (as opposed to the urbanized male sensibility) comes into play in such immensely oral refrains. The conflation of two registers suggests the relationship of a possible exchange between the *desi* and the classical, between the subaltern and the national.

The local heroine is raised to the level of a national icon; the oral nationalism combines with the printed one. Instead of going back to the prehistoric or proto-historic mythical narratives to assert the indigenous basis of nationalism, Chauhan chooses to dwell upon a woman protagonist from the not-so-remote past. But the historicity of the poetic narrative is soon lost or sufficiently compromised as the propensity to deify Rani overtakes the poet in moments of nationalist assertion. Rani is projected as a Hindu warrior-goddess:

> Lakshmi or Durga, she was in her own right, an avatar of bravery
> Marathas felt elated looking at her fencing skills
> Breaking through mock military stratagems, hunting,
> Encircling armies and destroying forts, were her favourite sports (ibid.)

Rani's bravery is transformed into masculine valour. In the process, she is denied her ordinary female aspirations: 'you were just twenty-three, you were not human being, but the very incarnation of the divine' (ibid.).

The poem does take its woman protagonist out of the inner and insular corset of the home, but it takes her straight to the battlefield. The engagement of the woman protagonist with the intermediate world of intelligent negotiation between the home and the battlefield goes without representation, implying thereby, that the choice is either to be a docile faithful queen or a warrior-woman who can match and even outdo male warriors. Both heroism and domesticity demand sacrifice and self-denial, and thus deprive the women their participation in mundane state affairs hitherto reserved for males. In this sense, both home and battlefield complement each other in excluding the women from the political processes of nation-making.

Chauhan's nationalism, instead of offering a female counter-perspective, ends up in the assertion of adult male militaristic values. The subaltern does not speak at all. Rani's best friends in her tender years were not dolls and toys but 'spear, shield, sword, dagger' (ibid.). The aged India regains its virile youthfulness in 1857: '*budhe bharat mein bhi aayi phir se nayi jawani thi*' (ibid.) ('ageing India regained its youth all over again'). In the context of the poem, the issues of gender and age combine to yield a paradigm of masculine nationalism that has little room for its women. The duality between nationalism and statism that hounds the poets of the Dwivedi period does not bother Subhadra Kumari Chauhan as much.

IV

By the time Suryakant Tripathi 'Nirala' descends on the poetical scene, Hindi nationalism seems to attain a rare degree of self-reflexivity. It begins to re-write its own cherished nationalist idols in terms of their vulnerabilities and moments of self-doubt.[20] As the challenges of inventing a secular nationalism within the *topos* of tradition begin to nag the nationalist elite of the late 1930s, it revisits mythical narratives and the archetypal frames of cultural nationalism with humanist pretensions. Although Nirala chooses overtly mainstream Hindu co-relatives to articulate his vision of struggle for freedom, personal as well as national, yet his attitude towards them is reflective and critical.[21] As Hindu myths, metaphysics and morality undergo a process of critical re-visioning from within, the process of the humanization of the iconic and the sacred begins to take place. The mythical and the humanist begin to impinge upon each other in ways that mark the promise of sufficiently moderate, if not fully secularized, versions of nationalism.

Nirala's 'Ram ki Shakti Pooja' (1988a [1936]) can be heralded as an allegory of self-reflexive Indian nationalism in which the poet seeks to re-invent *shakti*, the power of the self, afresh (*shakti ki karo maulik kalpana*) in its fight against the formidable Empire. In terms of its linguistic portfolio, the poem begins in sanskritized Hindi (*tatsam*) before it lapses towards the end into the ordinary standard lexicon. The change in the nature of diction mirror-images the floundering morale of Ram in his battle with his arch rival Ravana. Right at the outset, the poem attempts very ambitious structures, containing a series of *samasa*s (compound words), forgoing the employment of verbs:

> *pratipal-privartit-vyooh, bhed-kaushal-smooh,*
> *vicchuritvahni-rajeevnayan-hut-lakshay-baan*
> *lohitlochan-ravan-madmochan-mahiyaan . . .* (1988: 97–98)

> (changing every moment the stratagem, skill-secrecy combine
> going astray the arrows of fire-filled lotus-eyes.
> Blood-shot eyes of Ravana, frenzied on high trip . . .)

The poet changes linguistic registers when it comes to conveying the final message without any make-up, to admit:

> *dhik jeevan ko jo pata hi aaya virodh!*
> *dhik sadhan jiske liye sada hi kiya sodh!* (ibid.: 106)
>
> (O how cursed is this life that always found opposition!
> cursed are the means which were always researched!)

The descent from elevated lofty beginning to down-to-earth denouement points towards the limits of sublime sanskritic nationalism.

The poet employs the central Hindu trope of Rama versus Ravana to underline the enormity of the colonial combat, but unlike the traditional stereotypes, he infuses a rare streak of humanism in his characters. The episode re-explored in the poem does not belong to Tulsi's *Ramcharitmanas*; rather it is lifted from the Bangla *Ramayana* written by Krittbas. Such a deviation from the mainstream suggests the anxiety of the nationalist elite to look beyond the popular narratives of the Hindi heartland to understand the dynamics of a colonized nation. The episode pertains to the invocation of *Shakti* by Rama who is otherwise doubtful of defeating Ravana. To please the goddess *Shakti*, Rama prepares to offer a certain number of lotus flowers to her, some of which disappear; this reminds Rama of his *kamalnayan* (lotus-eyes). As he prepares to pluck out one eye to complete the required number of lotus flowers, the goddess is pleased and prevents his hand from performing the supreme sacrifice.

In the poem, Rama is portrayed as an extremely tentative warrior who is uncertain about the outcome of his battle with Ravana:

> Stable Rama is repeatedly rocked by doubt,
> Ravana's hailed dread keeps haunting life.
> A heart that never was foe-tamed, exhausted
> that remained unconquered in thousand trials
> is disconcerted at taking on the enemy
> In the weak heart, a sense of defeat comes . . . (ibid.: 99)

Rama is retrieved from his image of *maryada purshottum* that the successive cultural nationalists constantly imposed on him. He is at his frail human best as he remembers, rather romantically, in a flash back, his wife Sita, a captive of Ravana in Ashok Vatika:

> Eyes meet eyes in secretive communion;
> eyelids on new eyelids, their maiden rise-fall,

> trembling shoots of foliage, undulating pollen
> singing birds heralding new life, Malabar-trees all around
> heavenly light-fall as though the image of my first love
> Janaki's desirous-eyes first quivering trance . . . (ibid.)

The poem mirrors Rama's conflict, as it alternates between a war scene and a cherished moment of love, a flicker of hope with a fear of loss. The poem maintains the typical nationalist male distinction between *ghar* and *bahir*, yet the very memory of Sita in the battlefield suggests the intervening capacity of the former in the latter, and that the two domains cannot be easily segregated from each other.

The unassailable Rama of Tulsi's *Manas* undergoes a bout of existential anxieties; he literally weeps: 'then he listened—Ravana's raucous laughter/from the sentimental eyes dropped two watery pearls' (ibid.: 156). Vibhishana exhorts Ram to keep up his morale:

> Pride of *raghukul*, you are becoming small in this moment;
> you are turning your back when it is a moment of victory.
> How much effort has gone waste! When you are all set to meet
> Sita, you are mercilessly withdrawing your hand from her! (ibid.: 102)

The 'small Rama' of Nirala later on in post-independence Hindi poetry paves the way for the 'small man' (*laghu manav*) as its protagonist. In words that behove ordinary human beings, Rama expresses his despondency:

> Spake Raghumani—friend, war we shall not win
> for it is not just a war between devils and men-monkeys.
> *Mahashakti* itself has descended on the scene on Ravana's calling.
> Where there is injustice, *shakti* is on that side! (ibid.: 102)

Rama's dwindling morale corresponds with the tentativeness of the nationalist elite of the late 1930s.

In the face of utter hopelessness, the impeccable divine lord is exhorted by his subordinates to re-invent *Shakti* so that it no longer sides with imperial forces. Jambvan's intervention is significant:

> Answer devotion with firm devotion.
> Win over your own body with restraint.
> If Ravana by being impure can cause distress
> then, surely you by attainment will destroy him.
> Worship, imagine *Shakti* all over afresh. (ibid.: 103–4)

Nirala's re-invention of *Shakti* in poetry in a very subtle sense parallels Gandhi's endeavour to redefine *swaraj* in politics.[22] The control over one's self is one supreme precondition of winning (over) *Shakti* as well as *swaraj*. Towards the end of the poem, *Shakti* is won over, and despair turns into optimism: 'win, you will win, O new being, the best among men/saying this *mahashakti* dissolved into the body of Rama' (ibid.: 107).

'Ram ki Shakti Pooja' thus culminates in the rejuvenation of *Shakti*. It is through sheer devotion and commitment that Rama secures the favour of *Shakti*. This in a way is also suggestive of the trajectory of Indian nationalism that harnessed western knowledge to its advantage through its hard work and commitment. Also, that Indian nationalism was never simply derivative, it was a new form of nationalism, a reinvention of its dormant *shakti*.

V

The project of Indian nationhood becomes much more intricate and challenging after independence, because until 1947, the Empire emerges as an identifiable adversary, and the poetics of protest could safely be formulated in terms of the broad postcolonial binary of the self versus the other. In the post-1947 scenario, nation-making becomes more an enterprise of self-critiquing than pillorying against colonialism. In moments of self-criticism, the 'otherified' India begins to ponder over its own contradictions, and the structures of social discrimination within. Hindi poetic imagination, that until 1947 relies heavily on nationalist fervour or anti-colonial sentiment, seems to discover new grounds of discontent and dissent to carry forward its radicalism. The anti-colonial impulse in the post-independence phase continues as it identifies internal forms of oppression that remained obscure in the 'larger' nationalist struggle. The so-called 'side-issues' postponed during the 'larger' enterprise of the freedom struggle soon begin to surface.[23]

After having written his nationalistic narratives *Kurukshetra* and *Hunkar* during the peak of the colonial period, Dinkar, just after independence, settles down to write an epic in seven cantos (*sargas*) on Karna entitled *Rashmirathi*. As issues of social justice and dalit emancipation begin to gather greater urgency beyond the political freedom attained in 1947, the poet turns inward and begins to probe structures of caste-hegemony from within the emerging nation-state.

In his introductory remarks to *Rashmirathi,* Dinkar reveals a shift in his stance as he begins to take on the role of a post-independence poet-activist: 'This is an age of emancipation of dalits and the have-nots. Therefore it is natural that the socially-conscious poets of the nation are attracted towards those who stand as silent symbols of the neglected and defamed humanity since ages' (1960: iii).

Written in *charit-kavya* form, *Rashmirathi* covers the entire trajectory of Karna's life as that of a benevolent dalit leader who has no moral scruples in aligning with Duryodhana in his fight against the hegemony of the brahmanical elite represented by Guru Dronacharya and the Pandavas. The entire poem can indeed be read as an allegory of complex pre- and post-independence caste politics, with Ambedkar masquerading as Karna, Gandhi as Krishna, Nehru as Arjuna, Kunti as Mother India and Duryodhana as the British Raj.[24] In this creative interface of history and mythology, the cultural nationalism of pre-independence gives way to what might be described as 'religious humanism'—humanism circumscribed by high religious/spiritual imperatives.[25] The mythical characters are subjected to human scrutiny as the veneer of cultural nationalism thins down, but their subversive caricaturization is still out of mind.

Dinkar's Karna is not in any sense a modern-day strategic transgressive subaltern, for he invokes larger humanist ideals for his emancipation:

> Hey Lord, sheer labour reverses the figures of destiny.
> And the dice of fate is defeated by virility.
> And high ambitions are but strengths of human beings
> they keep us on our toes, waking us . . . (ibid.: 66)

In terms of his demeanour, Dinkar's Karna is too sanskritic to be identified with an ordinary native dalit. Except for his caste, he bears a perfect royal persona: 'Bodily, he is warrior, mentally he is emotional and by nature he is philanthropic/ . . ./ has adequate practice of meditation, scriptures and armaments' (ibid.: 2). His speech has classical restraint and decorum.

The predicament of Dinkar's Karna is not very different from that of Ambedkar and vice versa. Both tend to fight discrimination but within the over-arching frame of the high Hindu ideal of renunciation. If Ambedkar seeks redemption in Buddhism, Karna is philanthropic to the extent of absolute selflessness:

> People like me
> never carry the burden of gold.
> They earn to fritter away.
> The diamonds that they bring are squandered
> They never take anything from the world.
> They even give their hearts in charity. (ibid.: 54)

Both, despite vehement differences with the *savarna* order, shy away from forging a separatist dalit ideology and succumb to the pressures of dominant Hindu nationalism. In fact, despite siding with Duryodhana in the great battlefield, Karna does not want to augment the sorrow of the exiled Pandavas. He asks Krishna not to disclose to Yudhishthira his 'story of birth', otherwise:

> He would never accept the empire
> and would pass on all property to me
> which I shall never be able to keep with me
> and would hand over to Duryodhana
> Pandavas shall thus remain deprived
> Never shall they get over their sorrow. (ibid.: 57)

Despite the Pandavas being his adversaries in the battle, Karna thinks of their well-being. Duryodhana is not his ideological choice, but a strategic one.

Dinkar's Karna does not spare his mother Kunti, much against the nationalist imperatives of unqualified motherhood. Mothers, step- or real, are to be respected and revered, irrespective of what they do to their wards. Karna evinces little *maryada* of a twice-born Hindu as he takes on his indifferent mother:

> Why didn't she die herself, after killing her son?
> Wanted to live by turning indifferent, cruel and tough—
> what should I say O devi? I was simply unwanted.
> But mother what character you lived? (ibid.: 93)

The nationalist archetype of the self-effacing Mother India is turned upside down as Kunti is castigated for being apathetic to her low-caste son. Kunti is forced to admit her crime:

> Son, I am indeed a big sinner
> I am a vicious female-snake in human-form
> Can there be another woman on this earth
> Murderess, crooked, sinful as I am? (ibid.: 101)

The descent of Kunti from 'mother' to 'murderess' is so melodramatic that Karna simply relents and falls at her feet, thus postponing the possibilities of an all-out aggressive dalit discourse. He is easily co-opted by the nationalist discourse that after independence operates under the mask of secular humanism.

The discourse of *dharma* runs supreme, and the tyranny of the so-called sacred is seriously challenged but never reversed:

> Karna, how pure his character is! As long as he was in the battlefield, his mother's animate image remained haunting his mind.
> Having brought Sahdev, Yudhishter, Nakul, Bhim under his noose repeatedly
> he let them go with a laughter, receiving as though some intimation from inside. (ibid.: 137)

Dinkar's Karna, portrayed as a dalit hero, thus fails to puncture the miasma of rarefied nationalist discourse in a clinching manner. His war with his high-caste adversaries, though staged for the restoration of his honour, turns out to be no more than a mock-fight.

Rashmirathi as a poem thus marks a crucial stage in the making of India as a nation-state. The fact that Karna takes centre stage signals the rise of discontent among the margins of the new Indian state. Mere *dharma*-based nationalism is not adequate unless the state provides a space of honour to its low-caste people. Since the poem stops short of radical social engineering, it is not dalitist by radically separatist post-nationalist standards. The sanctity and supremacy of nation, *dharma*, family, etc. are maintained rather steadfastly, without really disturbing the so-called social equilibrium in a fundamental way. Hegemonic nationalism does question its politics of exclusion, but never gives in.

VI

The nationalist imagination continues to operate through mythical archetypes even as secular and statist imperatives begin to impinge on post-independence politics. Dharamveer Bharati's *Andha Yug*, a five-act poetic play written in the wake of the partition, denounces the self-destructing violence in which cultural nationalists indulge to defend and consolidate the arbitrary divisions drawn by the colonial powers.[26] Invoking the classical metaphor of *kalyug*, Bharati restages the trauma of partition's violence and politics through the familiar allegorical frame of the *Mahabharata* war. Such a teleological extra-polation brings the nation-centric postcolonial present in contact with the supranational civilizational past. The resultant nation-nationalism overlap not only explains the complex making of India, but also its hybridized predicament.

The Kauravas and the Pandavas as the two warring factions of the same clan are like Jinnah's Muslim League and Gandhi's Congress, battling for supremacy over each other right at the stroke of India's imminent decolonization. The guards pacing up and down the desolate corridors of power—defending 'nothing' (2005: 28)—remind us of Matthew Arnold's poignant image of 'ignorant armies/clashing by night' (1971: 131) in the high tide of European nationalism. Dhritarashtra (most probably modeled after Jinnah) represents the blind rage of narrow nationalism that he accounts for in terms of his being 'born blind' (2005: 34):

> My senses were limited by my blindness.
> They defined the boundary of my material world.
>
> . . . .
>
> My love, my hate, my law, my dharma
> has evolved out of my peculiar world. (ibid.: 33–34)

The Pandavas, led by Yudhishthira (probably Nehru), stand for op-portunistic and manipulative nationalism. Yudhishthira kills the invincible Guru Dronacharya through half-truth; Ashwatthama alleges, 'Yudhishthira's half-truth killed him' (ibid.: 52). In Bharati's scheme, neither of the two warring parties could claim moral superiority over the other. Eyes with or without sight lacked vision; therefore, the poet-playwright deploys the metaphor of blindness.

Krishna as Gandhi is trying to hold on to his stereotypical moral-metaphysical stance, though he is portrayed as a vulnerable human figure who could be 'cursed, loved, worshipped, abandoned and killed' (Bhalla 2005: 3). The portrayal of Krishna as a tentative god is in keeping with the general post-independence mood of humanizing the mythical. Krishna's speech has all the moral predilections of Gandhi, the philosopher-politician:

> In this terrible war of eighteen days
> I am the only one who died a million times.
> Every time a soldier was struck down
> Every time a soldier fell to the ground

> it was I who was struck down
> it was I who was wounded
> it was I who fell to the ground. (Bharati 2005: 123)

Balarama address Krishna as 'an unprincipled rogue' (ibid.: 79). Gandhari, the mother of the Kauravas, in fact curses Krishna for being partisan and unfair to Ashwatthama and the other Kauravas: 'you will return to this forest/only to be killed/like a wild animal/by an ordinary hunter!' (ibid.: 122–23). The play indeed dramatizes the death of Krishna by a hunter, as cursed by Gandhari. In the very partition of the nation, the seeds of Gandhi's death were sown.

The bloody arrival of the two nation-states in the debris of a cohesive civilizational past leaves the poet-playwright extremely pessimistic. Yudhishthira, though victorious in the war, is worried about the legacy of the bloody and treacherous war:

> Behind the throne I won
> stretches a long and unbroken
> tradition of blindness and stupidity.
> The people are still cast
> in the ugly mould of the old regime. (ibid.: 129)

He is extremely sceptical of the governing prowess of his fellow nationalists: 'My brothers/are ignorant or foolish/insolent or weary' (ibid.). Bhima insults Yuyutsu who 'dared to stand up against his family' (ibid.: 131) and fought on the side of Yudhishthira. Yuyutsu could be identified with either Abdul Gaffar Khan, Frontier Gandhi or Maulana Azad who opposed the idea of partition until the very end and did not endorse the Muslim League's separatist plans. He sided with the Truth (of united India). After the war, Yuyutsu is condemned as a traitor by both sides as he makes a theme-statement thus: 'In the final analysis/whether you uphold truth/or untruth/you are damned' (ibid.: 75).

The survivors from the side of the Kauravas are equally condemned. They are the latter-day war-obsessed military rulers, infatuated with beastly passions. Ashwatthama is one such survivor from the Kaurava clan:

> —foul as the spittle
> stale as the phlegm
> left in the mouth

> of a dying man—
> I, Ashwatthama
> am the only one
> alive today. (ibid.: 53)

Ashwatthama's only dharma is 'Kill, kill, kill/and kill again' (ibid.: 54). In the politics of the partition and after, it was difficult even to act neutrally. Sanjay too has his inner set of contradictions: 'Trying to show the truth/to the blind/must I too become blind?' (ibid.: 106).

Andha Yug, thus, is a kind of dramatic dirge for decadent and immoral postcolonial nationalism, coming as it does in the wake of the worst play of communalism. The poet-playwright does not foresee any future for India as a modern nation-state unless it hinges itself to the values of *dharma*. *Dharma* in the scheme of the play stands for truth, social harmony and mutual co-existence. Bharati traverses along the delicate path of *dharma* that does not divide the people of an integrated cultural past into antagonistic communal forces. Hindi imagination comes out of its narrow cultural nationalist mould as it presses for a secular *dharma*. The sacred that Bharati implicitly seeks to restore is not sectarian or religious; it derives its legitimacy from the assimilative and composite civilizational past.

VII

By the mid-1960s, the mood of disillusionment (*mohbhung*) peaks in Hindi poetry and the metaphor of darkness continues to haunt the embattled poetic imagination. The search for people-centric (as opposed to the failed mythopoetic) nationalism begins to bother the Hindi poets. Having exhausted the cultural archetypes, the new poets of the Ajneya-Muktibodh generation begin to probe the possibilities of the secular and progressive (as opposed to the sacred, retrogressive) narratives as viable frames of nation building. Muktibodh, in his long poem, 'Andhere Mein', does away with the need of sustaining his poetic impulse through a ready-made cultural correlative. As a poet influenced on the one hand by a very profound *chhayavad* and an equally powerful *prayogvad* on the other, he presses forth his subterranean self onto a critical journey—as the very site of a nation critiquing itself. The way he incorporates the cultural signposts of his times in his intensely inward and personalized narrative speaks of the emerging national consciousness that, too, was undergoing the same process of inner interrogation through the touchstones set by the nationalists.

The poetic self, chronicling as though the history of the nation, passes through a cavalcade of images, signifying its tryst with various tropes of nationalism. The poet invokes the image of Manu as one possible form of his unfulfilled absolute self:

> On its own
> a face emerges from the wall
> sharp nose
> glorious forehead
> firm jaws;
> some familiar, un-familiar shape
> which is seen
> but not recognized
> Who Manu? (1991: 127)

Howsoever tentatively interposed in the very beginning of the long poem, Manu's very presence points towards his regular Hindu intervention in the post-independence nationalist unconscious. As an arch-symbol of revivalist nationalism, he is difficult to ignore. As the first mythical man, Manu is bound to figure as one of the poetic possibilities of absolute self, the ideological propensities of the poet notwithstanding.

Soon, the reader is transported to a series of secular images drawn from a variety of discourses signifying the ever-expanding horizons of Muktibodh's nationalist expression. As the poetic self moves forward, a Tolstoy-like person—presented by the poet as 'one end of some inner strand of his being', as 'one seminal emotion of his unwritten novel' (ibid.: 135)—counters it, reminding it of its unrealized potential. The sudden shift of imagination from Manu to Tolstoy suggests the opening up of the canon from the narrow Hindu-centric nationalism to that of socialism. The transition is not smooth as the poet runs into a strange procession of the comprador ruling elite 'on the black horses wearing *khaki* military dresses/half the face is saffron/half black as coal-tar' (ibid.: 137).

Another image that follows is that of the 'dark dome-like/fearsome banyan' (ibid.: 140) tree that the poet holds to be the natural 'sanctuary of all the deprived and the downtrodden' (ibid.: 140). The banyan tree is a symbol of vertical roots as well as of horizontal expanse. In this home there lives an eccentric mad man who is self-critical:

> What life have you lived so far?
> What have you done so far—
> took more, gave less?
> As the nation died, you survived!! (ibid.: 142)

The self-preserving and opportunistic credo of the native nationalist elite is exposed with a postcolonial zeal. The whole project of the freedom struggle led by Tilak, Gandhi and other nationalists stands subverted. Tilak, a votary of extreme nationalism within the Congress, shakes the middle-class persona out of complacency: 'someone is chiselling my own self from me/some dangerous urge wakes me up' (ibid.: 150). Tilak's nationalism, clouded as it is by some kind of Hindu nationalism, might once again give an impression that the poet is momentarily seduced by the idea of a Hindu nation. But soon Gandhi, lamed and beleaguered, appears on his mental-scape.

With the appearance of Gandhi, another variant of national-ism enters into the poet's search for the elusive 'absolute expression' (*paramabhivyakti*). Gandhi, badly bruised and tattered in postcolonial India, underscores the need of taking people into confidence for the making of the nation: 'In a lump of mud, there are radiant atoms/of quality/only in the people's merit lies/the evolution of future' (ibid.: 152). Instead of the semi-spiritualized nationalism with which Gandhiism is often associated, the poet relocates it in a people-centric nationalism. The intimate encounter lends a rare combative edge to the intimidated inner self. Suddenly, it finds itself armed. Meanwhile, the murder of an artist by the powerbrokers in their underground cross-examination cells sets the poetic self into agitation. The artist is Muktibodh's repository of creative nationalism.

In the long poem, as the atrocities of the comprador intelligentsia mount, the secluded self of the poet braces itself for violent struggle. He announces: 'now onwards, the dangers of absolute expression will have to be taken/all centres of power will have to broken' (ibid.: 161). The Marxist strain comes to the foreground:

> The present society cannot work
> as the capitalist's heart cannot change,
> one who espouses freedom
> cannot betray its liberal mind
> people. (ibid.: 164–65)

Towards the end, the poet advances towards the dissolution of his solitary self into the mass of people protesting outside. The absolute self of the poet is ultimately discovered in the common man: 'Suddenly I saw that man,/ In the streets, on the roads, in the people's crowd' (ibid.: 170). Muktibodh's nationalist journey thus begins with Manu and ends on 'man'. The individual becomes the very locus of social emancipation. The poem in a way heralds the urge for people's nationalism in Hindi poetry after independence.

VIII

Writing under the influence of the naxalite movement of the 1970s, Sudama Pandey Dhoomil launches a frontal attack on India as a nation-state, its police, Parliament and judiciary in particular, in a poetic expression that is exceptionally militant, combative and even indecent. The progressive strain of Muktibodh attains a higher pitch by the time Dhoomil descends on the poetic scene. The complicity of the postcolonial state with upper-caste feudal lords disturbs the young poet most as he sets out to expose the politics of exclusion of the lower castes and also of the poor rural peasantry from the processes of nation building. The subaltern speaks in the first person in the poetry of Dhoomil with a candour and courage that even mainstream dalit writings cannot possibly match.

In Dhoomil's 'Mochiram', a poem of about 150 lines included in his much-discussed collection *Sansad se Sadak Tak*, the cobbler takes centre stage as he evaluates the character of the so-called citizens of the state in terms of the size, shape and design of their shoes:

> Babuji, if you believe me—in my eyes
> neither one is big
> nor small.
> For me every man is a pair of shoes
> standing before me
> for repair. (1980: 36)

The poet, for the first time perhaps in Hindi poetry, not only bestows the powers of intelligent analysis to the illiterate have-nots, but also grants them a rare sensitivity and self-reflexivity denied to them by the national elite. The cobbler does not want to tag additional patches onto an already worn-out, frustrated shoe, yet he obeys the dictates of his profession:

> I feel—a voice comes
> from within—'what kind of a man you are?

> you spit on your own caste.'
> Believe me, at that time
> I stitch eyes on the patches
> and with great difficulty
> fulfil my professional obligations. (ibid.: 37)

The distinction between the human and the professional self is carefully maintained in the poem.

The cobbler has his own silent but decisive ways to avenge his exploitation by the ruthless capitalists. As one of them, without paying the cobbler his due, crosses over the road, the cobbler as protagonist hits back in his own surreptitious style:

> Whenever my profession is hit
> somewhere a hidden nail
> remains embedded
> which on the ripe occasion
> comes to the surface,
> and pierces through the fingers. (ibid.: 38)

Except for this rare moment of angry lapse, the human aspect of his profession remains paramount to the cobbler. The cobbler contradistinguishes his labour with those power brokers who either sell religion or sex:

> And babuji! The fact of the matter is
> that if there is logic to right living
> then, there is no difference between
> those who sell Ram's name or those
> act as pimp for their earning. (ibid.: 39)

Dhoomil's protagonist, instead of hankering after non-productive middle-manship or Vedantic mysticism—the two privileged principles of nation building so far—thus underlines the significance of material production in the making of the nation.[27] Nation is not an abstract notion enshrined or spelled in some Vedic *mantra*; it is a real concrete entity that needs to be supported through manual labour.

The cobbler takes exception to those who confuse profession with caste. As someone describes him 'less of a cobbler, and more of a poet', he retaliates: 'In fact he is a victim of a wrong notion/who thinks that profession is a caste/and that language is a monopoly of a caste/and not of humanity at large . . .' (ibid.: 40). Mere literacy is not enough for awareness. Those who have access to words, due to compulsions of existence, remain blind to injustice. The cobbler acknowledges the role of 'intelligent silence' as crucial as that of 'a vehement cry' (ibid.: 40) in the shaping of the nation. From a fundamentalist dalit position, Dhoomil's 'Mochiram' may not be described as a 'dalit poem', but for the subsequent rise of dalit literature and consciousness, such interventionist poems do play a seminal role.[28] 'Mochiram' is a precursor to the radical dalit poetry that erupted around the mid-1970s in Maharashtra and other parts of India.

IX

From the high-pitched sanskritic nationalism of pre-independence, Hindi poetic imagination thus veers towards subaltern nationalism, negotiating in the process the demands as well as anxieties of statism. It unleashes different configurations of nationalism as much as it is animated by them. If in pre-independence Hindi poetry the endeavour is to work out a duplicitous poetics of nationalism (of resistance and collaboration), in the post-independence phase the self-critical poets question the politics of forging such an ambivalent form of nationalism. The people-centric imperatives, operating for a while under the pressures of high nationalism, come forth in the open as its quasi-spiritual illusions fail to lull them into obedience. Hindi poetry takes an ideological turn, from a statist position, it moves towards the societal one. Nationalism, statism, and finally, people-centric socialism are thus the three stepping stones in the broad evolutionary trajectory of Hindi poetic imagination.

Notes

1. It is authentic for two reasons primarily. One, the process of standardization of Hindi as a possible national language coincides with the early nationalist clamourings of the emerging Indian elite post-1857. Two, in comparison to Bangla and Indian English, the two language-literatures which have almost monopolized the literary space as truly national literatures, Hindi literature has always enjoyed a larger constituency, both in terms of authorship and readership.
2. The nation-state and nationalism are often treated as mutually co-extensive terms without any significant distinction. This happens because in any construction of nation-state, which historically speaking is modern and recent than ancient and even agrarian nationalism, the arbitrarily constructed 'immemorial past' is always invoked. 'Nation' in the frame of the chapter

stands for the institution of nation-state; nationalism is more a sentiment that may translate into a nation-state, may transgress it, may even counter it. Bhabha refers to this elision of meanings: 'The distinction (between modern nation-state and "something more ancient and nebulous *natio*—a local community, domicile, family, condition of belonging") is often obscured by nationalists who seek to place their own country in an "immemorial past" where its arbitrariness cannot be questioned' (1990: 45). Nation-state, as defined by Giddens 'is a set of institutional forms of governance maintaining an administrative monopoly over a territory with demarcated boundaries, its rule being sanctioned by law and direct control of means of internal and external violence' (1987: 121), but in the postcolonial context, it is not fully institutional as it involves a dialectic between the traditional and the modern. It is as much construction, 'an imagined community' (Anderson 1996: 6), as it is a working structure of a living and tangible tradition. Models of nationalism vary so much that it no longer remains a homogenously defined singular category. In the context of the Third World, along with the 'modular' western types identified by Partha Chatterjee as 'creole', 'linguistic' and 'official' (2005: 20), indigenous paradigms of nationalism—Sanskritic, composite, native/popular—produce a cacophony of nationalist discourses, each claiming to be more authentic and comprehensive than the other. Therefore, instead of retaining nationalism in the singular, its plurality is suggested in the parenthesis. The texts selected in this chapter have enjoyed critical acclaim for their subtle negotiation of the idea as well as structure of India as a nation. Also, the poetic-plays included—such as *Bharat Durdasha* and *Andha Yug*—have often been counted as poetic milestones, than as poetic plays.

3. Poetry is a potent discourse of (re-)historicizing reality. New historicists have insistently pointed out the falsity of the binary constructed between poetry as fantasy versus history as empirical truth. Hayden White, in his path-breaking work on historiography, *Tropics of Discourse*, writes in so many words: ' the discourse of the historian and that of the imaginative writer overlap, resemble, or correspond with each other' (1985: 121). Therefore, in the scheme of the chapter, poetic discourse and the historical one are seen to be concurrent with each other. History provides context to poetry as much as poetry re-writes history.

4. From Lukacs to Bakhtin, a whole range of theorists view epic as the genre of the complete rounded self that is beyond the pale of history. Its 'disintegration', according to Lukacs, 'is the pre-condition for the existence of art and its becoming conscious' (1971: 38). In the chapter, the long poem and its variants such as *prabhandha kavya, kavya-natak, prahasana*, etc., are genres of the 'becoming' of the nation, rather than of its 'being'.

5. The year 1857 is an important marker in the construction of the nationalist history of India. In the words of Bernard C. Cohn: 'The war [of 1857] led to redefinitions of the nature of Indian society, the necessary and proper relationships of the rulers and the ruled, and a reassessment of the goals of

government of India, which in turn led to continued changes in the institutional arrangements required to implement these goals' (1992: 179).

6. The pre-1857 nationalism, non-official, non-elitist as it was, relied 'more on the traditional organization of kinship and territoriality . . . more violent . . . more spontaneous . . . realized in its most comprehensive form in peasant uprisings' (Guha 1982: 4).

7. Urdu words/expressions such as *ek jindagi hazaar nayamat, amaldaari, hakim, fauj*, etc., occur frequently in the skit. Bhartendu also quotes Sanskrit sayings from the *Bhagvata Gita* at least thrice in the skit.

8. Bhartendu, in his 'Hindi ki Unnati par Vyakhyan', a poem written in ninety-eight dohas, insists on having 'a national language' (*nij bhasha*) which he holds to be essential for 'national progress'. He acknowledges the respective richness of Sanskrit, Persian and English, but he favours Hindi as the possible national language for it is the language of the intimate domestic domain: 'but this very mother, without Hindi/knows nothing at all/and so one's own language is ahead of all' (1951b: 733).

9. Ramvilas Sharma, for instance, discovers in Bhartendu's Hindi, seeds of assimilative nationalism (*ek sammilit rashtra ki kalpana*), mature enough to ward off sectarian or communal nationalisms (1975: 43). Benedict Anderson however employs the term 'print capitalism' to denote 'the expanding vernacular print-market being created by capitalism' (1996: 40).

10. The shift towards Khari Boli as the basis of Hindi was very much embedded in the communal politics of the times. Harish Trivedi's observation is pertinent: 'An obvious factor was the felt oppression of Hindi by Urdu, along with the frequent charge by the champions of Urdu that Brijbhasha and Avadhi and the other dialects that comprised Hindi were vulgar, rural and unrefined' (2004: 984).

11. This kind of unqualified adoration of the Indian ancient past is one of the common features of various Indian literatures produced in the wake of the so-called Indian renaissance. This is how Henry Vivian Derozio, hailed often as the first Indian poet in English, invokes India: 'My country! In thy day of glory past/A beauteous halo circled round thy brow,/And worshipped as deity thou wast/. . .' (2005: 7)

12. The first idiom was provided by the 'British presence in the country, their concepts, institutions and the terms of their critique of Indian-Hindu culture. . . . The second idiom, the "classical" Indian which sought to reduce the multiplicity of classical traditions on the subcontinent to a unitary tradition, which for all ideological purposes amounted to the Aryan-Hindu. . . . The second idiom then, practically bypassed the Muslim era . . . the third idiom . . . included both the traditional and the reformist formulations' (Dalmia 1997: 430–31).

13. 'Adapted into colonial discourse theory by Homi Bhabha, it describes the complex mix of attraction and repulsion that characterizes the relationship between colonizer and colonized. The relationship is ambivalent because the colonized subject is never simply and completely opposed to the colonizer.

Rather than assuming that some colonized subjects are "complicit" and some "resistant", ambivalence suggests that complicity and resistance exist in a fluctuating relation within the colonial subject' (Ashcroft et al. 2004: 12–13).

14. Under the statist approach, the state is seen in quintessential organizational terms.

15. Ironically enough, Gupt's overtly sanskritist poem is modelled after Hali's *Musaddas*—a long poetic text that contained translations of Quranic verses or of Hadith and some images of the present state of the Indian Muslims. Also, in his construction of Hindu nationalism, Gupt borrows tools, categories and even research findings of the colonialists to the core.

16. This is how Gupt endorses the Raj:

> Really British Empire has given us so much
> Showed us the glory of science, made us time-conscious
> Has been beneficial in spreading our past glory
> Many ancient signs of ours have been redeemed. (1989: 81)

> This is the grace of British rule that we woke up
> We are free to choose our religion, our all apprehensions gone
> We have started recognizing our own self somewhat—
> we have started accepting India as our own nation. (ibid.: 176)

17. According to Partha Chatterjee, early nationalists separated the domain of culture into two exclusive categories of the inner versus the outer, *ghar* versus *bahir*, wherein the former stands for spiritual growth, the latter for material advancement. The former is occupied by women; the latter by men. The former must always be protected from outer influence as it forms the core of culture. Chatterjee sums up: 'Once we matched this new meaning of the home/world dichotomy with the identification of social roles by gender, we get the ideological framework within which nationalism answered the woman's question' (1993: 121).

18. Subhadra Kumari Chauhan was 'involved in Congress propaganda among women both in the town and in the district, and was one of the few middle class women who did not observe parda. First arrested during the flag satyagraha in 1923, she was jailed again in 1941 for individual *satyagraha*' (Orisini 2002: 393).

19. Partha Chatterjee interprets this change in the following terms: 'Modernization began in the first half of the nineteenth century because of the penetration of Western ideas. After some limited success, there was a perceptible decline in the reform movements as popular attitudes toward them hardened. The new politics of nationalism "glorified India's past and tended to defend everything traditional. . . . Consequently, nationalism fostered a distinctly conservative attitude"' (1993: 116).

20. Re-writing has been one of the mainstays of modern Hindi poetry. A whole range of texts—Harioudh's *Priyaparvas* (1947), Maithilisharan Gupt's *Saket* (1974), Dinkar's *Kurukshetra* (1946), Prasad's *Kamayani* (1936), etc., were written during the nationalist period with a discernibly different orientation

from their original texts. The emphasis in re-writing shifts to women characters in a noticeable manner. Also, most of the texts re-written were based on the *Mahabharata*, than on the *Ramayana* or *Ramcharitmanas*, which not only speaks of the different possibilities of re-writing these two classical texts offer, but also the relatively non-*maryada*-centric attitude of the poets.

21. Nirala's many long poems such as 'Panchvati-Prasang' (1949b), 'Shivaji ka Patra' (1949b), 'Tulsidas' (1938), 'Jago Phir Ek Baar I & II' (1980a), etc., rely primarily on canonical Hindu narratives. In these poems Hindu nationalism and Indian nationalism tend to coincide.

22. Self-rule/home-rule, defined in derivative terms prior to Gandhi's arrival on the national scene, stands re-defined in *Hind Swaraj* in indigenous terms. Nirala's invocation to *Shakti* is in keeping with Gandhi's call for realizing *swaraj* as inner feeling: 'It is Swaraj when we learn to rule ourselves. It is, therefore, in the palm of our hands. Do not consider this Swaraj to be like a dream. Here there is no idea of sitting still' (Gandhi 1997: 73). Nirala's Ram, thus, in a way is a Gandhi exploring *swaraj/shakti*.

23. Nehru was greatly annoyed with Gandhi for giving extraordinary attention to the dalit issue. When Gandhi announced from prison that he would go on a fast to protest against the grant of a separate electorate to the 'Depressed Classes', Nehru expressed displeasure for choosing such an untimely 'side-issue for [his] final sacrifice'. He asks, 'What would be the result of our freedom movement? Would larger issues fade into background for the time being at least?' (1936: 370).

24. It is interesting to note that Shashi Tharoor, in his political allegory, *The Great Indian Novel* (1993), assigns the role of Karna to Mohammad Ali Jinnah.

25. 'In summary, religious humanists viewed religion as a human creation to contribute to both personal and social well-being. Unlike the traditional understandings of religion, even the more liberal ones, it repudiated belief in God, the belief that humans could not be moral without the concept of God to support morality, and the belief that humans were immortal in any personal sense' (Olds, see www.humanistsofutah.org/1996).

26. Alok Bhalla, in his 'Introduction' to the translation of *Andha Yug*, contextualizes the poetic-play in partition violence: 'Given the intensity of the moral anxieties *Andha Yug* evoked, it was obvious that the play, written soon after the carnage of the partition of the Indian subcontinent, which nearly erased a form of life and civilization . . . still had the power to make us realize how we live to the borders of nightmares' (2005: 5). According to Ramswarup Chaturvedi, a noted Hindi critic, the play exceeds any topical context as it raises fundamental questions 'about the difference and proximity between faith and non-faith' (1973: 103). Many other critics tend to situate the play in the global context as they hear the resonance of World War II in it.

27. Frantz Fanon, the Algerian revolutionary, also comments on the non-productive character of the national bourgeoisie: 'The national bourgeoisie of under-developed countries is not engaged in production, nor in invention, nor building, nor labour; it is completely canalized into activities of the

intermediary type. Its innermost vocation seems to be to keep in the running and to be part of the racket' (1990: 120). The concluding lines of Kancha Illaiah's essay, 'Towards Dalitization of the Nation', are also pertinent here: 'A nation is not merely a notion, but a living reality of people. Brahminism is to this day attempting to construct the Indian nation in the image of fantasy. On the contrary, the Dalitbahujans want to build the nation on the basis of its productive culture and consciousness' (1998: 290).

28. The fundamental dalit position as asserted by some of the post-Ambedkarite dalit ideologues and activists is that only dalits can speak about dalits, and only such a writing could be described as 'dalit': 'Dalit literature is that literature which is written by one who is Dalit by birth. . . . It is not possible to convey imaginatively the caste-specific experience of Dalits' (Limbale 2004: 105).

2

De-fetishizing Home/Homelessness: 'Nation' in Post-1990s Hindi Poetry

Harish Trivedi, a well-known bilingual critic, while charting out the contribution of Hindi in the making of India as a nation, makes a seminal observation: 'The new national identity of India, whether in the colonial first half of the twentieth century or in the postcolonial second half, thus had Hindi as one of its defining components' (2004: 961). One wonders whether such an assertion would hold true at the turn of the millennium, as both players of the game, that is, Hindi as well as the nation, have undergone drastic semantic shifts, if not dismemberment from within. A fresh appraisal of the relationship of Hindi and India as its home/nation, therefore, becomes very pertinent as both the discourses from the late 1990s onwards are on the back foot, virtually fighting for their survival against the hyped discourse of English as an international language on the one hand, and globalization as the new *mantra* of the international economic order on the other.[1]

Hindi as a language has undergone fundamental changes. From Khari Boli to Hindustani, and then from sanskritized *chhayavadi* diction to cosmopolitan 'school textbook Hindi', it has taken a postmodern character.[2] In the media, it is almost half-anglicized, as disco jockeys in their accented Hindi play re-mixes of Hindi songs of the the melodious 1960s. Hindi newspapers use English lexicon without any purist hangover. India as a nation, too, is desperate to hitch itself onto the global bandwagon, notwithstanding its atavistic lapses into the sanskritic past now and then. The political consensus on globalization as panacea for the ills of the nation is mind-boggling. Fukuyama's polemical gospel of the 'end of history' and the final victory of capitalism seems to have seduced the academic elite beyond recovery.[3]

The present chapter seeks to investigate the relationship between Hindi poetry and 'nation' in the extremely 'volatile period of the 1990s' in terms of the responses of the poets to new 'global' realities.[4] In view of some of the fundamental structural changes that the nation-state has undergone from within and without, the 1990s have been identified as the most crucial and even cataclysmic period of contemporary history. The collapse of the erstwhile USSR, the arrival of late capitalism in the age of multinational global economics, the explosion of information worldwide, the rise of global terrorism, the rise of the ultra-right, the demolition of the Babri mosque, the simmerings of the subaltern, etc., have been some of the seminal developments which shape contemporary creative imagination at the very level of the unconscious. In the wake of the post–Cold War international politics of new trans- as well as sub-national civilizational re-alignments, the very co-ordinates of political as well as poetical imagination have undergone a paradigmatic shift.

Do Hindi poets of the 1990s continue to valourize the nation in familiar semi-oriental, quasi-spiritual terms as their '*chayavadi* predecessors' did?[5] Are they caught in some nativist time-warp? Or do they take their nation for granted as their permanent, unalterable address? Or do they, under the spell of globalization, endorse the borderless barrier-free nation? Are they comfortable with apocalyptic pronouncements ranging from the death of the nation to the death of history? Do they give up the nation altogether? More importantly, is there a consensus on the idea of nation? The post–*Taar Saptak* breed of poets suddenly finds itself amidst a medley of new critical debates and social imperatives; it realizes the inadequacies of both experimentalism (*prayogvad*) and rhetorical progressive poetics (*pragativad*) to negotiate with the emerging dynamics of the post-1990s world order. The space they write in and for demands participation and even intervention at a level where boundaries of poetical and political activism simply blur.

I

Contemporary Hindi poets as postcolonial participants in the processes of the nation reveal keen awareness of the politics of location that implicates their home/nation in the 1990s. They observe and acknowledge the strategic shifts that the location, the address and the identity of nation/home has undergone with varying degrees of concern. The hitherto unqualified idealization of 'nation as a possessive space' has definitely given way to its critical understanding as a space that is undergoing immense contestation from within and without.[6] As multiple margins 'interrupt and transgress' the granted cartography—both geographical as well as cultural—of the overbearing nation-space, its traditional authority suddenly appears untenable, but not utterly unwanted.[7] Nation is cherished, but uncritical monolithic nationalism receives little poetic support. The body itself becomes the locus of the nation but it is dysfunctional: 'just like the existence of a state/our body too relies on infinite coincidences and possibilities . . . a problematic structure carrying the burden of its history and diseases' ('Shareer', Prakash 1998: 28–30).

Despite the possible fears of lapsing into the inflationary rhetoric of cultural nationalism, most of the poets tend to retain the institution of nation as a desirable vantage point for warding off the seductions of globalization. Home, before it is forever lost in the wilderness unleashed by global economy, is to be frenetically re-searched. Arun Kamal's title poem, 'Naye Illake Mein', for instance, is a sordid dirge on the increasing confusion on the home's location in the new global market place. In the jungle of new localities, the sense of direction goes haywire and pathways to home are often missed, 'old markers often betray' and 'memory does not work', yet identifying one's home/ nation is an enterprise and a challenge that must be undertaken: 'this is the only option now/knock at every door and ask—is this my home?' (1999: 13–14).

While the possibility of return to some imagined pure national past is ruled out, the necessity of home as a refuge for the battered self is, however, underlined in the following poem by Arun Kamal:

> Loitering through the day, tired
> I returned
> to where my home used to be
>
> instead there was
> a huge mansion, iron gates and gatekeepers—
> here it was my house, my father, my mother
> where is my house
>
> the gatekeepers laughed—
> which previous birth are you talking about?[8]
> ('Haat', 1999: 20–21)

The sudden transformation of the familial 'nation-space' into a well-guarded estranged mansion is regretted as the poet seeks to discover his organic roots. The exigencies of the new economic order have suddenly outdated any notion of even a working fixity in life. Uday Prakash, in his poem 'Ghar' (1998: 54), declares emphatically, 'I intend to go home'; yet as he self-reflects he wonders how he could produce this cohesive syntax in times of post-structural chaos.

Undeterred by the fashionable rhetoric of exhaustion, Krishan Mohan Jha continues to hear echoes of the secular sacredness of his home/nation. Nation exists as an ambience, a feeling and a prayer: 'Present in this house/is the sacredness of those prayers/sung hundreds of years ago' ('Es Ghar Mien', 1998: 20). There is an acceptance of life in terms of its essential continuities which even time's arrow cannot pierce through. In the poem quoted next, if 'the man' is seen as the locus of nation, the possibilities of its absolute demise are minimum:

> With so much effort
> the earth that crafts a man
> the rivers that water him
> the time that sculpts
> design on his body day and night
> how can all these
> let a man go absolute alone
> in his last moments . . .?
>   ('Akale hi Nahin', ibid.: 14)

These assertions of the pastness of the past are definitely far from being revivalist. Quite significantly, what sustains the poet in the hour of his dispersal is not religion, or even mythos; it is his allegiance to his surroundings and nature. The metaphysics of flux is not absolute as the poet says, 'This time/fails to liquidate many things/whatever you do/these things cannot be emptied' ('Saari Cheezein Nahin', ibid.: 18). Though the mirror of memory has lost its sheen, the poet Boddhisatav struggles to retain the clear image of the home in it: 'and here I am, who with effort has kept it decorated/in that fading mirror of the home' ('Ghar Mein', 2000: 58).

In a poem 'Ghar', Aikant Srivastav, another poet of the 1990s, while recounting days of his intimate past in the confines of his home pledges not to let it fall under any circumstance: 'This home/our most intimate relation/stood by us/through thick and thin/would it fall so easily/O home/I shall not let you fall' (1994: 44–45). The trope of nation as motherland—from *Vande Mataram* to *Bharat Mata* —continues to operate but only at a residual level. Leeladhar Mandloi, for instance, wants to rest on the pillow which retains some of the resonances of mother's lullaby. Here, the pillow is not simply a resting couch for the beleaguered mother-less postcolonial self; it is a kind of maternal support:

> one simple pillow is necessary for a suitable sleep
> even if it is badly mutilated or old, or it smells foul
> it does not really matter.
>
> after mother's departure the lullabies I lost are found near it
> ('Mera Takiya Ccheen Liya Gaya', 1995: 24)

The pillow is the beholder of mother's soothing lullabies. The nation, despite, its being dirty and archaic, is the poet's ultimate refuge. It is his familiar zone of comfort.

There is a latent desire to re-discover history, language, narrative, which the West thinks are irretrievably lost. The voices, though subdued, continue to appear that seek 'meaning' in life as against the polemics of its constant deferral. Dinesh Kumar Shukla believes that 'the words would over-brim with meanings' and 'the language of the lake/would come alive/with the waves of dialogue' ('Vahan Jana Hoga', 1999: 39). The poet steers clear of the seductions of the postmodern hyperspace as he reposes confidence in the history of human experience. The modern symbol of the flag co-exists with a medieval legend to resist the excesses of postmodern tentativeness. In the face of the rhetoric of history's so-called end, 'one girl writes/secretly/a love-letter', 'a farmer hums in low voice/one sad song', 'the engine of rail/keeps running/in its own rhythm', and more importantly, 'the poet/decides/to come back' ('Avaidhya Nahin hai Kavi', ibid.: 102).

Hindi poets of the 1990s react sharply against the 'end of history' syndrome as propagated by the capitalist West. The histories of post-colonial societies and nations cannot be wished away in favour of the grand and spectacular victory of capitalism. Katyayni writes a series of poems on Fukuyama's prophetic polemics that history has come to a dead end with its abject surrender to capitalism. In her poem 'Ve Nahin Sochte', she counters the propaganda of 'endism' thus:

> science did not burn with Bruno
> nor did it surrender with the apology of Galeleo
> songs did not die
> even in the torture chambers of Nazis
> after all why can't they think
> that reversals come about often

> but hardly could they become
> the norms of history
> (1999: 111)

In another very direct poem, 'Na Rookna', she insists on the flow of life even in the face of natural catastrophes: 'The building of houses/ would not stop/even if they crumble in flood, in storm/and in the earthquakes' (ibid.: 89). In yet another response to the 'end-of-history' debate, she approaches history as a discourse comprehensive enough to subsume its own notional end; 'In history itself/the slogan of end-of-history is laid to rest/this is as grand a truth/as the end-of-idea is/ which in itself is an idea' (without title, 2002: 48). The various endgames—from the end of ideology to the end of history—being stage-managed and orchestrated by the metropolitan academia are thus largely resented by the Hindi poets as they refuse to be swept off their feet against the tide of extremely seductive western theory. Thus, the nation survives in the Hindi imagination but its survival is precariously poised.

II

The nation/home is cherished, but nowhere is it lionized as a space of eternal wisdom or absolute purity. Closed nationalism is as much a threat to the postcolonial self as multinational globalism is. Kumar Ambuj's poem 'Janjire' dwells on the politics of cultural nationalism as it fetters the human self in the rusted chains of archaic morality and ritualistic past; these chains masquerade as dormant *samskaras* that come alive at the slightest provocation: 'one could see them lying on our door-frames/with minor mining they had begun to surface/out from our own selves, heavy and rusted'. The dissonances that these chains generate 'fill[s] one group with happiness, the other with fear'. And this is what defines the process of social change: 'this process has changed into a process of social progress' (Kumar 1998: 191). The poet warns us against the dangers of invoking a defunct and fossilized past with all its ceremonial baggage, for once it is legitimized it over-whelms the space with its antediluvian mindset. The relapse into a dead past is, ironically enough, projected as a new principle of social change and progress by the votaries of cultural nationalisms; the poet instead discovers in this politics of revivalism the seeds of com-munal divide.

Writing in the times of siege, the Hindi poets of the 1990s question the intervention of various religious/communal organizations in the day-to-day working of the nation-space. Kumar Ambuj exposes the politics of the so-called godly outfits, which seek to drag the modern nation-state back into the mould of medieval supra-territorial religious empires:

> Hoisting their flags on the ramparts
> they stone at the multi-coloured history they are ashamed of
> they seek to take pride at their birth
> which they had no control on
> they want to forge a new embryo
> in the womb of a dead language
> along with the wrong words of their live language
> they all are a godly organization, now.
> ('Ishwariya Sangthan', 2002: 114)

The nation is literally competing with so many caste and community gods/icons that retaining a secular human/national identity has become a challenge. The violent designs of the godly organizations are no longer camouflaged.

In his poem, 'Ghar ki Aitihasik Yaad', Leeladhar Jagudi traces the process of the communalization of the domestic space as it is carved out of the unbound space of the open skies and limitless earth:

> We build house as we make an idol
> a mixed idol of jungle, animals and their caves
> against the formless and the attribute-free, we make our house
> temples, mosques and churches we build
> we communalize styles as well.
> (Kumar 1998: 22)

The jingoistic madness of cultural nationalism even drives the poet to question the very idea of nation as such. The high-pitched 'iconolatry of home' disenchants the poet so much that he tends to relapse into the primordial pre-society state.

III

Hindi poetry of the 1990s offers a vehement critique of globalization as it is approached as another subtle manifestation of capitalism/colonialism. While these poets concede change, they regret the nation's total surrender to multinational global forces that are all set to swallow the small domestic players: 'when vultures hover all over the sky/ . . ./I walk on roads like/an easy prey'. The poet seems to shrink back into an ascetic mould; 'We have to earn the happiness/of retrieving our souls/from the terror of unholy desires' (Chaturvedi 1998: 12). The consumerism unleashed by globalization has only augmented materialist desires. Malay, in his poem 'Bazaar', forewarns against the glittering spectre of free economy that robs the individual of his innate self/space: 'In the shops/as we change clothes/of one fashion to another/undressing ourselves time and again so much/ that on going back to our homes/we are in a dizzy,/gasping and faltering/we are caught in the cyclones rising from our hearts,/ loosing control of our own selves' (2002: 113–14). Commodity fetishism is another fall-out of the global economy of mass production. Too many things would simply glut the market: 'Things one day become so powerful/that they create their autonomous authority/then man does not decide, things determine man's destiny!!' ('Vastuon Ke Bare Mein Ek Kathan', Joshi 1994: 60).

The ubiquitous presence of the market economy has commercialized the inner-most recesses of our soul. The 'so-called insular interior landscape' has been invaded by the new market forces reducing the nation into a perpetual transactional space:[9]

> At every step we see a bazaar
> every moment we pass through a bazaar
> we often forget
> when we are in the bazaar, and when we are not
> where there is slight settlement, a bazaar could be seen
> we see that where two people meet
> a bazaar springs up
> now bazaar is one minor event
> that happens every moment as
> routine in this world
>
> ('Ek Baar Phir', Ambuj 2002: 56)

Bazaar knows no boundaries—internal or external. The economy has overtaken all other aspects of life as people meet only to enhance material profits. The fluctuations in the stock market tend to control the heart beat of the nation. From the Gandhian era of co-operative competitiveness, we entered into the speculative realm of profit-making. Nirmala Garg articulates the craze thus: 'After Mahatama

Gandhi, it was share only that undertook the Dandi march/right from the paanwalla's hut/to the multi-storeyed flats' ('Share', 2002: 34).

Dinesh Kumar Shukla's poetry is also full of postcolonial anguish and anger. Taking a dig at the new international patent regime under the World Trade Organization (WTO), the poet confronts the complicit postcolonial peddlers of globalization for mortgaging the nation's soul to market forces:

> because now neem and turmeric
> are your patents
>
> this morning is yours,
> this evening too is yours.
>   ('Buddhi ka License', 1999: 32–33)

Globalization is seen as a process that appropriates the unpatented community-owned intellectual property of the Third World. It amounts to robbing the poor of their organic wisdom. The local technologies that were once invented by the tribes and other grass-root communities centuries ago are being patented by the mercantile West; the poet fears this would deprive them of their basic natural rhythms.

Mithilesh Srivastav also raises his voice against market forces, even if it entails total marginalization of his own products. He refuses to be beguiled by the razzmatazz of the new market-driven economy 'if they do not like the sad colours, let them not/I cannot make the colours on my canvass brilliant' ('Bazaar ke Khilaaf', 1999: 9). The barrage of advertisements that come from practically every possible space of the nation—private or public—has totally taken over the reality of life. A virtual world has relegated the real into oblivion: 'In the mad-mad world of ads/the real taste of colours/is forgotten' ('Kucch Na Kucch', Shukla 1992: 31). There is a fear that the nation would abdicate itself totally. Aikant Srivastav writes on the WTO agreement: 'Only one signs the deed/and we lose/our country' ('Hastakshar', Kumar 1998: 203). Globalization is perceived to be a gateway to re-colonization.

Globalization is the economic order of the trans-national elite, which has scant regard for rural economy. Its promised prosperity would bypass rural India. Viren Dangwal takes exception to globalization's overarching logic of prosperity: 'Let the globe become village/but all the villages remain outside from it/this should be the feat of computer' ('March ki Ek Sham Mien IIT Kanpur', 2002: 19).

The apprehension is that the superhighways of information shall circumvent the by-lanes of rural poverty. The hyperspace shall have no contact with the socio-cultural space of the nation; it might also have no rivers to flow under them: 'how unfortunate are those bridges/ which are just passages/under which no river flows . . .' (ibid.).

IV

Hindi poetry of the 1990s enters a new phase of subaltern activism. Furthering the credo of the preceding generation of progressive poets, the new poets expose the hegemonic politics of representation which relegates people—the real players of history—to the margins. History is nothing but an account of the chosen few plunderers who steal the limelight. Major landmarks are named after them. Sanjay Chaturvedi fears that these false gods might appropriate our future too: 'Whenever this town would be dug up/these plunderers would become [players of] history/they shall swallow our future' ('Lutere Bankar Itihaas', 1993: 57). The poets of the 1990s have taken upon themselves to speak along with the subaltern. Poetry is a perpetual correction of official history. Ashok Vajpeyi articulates his enchantment against the made-up history of the nationalists. The poet joins the company of the sub-alterns thus:

> On the margins of glitter and pomp,
> outside the glossy edifice of history
> people who are standing there
> in their own places
> with me, the poet
> I open only one window for them.
>   ('Shatabdi ke Ant ke Kagaar Par', 2000: 13)

The nationalist histories put people on the margins in favour of a semi-spiritualized account of the nationalist elite.[10] For Manglesh Dabral, these margins constitute the dwelling space of the poet wherein 'he scribbles some words/draws some figures of animals, vegetation and clothes drying on the wire outside/registers his duties/leaves some signs of red colour' ('Hashiye ki Kavita', 1995: 40).

Leeladhar Jagudi's 'Itihaas Mein Ghaas' is a poem which challenges the hegemonic discourse of nationalist historiography from a sub-altern perspective. In the poem, 'grass' emerges as a symbol of the downtrodden and the unprivileged. The poet argues that despite efforts to obliterate the subalterns from the hegemonic narrative of nationalist history, the subalterns survive to script alternate histories, histories of the people from below: 'The grass proved to be smarter than the grass-cutter/whenever it was cut, it remained with us . . ./ and with whatever it was left, it scripted history' (1999: 18). 'Grass' has been our mainstay against any onslaught, military or cultural. Against the official histories, the counter-histories narrated, sung and written by the people are far more trustworthy and reliable: 'In our history, more than history, it was grass that helped us more/without any cost-benefit analysis, it paved way for crop-cultivation/whose one witness is that hunger-satisfied animals are not against us' (ibid.). Grass has been our saving grace, despite the official machinery's efforts to erase it: 'Many a times the grass grown on the edges saved us from falling and sinking/while we have been doing our utmost to uproot it . . .' (ibid.).

The poets of the 1990s discern potential unrest at the roots of the grass. Hamant Kukrati decides to abandon his life in the dense grass, instead of any holy river: 'just stroked the grass/stroked and realized it too had fire/is there anyone who shares its heat?' ('Ek Garam Shaam Ghaas Par', 2002: 63). Grass, the conventional Whitmanian hieroglyph, thus undergoes significant semantic mutations in the 1990s as, increasingly, it becomes a signifier of the people at the lowest rung of the social hierarchy whose presence cannot be wished away any longer.[11] From being a symbol of mystical oneness, it turns into the sword of political activism. A rare energy is thus bestowed upon this rather dormant symbol of everyday life.

In a poem, 'Ghaas-Bans-Birudavali', Dinesh Kumar Shukla addresses the blade of grass 'as life's simplest creation' (1999: 35) that refuses to vanish against all odds. It took the form of river grass, sugarcane, elephant grass, wheat, bamboo tree, etc., to confront the elitist world. It exists even in deserts: 'it is said/sands of desert/have the most developed species of grass/which is now/found only in dreams' (ibid.: 38). Naresh Saxena also locates the potentials of subaltern unrest in the grass, which if at one level sustains life, '[Something] that runs through the veins of a horse as blood/that bursts forth as milk from the nipples of a cow/that carpets the earth', at another, if trampled, 'sprouts forth/on the minarets of palace and walls of fort/ heralding the beginning of new demolition' ('Ghaas', 2001: 37).

The innocuous looking grass is invested with rare powers of subversion. Its animating powers are acknowledged as proof of its revolutionary potential.

If 'grass' emerges as a symbol of the subaltern in the poetry of Leeladhar Jagudi, Pankaj Chaturvedi and Dinesh Kumar Shukla, the onion is the chosen metaphor of subaltern alignment in the poetry of Rajesh Joshi. In his poem, 'Pyaaz Ek Sanrachna Hai', the poet compares the structure of the onion with a series of images from the subaltern world:

> Onion is a structure like
> our people around the fire
> like farm-labour taking
> its mid-day meal
> in a group
> sharing *roti* and salt.
>
> onion is a structure of
> fist held tight in anger and resolve . . .
>
> (2002: 52)

The onion is the food as well as the fuel of subaltern masses. It, like grass, also sprouts from the womb of the earth—the intimate hub of the subaltern.

Besides the onion, Rajesh Joshi also deploys images such as 'unfinished poems', 'auxiliaries', 'crickets' to articulate the concerns of the small and the peripheral. He addresses the marginalized subalterns as 'et cetera' who 'were everywhere but there names could not be included anywhere/et cetera could be seen often in the poems of some mad poets. . .' The unrecognized contribution of 'et cetera' to the making of the nation is further stressed:

> The et cetera used to do all work
> that runs the nation and the world
> yet they believed that
> the work they do is
> only work for the sake of their family.
> ('Ityadi', 2000: 13–14)

As a poet of unfinished poems, Joshi discovers possibilities of resistance in them. They may not have attained the sophistication and finesse of the finished ones, yet they do assert their presence in their own half-heard, half-understood tongue:

> They do not speak, yet they seem to say something
> we are unfinished alright
> but which poem has descended on this earth as finished?
>
> by the way we are greater in number in this world
>   ('Adhoori Kavitain', ibid.: 12)

The unfinished is innate, spontaneous, organic and even unorganized —these precisely are 'the characteristics of the subaltern'.[12] The auxiliaries are not major units in a sentence structure, yet in functional terms they are indispensable. They may not have their own autonomous meaning, yet they sustain the suggestions conveyed by the whole structure. Through the image of 'auxiliaries' Rajesh Joshi conveys the message that small is neither insignificant nor shameful: 'the jugglers of language tried their best/to oust them from their sentences/but in the life's wider prose, they continued' ('Sahayak Kriya', ibid.: 15–16). The jugglers of language are the manipulators of social realism who fail to silence the sound of the auxiliaries.

The women poets also find home too patriarchal and male-dominated. As a subaltern subject, the woman protagonist in the following poem is all set to leave the 'comforts' of nation-space:

> Just, one day all of a sudden
> she raised an innocent question
> can there be a female without home
> or is there any structure
> other than the home
> wherein she can live
> happily
> wherein a woman could remain a woman,
> and a home, a home . . .
>   ('Aurat Aur Ghar', Katyayni 1999: 69)

More than anything else, it is the nation that exiles its own women. As a subaltern subject, she seeks positive empowerment; the so-called national identity in itself does not redeem her lot.

V

While articulating the concerns of the subalterns, the poets are acutely aware of the possible misuse of the subaltern space both by the subalterns themselves and their non-subaltern spokesmen from outside. Kumar Ambuj expresses his reservations on the new slogan of the subaltern, particularly its appropriation by the non-subaltern elite; in one of his poems, he apprehends, 'that it could be used to wipe off/ our own black deeds' ('Aadarshviheen Samay Mein', 2002: 79–80). The credo of the subaltern is not used as an excuse to promote exclusive nativism or narrow provincialism. Rajesh Joshi himself warns against the polemical use of subaltern poetics and politics both. Dissent is manufactured in the workshops of subaltern literature:

> now plays would be prepared in workshops
> poems would be written in the workshops
> novels would be written in the workshops
> all arts would be prepared in the workshops
> as per directions
>
> that it is new phase
> of workshop culture.
>
> ('Mahan Kala-Mulya', 2002: 163)

In the poem, the poet cautions against the vulnerability of the subaltern movements to the forces of global militarism. The subaltern locations can be used for strategic military installations by the superpowers.

The son-of-the-soil theory disturbs most of the contemporary poets for it not only inhibits the dynamism from within, it also breeds the forces of narrow provincialism. Hindi poets do not evince any regional fanaticism or any narrow hegemonic Hindi nationalism; they are eager enough to traverse across the whole nation-space without being branded as outsiders or insiders:

> Kamal, listen Kamal, do not be sentimental
> somewhere you will have to go
> somewhere you will to search livelihood
> just think Kamal, think about me
> think I went to Imphal
> you described me as outsider,
> then I came to Delhi
> and Delhi declared me outsider too
> then I came back to my Patna
> and Patna said that you were not born here . . .
>
> ('Svagat', Kamal 1989: 75)

The reference to Imphal in the poem extends the conventional cartography of the post-1990s Hindi imagination which otherwise remained within the confines of the so-called holy cow belt. Not only are the new imperatives of economic and the concomitant social change accepted, the possibilities of going back to an absolute past are also ruled out.

The new poets seek to cover the entire nation-space in their stride, without being possessive of their regional loyalties. Migration within the nation should not be seen as displacement, nor should it be seen with distrust. The poet Mohan Kumar Daheriya recounts the natural landmarks of the nation-space as he seeks a room of his own: 'always I made a request to/the deserts of Rajasthan, the snows of Shimla, the chinars of Kashmir/don't smell me like hunting dogs' ('Visthapan', Kumar 1998: 233). The sameness of the soil is also expressed: 'I am made up of the same soil/which is under your boot-soles' (ibid.). What the poet seeks quite modestly is a small piece of land irrespective of the region in which it is located. Once again the poem is remarkable for its geographical expanse, extending the frontiers of Hindi nationalism. The poets of the 1990s seek open and dynamic nationalism, which is not unduly regimented from within and without. Not only should the walls crumble, even the doors should be chopped down for being stationed at one place: 'they only toss up the delicate time in and out' ('Darwaazon ko Chalna Chahiye', Chaturvedi 1998: 41).

Malay, another poet of the 1990s, also seeks to break across the walls of saffron nationalism.

> When shall the eyes be alert?
> when shall the coming generations see
> beyond
> and think correctly
> when shall the walls collapse
> when shall the dawn come
> to these eyes . . .
> ('Paanv Vali Deevarien', 2002: 63)

'Beyond' in the poem is not a marker of post-national identity; even nationalism—both critical and creative—demands a degree of self-enlargement and constant self-re-validation so as to meaningfully meet the new challenges of life as a whole.

VI

Hindi poets of the 1990s are, thus, not satisfied with either the cultural
or the post-national brands of nationalism being currently championed
in the political arena. Subaltern is definitely its constituency but, as we
have seen, it is not romanticized beyond a point for, at times, it turns
overtly polemical. Even the modernist 'statist model of nation' is
strongly resented for its being bureaucratic in structure.[13] Both colonial
indifference and feudal arrogance combine to usurp people of their
right to protest. In his poem, 'Jiladheesh', Alokdhanva underlines how
the post-independence indigenous bureaucracy with its intimate
knowledge of the native space could be far more deceitful in depriving
people of the benefits of independence:

> He can keep us away from
> our independence
> tight,
> we should keep a tight
> vigil
> on this mind of the government.
> (1998: 48)

The bureaucratization of the nation-state, along colonial lines, is clearly
not the way endorsed as a strategy of postcolonial emancipation by
the Hindi poets of the 1990s.

The statist approach pins down organic nations to rigorous
cartographies of space and mind, both. Maps—even the most detailed
ones—often miss out people:

> In the map, there are jungles, but no trees
> In the map, there are rivers, but not water
> in the map, there are mountains, but not stones
> in the map, there is a nation, but not people
> you must have understood that we all live
> in a map.
> ('Nakshe', Saxena 2001: 92)

Not only have the macro-level outer details been mapped out, the
blueprints of the inner micro-level body parameters have also been
prepared:

> From our pants and chappals
> to our parentage and body marks
> our pulse rate, blood pressure and temperature
> dreams and memories included have
> also been measured out
> and the maps are ready
>
> (ibid.: 92)

The poet does not scramble for a space on the map, but he also does not want to be left out. As he bemoans the excessive zeal for cartography, he imagines someday 'some joker would just fold this unrelenting map in his pocket and disappear' (ibid.: 93).

In his poem, 'Almaari Jaisa Ghar', Hamant Kukrati also disparages the whole notion of dividing the organic space into segregated zones of region or language, in the process reducing the living space into an inflexible grid of blocks:

> all have been rendered so isolated
> for the release of pent up breaths they
> run away from their own shadows . . .
>
> it was less a house than an almirah stacked with people
> people, who had become shelves of this almirah
> each with distinct lock
> all closed
> all keys lost . . .
>
> (2002: 61–62)

VII

Thus, across the variety of responses—from rejection of the new-fangled idea of post-nation to the continuation of nation as an institution more answerable to its margins—the Hindi poets of the 1990s and after positively rebuff both globalization and cultural nationalism, the two most hyped paradigms of possible postcolonial recovery. This rebuff constitutes the bottom-line of response that Hindi poets of the 1990s evince towards the relevance and future of the nation in human affairs. Neither closed nationalism nor barrier-free globalism nor even separatist subalternism is endorsed as these poets clamour for a negotiated nation-space that caters to the material, intellectual and emotional needs of everyone living within it.

Notes

1. In the emerging global context, the microcosmic 'home' bears a homologous relationship with the macrocosmic nation. At an intermediate level, it also stands for the determinate native foregrounding of the self/body. In this chapter, 'home' is as much a signifier of the private self, the native-space and the nation as 'nation' is the signifier of the home, the self and the native-space.

2. Alok Rai, in his book *Hindi Nationalism* (2001), traces the evolution of Hindi from pre-independence Hindustani to what he terms as 'school Hindi' which is as alien as the so-called 'second-language'.

3. Francis Fukuyama posits a theory according to which, after the liquidation of USSR, there is nothing left in history to accomplish. The victory of capitalism is universal and final, and this marks the very end of history. He argues, 'a remarkable consensus concerning the legitimacy of liberal democracy as a system of government had emerged throughout the world over the past few years, as it conquered rival ideologies like hereditary monarchy, fascism and most recently communism . . . that liberal democracy may constitute the "end point of mankind's ideological evolution" and the "final form of human government" and as such constituted "end of history"' (1992: xi).

4. From V. S. Naipaul's *India: Million Mutinies Now* to Gurcharan Das's *The Elephant Paradigm*, a number of books written on India identify the 1990s as the most volatile phase of the country's history. Naipaul finds India of the 1990s suddenly changed: 'It made the independence struggle seem like an interim . . . ; now there were many revolutions within that revolution' (1997: 4). In Sunil Khilnani's *The Idea of India*, India of the 1990s is seen to be 'poised for dramatic change, yet never quite accomplishing it' (1997: 11). Shashi Tharoor's observation also underlines the significance of the 1990s: 'As the country nears the fiftieth anniversary of its independence, it is undergoing a period of ferment in which profound challenges have arisen to the secular assumptions of Indian politics, to the caste structures underpinning society, and to the socialist consensus driving economic policy' (1998: 323–24). Gurcharan Das, in his *The Elephant Paradigm: India Wrestles with Change*, describes the 1990s as 'our liberating nineties' (2002: 3).

5. For instance, Sumitranandan Pant's poem, 'Bharat Mata', from his collection *Gramya*, concludes on a note of spiritual resignation:

> Today her self-denial comes to fruit
> she nourishes us from her breast
> with the nectar of *ahimsa*.
> She banishes the people's fear,
> Their error and delusion:
> life's evolving spirit, she,
> mother of the world.
> (Rubin 1998: 142)

6. Nation continues to be the 'possessive space' even after *chhayavad*. Naresh Mehta, a *Taar-Saptak* poet, for instance, locates the cosmic in the national:

    > Touch this land anywhere,
    > a magical invocation, it engenders.
    > Doesn't the majestic height of pines
    > look *upnishadic?*
    > Don't you realise
    > a Vedic touch
    > in the leaves of birch-tree . . . ?
    >   ('Mantra-gandha aur Bhasha', 1979: 49)

7. Homi Bhabha, a leading postcolonial post-nationalist uses the expression 'interruptive interiority and transgressive exteriority' (1990: 5) to account for the new tensions that a nation undergoes in the postcolonial phase of transaction and exchange.

8. The quotes of Hindi poetry included in the main text of the chapter have been translated by myself. These translations are of working nature only.

9. One of the ill-logics of the 'complicit' nationalist elite during the colonial period was that national space was divisible into two insular domains of the inner and the outer in which the former stood for the unalterable spiritual core, and the latter signified the mundane materialist necessity. Partha Chatterjee sums up the politics of the inner versus the outer: 'The discourse of nationalism shows that the material/spiritual distinction was condensed into an analogous, but ideologically far more powerful dichotomy: that between the outer and the inner. The material domain, argued nationalist writers, lies outside us—a mere external . . . the spiritual is true self . . . genuinely essential' (1993: 120).

10. Ranajit Guha writes: 'The history of Indian nationalism is thus written up as a sort of spiritual biography of the Indian elite' (1982: 2).

11. Walt Whitman, in his 'Song of the Self', lends rare metaphysical dimensions to the leaves of grass. Grass is not only a 'uniform hieroglyph' (1973: 33), it is the 'handkerchief of the lord' (ibid.: 34) as well.

12. Ranajit Guha explains mobilization among the subaltern as 'violent' and 'spontaneous' (1982: 4–5).

13. The statist approach invokes the authority of Weber according to whom, 'the state is seen in quintessential organizational terms: actual arrangement with distinctive interests and goals that influences the politics of society as a whole' (Hasan 2000: 13).

3

From Hyphen to High-fun: Towards a Topology of New Indian English Diaspora Poetry

Gone are the binary oppositions dear to the nationalist and imperialist enterprise. Instead we begin to sense that old authority cannot simply be replaced by the new authority, but that new alignments made across borders, types, nations, and essences are rapidly coming into view, and it is those new alignments that now provoke and challenge the fundamentally static notions of identity that has been the core of culture during the era of imperialism.

(Said 1993: xxxiv–xxv)

The boundaries of the diaspora and the native blur in Indian English poetry as most of the poets claim both the spaces without any guilt of cultural contradiction. Yet, despite this general contamination or conflation of categories, a definite topology of this poetry can be worked out to map its shifting locations as well as its terms of cultural encounter. This chapter, therefore, is divided into three broad sections, each dealing with a distinct generation of new Indian English diaspora poetry and its dynamic *topos*/politics of space. Of the post-independence diaspora poets, which Vijay Mishra terms as 'new (border) Indian diaspora' (1996: 422), the poets of the pre-1990s, Dom Moraes and A. K. Ramanujan are bunched together in the first section, and the poets of the post-1990s comprising Vikram Seth, Sudeep Sen, Sujata Bhatt, Meena Alexander, Jeet Thayil, Suniti Namjoshi and others have been discussed in the third section.[1] The second section is devoted exclusively to the latter poetry of Agha Shahid Ali that he writes in the emerging context of the pre- and post-polemics of civilizational clash. As a poet locked between two generations of the new diaspora and its shifting moods from 'hyphen to high-fun', Shahid Ali charts his own unique course that provides significant transitional linkages as well as departures from his predecessors and successors, both.[2]

I

The post-independence generation of Indian English diaspora poets, though quite limited in number, does not offer any singular cohesive approach to the issues of cultural displacement. Most of the poets happen to go to different destinations in the West as academics/research students on fellowships and scholarships on personal initiatives, rather than as part of any discernible social movement, at different points of time between the 1950s and 1980s, that is, just after independence and just before the arrival of the new multinational world order in the late 1990s. Most of these poets are diaspora poets in a partial sense only as they start their poetic careers in India much before they sail abroad. Some actually cease to be diaspora poets as they come back to their motherland and settle there till the very end. In terms of approach they evince remarkable differences; some simply adapt to the alien ways of life without experiencing much cultural incongruity, while others negotiate their stay abroad in ways that are essentially dialogic. However, what really binds them into a common frame is their inherent bicultural situation. The two major diaspora poets of the first generation—the earlier Dom Moraes (till 1967) and the latter A. K. Ramanujan (after 1970) offer two contrasting perspectives on their bicultural diasporic situation.

i

Dom Moraes's earlier poetry which he writes in his twenties during his stay in England does not evince either much of what is today valourized as 'diasporic consciousness' or the so-called postcolonial anguish/pain.[3] It is a kind of poetry in which biculturalism remains rather vague and un-stressed as the poet writes in the great English tradition of romanticism from Keats to Dylan Thomas. Here, Bruce King's observations are significant:

> From the first, Dom Moraes was a poet thoroughly immersed in the themes, languages, conventions and attitudes of poetry, especially of the English poetic tradition. . . . He did not go beyond older literary conventions nor place his emotions within a larger cultural context. (1991: 7–8)

The sense of exile or loneliness that the poet often experiences is approached more in terms of existential alienation or romantic disillusionment than cultural estrangement. The themes of loss, love, death, etc., appear in his earlier poetry in an intimate autobiographical context, or as the poet puts it, 'in the private darkness' ('Figures in the Landscape', 2004: 3).

As a young man away from his parents and homeland, Moraes is lost in the world of dreams and their failures. The pipers, the dancers, the flute-wizards and the bells generate a choreography of desolation. A Keatsian mood of 'half in love with easeful death' ('Ode to a Nightingale', 1970: 529) is evident in the following lines from one of his earliest poems thus:

> 'Dying is just the same as going to sleep,'
> The piper whispered, 'close your eyes,'
> And blew some hints and whispers on his pipe:
> The children closed their eyes (ibid.)

'Imagining death' is the isolated poet's preferred way of looking at life. In fact, he longs for death: 'And wondered would a stranger come that way/To take his hand and say, I long to die' (ibid.). Dying, dreaming and sleeping flow into each other as one continuous experience: 'There dying would only be the trek to sleep/or waking through tall mirrors of a dream' ('That Was', ibid.: 18). The poet's propensity to worship death is patently personal, as it does not spring from any larger cultural complex of inheriting a colonial past, or of living in a country which colonized his motherland not long ago.

Most of the poems of the first collection, *A Beginning*, end on a note of death, the poet 'Trying vaguely to conceive eternity' ('Moz', ibid.: 7). 'Shyness' concludes on a note of pro-creation of another life through death: 'By an act like the act of lovers who,/Riding through death upon each other's thighs,/Create, within their death, a life, a voice' (ibid.: 6). In another poem, he compares dying to the setting of the sun, which eventually would rise up again the next morning. The poet exhorts the dancer holding a gun 'against the archaic horror': 'O dancer, when beneath the brass fist's weight/Your skull fluffs out in blood, be not afraid./O imitate the sunset as you die' ('Words to a Dancer', ibid.: 8). Another poem ends on a more metaphorical climax: 'At a river's end/Streams gulp and sweat, expiring in the sand' (ibid.: 18). But the poet's tryst with death is more romantic than metaphysical. There is no such thrust or nationalist anxiety to Indianize the theme by way of overtly sanskritizing/orientalizing it.

The autobiographical is the staple source of poetic metaphors in Indian English poetry in general, but in the poetry of Moraes this is so pronounced that it borders on self-indulgence:

> I have grown up, I think, to live alone
> To keep my old illusions, sometimes dream,
> Glumly, that I am unloved and forlorn,
> Run away from strangers, often seem
> Unreal to myself in the pulpy warmth of a sunbeam.
>
> ('Autobiography', ibid.: 25)

The self of the poet is so secluded and solitary that it fails to make tangible connections with the outer world. This kind of self-involvement does lend an element of lyricality and also authenticity to the poetic idiom, but it denies the possibilities of postcolonial participation. The insecurities that the poet harbours have more to do with his displaced childhood and youth than with his cultural displacement. The romantic in Moraes is more saturnine than celebratory, more defeated than triumphant, more elegiac than panegyric.

The poetry that the vulnerable young poet creates is too personalized in the sense that it is written primarily for self-preservation and self-survival. As such, Moraes's poetry is not as much a product of cultural encounter, of civilizational clash, of colonial-postcolonial antagonism, as it is poetry of psychological stalemate. Poetry provides a personal protection: 'Till locked locked locked with the body of the poem/ I voyage past my darkness into light' ('Shyness', ibid.: 6). Poetry is the poet's own intimate space of belonging: 'I have grown up, hand on the primal bone,/Making the poem, taking the word from the stream,/Fighting the sand for speech, fighting the stone' ('Autobiography', ibid.: 25). The psychological feeds the literary, circumventing in the process the pressing imperatives of biculturalism.

It is through dreams that Moraes engenders in his verse the much-needed penumbral eeriness. More than the dreams, it is their lingering reminiscences that mark the ending of some of his poems. The stranger in the dreams is Moraes's death-angel: 'Waking in lonely fields at break of day/He remembered a dream, looked at the sky/ And wondered would a stranger come that way . . .' ('Figures in the Landscape', ibid.: 3). In another poem the stranger could be the ever-evasive beloved:

> My dream was broken by the knock of day.
> Yet within my mind, these pictures linger:

> I touch her with my clumsy words of love
> And sense snow in her eye,
> Mists, and the winds that warn, Stranger, O Stranger!
> ('Snow on a Mountain', ibid.: 17)

Neither dream, nor reality, in a way, are exclusive to each other in Moraes's poetic realm. The in-between space of dream and reality is where the tentative poetic self dwells most. But the dreaminess in Moraes, despite its grey shades, does not have the postcolonial political wherewithal of 'magic realism', for it is magical, but not real enough.

In Moraes's next collection, simply entitled *Poems*, following the poet's failed relationship with a British actress Dorothy, the confessional streak aggravates: 'There's a child in my body: it longs to confess' ('French Lesson', ibid.: 30). As 'she' announces her departure ('I must go'), almost like a teenager the poet sulks: 'And absence came upon the land,/Cold, foreign, like the drifted snow./The rose had shrivelled in my hand' ('Girl', ibid.: 33). The poet's encounters with his beloved are too transient to lend him a sense of stability. In terms of its stereotypical rose-imagery and rhymes—'go/snow', and 'land/hand', the poem has all the trappings of pre-Raphaelite decadent romanticism. The concluding lines of the 'The Final Word', confirm the rawness of the romance: 'I have furnished my heart to be her nest/ For even if at dusk she choose to fly/Afterwards she must rest' (ibid.: 58). This is aesthetic compromise, if not withdrawal; it is a solipsistic way of negotiating un-fulfilment in love, a characteristically pre-Raphaelite poetics of unsatisfied longing.

The poet invents his surrogate ways of realizing love, which may not be morbid, but they stop short of action. One of these ways is expressing his love to birds: 'Glumly I wait to marry dust./It grieves me only that I must/Speak not to you, but to a bird' ('The Garden', ibid.: 45). A tone of languorous melancholy marks Moraes's love-poetry. The sentiment of love is more camouflaged than expressed:

> The angles of my love rose to my eyes.
> I was embarrassed to display them, so
> I put dark glasses on for a disguise
> And climbed away through pines, towards the snow.
> ('The Climber', ibid.: 34)

Renunciation, before participation, is patently pre-Raphaelite. The gestures of renunciation appear to be inevitable, sometimes compulsive. Another surrogate way to realize love is writing poetry about it. The poet is shy enough to express his love directly:

> And I by shyness am undone
> And can't go out for fear I meet
> My poems dancing down the street
> Telling your name to everyone.
> ('The Garden', ibid.: 45)

It is in his dreams that he tends to be passionate and bold: 'My dreams, I thought, lacked dignity./ So I got drunk and went to the bed' ('Gone Away', ibid.: 49). Moraes's swings from bohemianism to renunciation deny him the possibility of transforming his affair with Dorothy into an encounter of cultures (of East versus West).

Most of the poems invoke broken relationships, historical as well as mythical, such as those of Yeats and Maud Gonne, Catullus and Lesbia, Hamlet and Ophelia, either at the sub-textual or at the conspicuous textual level as Moraes negotiates his own unsteady relation with his British beloved Dorothy. Having failed in attracting Hamlet, Ophelia's suicidal plunge in the sea—one of the favourite subject matters of pre-Raphaelite painters, invites wholesome praise of the lovelorn poet: 'Her driftwood shape will travel far./Never will it seek land, for she/ has fled our tributes and our war' ('Ophelia', ibid.: 59).

The confessional and the autobiographical collapse into each other as Moraes rather instinctively goes back to the days of his childhood and youth to dig up metaphors and situations for his poetic enterprise. The autobiographical poems in the second anthology pertain more to his turbulent and tumultuous adulthood. The loneliness of childhood compounds with a broken love affair:

> Three winters I was drunk: one early spring
> Brought me first love for you, my great good news:
> Then my excuse to play the drunken king,
> Staggering through bars, became a bad excuse.
> ('A Letter', ibid.: 44)

The dream of eternity is suddenly shattered, as the young poet realizes: 'Tombstones are a trouble/Others must endure' ('Voices', ibid.: 46). The solution to disillusionment lies in being bacchanalian: 'Nothing that double/Brandy will not cure' (ibid.). Moraes fails to politicize his personal self, which in the postcolonial context would not have been utterly unwarranted. The subject position of a diasporic Catholic Indian Christian has not been exploited for poetical/political ends. The anxiety to internalize and approximate British poetry, from Romantic to pre-Raphaelite, is so overwhelming that there is hardly any room left for the postcolonial assertion of political difference.

The Dionysian drift continues in 'John Nobody' as the poet frequents the bar: 'That day, bored with myself, I leant upon/ The chipped bar, chinking thoughts together like/A late drink twopence short of busfare home' ('Dedicatory Sonnets: Finch's', ibid.: 63). The bar is the banished poet's new abode: 'The heart that bleeds but does not really ache./Wandering the world, it finds nowhere to hide/Save in a bottle bought with a bad cheque' ('After Hours', ibid.: 65). The bar's bleak ambience complements well with the poet's private darkness:

> The shadows in the bar cling to the shapes
> Of lonely drinkers whose hunched shoulders touch.
> One of them hides his tired eyes and weeps
> Unnoticed, till the barman starts to bitch. (ibid.)

The bohemian streak does not really expand the poetic self; it induces greater inwardness: 'I milk smoke from my cigarette, and puff/ Inexpert rings at it, and startled, see/Through a blurred haze of whisky, smoke and love' ('John Nobody', ibid.: 102). Such escapades rule out the possibility of voluntary and volitional cultural contact that otherwise is so intrinsic to the discourse of diaspora. Moraes acts more like a broken lover than a displaced expatriate. Even within the bar, there is no sign of cultural mixing; even the boozed private refuses to become public.

As the poet grows inward, his romance of easeful death turns into a bloody nightmare. As he himself puts it, he had never 'dreamt that he/ Would be probed from anus to throat by a spear' ('The General-III', ibid.: 76). The benign images of childhood appear ghastly and ghostly, both: '. . . , the children in surprise/Stared up as their invited visitor [Santa Claus] / Lifted his claws above them, holes for eyes' ('Christmas Sonnets-I', ibid.: 70). A family dinner in which a 'spraddled turkey' is all set to be butchered wets 'each child's eye/While the gross father, with the whisky flush/Deepening in his cheeks, prepares the blade/To pare off from the bone the warm white flesh' ('Christmas Sonnets-II', ibid.: 71). The images of archetypal violence, bloodshed and slaughter begin to haunt the poet.

Some of the poems provide gory and gruesome details of death by violence; the veneer of soft lyricism is ruptured. The romantic turns almost into the gothic, monstrous and bestial. '. . . fingers work/ Crablike upon her white throat, killing her' ('Melancholy Prince', ibid.: 80). The delicate notes of the piper give way to 'hound notes': 'Of the hounds dying out on the wintry sky./O blood dropped in the fern, O dripping throats' ('Hound Notes', ibid.: 92). A poet of meadows, Moraes suddenly looks upon trees as raw material for paper on which he could inscribe his 'murderous kiss of ink' ('The Images', ibid.: 84). The images of rape, violent love and lust suddenly become pronounced, revealing the poet's growing insecurity: 'Soon in the dark a stepfather will ride/His handsome mother like a randy mare' ('Melancholy Prince', ibid.: 80). When a captive girl is raped on the battlefront, the poet feels his hymen is broken: 'They [the troopers] will never heal/The hymen in me, burst in blood and fear' ('The General-I', ibid.: 74).

The images of hunting and being hunted, of butchering and being butchered, of killing and being killed begin to dominate Moraes's dark poetic scroll. Near the lake the poet watches 'an archer's shaft/ Startle an outcry from the cygnets, shift/The red deer down the mountainside to die./I saw a boy destroy the wild swan's wings' ('Lake', ibid.: 98). The violence is cyclical in nature; 'the fallen skull' becomes a minefield of food for the ants, till it is completely hollowed into 'a cup for dew', which then 'the field mice' sip in the day, and finally the skull furnishes 'the nightwork for the owls to do'. The poet sums up this series of activity thus: 'In all this labour nothing went amiss/ Each cycle moved as strictly as a dance' ('The Watcher', ibid.: 94). The poet is a mere watcher who in another poem masquerades as 'a mad prophet of that land/Who mewed for more blood under a white moon' ('Local History', ibid.: 87). The stasis, which one discovers in the poetry of Moraes, is thus very deceptive, for it has its dance-like movements within.

The outer acts of butchering trigger off self-stripping. The poet internalizes external violence and even as an animal is hunted or killed for religious ceremony he feels his own self sacrificed:

> Obediently he stretched out while I stropped
> Blade upon blade, and while the blades were drawn
> Through flesh, till in the gap which they had torn
> I saw his wild heart falter, not yet stopped.

And from his gentle eyes two slow tears dropped.
In this fashion I killed my unicorn.

('Vivisection', ibid.: 73)

The unicorn in the passage is probably the poet himself. The killer is the killed too. In the collection, the poet suffers from 'This ignominy of being clad in flesh/This inability to strip the flesh off' ('The General-IV', ibid.: 77). The Yeatsian bold 'enterprise' of 'walking naked' ('A Coat', 1957: 320) is taken a step ahead as the poet wants to be fleshless, naked to the bones.

In *Beldam Etcetera*, the poet's fourth collection, Moraes does address his mother and motherland in a rare bout of nostalgia, but the tone is accusatory. In so many words, the poet writes: 'You [mother] do not understand me' ('Letter to My Mother', 2004: 105). The estrangement is more with the motherland than with the land of affiliation. Due to an unhappy childhood on account of an indifferent mother the poet suffers guilt: 'I am ashamed of myself/Since I was ashamed of you' (ibid.). The rhetoric of belonging, therefore, does not allure the poet. The journey back is not sustained. There are occasional trespasses and these too are very harsh and uncharitable. The poet discovers the whole motherland lost in prayers: 'a defeated dream/Hiding itself in prayers' (ibid.: 106). The spiritual stupor disenchants the poet all the more: 'Your dream is desolate/It calls me every day/But I cannot enter it' (ibid.).

The homeland is a temporary distraction; the poet soon relapses into his usual quasi-romantic dark dreamy world that becomes increasingly macabre and morbid, revealing the repressed underside of the poetic self as such. The poet is served by his servant 'A folded napkin on a tray,/A soupspoon and a bowl of blood' ('Craxton', ibid.: 119). The poem 'Jason' has all the trappings of Coleridge's mysterious poem 'The Rhyme of the Ancient Mariner', except that instead of an albatross, what tugs the poet-as-sailor on is the 'disquieting shape' of a fleece:

Through the ship's planks I heard the finned
Sea monsters thrash. I dreamt of the
Fleece running wild where our wake was.
My crew and I were beardless boys
But driven by a mystery.

('Jason', ibid.: 111)

To his dismay, later on the poet discovers, 'That the bright fleece turned out to be no more than a burst quilt someone had left/To ooze its heart out on the shore' (ibid.: 111). The early phase of Dom Moraes's poetic career is thus marked by strong private fantasies—from very mellow and soft to grotesque and ghoulish. The diasporic consciousness, if any, is subsumed within the sense of general alienation that the poet suffers on account of his lonely childhood and youth. The possibilities of biculturalism, which otherwise are very potent in the case of culturally displaced poets like Moraes, remain, therefore, almost understated, if not unexplored.

ii

In the poetry of A. K. Ramanujan, a distinct configuration of diasporic experience emerges that eventually sets the tone and direction for Indian English (diaspora) poetry as a whole. In his poetry, the native and the alien, the inner and the outer enter into a dialogic relationship, whose poetics is invariably that of parody and subversion. Unlike Dom Moraes, Ramanujan's nostalgic trips down memory lane are not mere trespasses into the native zone. In his earlier poetry, most of which was written prior to his departure to the United States, Ramanujan gives an insider's perspective of his native landscape. In such poems, Chicago, as an adopted abode of the poet, is missing altogether. These poems offer a perspective of 'home' from within.

In Ramanujan's later poetry, one finds the simultaneous presence of landscapes from both Chicago and India, in a relationship, which is at best contrapunctal. In a contrapunctal relationship, the 'effort is to draw out, extend, give emphasis and voice to what is silent or marginally present or ideologically represented' (Said 1993: 66) in one standpoint from a reference which is external. Such is the plurality and mobility of Ramanujan's experience that no private space can claim its perfect insularity from the corrupting outer space. Each self-assumed space of privilege punctures and is punctured by another equally self-validating space. Chicago parodies native Karnataka, and native Karnataka parodies Chicago. This two-way inter-spatial traffic of ideas and experiences within Ramanujan's poetic universe necessitates an extraordinary inter-textual framework of parody to contain and express the experienced heterogeneity.

Chicago provides the necessary intellectual distance to look back mockingly at the native past. No wonder then, it is in Chicago only that the poet's 'estranged wife and her brother' start 'one of your [their] old drag-out fights/about where the bathroom was' ('Love Poem for a Wife-I', 1995: 66) in their ancestral house. The reconstruction of the house through a funny speculation on the whereabouts of the 'bathroom' in that house has parodic undercurrents. The bathroom was either to the 'north or south of the well/next to the jackfruit tree/ in your [their] father's house/in Aleppey' (ibid.: 66). Aleppey becomes a 'strange' ridiculous terrain from the high modernistic perch of Chicago.

Chicago appears as the most anomalous space from the surer vantage point of native Karnataka. In 'Take Care', Ramanujan presents a topsy-turvy image of Chicago where even 'Small flies sit/on aspirin and booze' and 'Invisible crabs/scuttle the air' (ibid.: 103). The poet advises:

> not to stare
> At the peppergrinders,
> Salt shakers, or the box
> of matches on the black
> and white squares
> of your kitchen.

Because:

> They take on the look
> Of meat grinders,
> Cement shakers,
> Boxes against boxes
> In the grilled
> City: intersections
> Of wet black splinter,
> Of houses burned. (ibid.:104)

Chicago as the meat capital of the U.S., along with its skyscrapers and racial violence becomes a monstrous version of relatively placid and vegetarian native Karnataka. 'Ramanujan's warnings about the life that is lived in Chicago bespeak his moral judgement and Indian ethics' (Mohanty 1994: 39). Chicago proves to be a rather secular and non-sacred parody of the poet's native land where 'the dry chlorine water' replaces the holy Ganges and 'the naked Chicago bulb' becomes 'a cousin of the Vedic sun' ('Extended Family', 1995: 169). Such parodic tropes belittle both the postmodern Chicago and equally conservative native Karnataka.

Ramanujan's poetic consciousness permeates primarily between Chicago in the foreground and Karnataka in the background in a way that uproots the poet eternally. This uprootedness engenders in him a double voice, a dialogic vision characteristic of the postcolonial condition. In the poem, 'Waterfalls in a Bank' (ibid.: 189–90), for instance, one can see Ramanujan's bifocal vision at play thus:

> And then one sometimes sees waterfalls
> as the ancient Tamils saw them,
> wavering snakeskins,
> cascades of muslin

Here, Jahan Ramazani's explication on this relationship of waterfalls with snakeskin/muslin is very pertinent: 'Ramanujan decommodifies and Indianizes the confined waterfall in an American bank, putting metaphor to work in a kind of reverse colonization. The ancient Indian vehicles of snakeskin and muslin paradoxically enliven with danger and wonder an image hackneyed in Western poetry' (2001: 78). It is, however, very difficult to say whether Ramanujan enlivens the hackneyed America or modernizes ancient India by employing cultural metaphors of two civilizations in such a dialogic frame.

In the same poem, that is, 'Waterfalls in a Bank', Ramanujan, while looking at the waterfalls, is suddenly reminded of a childhood image of a brahmin sadhu pissing in the open. The Chicago waterfalls and a sadhu's stream of urine bear a parodic relationship. The poem reaches its parodic climax when the poet lets the trajectory of the sadhu's urine gleam like diamonds in a semi-arch, in the light-beam of a car headlight thus:

> Headlights make his arc
> a trajectory of yellow diamonds,
> scared instant rainbows, ejecting spurts
> of crystal, shocked
> by the commonplace cruelty of headlights. (1995: 190)

How a sadhu's stream of urine attains a glamorous hue in the glitter of Chicago speaks volumes of the spiritual impoverishment of the West. This in no way signifies an easy compatibility or convergence of East with West, the traditional with the modern. Ramanujan has an uncanny knack of raising the mundane to the level of transcendental, momentarily and even precariously in 'the commonplace cruelty of headlights'. The divine claims of a sadhu are thoroughly exposed in Chicago lights.

Both Chicago and the deep Indian South act as external standpoints for each other; one brings out the strengths and weaknesses of the other. In 'Chicago Zen' (ibid.: 186–88), a Himalayan river and Lake Michigan are locked against each other. Chicago traffic with a deluge of 'orange' headlights gives the poet a 'vision of forest fires', which in turn reminds him of the 'rapid' river back home:

> you fall into vision of forest fires,
> enter a frothing Himalayan river
> rapid silent
> On the 14th floor
> Lake Michigan crawls and crawls
> in the window. . .

Once in America, the poet negotiates his estrangement through two ways—one, by way of imagining Indian equivalents among things/situations foreign, and two, by way of juxtaposing them with the alien landscape. Chicago traffic lights are likened to a rapid Himalayan river, which is then contrasted with the calm and still Lake Michigan. Such equivalences or contrasts, overarching as they are, while bringing the two cultures in one frame, serve more importantly as reference points for their mutual reviewing. It becomes very difficult to conclude as to what is redeemed and what is ridiculed in such a frame of juxtaposition.

In 'Extended Family', the contrapunctal inter-locking of the alien with the native is terse and pointed:

> the dry chlorine water
> my only Ganges
> the naked Chicago bulb
> a cousin of the Vedic sun (ibid.: 169)

In such a dialogic frame, while the poet seems to make his adjustments in the alien landscape through the strategy of equivalences, he is also hinting at the limitations of such an enterprise. The 'naked Chicago bulb' is his working equivalent of the 'Vedic sun', yet it is too facile an object to be compared with the 'Vedic sun'. Similarly, the Ganges is discovered in 'the dry chlorine water', yet the equivalence is absurd and remote. The poet not only belittles the mechanical Chicago life, he also ridicules the obsessive brahmanical life-style back home. It is not that Ramanujan cannot think independently about his cultural landscape; he employs Chicago not to assert any 'fundamentalist' or rank 'nationalist' association with his 'home'. Both the landscapes are juxtaposed, and yet none is redeemed. This in a way belies Jameson's exaggerated account of the encounter of Third World cultures with First World capitalism, wherein he says: 'none of these cultures can be conceived as anthropologically independent or autonomous, rather they are all in various distinct ways locked in a life-and-death struggle with first-world cultural imperialism' (2000a: 318).

Straddling between two 'rich' cultures, Ramanujan does not think in exclusive terms as one culture becomes a ready critical frame for another. In 'Take Care' (1995: 103–4), the poet presumably concentrates on life in Chicago, but at the back of his mind his native landscape works as the reference point. Here in Chicago, the native Kannada 'pepper grinders' or 'salt shakers' take on 'the look/of meat grinders,/ cement shakers'. The 'black/and white squares/of kitchen cloth' appear as 'boxes against boxes/in the grilled/city'. If the native landscape provided time enough 'to stare', in Chicago there is 'no time/to stand and stare'. A comparative frame is so inseparably inter-locked in the entire fabric of the poem, that while being a poem on Chicago, 'Take Care' becomes as much a poem on the native landscape.

Through his oft-quoted poem, 'Small-Scale Reflections on a Great House', Ramanujan gives an extended account of the history of home/ nation in terms which are ambivalent and self-critical. He looks back at home/nation as a trope of cultural recuperation and dissipation both. It is a matter of concern as well as contempt.[4] Its present state of inertia is a matter of deep concern. If the poet describes it as a perfect breeding ground for insects, he does so with a sense of loss. In the sleepy space of this human habitation, in the absence of real human activity in the form of frequent family get-togethers, only insects lend life and momentum:

> Unread library books
> usually mature in two weeks
> and begin to lay a row
> of little eggs in the ledgers
> for fines, as silverfish
> in the old man's office room
> breed dynasties among long legal words

> in the succulence of
> of Victorian parchment. (ibid.: 96)

Here 'unread library books' in 'the old man's office room' become the poet's chosen tropes for the decrepit home. Home, a traditional referent of stability and security, at once stands inverted as a referent of stagnation and unhealthy stasis.

Home, hitherto regarded as the dynamic centre of culture, is under-played as the hub of routine life. As against the challenges of exiled living, it offers a course of life well laid out by family traditions and customs. In Ramanujan's world-view too, 'home' is the domain where women 'who come as wives/from houses open on one side/to rising suns, on another/to the setting' become 'accustomed to wait and to yield to monsoons . . .' (ibid.: 97). The poet has utmost disregard for women as wives, as they easily fit into the scheme of the great house. At the same time, the poet could be seen as a sympathizer of women as wives, as they are compelled to bear the tyranny of the great house offering little space for the assertion of their individuality.

To Ramanujan, home, at one level is a kind of a prison or just a ghetto one is eternally a captive of, at another level, it is a meeting ground of distant relatives. On the one hand, the poet berates the tyrannical centripetal pull of the home that does not allow an individual any independent and free thinking space, on the other, he acknowledges home as the site of realizing the communitarian self. It is as much an institution of self-fulfilment and self-recovery, as it is an institution of self-curtailment and self-erosion. To Ramanujan, it is a kind of black hole that swallows all the (p)articles that fly around it: 'Sometimes I think that nothing/that ever comes into this house/goes out. Things come in every day/to lose themselves among other things/lost long ago among/other things lost long ago' (ibid.: 96). Home's invitational pull yields joy and regret at the same time.

Home is as much a refuse as it is a refuge. 'Nothing stays out: daughters/get married to short-lived idiots;/sons who run away come back' (ibid.: 98). Even the songs of the beggars keep on re-visiting this home: 'A beggar once came with a violin/to creak out a prostitute song/that our voiceless cook sang/all the time in our backyard' (ibid.). Here the word 'prostitute' has serious semantic connotations. It at once relates home to some kind of a brothel visited and revisited by its clients, namely the family-relations, to get an emotional kick now and then. Home is thus the site of both permanent ever-lasting emotional bonds and ephemeral one-night relationships. This prostitutional value of home ruptures the noble notion of home as a sacred space.

Home is as much a cultural junkyard as it is a place of roots. It is a place where 'ideas . . ./once casually mentioned somewhere/ . . . come back to the door as prodigies' and where 'Letters mailed/ . . . [find] their way back/with many re-directions to wrong/addresses and red inkmarks/earned in Tiruvella and Sialkot' (ibid.: 97). Its seminal functional value is that it provides one a 'permanent address'. It is a rarefied confession box where the poets can easily shed off their sins without any fear of backlash or accountability. They tend to take home as an innocent space—a space too inane and sentimental to counter-argue, to lay its own demands on its inhabitants. There is a tendency to take home for granted. To Ramanujan, home perhaps stands for abstention as well as inescapable participation in life. When the high modernism of the West impinges upon Ramanujan, he prefers to retreat to his 'particular hell only in my [his] hindu mind' ('Conventions of Despair', ibid.: 35), not for cultural recuperation or cultural assertion as such, but for temporary relief and respite.

In Ramanujan's double-edged poetic discourse, home is thus raised and erased simultaneously; it is desired and shunned in the same breath. It turns towards the nation, as much as it turns away from it.[5] In his topsy-turvy vision, stability is also a synonym of stagnation; security is as much a semantic equivalent of complacency; tradition could well be an excuse not to change. The poet never shows the nationalist anxiety of a persona-in-exile, for no space to him is absolute and perfect. In terms of the poetics of home, Ramanujan's poetry is a poetry of understatement and critical nostalgia, very much distinguishable from the rabid and overstated 'poetry of exile'.

II

Agha Shahid Ali, as a poet of Indian diaspora, undergoes multiple mutations, which on the one hand point towards the vulnerabilities of the displaced self in the grossly identitarian politics of the times, and on the other raise possibilities of poetry attaining new semantic promise. The poet moves from local to global, before finally lapsing into a transnational religious identity. From the interstitial space of Indo-American, the poet in the post-national era turns towards a more glocalized identity of Kashmiri-American. As the politics back home enters a phase of fierce nationalist struggle, the poet tends to take on the role of 'the national [as against the nationalist] poet of a future independent Kashmir' (King 2001: 273).[6] But soon, Islam as his religion eclipses Kashmir as his region. As international politics drifts, albeit polemically, towards a mode of civilizational clash, the poet in a self-sacrificial way declares himself to be the very voice of Islam: 'Call Me Ishmael Tonight'. The native Kashmiri self loses its local vector to merge into the larger civilizational frame of Arabic culture/Islam as such. Chechnya, Sarajevo, Armenia, Palestine, Kashmir form one continuous site of larger transnational human tragedy. The three post-1990s collections— *The Country Without a Post Office* (2000 [1997]), *Rooms are Never Finished* (2002) and *Call Me Ishmael Tonight* (2004), chosen for analysis here, suggest a swift strategic transition in the poetic make-up of Shahid Ali.

i

In the wake of Kashmir's 'on-going catastrophe' and 'devastation' due to the eruption of a 'full-scale uprising for self-determination' (Ali 2002: 14), *The Country Without a Post Office* turns out to be an extended dirge over its loss as the fabled paradise. Though Kashmir has been one of the patent obsessions of the poet, yet in his earlier collections he devotes as much space to the country of his exile, that is, America. If in his *The Half Inch Himalayas*, it is the resplendent un-ravaged Kashmir that beckons the displaced poet—'Kashmir shrinks into my mailbox,/my home a neat four by six inches./I always loved neatness./ Now I hold the half-inch Himalayas in my hand' ('Postcard from Kashmir', 1987: 1)—in his *A Nostalgist's Map of America* (1991) he is anxious to advance his credentials more as an American poet than even the hybridized Indo-American one. The following lines from one of the poems in the collection can as well be mistaken with Vikram Seth's *The Golden Gate* for their overt American-ness:

> this, the least false: 'You said each month you need
> new blood. Please forgive me, Phil, but I thought
> of your pain as a formal feeling, one
> useful for the letting go, your transfusions
>
> mere wings to me, the push of numerous
> hummingbirds, souvenirs of Evanescence
> seen disappearing down a route of veins
> in an electric rush of cochineal.'
>
>   ('A Nostalgist's Map of America', 1991: 37)

But as the poet confronts the volatile 1990s, his compulsive Kashmiri past re-surfaces with the difference that it is no longer celebratory; rather it is saturnine and despondent. The poetic form changes consequently from that of *qasida* (panegyric poetry) to *marsia* (elegiac poetry). The outward leap before it stretches itself beyond the native past, relapses into fatalistic inwardness that is as much political as it is religious and literary: 'I hid my pain even from myself; I revealed my pain only to myself' ('Farewell', 2000: 9). 'I' here operates at three levels—the poet's own narcissistic self, his Kashmir and his rather besieged religion Islam—each sustaining the other in a mutually enhancing continuum.

The inwardness, from the diasporic location, strikes its own selective cross-cultural horizontal affiliations making it distinctive from purely native, non-diasporic inwardness. In the very opening prologue to *The Country Without a Post Office*, Shahid Ali, invoking the Russian rebel poet Osip Mandelstam's urge for his lost Petersburg, re-invents his own 'homeland, filling it, closing it, shutting himself in it' in a 'craft' of sheer 'heartbreak' ('The Blessed Word: A Prologue', 2000: 3). The epigraphs of Ali's poems lend a multicultural dimension to his otherwise centripetal poetry.[7] The lines from Yeats's famous 'Easter 1916' (1957: 394)—'Now and in time to be,/Wherever green is worn, . . ./A terrible beauty is born'—bring together Kashmir's oxymoronic predicament with that of Ireland in Ali's 'I See Kashmir from New Delhi at Midnight': 'The City from where no new can come/ is now visible in its curfewed night/that the worst is precise' (ibid.: 10). The poet's native space seen from above, from the plane, generates its own 'terrible beauties': 'I'm sheened in moonlight, in emptied Srinagar' (ibid.); 'snow begins to fall/on us, like ash' (ibid.: 11). The poet is unable to distinguish between 'autumn's last crimson spillage' and the 'flames clinging to a torched village' ('I Dream I am the Only Passenger on Flight 493 to Srinagar', ibid.: 20) as his plane touches down on the ashen tarmac.

The paradoxes of return continue to seize the poet's inward imagination at least in the first few poems—the pre-return poems—of *The Country Without a Post Office*. One of the odd ironies of return is that the news of death comes before the actual return:

> We'll go past our ancestors, up the staircase,
> holding their wills against our hearts. Their wish
> was we return—forever!—and inherit (Quick, the bird

will say) that to which we belong, not like this—
to get news of our death after the world's.
('A Pastoral', ibid.: 24)

What haunts the poet perennially is his death before the return to the so-called paradise: 'On everyone's lips was news/of my death but only that beloved couplet,/broke, on his:/"if there is paradise on earth,/ it is this, it is this, it is this"' ('The Last Saffron', ibid.: 15). The untimely return is not a moment of respite, it is another bout of alienation: 'Mirror after mirror,/textiled by dust, will blind us to our return/ as we light oil lamps' (ibid.: 24). The hell-heaven binary begins to blur: 'I am being rowed through Paradise on a river of Hell' ('Farewell', ibid.: 8).

But once the poet returns to his proverbial paradise, the inwardness attains incantatory solemnity; the tragic takes over the ironic, though not without its own poignant and painful paradoxes. Sung in a hushed tone, the reverberating refrain is 'Everything is finished, nothing remains' ('The Country Without a Post Office', ibid.: 26). Shahid Ali's poetry breaks free from minimalist poetic fads that his contemporaries make much ado about; it returns to quasi-romantic, quasi-mystical strains that bemoan the demise of the divine in the valley.[8] Ghazal emerges as the natural genre of intimate tête-à-tête with the de-solation all around:

> *Lord*, cried out the idols, *Don't let us be broken;*
> *Only we can convert the infidel tonight.*
> . . . .
> In the heart's veined temple all statues have been smashed.
> No priest in saffron's left to toll its knell tonight . . . .
('Ghazal', ibid.: 21)

On his return, the poet discovers to his dismay that the voice of muezzin, the postman of the divine, has long been silenced: 'When the muezzin/ dies, the city was robbed of every Call' ('The Country Without a Post Office', ibid.: 25). As he is impelled to take over the role of the dead muezzin 'that archive for doomed/addresses' (ibid.: 25), his poetry attains a touch of combativeness: 'The entire map of the lost will be candled./ I'm keeper of the minaret since the muezzin died./ Come soon, I'm alive. . . ' (ibid.: 27). And as he opens the 'vanished envelopes' in the entombed minaret, he is already in the thick of fire: 'I'm inside the fire. I have found the dark' (ibid.: 27). The diaspora poet on his return is, thus, 'utterly transformed' into the new postman of the divine in the desolate homeland.

Shahid Ali's increasing inwardness is not a sign of his withdrawal or resignation; it is rather a sign of his gritty confrontation. In the face of destruction, the poet has the courage to say:

> When the ruins dissolve like salt in water,
> only then will they have destroyed everything.
> Let your blood till then embellish the slaughter,
>
> till dawn soaks up its inks, and . . .
>
> ('A Villanelle', ibid.: 61)

As blood becomes the new password in the valley, Ali's poetry acquires revolutionary fervour, though not without the apprehensions of losing a cultural past:

> Was there, we asked, a new password—
> blood, blood shaken into letters,
> cruel primitive script that would erode
> our saffron link to the past?
>
> ('The Floating Post Office', ibid.: 29)

Faiz Ahmad Faiz, the master-poet, translating who Shahid Ali grows as a poet in his own right, seems to be the primary source behind such stark violent images.[9] The following lines from Faiz's 'In Search of Vanished Blood' lend a contextual richness to Ali's blood-laden imagery: 'From the beginning this blood was nourished only by dust./ Then it turned to ashes, left no trace, became food for dust' (1991: 63).

ii

In the next collection, *Rooms are Never Finished*, the sense of tragic compounds as the death of the mother conflates with that of the motherland: 'I'm piling/Doomsday on Doomsday' ('Above the Cities', 2002: 33). The experience of expatriation turns into that of exile. Kashmir stands transmuted into the archetypal Karbala, with Muharram its permanent season, and the poet as its Hussain, the Prophet's chosen martyr: 'Only Karbala could frame our grief:/The wail rose: *How could such a night fall on Hussain?*' ('Summer of Translation', ibid.: 31). The sublimation of the regional into the religious not only obliterates the difference between the secular and the sacred, it also fuses the mythical with the personal. Also, disparate time zones collapse, generating complex topologies of space: 'At dawn, my mother heard, in her hospital-dream of elephants, sirens wail through Manhattan like elephants/forced off Pir Panjal's rock cliffs in Kashmir' ('Lenox Hill', ibid.: 17). As the poet's mother 'sleeps in Amherst. Windows open on Kashmir' (ibid.: 18). The outer world is thus brought indoors: 'What city's left?/I've brought the world indoors' ('Rooms are Never Finished', ibid.: 55).

Shahid Ali, in his moments of intense inwardness, ironically enough acquires more inter-textuality. From one sub-tropic stroke, he shifts to another—complementary as well as contradictory—building his poetic argument in a non-chronological sequence. From Faiz's 'Memory', the poet moves on to 'hear Begam Akhtar enclose—in Raga *Jogia* —"Not all, no only a few return as the rose/or the tulip"' ('Summers of Translation', ibid.: 31). The romantic ghazal—which is more like 'the wound-cry of the gazelle'—is immediately juxtaposed with a stark news headline: 'PARADISE ON EARTH BECOMES HELL'. The inwardness is further accentuated by the call to prayer which breaks the night in two: on the one hand he hears his mother wail like Zainab, on the other he remembers her singing a song from a black and white film—*'Dark Krishna,/ don't let your Radha die in the rain'* (ibid.: 31).

From a film *bhajan* to Ghalib's couplet—everything that the poet happens to hear on his way back to Kashmir, carrying the dead body of his mother, lends richness to the mood of despondency. The film *bhajan* begins to sound like the desperate last prayer of the dying mother: 'only take this vow I am yours dark god/dark god you are all you are all I have/swear only swear I am yours I am yours' (*'Film* Bhajan *Found on a 78 RPM*, ibid.: 41). A Bombay film song (*'Whom the flame itself has gone searching for, that moth—just imagine'* ['New Delhi Airport', ibid.: 38]), a Koranic gospel (*'There is no god but God'* ['Srinagar Airport', ibid.: 42]) followed by Ghalib's laconic wisdom (*'Doomsday had but—but barely had—breather its first/ when I again remembered you as you were leaving'* ['The Fourth Day', ibid.: 47]) keep haunting the bereaved poet as he returns to his homeland.

Ghazal as a form of poetry begins to appear more regularly in Shahid Ali's later collections. Even poems which are not patently ghazals are sufficiently ghazalesque in the sense that in terms of mood and style there is a controlled and well-modulated articulation of emotional outburst.[10] The typical moth-flame ghazal trope is used with the necessary poetic tension thus: 'Moths, one by one,/ dive into light, dive deep to catch the light,/ then return to keep the halo' ('The Purse-Seiner', ibid.: 75). In lines such as these—'Even You don't give me a shadow. Your Light—/ all the lights of heaven—are dimmed tonight' ('A Secular Comedy', ibid.: 61)—the poet seems to be on the edge of breaking into a ghazal with 'tonight' as its possible *radeef* (refrain). Ali's poetry in general derives its tropical strength from stereotypical ghazal-motifs of 'union and separation, ecclesia and monastery, the censor and the guard of faith, the beloved and the idol, the lover and the rival, the messenger and the confidant, the tavern and the cup bearer, and so on' (Rahman 2002: 117).

In the hands of Shahid Ali, the *ghazal*, which is traditionally used for intimate exchanges of soft sentiments by lovers, undergoes a functional change; it is increasingly deployed for political purposes: 'And who is the terrorist, who the victim?/We'll know if the country is polled in real time' ('Ghazal', 2002: 68). The accent on 'real time' which happens to be the *radeef* of the ghazal suggests its engagement with bold political issues including that of the demand of plebiscite in Kashmir. In another ghazal inspired by Mahmoud Darwish's couplet, *'Where should we go after the last frontiers,/where should the birds fly after the last sky?'* (ibid.: 72), Shahid Ali sums up the predicament of Palestinians: 'In Jerusalem a dead phone's dialled by exiles./You learn your strange fate. You were exiled by exiles' ('Ghazal', ibid.).

In Shahid Ali's poetry, the pull of inwardness is so overwhelming that epigraphs travel into the very body of the poems they presumably inspire. The poems carry lines from other sources in inverted commas, italics and parenthesis with such organic ease that the gap between the original and the derived begins to vanish. The translations of the poet are no less than his 'original poems' and as such they are included in the poetic collections more as poems by the poet than as his translations of the other poets.[11] The translated poems of Faiz, Ghalib, Pushkin and Darwish have been appropriated as his own for they carry the stamp of Shahid Ali more as a free poet-translator than as a fastidious translator. In his 'Preface' to the translation of Faiz's *The Rebel's Silhouette*, he declares boldly: 'This is not for the purists' (1991: not paginated).

The collection *Rooms are Never Finished* in its last section includes 'Eleven Stars Over Andalusia' which is not as such the translation of Mahmoud Darwish's 'Eleven Stars' as it is a 'version' of it. A poem in eleven parts, it is an extended elegy over the expulsion of the Moors from fifteenth-century Spain.[12] Darwish invokes their obscure history in the context of the present predicaments of Palestine, and Ali reversifies and appropriates Darwish's poem so as to create a continuous discourse of exile that Muslims have suffered from the days of the conquest of Garanda by the Catholic monarchs in 1492 to the ghettoization of Palestinians in their homeland, to the present-day Kashmir crisis. The continuity of concern overrides the issues of authorship. The poet and his translator become one consolidated self, difficult to distinguish from each other. Ali becomes as much an author of these poems as Darwish is. Such a conflation sets new touchstones for the translation of poetry.

The endeavour is to retrieve oppressed histories through poetry. It is an endeavour, which both Darwish whose village Berweh was totally wiped off the map by the Israeli forces in 1948, and Shahid Ali, whose native Kashmir is equally ravaged from within, share and endure. The first part of the poem cautions against the politics of historiography:

> Soon we will search
> in the margins of your history, in distant countries,
> for what was once *our* history. And in the end we will ask ourselves
> Was Andalusia here or there? On the land . . . or in the poem?
> (italics not mine, 2002: 79–80)

The history of the community of the exiled Andalusia becomes a befitting objective correlative for the exiled Palestinians. Ali seems to speak through Darwish about his own double exile: 'I am Adam of the two Edens, I who lost paradise twice' (ibid.: 82).

In the fourth part of the poem, the references to the present-day Palestinian crisis become more pronounced as the poet (Darwish) makes an issue of the 'peace accord' that Arafat signed with Israel towards the fag end of his life: 'and no love can redeem me,/for I've accepted the "peace accord" and there is no longer a present left/to let me pass, tomorrow, close to yesterday' (ibid.: 83). The veteran leader is caricaturized, if not derided, for his unilateral agreement:

> And I am one of the kings of the end. . . . I jump
> off my horse in the last winter. I am the last gasp of an Arab
> I do not look for myrtle over the roofs of houses, nor do I
> Look around. No one should know me, no one should recognize
> me, no one who knew me. (ibid.)

Darwish, once a close associate of Arafat, turns out to be his critic for the arbitrary ways in which the late leader sold out the interests of his people. In the sixth section of the poem, the poet almost accuses Arafat for not staking his life for the cause of Palestine thus: 'You didn't fight, afraid of martyrdom. Your throne is your coffin./Carry then your coffin to save the throne' (ibid.: 86). The poet concludes the section on a more belligerent note: 'Everything is fixed for us:/why then this unending conclusion, O king of dying?' (ibid.).

Darwish looks upon Granada as a zone of inter-civilizational contact, and its culture a mixed harmonious one: 'I was the words/of the singers, the reconciliation of Athens and Persia, an East embracing a West/embarked on one essence' (ibid.: 84). This is much like Shahid Ali's description of Kashmir in terms of its secular past: 'In the lake the arms of temples and mosques are locked/in each other's reflections' ('Farewell', 2000: 8). Darwish and his poet-translator weep in unison over the loss of the homeland: 'Violins weep with gypsies going to Andalusia/Violins weep for Arabs leaving Andalusia' (Ali 2002: 92). The poet as well as his translator love the homeland in moments of its loss: 'In the exodus I love you more. . . . In departure/ we become only the birds' equals' (ibid.: 89). 'Eleven Stars over Andalusia' thus marks not only the blurring of distinction between the original and the translated, but more importantly, it brings the history of Granada, Palestine and Kashmir into one continuous frame of exodus and exile.

iii

In his last collection, *Call Me Ishmael Tonight*, as Shahid Ali confronts his own death, he breaks into ghazals exclusively, scripting in a way his own poetic elegy. An element of self-indulgence is inevitable to the very form of the ghazal as the poet's signatures form an essential part of the *maqta*, the concluding couplet(s):[13]

> Yours too, Shahid, will be a radical departure.
> You'll go out of yourself and then into my word
> ('My Word', 2004: 41)

> You've forgiven everyone, Shahid, even God—
> Then how could someone like you not live forever?
> ('Forever', ibid.: 78)

The self-indulgent poetic enterprise is more than redeemed not just by its rigorous aesthetic meticulousness but also by its serious implications in the discourses of Islam, nativity and diaspora. The motif of self-annihilation or exile from life operates at different levels— personal, national/sub-national and religious, simultaneously. The personal is elevated into communitarian/communal, and the regional into civilizational/transnational. From a culture-specific Kashmiri identity, the poet heads towards an Arabic identity:

> The sky is stunned, it's become a ceiling of stone.
> I tell you it must weep. So kneel, pray for rain in Arabic.
>
> At an exhibition of Mughal miniatures, such delicate calligraphy:
> Kashmiri paisleys tied into the golden hair of Arabic.
>
> ('Arabic', ibid.: 24)

Arabic is not just a language, it is a homeland for the exiled, a space of ultimate belonging, the last shelter: 'Territorialize each confusion in a graceful Arabic' (ibid.: 25). 'Arabic' is the *radeef*, that is, the refrain of the ghazal.

In the ghazals of Shahid Ali the personal feeds the political, and vice versa, engendering a streak of aesthetic activism in their otherwise delicate texture. Caught between the quotidian space of his everyday existence (America) on the one hand, and the possessive space of his religion (Islam and the Arab world) on the other, the poet gravitates towards the latter, questioning the neo-imperialist designs of the former: 'The birthplace of written language is bombed to nothing,/ How neat, dear America, is this game for you?' ('For You', ibid.: 26). The poet's political interventions are deliberately interrogative for such a stance lends necessary open-endedness to the poetic expression: 'Outgunned Chechens hold off Russian tanks—/They have a prayer. Are you listening, God?' ('God', ibid.: 75). Sometimes his ghazals turn deliberately brusque in expression as well as intent, revealing his growing unease with the politics of persecution of the people of his community/religion: 'You play innocence so well, with such precision, Shahid:/You could seduce God Himself, and fuck the sexless angles' ('Angels', ibid.: 45). The legacy of Faiz and Ghalib beckons the poet in such couplets. If Faiz brought revolutionary fervour into the ghazal, Ghalib could use the form for non-romantic purposes in his half-serious, half-comic manner.

The form of the ghazal, which Shahid Ali ultimately settles on, goes on to consolidate the identitarian drift of the poet towards an Islamic identity. Being the primary form of Arabic, Persian and Urdu poetry, the ghazal is a kind of formal home for the exiled poet. The poet who experimented with various kinds of literary forms—from Italian canzone to Persian ghazal—both from the western and the Indian traditions, becomes singularly conservative towards the end, which at one level engenders a rare degree of fastidiousness in the execution of the ghazal, and at another level blocks the possibilities of hybridization.[14] Despite being written in English, Shahid Ali's ghazals are least hybridized as the form becomes more powerful than the language in which they are executed or realized. English is fairly Persianized/Arabicized and the resonances of native Urdu can be easily heard in the English ghazals. The poet goes beyond English, through English: 'Go all the way through *jungle* from *aleph* to *zenith*/ to see English, like monkeys, swung beyond English' ('Beyond English', ibid.: 68). In the *maqta* of the ghazal, the poet sums up his struggle of going beyond English: 'If someone asks where Shahid has disappeared,/ he's waging a war (no, *jung*) beyond English' (ibid.: 69). Arabic is the poet's language of cognition: 'I too, Amichai, saw everything, just like you did—/In Death. In Hebrew. And (please let me stress) in Arabic' ('In Arabic', ibid.: 81). Arabic is the language of the poet's subconscious, he sees everything scribbled in Arabic: 'When Lorca died, they left the balconies open and saw:/On the sea his *qasidas* stitched seamless in Arabic' (ibid.: 80).[15] If the barriers of language are set aside, Shahid Ali is a worthy descendent of ghazal-maestros like Ghalib, Faiz or Firaq.

III

The young breed of 'rootless' Indian English diaspora poets of the post-1990s disentangles itself from the polemics of identitarian politics of the nation, the native-land and ethnicity as it harnesses multiculturalism to its creative ends with the openness of global foresight.[16] Suddenly, the anxiety of negotiating working alignments—which has otherwise been one of the major obsessions of Indian English diaspora poetry of the earlier generation—gives way to a willing acceptance of multiculturalism. The so-called 'diaspora' as an embattled bicultural condition appears to be anachronistic and redundant. From a bicultural world-view of the earlier diaspora poetry, what these new poets offer is a view of distracted and playful inter-textuality that cuts across civilizations and cultures in both time and space. In this section, 'a poetic collection' each of Vikram Seth, Sudeep Sen, Meena Alexander, Sujata Bhatt, Jeet Thayil, Suniti Namjoshi, Rukmini Bhaya Nair et al. has been critically focused upon.

i

In his poetry, Vikram Seth reveals a rare felicity of extrapolating himself to 'other places' as well as speaking in 'other voices' across a wide spectrum of cultures never charted before in Indian English poetry. If *The Golden Gate*, the poet's acclaimed verse novel, is overtly American (to be specific, Californian), with no apparent marker of the so-called Indianness in it, his *Three Chinese Poets* offers rare glimpses of the not-so-accessible Chinese culture, including that of forbidden Tibet. The way the poet withholds his own nativity in these texts, varied in their cultural configurations as they are, makes him a truly internationalist (as against merely the international) poet. For the purposes of focused discussion, the present section, however, con-centrates on his post-1990s poetic collection *All You Who Sleep Tonight*. The collection may not have the artistic merit of *The Golden Gate*, yet it provides us ample clues about the multiple locations of Indian English diaspora poetry as a whole.

The collection is divided into five parts—*Romantic Residues, In Other Voices, In Other Places, Quatrains* and *Meditations of the Heart*. The very first poem takes us to the airport—the hub of fleeting relations in the emerging global arena. 'A brave suitcase, red and small', a residue of the poet's romantic encounter with his ex-girlfriend who he 'hadn't met in seven years' ('Round and Round', 1999b: 151) appears on the carousel. Before he could focus his attention on this residue, 'My [his] memories chimed and chattered./ An old man pulled it off the Claim./ My bags appeared; I did the same' (ibid.: 151). 'The protocols of friendship' ('Protocols', ibid.: 152) break, for there is no room for sustained relationships. The overwhelming question is 'Were we to become lovers/Where would our best friends be?' ('A Style of Loving', ibid.: 153). The love, if at all there is any, is due to a 'mistaken smile': 'We found we'd been mistaken all the while/From that first glance, that first mistaken smile' ('Mistaken', ibid.: 156).

Instead of the usual tête-à-tête with the beloved, what the poet as lover seeks is 'No need for wit; just talk vacuities, and I'll/Reciprocate in kind, or laugh at you instead'; 'Twenty minutes' rendezvous will make my [his] day' ('Sit', ibid.: 157). Vikram Seth's romantic take-offs are marked more by departures, farewells and evictions, than by intimate moments of togetherness: 'Now it is the time to serve/ Eviction upon me' ('The Room and The Street', ibid.: 158). The farewells are contrived too: 'Then stand and frown awhile./At my express demand. You undertake to smile' (ibid.: 159). Distraction is in the environment itself:

> Great city, harsh and tall,
> In the cold throes of spring—
> Numb and distract us all
> That love may lose its sting. (ibid.)

The residues also tend to evaporate and diffuse in the postmodern ethos of distraction. Most of the poems in the first section do not suggest specific geographies. Love is a twenty-minute hometown—a place too transitory for life-long relationships.

In the second section, *In Other Voices*, Vikram Seth 'attempts to retrieve some of the suppressed voices from history' (Baral 2004: 81). The poet looks beneath and beyond constructed histories—both national as well as of the world. A medley of voices from zones as different as Auschwitz, Lithuania, Hiroshima and other places overtake the poet's authoritative voice, lending a non-provincial edge to his imagination. The remarkable aspect of this set of poems is that the poet, *a la* a playwright, takes the backseat, as his multiple personas choose to speak for themselves. In the first poem, the poet takes on the garb of a rabbi Ephraim Oshry, hearing the case of a woman-victim of the Nazi Germans: 'A woman of a good family in Kovno/Came to me weeping, comfortless. The Germans/Had raped her and tattooed on her arm/The legend, "Whore for Hitler's troops"' ('Lithuania: Question and Answer', 1999b: 163).

In the very next poem, there is a reversal of roles as the poet, instead of speaking on behalf of the much-empathized Jew, takes the role of a reluctant Nazi officer. Killing is not a happy choice for the Nazi Commandant:

> My wife ascribed my gloom to some annoyance
> Connected with my work but I was thinking,
> 'How long will our happiness last?' I was not happy
> Once the mass exterminations had started.
>
> ('Work and Freedom', ibid.: 165)

The protagonist, smarting under an excessive sense of duty, is traumatized so much that 'Often at night I [he] would wander through the stables/and seek relief among my [his] beloved horses' or 'would walk out and stand beside the transports' (ibid.). The officer feels helpless in the situation; he himself feels unsafe in the dreaded camps:

> My work, such unease aside, was never-ending,
> My colleagues untrustworthy, those above me
> Reluctant to understand or even to listen—
> Yet everyone thought the commandant's life was heaven. (ibid.)

When he is given an option of transfer from Auschwitz, the officer is too glad 'to gain my [his] freedom' (ibid.: 166). Vikram Seth thus enters the soul of different characters—both the victims and the victors—to retain the drama of life in its paradoxical entirety. The intimate German connection of the poet comes alive in his semi-autobiographical *Two Lives*. The new poets do not just intellectually extrapolate themselves in multicultural situations; as compulsive travellers, they have first-hand experience of sites and people.

In another poem, both the place and the persona change rather swiftly. The poet takes us through the journal entry of a Japanese doctor, victim of atomic attacks in World War II. The details of the tragedy recounted in the first person, take the reader straight into the vortex of events:

> I saw the shadowy forms of people, some
> Were ghosts, some scarecrows, all were wordless, dumb—
> Arms stretched straight out, shoulder to dangling hand;
> It took some time for me to understand . . .
> ('A Doctor's Journal Entry for August 6, 1945', ibid.: 170)

Vikram Seth and the other poets of his generation are part reporters, part historians and part anthropologists, digging out details of international events/culture in poetic metaphors. They claim access to the most private and obscure information about events as varied as the Holocaust to the bombing of Hiroshima and Nagasaki, which subsequently is transformed into a poetic subject.

Ghalib is a recurring presence in the Indian English poetry of the post-1990s which proves not only Ghalib's popularity beyond Urdu, but more importantly, the cross-linguistic range of Indian English poetry as a whole.[17] Seth fashions himself to be Ghalib writing a letter to Yusuf Mirza two years after the mutiny. Through the letter, Seth as Ghalib recounts the decline of Moghul culture in the wake of the failure of the 1857 mutiny:

> My brother died insane; his children and his wife
> Stranded in Jaipur, eke their pittance of a life.
> The children of high lords go begging in the streets.
> My household, God knows how, finds just enough to eat.
> (Ghalib, Two Years after the Mutiny, ibid.: 167)

The poet not only captures the mood of despondency that is evident in the later poetry of Ghalib, he is able to retain the subtleties of irony, so characteristic of the great master's poetic craft. The transition from a 'journal entry of a Japanese Doctor' to a letter supposedly written by Ghalib is effortless, with no evidence of rupture. The poet can ghost-write for anyone across cultures with a confidence unparalleled in Indian English poetry as a whole.

The third section of the collection offers a vivid range of landscapes from across the globe as though the entire earth is the terrain of the poet-traveller. Geography enamours the poet more than nationalist cartographies. The continuity of the landscape defies political divisions:

> As shadows, then as mass,
> The mountains of Garhwal
> Serrate and curve by pass
> And peak towards Nepal.
> ('Hill Dawn', ibid.: 177)

From the crests of the Upper Himalayas, the poet descends to the parks of China, where 'The humans rest in a design/One writes, one thinks, one moves, one sleeps./ . . ./And each is in his dream alone' ('Suzhou Park', ibid.: 178). Not only does the quiet night by the sea in Qingdao 'nullify the heart's distress', it compels the poet to break into lyrical poetry: 'I touch the insight, but a bent/Of heart exacts its old designs/And draws my hands to write these lines' ('Qingdao: December', ibid.: 182). For Seth, poetry is a playful acceptance of life irrespective of the nationality of places, persons, events and situations it revolves around.

The Golden Gate continues to be Seth's favourite site of suicide: 'What happier place/to quit that over-salted pie' ('On the Fiftieth Anniversary of the Golden Gate Bridge', ibid.: 189). On its fiftieth anniversary, the poet revisits it with a very positive frame as he discovers in the steel bridge an affirmation of life; it is heralded as 'That fine pendant on your God-/created breast'. The history and location of the bridge is so meticulously mapped out that the whole poem appears to be its poetic biography:

> Though courts twice threatened it, though storms
> Once washed away
> The trestles of his bridge, two forms
> Inched day by day (ibid.: 184)

The new poets do not just peer at alien objects/monuments with the fleeting interest of a tourist, they internalize the alien so much that the gap between the alien and the outsider no longer remains an issue of cultural contention; experience and observation consolidate the poetic expression.

The diaspora poets exploit both the indigenous and the international forms of poetry. Seth, otherwise a sonneteer *par excellence*, tries his hands at quatrains—a form which Ramanujan also tried with ample degrees of finesse, but with discernibly different dynamics. In Seth's 'Quatrains', instead of parodic reversals, there are residual impressions of a state beyond exhaustion:

> He dreams beyond exhaustion of a door
> At which he knocked and entered years before,
> But now no street or city comes to mind
> Nor why he knocked, nor what he came to find.
> ('Door', ibid.: 195)

The poet has entered in and out of so many doors that it does not matter which place he leaves and crosses over. The feeling of love (including that of love for the nation) has come to a stage when the poet's 'eyes will painlessly survey your [beloved's] face' (ibid.: 197). The pangs of passage are understood with an equipoise: 'The trees we see, the books we read, will go/ . . ./And we are fortunate that this is so' ('Passage', ibid.: 197). The aesthetics of diaspora—tragic or ludic—thus no longer remain as dramatic as to be defined in terms of an inordinate tension between the centripetal and the centrifugal.

ii

Writing from inside the basement of a partially restored fifteenth-century mansion 'Gartincaber' in Doune (near Stirling, Scotland), Sudeep Sen creates his own sparse and elongated 'archipelago of intent' which, as it ossifies into shape, remains no longer location-specific. In the half-sunken basement, a metaphor of the poet's inner being, various cultures of the world—from Latin American to American, from West Indian to Indian—meet, merge and mingle in a series of minimalist impressions, 'overheard phrases' and 'fragmented images' (2004: 202). The poem thus generated bears the structure of a human vertebra (as well as the 'long thin shape of Chile') in which 'sections and sub-sections join together like synapses between bone and bone' (ibid.: 205):[18]

> My thin country,
> my own spine.
>
> Locked dactyls,
> unconnected,
>
> stretched
> deeply fused.
> ('Indoors/ Outdoors-1', ibid.: 17)

It is no longer obligatory on the part of an Indian poet in English to map his great nation (i.e., India/Bharat) only. Also, there is no sacrilege committed in claiming his body to be a 'mobile republic' in itself.

Each section of the poem (twelve in all) contains a number of epigraphs from a whole range of sources lending textual richness to its cultural portfolio. Rilke's 'Death' provides the context for the mansion's outdoors: 'There stands death, a bluish distillate/in a cup without a saucer . . .' (quoted in ibid.: 15). As the humid and 'sticky heat [around the mansion]/tempt[s] the clouds/to change/their sex' (ibid.: 45–46), the poet is reminded of Derek Walcott, Donald Hall, Arvind K. Mehrotra, who in their own ways foresee rain. The gothic structure and 'the tower's/inner temple' (ibid.: 124) immediately invite inter-textual comparisons with Arun Kolatkar's description of Jejuri ('A low temple keeps its gods in the dark' [quoted in ibid.: 107]) and Picasso's observation on the human body ('Every human being is a colony' [quoted in ibid.]).

Whether inside the mansion or outside it, Sudeep Sen is carried adrift by the transnational poetic impulse inseminated by poets across cultures. The epigraphs actually travel into the text effortlessly, without any sense of insertion. To use the poet's own terms: 'juices spill/cautiously/like preserved semen/anguishing/to let go'.(ibid.: 17). The inter-texts do not lurk beneath; they appear on the surface as part of the whole experience. The epigraph drawn from Ann Blandiana's 'Condition'—'I am like sand in the hourglass/which can be time only in falling'—becomes part of the poem under the sub-title 'Sand Time' (ibid.: 69–70). This is how the poet culminates his section entitled 'Passion': 'I want/to do/with you/what/spring does/with the/cherry trees' (ibid.: 105). This also happens to be the epigraph taken from the poet's favourite poetry by Pablo Neruda. In the poetry of the post-1990s, the gap between the epigraph and the poem, the inter-text and the text collapses as cultures coalesce and comingle in one sustained poetic experience.

The poet's archipelago/body is 'addressless/and unmapped', not sure of its future. It is 'an errant/outcrop of land—/a floating island/ without future/or anchor' whose 'terrain/is ever-shifting' (ibid.: 186–87). The sense of insecurity or alienation—'I am/an outcast' (ibid.: 183)—is soon overcome:

> and I am glad
> not to
>
> get caught in
> the quagmire
>
> of poetry
> and pretence
>
> of ambition
> and intellect,
>
> of life
> and death.
> ('Archipelago', ibid.: 188)

The poets of Sudeep Sen's generation no longer suffer the dilemmas of diasporic existence, for exile is a permanent condition of life; it is more inside than outside: 'I am/an exile/everywhere—/within/my own self' (ibid.: 183). Exile provides 'transitory freedom'—'enough for/a dreamer' (ibid.: 187). The young diasporic poet does not look for any lofty spiritual salvation, nor does he seek easy resolutions of dualities: 'All I'm left/with/is my fatal/imagination,/ the conjured/ dreams, and/a summer of metaphors' (ibid.: 74).

'Fission' (as against the conventional 'fusion') is the poetics of the distracted diaspora: 'That's all/I really need/Rest is uncontrolled . . .' (ibid.: 74). Everything seems to explode into infinite directions:

> the ink
> blots
>
> as this line's
> linear edge
>
> dissolves
> and frays—
>
> like capillary
> threads
>
> gone mad
> twirling . . .
> ('Offering, Fluids', ibid.: 80)

There are no full stops, definite destinations or moments of arrival in Sudeep Sen's fleeting journey. It is marked by 'only beginnings' (ibid.: 81). Even the 'mattress' which the poet shares with his beloved breaks the anchor, defies 'current/gravity, and/electricity' (ibid.: 86). The two are like 'vessels buoyant/on different shores' (ibid.). The mattress becomes the 'the ocean bed', 'its pulses/uncontrollably/rocking the water,/ the bodies/the dreams' (ibid.: 87–88).

iii

Meena Alexander's splintering credo is not fundamentally different from Sudeep Sen's dreamy distractions. She too takes a vast geography—inter-continental as well as inter-civilizational—in her poetic stride without ever overplaying the differences. The poets of the post-1990s celebrate the sheer array of their hometowns:

> Place names splinter
> on my tongue and flee:
>
> Allahabad, Tiruvella, Kozhencheri,
> Khartoum. Nottingham, New Delhi,
> Hyderabad, New York,
> the piecework of sanity—

> stitching them into a single
> coruscating geography . . .
> ('Gold Horizon', 2002a: 49)

The poet compares the breathless dimensions of her expanse with 'a long drawn breath/in an infant's dream' (ibid.). Various sites are patch-worked into a glittering 'location-free' space whose sheen is occasionally 'ruined by the black water in a paddy field' (ibid.).[19] Belongingness is a kind of fundamentalism, an insanity that the new poets constantly shy away from in the age of global citizenship. They are globetrotters rather than settlers.

The waters of rivers are not the preserve of nations they flow through. In Alexander's fluid universe, the rivers of the world bear same degree of holiness for the distinct civilizations they support; rather they are extensions of each other:

> Holy, the waters of the Ganga, Hudson, Nile,
> Pamba, Mississipi, Mahanadi.
>
> Holy the lake in Central Park, bruised eye of earth
> mirror of heaven.
> ('Indian April', ibid.: 57)

Lest the holiness is spiritualized, the poet brings in the quotidian presences around these watery heavens: 'the pointed reeds, spent syringes,/ pale, uncoiled condoms' (ibid.). The new poets establish global connections, but they do not create wishful arcadias. The juxta-position of the holy with the profane is a reminder of their complexity of vision.

In the diaspora poetry of the post-1990s, the specificities of culture give way to their free transposition across different landscapes, morphing the whole spectre of culture irrevocably. Allen Ginsberg could be seen 'naked in a doorway in Rajasthan' ('Indian April', ibid.: 54), he could be found on the ghats of the Ganga as well, 'young again/ teeth stained with betel and bhang,/nostrils tense with the smoke of Manhattan' (ibid.: 57), his 'flesh is indigo,/the color of Krishna's face' (ibid.). The thirteenth-century Sufi poet Rumi could be heard on the phone line doling out his bits of wisdom: '*The way of love/is not a subtle argument,*/Rumi sang. *The door/there is devastation*' ('Reading Rumi as the Phone Rings', ibid.: 19). Meena Alexander invokes the myth of Iphigenia's sacrifice to recount perhaps her own at the hands of her father. As she is reminded of Agamemnon, she self-reflexively asks: 'How can I bring the Greeks and Indians like this?'. It is not mere Indo-Greek historic past, as the poet adds: 'Menander will not help./He will not answer questions put to him' ('An Honest Sentence', ibid.: 52).

There is a latent desire to speak in multiple tongues. The Muse comes to the young poet like 'a bird shedding gold feathers,/each one a quill scraping my tympanum'. This is what she whispers to her:

> Alphabets flicker and soar.
> *Write in the light*
> *Of all the languages*
> *You know the earth contains,*
> You murmur in my ear.
> This is pure transport.
>   ('Muse', ibid.: 24)

Instead of generating linguistic chauvinism, other languages add to the linguistic portfolio of the new poets. As the poet descends on Port Sudan, she hears Arabic sounds much to her delight:

> Someone cried *Kef Halek!*
> My skirt spun in the wind
> and Arabic came into my mouth
>
> and rested alongside
> all my other languages.
>   ('Port Sudan', ibid.: 10)

Translations conceal truths: 'Now I know the truth of my tongue/ starts where translations perish' (ibid.). Therefore, the poet seeks to acquire as many languages as possible. Whenever the translated sensibility fails, the poet resorts to the originals with their meanings sometimes in the parenthesis or notes.

In the small collection *Illiterate Heart*, containing not more than thirty-five poems, Meena Alexander uses fragments of expressions from as many as nine languages including French, Arabic, Japanese, Hindi, Sanskrit, Bangla along with her mother tongue, Malayalam— a range, which is only matched by Sujata Bhatt, another expatriate poet. The expressions quoted from other languages are scriptural, official as well as popular. From the national song's opening line *jana gana mana* to the popular film song *choli ke peeche*, to classical expressions such as *gnanam, dhanam, kavya,* etc., Meena Alexander's poetry is replete with multilingual lexicons. These expressions are so strategically inserted in the poetic argument that they acquire a centrality that forces the other language readers to explore them in their respective traditions. The multicultural impetus is derived from culture-specific expressions such *Almav, Ai, Kaddish,* etc.

If Sudeep Sen incorporates lines/images from various poets of different cultures in his long poetic text *Distracted Geographies,* Meena Alexander writes 'notes' for her international audience to provide clues for various culture-specific images/tropes/mythemes used in her poems. T. S. Eliot faced the same dilemma when he rather reluctantly wrote his multicultural poem *The Waste Land.* 'Notes' now seem to be a mandatory extension of poems, even while they suggest an element of intellectualism invading contemporary poetry in a rather un-concealed form. Some of the 'Notes' in the collection elucidate as well as consolidate the poems concerned. A 'Note' to the poem 'Daffodils' adds to the texture of the poem. It reads: 'This poem was inspired by Kasuya Eiichi's poem "Daffodils", but also running through my head was that other poem, William Wordsworth's "I Wandered Lonely as a Cloud", which I read as a child in India without ever having glimpsed these yellow-gold trumpets' (ibid.: 102).

iv

Another post-1990s poet, Jeet Thayil, too charts out the entire globe as his territory, which he sails across on the ship of his poems along the wavy path of yin-yang that epitomizes 'the twofold and comple- mentary character of the universe' (Chevalier and Gheerbrant 1996: 1140) in seven phases. In the prefatory 'Acknowledgements' to his collection *English: Poems* (2003), the poet explains the 'in- seven structure' of the book through a drawing that is modelled after Robert Wilson's seven-act play *Stalin.* The play, staged in 1973, had a twelve-hour duration in which Stalin is unfolded not through logic, but through fragmented phantasmagorical sequences. Thayil's poetic venture is as much phantasmagoric, dramatic and extravagant. Out of the seven sections, part 1 and 7, part 2 and 6 and part 3 and 5 'reflect' each other, part 4 is 'point of reflection' (2003: x). The 'Acknowledgements' serve the purpose of 'Notes', which, as pointed out earlier, become increasingly indispensable for the new multicultural diaspora poetry.

The first section is all about movement and dislocation not as much by force but by the poet's own volition. Very much like his fellow poets, Thayil chooses instability, freedom to float in water and air through means as different as a ship, a plane or even an auto. Once airborne, the poet is not ready to descend: 'My regenerate heart pumps like a bird,/ floating on auto, ever unwilling to land' ('Skewed', ibid.: 7). The earth holds no surprises: 'Only who married/earth was unsurprised' ('The Man Who Married Water', ibid.: 12). The poet would like to identify himself with other elements like water, fire and air that can engulf and overwhelm the poet beyond the sense of space. The water 'drowns', the fire 'consumes' and the air provides a vision of flying and falling:

> The man
> who married
> air, saw
>
> himself fall
> into a spiral,
> his hands
>
> gripped tight
> on the wheel
> of a plane
>
> hurtling
> down a
> plane that
>
> was
> not
> there. (ibid.: 11–12)

There is an unmistakable urge to 'bob/like flotsam/above the scene of future martyrdom' ('Afloat, the Immigrant Martyr Elect', ibid.: 8). The poet takes a dig at those who glorify immigration as some kind of martyrdom. Air is both the medium and the meaning. Jeet Thayil is a poet of take-offs in 'the pulverised air' ('About the Author', ibid.: 4), without ever knowing the art of descending downwards: 'I know how to fly/not how to land' ('Afloat, the Immigrant Martyr Elect', ibid.: 8).

In the next section, entitled 'Shapeshifter', Thayil expresses his intention of taking different shapes across a range of species. First, he seeks to shift to the other gender. As a girl that steps into his fantasies leaves the cubicle, the poet 'pull[s] on her things—shoes, underwear, jeans'. The primordial surfaces: 'Again/the sound of God's snake hissing;/sudden swell of breasts on my chest' ('How to Be a Girl', ibid.: 17). In another poem, the poet wants to turn into vegetation:

> Hold your breath until
> you are God's green thoughts.
> Stop Eating.
>
> air will suffice for food.
> ('How to be a Leaf', ibid.: 20)

The air is food for the leafy poet. In yet another 'shift', the poet seeks to become a crow: 'turn black/not nigga, black' ('How to be a Crow', ibid.: 22). To be a bandicoot is his next option so that he could 'Assume dominance/over the underworld' ('How to be a Bandicoot', ibid.: 23). It is, however, easier to be a satanic snake:

> This one is easy,
> let your grief take over.
> Enjoy salt.
>
> Forget the rest.
> When your skin falls off,
> sere as bone,
>
> laugh out loud.
> ('How to Be a Krait', ibid.: 24).

Most of the post-1990s poets tend to write 'animal-poems' as they endeavour to re-live a pre-political primitive past. The 'regression into bestial world' is a measure of their 'disgust for modernist universalism'.[20]

Jeet Thayil is not a poet of facile postmodern freedom. While there is a desire to celebrate, there is also the pain of not breaking through the stalemates, emotional as well as cultural. The poet 'long[s] to be' free, but the misery is 'my [his] race [is] obscure in a crowded sea/ shipwrecked' ('Sailor's Log', ibid.: 34). In the very first poem of the third section, 'Ache', holy matrimony is the subject of a spoof:

> Fool will sing,
> flea will suck,
> Fool will work,
> flea will pluck

> Both will learn
> the virtue of obedience.
> ('Fool and Flea', ibid.: 27)

'Obedience' stands for lack of creative enterprise as it checkmates imaginative wilderness and presses for a docile acceptance of norms and values which the new poets find difficult to abide by. The relationships are mere short-lived encounters in the poetry of these poet-travellers: 'He stops to stare on the wall,/remembers nothing but farewell too soon' ('The Air There is Crowded', ibid.: 28). The new diaspora poetry is more a poetry of farewells, than of re-alignments; stability of any kind—marital, vocational and locational—is out of the question.

The next section, 'The Genesis Godown', explores the 'genesis' of the wandering self not as much in its genealogical sequence as in its horizontal variety. The anxiety of being 'ruined by syntax' continues to bother the poet. Settling the issue of language in favour of English once and for all, the poet begins to locate the self in the airborne gristly insects, 'a flotilla of baby striders/afloat on the sticky green waters', 'near the ladies' latrine' so as to have a sense of airlift: 'Their joyous humming lifts /us afloat, airborne like our brothers' ('English', ibid.: 40). The moon is also a part of the poet's extraordinary non-nationalistic genetic inventory; like the moon, the poet too is 'turned by water, returned by crescent,/quartered and corrected by the many-maned ocean' ('Moon', ibid.: 43). The poet is smitten by the monsoon as a harbinger of 'true rains'; its 'random power/endowed with shower of bounty, whips wind/shreds vine . . ./and douses/the world in torrents of self-cycled water, maddened/by sea-rhythm . . .' ('Monsoon', ibid.: 44). Thus, the cycle of seasons, local winds in the form of monsoons, familial past, colonial English and small insects—a whole set of disparate entities—go into the making of the poetic self.

The succeeding sections of the collection mirror-image the first three ones, reinforcing the curvy trajectory of the journey. The 'Ache' comes back. If in the previous 'Ache', 9/11 is approached in terms of the burdensome habit of 'never looking up at the approaching sky' (September 10, 2001), in its reflected version, the burning of Australian missionary Graham Staines is seen as the death of vision: 'Daylight is worse by far' ('Meanwhile, Over in Orissa', ibid.: 52). Botero's fat figures and Akbar Padamsee's nudes are portraits that quarrel with themselves. The journey is mediated by bouts of boredom, frustration and pain: 'Listen: nothing, not even love, is true' ('The Boredom Artist', ibid.: 54). The section is marked by a mood of despondency and melancholy: 'Ash heaves/upwards. Bones fall, fill/the river, fat its oiled banks' ('Elegiac', ibid.: 56).

But in the last two sections, Thayil re-asserts his desire to acquire many tongues, shapes and sites. In 'The Unauthorized Autobiography of Rain', the poet speaks for rain as it comes in different ways in 'many continents': 'In Euro, I trilled nightly/a friendly anti-rhythm, unbound by time or rime' (ibid.: 63), and in Siam, I 'Heard my own forgotten name/from sources unreliable/Nothing prepared me for monsoon' (ibid.). From Kabul to Kathmandu to Kovalam, the poet travels across the entire Indian subcontinent before he lands in London, Doune and finally in Hong Kong. From zoo to temple, and from beaches to shores, the poet provides a range of vignettes, which the so-called native poetry circumscribed as it is by the geography of its own cannot ever match. The horizontal reach of the post-1990s poets is so over-whelming that it itself takes on the dimensions of the depth.

V

It is the wind, the window, the wings and the sky that enchant the new poets of the diaspora most—the tropes that are intrinsically poetic.[21] Besides an overt multicultural/multilingual display of metaphors and mythemes, what lends a rare kinesis to Sujata Bhatt's poetry is her skyward gaze: 'Who can look after the roses when the sky/ripples and throbs with so much passion?' ('Looking Up', 2000: 11). As the squirrels below fight with each other with 'raging lust', the poetess is overtaken by the borderless and boundless (female) sky above: 'The sky is naked,/it is a nude in its eloquence'. The violent rustle in the treetops engages the poetess as much:

> Even the air feels stunned
> from the constant noise of whipping.
> How the leaves slap the wind:
> they are reckless, careless,
> they don't believe they could ever be torn
> ('Squirrels', ibid.: 13)

It is this recklessness (suicidal as well as celebratory) that marks some of the not-so-self-consciously-written multicultural poems of Sujata Bhatt, as indeed the poetry of her generation in general. The over-metaphysicalized inwardness characteristic of Indianness suddenly gives way to looking outside: '*Augatora*/the gate opening towards the sun—/eyes watching for the wind' ('Augatora', ibid.: 16). The skyline is the trajectory of the poet's non-nationalist cartographic imagination:

> The sky is orange
> and so is the cat
> that ran just across the roof—
> Television antennae cut up
> her path—Everyone has hung up
> their laundry outside . . .
> ('Barcelona', ibid.: 22)

Skyscaping is one of the exceptional features of new diaspora poetry. The sky is not reduced to metaphysical nothingness, but it is seen in terms of its scintillating shades—sinister as well as supportive.

In the case of most of the woman diaspora poets, the politics of space conflates with that of gender. Diaspora no longer remains just a signifier of cultural displacement; it becomes as much a happy enterprise of trans-gender flights into the open sky. Sujata Bhatt has a direct tête-à-tête with the wind, the mother of the bird:

> I could be anything
> depending on the light:
> the owl, the tree, the woman—
>
> I know the sort of shadows
> the wind prefers—
> ('Vogelfrau', ibid.: 80)

The wings of birds—a common trope in women's poetry/literature— are not just accessories; they constitute the very country of the poetess in flight, howsoever transient and fleeting it may be:[22] 'That's when the feathers are/everything: my eyes, ears,/my lips, my brain—' (ibid.). The bird has a very different genealogy in Bhatt's universe: 'Broom married Wind/and gave birth to Birth'; both the Broom and the Wind have lost purity: 'Wind wears five little bells/In front of his mouth' and 'Broom wears a silver mask these days', the poetess claims: 'The only one/who speaks the truth/is Bird' ('Broom, Wind and Bird: Zeitwanderer', ibid.: 81). The flutter of the bird's wing is enough to spark a vision of emancipation.

From airborne birds to surreptitious snakes, Bhatt's poetry takes a plunge into the nether world for what it ultimately seeks to celebrate is the poet's combat against the forces of conservation as well as preservation, of stability as well as status quoism. The dread stands transformed into desire as the snakes turn into the birds of the underworld. In one of the poems, 'The Circle', 'the snake is a bird': 'How can you have a pink, polka-dotted cobra?/ I say it will be a flamingo' (ibid.: 99). The blowing wind enters into the hair of the poetess with all its rustling leaves and vines, which subsequently 'turn[s] into a small snake':

> Oh I was frantic,
> desperate with fear as the snake
> simply grew stronger
> and larger—constantly changing its colours—
> as if trying to win me over
> with its shimmering scarlets and blacks—
> then always slipping out
> of my grasp—and yet
> refusing to go away—
> ('The Dream', ibid.: 14)

The snakes, interestingly enough, 'drop down from trees' before they 'slide into the lake' ('A Swimmer in New England Speaks', ibid.: 26):

> . . . —and sometimes
> when one of them hangs, dangling
> from a branch, I've seen the half moons—
> red, yellow, brown . . . glistening down
> its belly—a rippling ladder,
> a necklace— (ibid.)

The snake becomes a ladder in the poetry of Bhatt, as indeed in the poetry of many of the post-1990s poets.[23] It emerges as an ambiguous symbol of trepidation and trance, of destruction and preservation, of nervous energy: 'a sudden bolt of energy—a black flash/darting out of my hands' ('The Snake Catcher Speaks', ibid.: 29).[24]

Bhatt seeks to relapse into the jungle age with Tarzan as her lover. Her 'homeland is always green', uncorrupted by the sophisticated languages that human beings have developed. For most of the new poets, civilization is a state of exile; the jungle is the original home. Tarzan's 'raw speech' has changed 'the way I [she] look[s] at tree,/the way I [she] hold[s] a stone—/the fruit I [she] eat[s]' ('Jane to Tarzan', ibid.: 57). The jungle-man pulls her into 'impossible positions' as she craves for 'endless aching', 'the clenching curl of it' (ibid.: 59). The poet is most animate in the company of animals. As she spends a night near a zoo, the poetess is all lost in the animal sounds: 'And the cries from the animals/in the zoo were like a steady storm/in my sleep—' ('A Room in Amsterdam', ibid.: 47).

As the poet steps out of the animal world into the domain of history and politics, she confronts a world utterly divided and fragmented. Having experienced a primordial belongingness in the bestial world, the poet fails to reconcile with political divisions. The question raised in the context of the partition of the subcontinent is hard-hitting:

> How could they
> have let a man
> who knew nothing
> about geography
> divide a country?
> ('Partition', ibid.: 34)

The poet acquires so many languages, without ever being aware of the provincial linguistic feuds that go with them:

> What happened when the Gujarati
> and the Marathi and the Hindi
> I spoke
> made room for the English words?
>
> Perhaps it happened quietly,
> easily—with the fragrance of magnolias
> filling the air—
> So no one noticed.
> So I can't remember.
> ('New Orleans Revisited', ibid.: 45)

The poet's mother, caught as she is in the cultural quandaries of her own generation, however, feels 'guilty' for her daughter's grill: 'How hard it had been for her/to watch me—/on the wooden bench/in the street car/in that sunlight—' (ibid.).

In a meta-poetical venture—which becomes increasingly rare among the diaspora poets of the late capitalist era—Bhatt does spell out the poetics of multicultural poetry. The new poets who take multiculturalism in their stride do not feel the urgency of explaining their (dis-)position. Bhatt, self-conscious multiculturalist as she is, however, tends to explain:

> [The multicultural poem] will not settle down.
> It will not be your pet
>
> It wants to be read at the border
> to the person who checks your passport.
>
> . . . .
> It speaks of refraction.
> It wants more dialogue
> between the retina and the light.
> It says, 'get rid of that squint.'
> ('The Multicultural Poem', ibid.: 101)

This kind of intermittent regression into 'conscious multiculturalism', despite its claims of refraction and dialogue, does broach in an element of exhibitionism in Bhatt's celebratory multiculturalism. The diaspora is not an effortless reflex as it is in the case of other rootless poets of her generation. But what redeems her occasional self-conscious multiculturalism is her naturalist way of defining the multiculturalism as 'a creature, a being/whose spirit breathes/like an orchid in the sun/ still wet from the rain/on a day when the garden tilts slippery, sublime—' (ibid.). As the poet matures, she does not showcase her multiculturalism in a pastiched play of tropes.

vi

Suniti Namjoshi, with her effusive fabulist imagination that is re-markably so consistent with the neo-primitive moorings of the new diaspora poets in general, breaks free from cartographic barriers—the nationalist as well as the post-nationalist. In her latest collection of fables and poems, *Sycorax*, she re-writes the Shakespearian romantic comedy *The Tempest*, not as much with a postcolonialist zeal, which it is often subjected to, as with a feminist orientation that defies loc-ational assertions. The usual claptrap of memory and nostalgia of the homeland that often reverberates the diaspora poetry of the 'classic' kind is missing; there is no visible attempt at assimilation or hybridization because the anxiety to negotiate relationships is already over. Her country/utopia, if there is any, is her gender that she sails into invariably with her army of animals, insects, birds, witches and other female spirits.

In the collection, the dehumanized witch Sycorax, who in the original *The Tempest* dies just before Prospero arrives at the marooned island, is resuscitated to confront male-dominance. She claims her space in bold letters:

> I'm able to say clearly that when Prospero
> said he took over an uninhabited island
> save for Caliban and the enslaved
> Ariel, he lied
> I LIVED ON THAT ISLAND.
> It was my property . . .
> ('Sycorax', 2006: 1)

Caliban is literally disowned for going 'with the gods who were only men' (ibid.). Except males, all kinds of animals—including bats, dolphins, lizards, sparrows, are the 'unacknowledged companions' of the aged witch who 'made tidy/whatever I [she] had been' ('The Hermit', ibid.: 36). This is how the poetess (as Sycorax) welcomes the grisly lizard: 'This is her home, her shack,/ and her planet. Her ancestors preceded mine' ('Visitors', ibid.: 10). Obviously, the time-scale that the poet uses is that of geology rather than mere history. Ariel's charming twin sister is invented so as to provide a happy female alternative to the arrogant twin bother.

The female birds and the beasts are Namjoshi's soul-mates as they keep intruding into her unconscious as shape-shifters: 'a hundred/ thousand mares now gallop/through my head' ('Mares', ibid.: 50). The bestial and the human collapse into each other in Namjoshi's post-diasporic arcadia, and the transition is too swift:

> [Old women] drift like owls not knowing what
> dreams they might light upon . . .
> . . . Sometimes they sleep like kingfishers
> on the charmed wave . . .
> . . . Or they slip like seals through black
> water from island to island and choose their dreams: . . .
> ('The Old Woman's Secrets', ibid.: 9)

The brave women are like trees, circled by gulls or 'dolphin[s] circling the gull[s]/ . . ./ inadvertently' ('For Anna Mani', ibid.: 77). The women—brave, old or bewitched—in Namjoshi's verse, personify the raw buzz of nature, as against the sophistications of culture.

The borders and the boundaries simply collapse in the ever-expanding vision of the new poets. Sky, oceans, forests are the limitless playgrounds of new poetic playfulness. A dip in the sea for Namjoshi is curiously enough an act retaining the shape of the self; rather than of its possible attrition or disintegration:

> In the sea she cannot lose her shape.
> Cold water curls over her body;
> skin is made aware of its own expanse;
> and fish pass by while she bobs like a cork,
> robbed of all her careful disguises.
>
> ('Submerged', ibid.: 108)

There is a desire to be anonymous. The post-diaspora consciousness borders on metaphysical self-annihilation; at least it provides a necessary take-off. The liquidation of the splintered self into the void no longer remains remote. Namjoshi's poetry gravitates towards a transcendental awareness attained through the diasporic experience:

> To hide a letter, enter a forest.
> To lose a letter, stash it away
> in a stack of letters, and in order to live
> in obscurity, be a pebble on the beach,
> looking very much like any other.
>
> ('Getting Anonymous', ibid.: 108).

The new diasporic poetry attains verticality through its horizontal proliferation. Its metaphysical climax is not that of a still *yogi* in trance, but of a traveller in transition. The process remains intrinsically human.

Suniti Namjoshi, ever-eager as she is to merge into the infinite realm, be it of the sea or of the sky, like her other female counterparts, Bhatt and Alexander, does look skywards. While Bhatt is overwhelmed by the site of 'Giant fireballs [hot air balloons] that dare to compete with the sun' ('Looking Up', 2000: 11), Namjoshi is aware of the mechanical endeavour involved:

> Then there are machine gods,
> balloonists and such,
> whose clever contraptions haul them up;

> but they're not reliable
> Should a string snap, a strut break,
> they hang in mid air,
> or drift skyward, which after all
> is awkward.
> ('Modes of Flying', 2006: 58)

The poet does not seek to fly on angelic wings either, for 'their mode of locomotion/is beyond [her] emulation' (ibid.: 57). Apsaras, as they descend down, have grace, but they are made of 'ethereal stuff' (ibid.: 58). The preferred way to fly beyond is Buddhist 'because in this mode everything I do/is light and easy/and even my messages fall like confetti' (ibid.). The Buddhist way is the existential middle course that involves the seminal role of human effort in the self's striving towards its emancipation.

In Namjoshi's primordial world, not only do the beastly and the womanly coalesce into organic symbiosis, generic divisions blur as much; fables lead to poems as much as poems lead to fables, effecting a flow of life from nature to culture and vice versa. Fabled creatures are re-invented and replenished with rare poetic vigour: 'Best be a giant who sometimes indites/poetry' ('Twelve ways of Looking at a Giant', ibid.: 139). The giant of a folk tale who 'kept his heart hidden away somewhere safe . . . in the tree' (ibid.: xii), is looked into in twelve different ways as Wallace Stevens (2000) does in his poem 'Thirteen Different Ways of Looking at a Blackbird' in a unique inter-textual exercise. The giants, along with the witches and the dwarfs in dreams, engender an element of fantasy in Namjoshi's poetry, liberating the reader at once from the tyranny of political divided territories. All these so-called 'disabled creatures' stand redeemed as they undergo a human predicament.

> It's not that he [the giant] belongs to another species.
> It's just that he's bigger and far more beautiful.
> Look at this statue I've made of him.
> ('The Artist Praises Him', 2006: 139)

Namjoshi's universe is fabulous, for the sheer experience of diaspora in her case defies ordinary co-ordinates of existence. Diaspora, as it increasingly turns location-free and multi-directional in the globalized era of the post-1990s, borders on fantasy that takes in its stride not only the tangible earth, but also the skies above and the netherworld below. The pre-lasparian and the post-diasporic begin to coincide.

vii

Another post-1990s poet, Rukmini Bhaya Nair, like Sujata Bhatt or Meena Alexander, may not have a formal status of a non-resident Indian, but as a fairly well-travelled poet she too lives on the interstices of cultures/civilizations.[25] In her *Yellow Hibiscus*, the poet virtually takes the reader through a poetic peep show of various 'territories' across continents in terms of their cultural peculiarities. The images or poetic snippets are no easy tourist postcards as the endeavour is to represent life at the level of experience of the backyard. The essence of Africa is captured through its tribal javelin-like weapon 'assegai'; for the poet more than a weapon it is a sound of wounded Africa hurled unseen: 'this is the sound of a forest wound ancestral/tribute cry heard among the granite foothills . . .' ('Assegai, Africa', 2004: 91). Far from exoticizing the Dark Continent, the poet, being a fellow postcolonial subject, portrays its hinterlands in terms of the pain and brutality that its virgin forests underwent during the colonial period.

Nair takes special interest in the Southeast Asian nations which once again goes on to prove that the horizontal vision of the new poets is no longer confined to the First World. Japan is seen through its sumo wrestlers—'Courteous/beyond recognition, elephantivorybellies/ embrace in pairs, beautiful and obscene' ('Sumo Wrestlers, Japan', ibid.: 93). Java is approached as a rain-hit island of temples. The torrential rain that produced dense tropical forests in the region is the 'Closest thing to a stoning'—'Small, stinging pebbles of rain/And then—fist-sized rock hammers/Loosed wrath of some invisible mob' ('Moondrop, Java', ibid.: 94). The temples in the poetic logic prove to be the rainproof shelters: 'Here is no rain, no splintering sound/A scarred grey boulder fills the place' (ibid.: 95). Thailand, another Southeast Asian nation, defies all horizons as 'so low it dips invisibly/ Whenever stork bends to drink' ('Enigma, Thailand', ibid.: 96). Buddha strides across its fields. The geography and culture of the nation are summed up thus:

> When the folds stopped
> Stork found many fish.
> Balanced on Thailand's
> Tilted rim, Buddha smiled. (ibid.: 97)

Singapore is presented in terms of its increasingly modernized structures: 'Wasteful colonial shacks replaced by prefabs (. . . .)/

For our good, true./ But—squares of high-rise window light resemble sugar cubes, . . .' ('Backyard, Singapore', ibid.: 98). Everyday culture and climate, the essence and the existence, as they impinge upon each other, inform the poetic description.

Though all the multicultural poets exposed as they are to various linguistic registers do invoke words, signs and mythemes from various cultures, as a professional linguist, Nair has a special sensitivity for the sound and the syllable. Each sound is the space of distinct culture in her poetry. Languages—natural, human and machine; written, un-written, spoken; native, alien; contemporary and classic—are turned into poetic metaphors. And as she hears a diverse range of sounds in the night, a whole range of theorists from cultures as different as Greek, Russian and Indian inform her. In a daring experiment she puts together the sounds and the sound-theorist against each other:

> Strange, how the night confuses Ladefoged (1970)
> Odd frequencies of sound, dog's Jakobson (1952)
> Deep growl, rasp of a rusty bolt Aristotle (c. 5th century BC)
> And infirm death Anandavardhana
> Rattling in an old man's throat Abhinavagupta
> ('Language Lessons', ibid.: 156)

The poet locates the play of cultures in the voices, and how these voices provide a perspective and boundary to human imagination.

Linguistic codes hitherto deemed necessary for intelligible human communication constrict the freedom of self. Very much like other poets of the post-1990s, Nair seeks to break into the unbridled natural:

> Nothing like the unpinioned dance
> Of cat and eagle, sun-entranced
> Can of our making, the limits
> Of our rules are in our voices.
> ('Leela', ibid.: 132)

The operative phrase is 'unpinioned dance'—that is, a frenzied movement with its own in-built harmony, but without a fixed stable anchor or platform. The urge is to go beyond clichés which travel from generation to generation and thus form the unsalted principles of society. Nair as poet first discovers freedom in multiple voices, then extending her urge further she seeks to go beyond the discourse of voices itself; the primal sounds not decreed by codes—religious or social—is her preferred destination:

> The routine talk learnt from clans
> Are our sole means of remembrance
> Patterns of birth, the interchange
> Of communities, are by words decreed. (ibid.: 133)

The verbal definitions of give and take, of home and exile, of loss and gain lack instinctive transparency and grace—the two virtues the poets of the 1990s clamour for.

The detachment that the new poets seek is not metaphysical, it is very much physical and is located in the body itself. The hyoid bone—'The only bone in the entire body/not tied to any other' ('The Hyoid Bone', ibid.: 140), becomes a metaphor of new diasporic detachment: 'Unannexed/freedom's territory deep within' (ibid.). Animals, rather than angels or divine spirits are Nair's epitomes of higher self. And these animals are not civilized pets, they are 'brutes' of a primordial world. A despicable cockroach wins the poet's admiration for being brave against her swipes at him: 'His sense of honour, of order, I wished I could/Surrender the darkness to him, tell him/I wanted to salute him' ('Cockroach', ibid.: 62). Mayflies are angelic: 'Radiant against electronic / beams, tiny flighted sprites/ Epiphanic with delight!' ('Mayflies', ibid.: 63). The spider is a delicate crafts(wo)man: 'Silicon sharp, never in focus/Smaller, softer than my eye/That views it, gossamer slews/Slung up like steel pitched high . . .' ('Arachnidaria', ibid.: 78).

Nair's inventory of brutes is chequered for it not only includes minor insects and flies, but also the 'leaping' tiger and the 'somnolent' cow. The animals emerge as metaphors of charged poetry, of a free (uni)verse, of imagination unbridled. They are not poetic subjects; they are rather poems in wild motion. The poetic syllables take the form of a bestial body. The tiger's pugmarks are imprints of poetic expression or vice versa. The tiger stands for poetry unleashed:

> Look tiger is about to leap.
>
> Abandoning mere metrical grace
> Rhythm, rhyme, that measured pace
>
> Tiger breaks free
>> ('Tiger', ibid.: 67)

The 'impassive' cow is exhorted for taking on the activist role: 'those killing horns, cow, belong to you/and poetry' ('Gomata', ibid.: 71–72). Nair's animals are multicultural too for she is inspired into poetry not only by the very Indian *gomata* (i.e., cow), but also by a central African Okapi or a Californian deer. The poet virtually takes the reader on a safari across various zoos and jungles of the world, as she negotiates her own movement in and out of the homeland.

IV

The dimensions of home thus expand continually in Indian English diaspora poetry. From being a negotiated space between two cultures—the host and the native—it takes on a multi-scalar character in the poetry of the post-1990s. Collectively, these poets seem to write a new 'epic' which is based more on epistemic cooperation, than either on some absolute objectivism or even relativism among different cultures of the world.

Notes

1. In his essay, 'The Diasporic Imaginary: Theorizing the Indian Diaspora', published in *Textual Practice* (1996), and later in another essay, 'Diaspora and the Art of Impossible Mourning', in *In Diaspora*, edited by Paranjape (2001), Vijay Mishra divides the diasporas into 'old and new, classic and late capital type respectively' (ibid.: 38). The two diasporas are 'historically separated diasporas'. 'The old Indian diasporas were diasporas of exclusivism because they created relatively self-contained "little Indias" in the colonies' (1996: 422).
2. 'Hyphen' as a term conveys pangs of dislocation and adjustment. 'High-Fun' suggests a state of celebration of the new multinational order, in which the anxieties of adjustment do not bog down the new diaspora.
3. Diasporic consciousness is described as being 'marked by various dimensions of dual or paradoxical nature. This nature is constituted negatively by experiences of discrimination and exclusion, and positively by identification with a historical heritage or contemporary world cultural or political forces' (Vertovec 2000: 147).
4. It is significant to note that Caribbean poet Walcott looks upon the expatriates as those who disdain their homeland more than they care for it:

> You spit on your people,
> Your people applaud,
> your former oppressors
> laurel you.
> The thorns biting your forehead

> are contempt
> disguised as concern
> still you can come home now. . . (1976: 88)

5. Significantly, Rushdie also underlines the relationship between 'nation' and 'writing' in similar terms—'If writing turns repeatedly towards nation, it just as repeatedly turns away' (1991: 67).

6. Once Amitav Ghosh remarked to Shahid Ali that 'he was the closest that Kashmir had to a national poet. He [Ali] shot back: "A national poet maybe. But not a *nationalist* poet; please note that"' (2002a: 355).

7. Shahid Ali's poems either begin with an epigraph, often from a trans-cultural source, or are dedicated to some fellow poets and friends from across cultures. These epigraphs and dedications not only provide a multicultural context to his poetry, but also constitute inter-textual linkages from within. Here are some interesting epigraphs of his poems—i. 'on the wall the dense ivy of executions' ('A Pastoral', 2000: 23) by Zbigniew Herbert, a member of the Polish resistance movement during World War II; ii. '. . . letters sent/To dearest him lives alas! Away' ('The Country Without a Post Office', 2000: 25) by Gerard Manley Hopkins, a famous Victorian poet; iii. 'Many of my favourite things are broken' ('Rooms are Never Finished', 2002: 55).

8. Fidelity to any single aesthetic, and in particular to the William Carlos Williams-inspired minimalism he felt dominated recent American verse, was utterly foreign to Shahid Ali's concerns as a poet. Pointing out the celebration of the ecstatic mode in the traditions he grew up with, he said he found Americans overly skittish about excess. 'I say, well, you've had Walt Whitman and you've had Emily Dickinson, what's your problem? I find Walt Whitman absolutely exces-sive, and why not? I think that's great. Why should one write in that minimalist fashion all the time, given the fact that Americans have those examples?' ('Interview' to Benvenuto, see www.massreview.org/07).

9. Indian English poets are bilingual and most of them actually translate poetries from their native regions into English. The act of translation travels into their creative process generating a unique complex of 'poet translator, translator poet'. Poetry in such situations is invariably post-translational. Shahid's translation of Faiz's *The Rebel Silhouette* is not an academic exercise for it talks back to the poet in moments of his creative unrest.

10. Two couplets from English ghazals bring out the role of restraining the effusive sentiment:

> Each syllable unwinds its shy request in time
> Speak slowly, show me what it means to rest in time
>> ('Ghazal', Fave 2002: 100)

> Each new couplet's different ascent: no good peak
> But a low hill quite easy to climb at the end.
>> ('Ghazal on Ghazal', Hollander 2002: 76)

11. There are number of poems to which Shahid Ali gives his own stamp of authorship, though they are either versions, translations or adaptations of poems written by other poets. An adaptation from Makhdoom Mohiuddin entitled 'Ghazal' occurs in *Country*; the translation of Faiz's 'Memory' and a version of Mahmoud Darwish's poem 'Eleven Stars' form part of his anthology *Rooms*. Vikram Seth also has this tendency. The translations of Faiz, Ghalib, Nirala and many Chinese poets occur in his poetic anthologies sometimes with information in italics at the top, and sometimes even without it.

12. Edward Said places the poems in the traditional Arabic form of *qasida* in his small note on Darwish ('On Mahmoud Darwish', see www.grandstreet.com/gsissues/gs48).

13. The *maqta* is the last (couplet) of a ghazal, a collection of Urdu poems, in which the poet's pen name is employed, often in very creative ways.

14. Canzone is an Italian term meaning lyric or song. It is used to designate such various literary forms as Provencal troubadour poems and the lyrics of Dante, Petrarch, and other Italian poets of the thirteenth and fourteenth century. This is what Amitav Ghosh has to say on the use of the form canzone in Shahid Ali's poem 'Lenox Hill': 'The poem was a canzone, a form of unusual rigour and difficulty (the poet Anthony Hecht once remarked that Shahid deserved to be in the Guinness Book of records for having written three canzones—more than any other poet). In "Lenox Hill", the architectonics of the form creates a soaring superstructure, an immense domed enclosure, like that of the great mosque of Isfahan or the mausoleum of Sayyida Zainab in Cairo' (2002a: 358).

15. Lorca being an Andalusian is revered in Arabic poetry. It seems that out of all the figures of western revolutionary poets whose poetry was looked upon in utter admiration by the leftist Arab poets in the 1950s and the 1960s, Lorca remained the last poet whom Arab poets continued to refer to in their poetic writings during the 1970s, 1980s and even the 1990s.

16. The diaspora in the age of late capitalism is hardly stable as it seeks more promising opportunities; it tends to be 'temporary' or 'rootless'. In the pre-globalization period, diaspora was relatively stable and rooted. Gurharpal Singh, in his Introduction to the edited volume *Culture and Economy in the Indian Diaspora*, employs the term 'rootless Indian diaspora' (2003: 6) in the context of its increasing 'transnational mobility' (ibid.: 5).

17. Agha Shahid Ali uses Ghalib's couplets as epigraphs as well as translates some of his ghazals. Ranjit Hoskote writes a poem, 'Ghalib in the Winter of the Great Revolt: Delhi, 1857' in which the great poet's 'ink well is empty, but your [his] dry quill/still claws at the fibres of the heart' (2006: 157). Ghalib's famous lines—*Dil hi to hai na sang-o-khisht dard se bhar na aaye kyon?* (It's but a heart, not a brick or marble; why shouldn't it fill with pain?—are invoked as epigraph to his poetic collection *Where Parallel Lines Meet* by Tabish Khair. The poet also transcreates a ghazal by Ghalib into what he terms as 'Delhi English' (2000: 25). Meena Alexander also writes a poem 'Ghalib's Ghost' in which the poet feels the great poet languishing under the burka thus;

'I saw leopards curled in heat / and Ghalib's ghost hidden in a burka, pouncing at crickets' (2004: 15).

18. Sudeep Sen himself informs: 'The form and structure of the piece is inspired both by the architecture of the human body, and the shape of Pablo Neruda's Odes that reflect the long thin-shape of Chile' (front jacket flap of Sen 2004).

19. Sudeep Sen draws on a variety of quotes as epitaphs to lend cross-cultural richness to his *The Distracted Geographies: An Archipelago of Intent* (2004). Quotes such as these—Derek Walcott's 'At the end of this sentence, rain will begin' (ibid.: 41); James Joyce's 'the soft tumult of thy hair' (ibid.: 75); Pablo Picasso's 'Every human being is a colony' (ibid.: 107); Arun Koltakar's 'A low temple keeps its god in the dark' (ibid.); Pablo Neruda's 'I want/to do with what spring does with the cherry trees' (ibid.: 75); Donald Hall's 'When the rain drives on the poppies they hold bright petals to the rain . . .' (ibid.: 51); etc.—distract as much as they hold the mongrel soul of the poet.

20. Joseph Brodsky has similar sentiments: 'In a dream, depending on one's mania or supper or both, one is either pursued or pursues somebody through a rumpled maze of streets, lanes, and alleyways belonging to several places at once; one is in a city that does not exist on the map' (1995: 35). Clifford Geertz once wrote, 'Every man has a right to create his own savage for his own purposes. Perhaps every man does' (1973: 347). From Lyotard to Baudrillard, a host of postmodern theorists have under-lined the necessity of creating a primitive otherness as pre-condition for interrogating the western present. In their works 'what ultimately matters is not the actual existence of primitives but their discursive presence, their function as theoretical place-holders, as abstract differend in a conflict with Western universalism' (Li 2002: 104).

21. These lines from a poem by Vikram Seth suggest the power of wind in the post-1990s: 'Against the wind, as it should be, /I walk, but in my solitude/Bow to the wind that buffets me' (1999b: 212).

22. In her essay, 'Do Women Have a Country?' (2002: 43–62) Ritu Menon uses a quote from Ismat Chugtai's *Roots* (2001b) as an epigraph to suggest the bird's wings constitute the only home of the displaced women.

23. In *Midnight's Children* also Rushdie effects a similar reversal; the snakes stand for ascendance and ladders for downfall: 'it is also possible to slither down a ladder and climb to triumph on the venom of snake' (1995: 141).

24. Arun Kolatkar's *Sarpa Satra* deserves an extended mention here. In the poem, crazy and megalomaniac Janamjeya is all obsessed with avenging the death of his father caused due to a snake bite by holding a *yajna* of mass killings of snakes to wipe out the species from the earth. The madness comes to a halt as soon as Astika, son of Jaratkaru, reminds Janamjeya of the danger his *yajna* might cause to the very existence of the earth as it rests on the Sheshanaga:

> Does not have to remind them
> that this
> planet itself this sphere our whole earth
> is resting

> balanced precariously,
> on the hood of a snake called Shesha. (2004b: 62)

The snake thus attains the dubious distinction of a killer as well as a preserver of all life on earth. The poem is a political allegory and can be read in the context of all those events of history that pertain to the mindless political persecution of rivals/races/communities in the name of ethnic cleansing right from the Holocaust to the post-9/11 so-called global war against terror.

25. Rukmini's bio-data from the opening page of her *Yellow Hibiscus* (2004) reads: 'Nair obtained her Ph. D. at the University of Cambridge in 1982 and has since taught and lectured at universities around the world'. Such an exposure lends sufficient internationalism to her poetry. The poetess occupies the space between the nation and the inter-nation.

Section 2
Re-writing Culture

Section 2: Introduction

[W]riting as rewriting encroaches upon the 'traditional' spaces of political agon (Moraru 2001: 156).

Under the pressures of nationalist anxiety, it is often assumed that 'culture is a one-time event which has survived untempered with from the past to the present' (Thapar 1987: 8). The present section contests such a fundamentalist assumption through the agency of poetry, which while operating through the given archetypes, symbols, mythical correlatives and other community-specific paradigms, tends to re-invent them in ways that continually extend, improvise, subvert, and possibly implode them.[1] Poetry, as it re-writes broader frames of culture, re-writes itself for it was poetry once which provided culture its seriousness. A poem once written re-visits itself in self-reflexive, hyper-signifying ways. Each poem has a pedigree and posterity, a pre-text and an after-life that ensures its continuous engagement with culture. Poetry, thus, is a continuous discourse, it may pre-date human history in terms of its origins, yet it travels though time, and has stakes in the flow of time.

Those who presume poetry to be a one-sided ahistorical tension-free monologic discourse simply overlook its creative dialogue with culture in the form of its continuous re-writings. Re-writing is not an 'evidence of imaginative parsimony, still less a symptom of creative exhaustion' (Greenblatt 1995: 229), rather it is poetics of engagement with re-newed energies. In this section, the endeavour is to underline poetry's continuous march across time and space through paradigms and myths that under the pressures of poetic imagination exceed and transgress their original implications. Poetry is never a mechanical sedimentation or reinforcement of stereotypes. It is not as much the revelation of the absolute as it is the realization of the relative, of the re-visited and replenished original. Poetry is as much a chronicle of life as it is an event in itself, which once it happens, reverberates till eternity. Kabir's couplets, Meera's *padas* or Ghalib's *ghazals* are not frozen events of history; they keep bouncing back in new permutations.

The section consists of four chapters entitled, 'From Nationalist Icon to Subaltern Subject and Beyond: Latter-day Meeras', '*Kissa* as the Locus of Cultural History: *Kissa Pooran Bhagat* in Modern Punjabi Literature', 'Translating Bhakti: Versions of Kabir in the Colonial/Early Nationalist Period' and 'Anxieties of Native Descent/Dissent: Bhakti Sub-text of Indian English Verse'. The thrust of these chapters, as is evident from their titles, is on medieval Bhakti and Sufi literatures and their latter-day re-writings. This accent on the medieval, instead of the much-orientalized ancient, is strategic and deliberate. Re-writing is not all that atavistic as is often believed; it too follows a logic of linearity in the sense that the so-called original must be available in the active memory of the culture. The proximity of the medieval with the modern, therefore, is more plausible and historically tangible than that of the ancient with the modern. The medieval, otherwise wishfully knocked out in the high-pitched nationalist accounts in favour of the glorious ancient, with its mediatory presence, redeems us from the cataclysmic re-writings of culture.

Re-writing, in the scheme of the book, is not as much a post-modernist radical rupturing of the so-called cultural values/icons/texts, as it is a measured and caliberated response to them. Engineering dramatic reversals in the classical is not as much artistic as engendering new semantic possibilities in the secular narratives. Extreme tropic twists not only suggest abruptions/aberrations in culture, but they also underplay its self-correctional powers and processes. In the chapters that follow, re-writing is seen as a continuous process in which each re-written text becomes original for its successive re-writing. Not only does the 'original' become fluid and dynamic, re-writing as an activity becomes open-ended and full of futuristic possibilities. Re-writing appears radical and cataclysmic if the intermediate texts between the 'original' and the 're-written text' are missed out. In the book, re-writing becomes the very mechanism of cultural evolution, and not of its spasmodic/arbitrary returns or of its mechanical re-runs.

The first chapter of the section explores the latter-day invocations/representations of Meera, particularly in the literary discourses of the nationalists and the post-nationalists. From Gandhi's Mira to the 'Meera' of modern Hindi poetry—the *chhayavadi* poetess Mahadevi Verma—and from a sweepress of the streets of Bombay to a lesbian research scholar in relation with Vrinda, the chapter includes a discussion of as many as eight latter-day Meeras. While the controversy between the historical Meera and the hagiographical one continues unabated, the biography of Meera as an icon travels from a high nationalist pedestal to a low subalternist one. The second chapter deals with a Sufi *kissa*—also spelt as *qissa*—of Punjab and its latter-day narrative configurations that bear a dialectical relationship with the changing contours of Punjab's socio-political history. As Punjab undergoes multiple cultural mutations from the post-independence hey-days of the Green Revolution to the bloody mid-1980s marked by terrorist violence, the local *kissa* of Pooran Bhagat is re-written in various permutations and combinations. The *kissa*, in its various re-written forms, provides a ready locus for the cultural history of the region.

Translation is first and foremost an act of re-writing culture. In a multicultural situation, it is a process of inter-cultural as well as intra-cultural dialogue. The translation of poetry, not as syntactical and formal as that of prose, offers far greater scope for exchange than hitherto possible through other genres. The third chapter undertakes a textual analysis of multiple translations of Kabir from 1860 to 1917 to bring out the dynamics of appropriation of the discourse of the saint-poet during the colonial period to the specific agenda of the translation or the sponsoring agency. The early colonial Indologists took up the task of translating the Bhakti poet primarily to underline fissures within Hinduism, and then to appropriate him within the re-formatory rhetoric of Christianity. The translations of Kabir, mostly undertaken on the margins of the official project of orientalism, ensure a resounding after-life to the saint-poet. The translations included for study in the chapter are those of E. Trumpp, Macauliffe, Ahmad Shah and Tagore.

The fourth chapter in the section discusses the all-important issue of nativity of Indian English poetry—an issue that invites extreme responses from its readers and critics. To some, Indian English poetry is just like 'Shakuntala in a Skirt', to others it is nothing more than 'plantation in the pot' (Mehta 1983: 15). Modern Indian English poets, however, seek descent from native traditions, and Bhakti poetry comes closest to their type of subversive, ironical, understated poetry. It is not simple coincidence that most of these poets have been translators of Bhakti poets of their respective regions, and in their interviews, articles and prefatory notes they openly declare their allegiance to local Bhakti traditions. The chapter establishes the organic linkages between Indian English poetry and the medieval Bhakti poetry.

Note

1. Harold Bloom, way back in the early 1970s in his much-discusssed book, *The Anxiety of Influence*, offered a theory of poetry in terms of 'intra-poetic relationships' (1973: 5). The critic identified six 'revisionary ratios' that operate in poetry inevitably. The ratios identified are: *Clinamen* through which the poet 'swerves away from his precursor' by an act of 'poetic misreading' (ibid.: 14), *Tessera* through which 'A poet antithetically completes his precursor . . . in another sense' (ibid.), *Kenosis* through which a poet realizes 'a movement towards discontinuity with the precursor' (ibid.), *Daemonization* through which a poet brings his 'personalized Counter Sublime in reaction to the precursor's Sublime' (ibid.: 15), *Askesis* through which a poet curtails the precursor's meaning, and finally, *Apophrades* through which a poet returns to the dead poet in a very overt manner so as to give an impression that 'the latter poet himself had written the precursor's characteristic work' (ibid.: 16).

4

From Nationalist Icon to Subaltern Subject and Beyond: Latter-day Meeras

With each turn in history, Meerabai, the woman saint poet of medieval India takes a new *avatar*.[1] While during the colonial period, she becomes one of the preferred icons of the non-violent nationalist imagination, in the postcolonial phase she emerges as an arch symbol of the marginalized and the subaltern. Her verses, trudging along the fault-line of devotion and rebellion—an oxymoronic poetics peculiar to Bhakti poetry as a whole—provide a suitable discursive space for any protest-poetics that is realized within the overarching scope of the sacred and the canonical. Latter-day poets, activists and feminists appropriate her name and legacy to lend native credence to their respective protests in contexts that perennially extend, if not exceed, 'her original discourse' in new situations.[2] As she is resurrected and re-invented, she undergoes strategic cultural transformations that quite significantly impinge on, and not just mirror the changing contours of culture in our times. This chapter restricts itself to the study of latter-day Meeras—the self-proclaimed, the critically designated and the creatively re-imagined ones—to understand the dynamics of the after-life of Bhakti poetry as a whole.[3]

I

Surprising though it may seem, but pre-independence Urdu poetry, during the high tide of the progressive movement, produced a Muslim male poet by the pen-name of Miraji.[4] Apparently, this Miraji had nothing to with the medieval saint-singer Meerabai, because as the story goes, Sana'ullah Dar renamed himself as Miraji after the name of some Mira Sen, a young Bengali woman he loved most. But once renamed as Miraji, the poet is inwardly drawn towards the discourse of medieval Meerabai to the extent that towards the fag end of his life he was 'reading and translating the poems of Mirabai, which he intended to publish' (Patel 2005: 241) under the title 'Miranjali'.[5] Meera as a name talks back to the person so-named, in ways that trigger off a creative vision which is inevitably implicated in the discourse of the medieval poet. In her rather extended study of the poet, Geeta Patel refers to a possible creative connection between Miraji and Meerabai: 'The problem with Miraji is that because of his name, "Mira", he is intertextual with and fits the expectations of other poetic lineages, namely the *bhakti* one' (ibid.: 245). In the opening sentence of his 'Incomplete Self Portrait', Miraji invokes Meerabai: 'This [Kathiawad, the place of my childhood] is the same place where, many years before, Queen Meerabai had given birth to the magic of her songs. I did not know her then, as I have come to know her [now]' (ibid.: 248).

Miraji and Meerabai shared a somewhat similar destiny to the extent that both were victims of speculative and even vicious historical constructions. If Meerabai was condemned for her unwomanly conduct in repudiating normal domestic course; Miraji was also castigated for adopting a female *takhallus*—a poetic name—and more importantly, camouflaging his sexual identity of being a male to his readers for long. Miraji was often described by his contemporaries as '*avara*, as an isolationist, drunk, dissolute, self-centered, pathologically sexual, morally bankrupt man' (ibid.: 243); Meerabai too was described as *raand*, a debouched and deviant woman, by the local Rajputs.[6] Meerabai's unconventional persona, at a sub-textual level, only adds complexity to an otherwise equally enigmatic Miraji.

Both the poets—Miraji and Meerabai—preferred the lyrical *geet* form for its exceptional qualities of oral reach. Miraji performed the singing of songs on the radio; Meerabai sang her songs in *kirtanas* primarily among a band of women devotees. More than mysticism, what brings Miraji close to Meerabai is the lyricism of love. In the poem quoted here, it is not difficult to hear the echoes of lovelorn Meerabai:

> Far off
> in the tall indigo jungle
> black, blue-black clouds crowed.
> In the forest, a black koel called
> black shadows on the ground
> black, wet eyes
> black, blue-black hair.
>
> Close by
> In the center of my heart. Slowly

slowly sighs rose
sorrow poisoned the nectar
sorrow's fierce, fiery glances . . .
    ('Movement', ibid.: 328)

The images of 'koel', 'clouds', 'poison', 'nectar', 'sorrow', etc., are typically Meeraesque as they recur throughout her songs. The following *pada* of Meerabai is evidence enough:

I am dying, swept by the poisonous waves,
The frogs, the peacocks and the rainbirds cry;
The koel also sings,
The clouds gather with greater forces
The flashing lightning frightens me.
Is there in the world any lover of God
Who could remove the pain of my heart?
    (Nilsson 1977: 32)

Love-in-separation remains the patent motif of both Miraji and Meerabai. Both poems/songs appear to be loose translations of each other.

In another poem by Miraji, the celebration of passion is fulsome and whole-hearted. The all-encompassing love has more than sexual/sensual implications as the lover seeks fulfilment of a higher kind. In the following poem, the male subject 'I' feminizes itself into a female lover, something so characteristic of Bhakti and Sufi poetry as a whole:[7]

I'm sitting
my veil slips off my head
I'm lost in thought,
someone will see my hair
the edges of joy's circle close in
Enough, let nothing new enter the circle of my joy.
    ('Rare Waves of Passion', Patel 2005: 326)

This could as well be the image of self-possessed forlorn Meerabai, who in her moments of inner joy does not want anything else to intrude into her private universe of ecstasy. Miraji appropriates Meerabai more as a lover than as a Krishna-*bhakta*. Such a partial or selective appropriation is in keeping with the tradition of pastoral romances in the Sufi and Persian narratives of which Miraji is equally a cultural claimant. The passion of love clouds, or rather eclipses, the passion for devotion, or spiritual enhancement.

II

In their search for authentic native nationalism, Gandhi and his followers appropriated Bhakti poetry.[8] Gujarati Bhakti poets like Meera and Narsimh Mehta form an inseparable sub-text of passive, semi-spiritualized struggle against the colonialists.[9] If Gandhi adopts Narsimh Mehta's hymn '*vaisnav jan to tene kahiye, pir parayee jani re . . .*' as his staple prayer-song, he names an English lady—Madeleine Slade—who comes to the *ashram* as his disciple, after Meerabai. By re-christening Slade as 'Mira', Gandhi adds another dimension to the discourse of Meerabai.

Gandhi's Mira, as the correspondence between the two suggests, was more of a daughter in awe of a spiritual father. By re-naming Slade as Mira, not only does Gandhi superimpose an indigenous frame on the foreign lady, he elevates himself to the position of Krishna as well.[10] As Mira enters Sabarmati Ashram, she becomes 'conscious of a small spare figure rising up from a *gaddi* and stepping towards [her]'. Immediately, lest the relationship is defined otherwise, Mira, in her 'Preface' to her compilation of correspondence with Gandhi, entitled *Bapu's Letters to Mira*, pre-empting speculations writes: ' . . . so completely overcome was I with reverence and joy, that I could see and feel nothing but a heavenly light. I fell on my knees at Bapu's feet. He lifted me up and taking me in his arms said, "You shall be my daughter." And so has it been from that day' (Gandhi 1949: 6).

Throughout their letters to each other, Bapu and Mira struggle to underline their 'sacred' relationship of a daughter and a father. The sensual and the sexual is intellectually controlled, if not suppressed, through metaphysical complements and rejoinders. The letters, particularly of the earliest phase, are replete with extended references pertaining to the controlling of passions, desires (including sexual) and senses. *Brahmacharya* continues to be a recurrent concern. This is how Gandhi explains to Mira his meaning of *brahmacharya*: 'Remember my definition of *brahmacharya*. It means not suppression of one or more senses but complete mastery over them all' (ibid.: 246).

In an otherwise conservative nationalist discourse, the bold relationship of a lover and his beloved is thus transmuted into hierarchal relationships such as that of husband and wife or father and daughter in which more than love, submission to the male becomes more significant. By invoking Meerabai in the pious nationalist context, Gandhi not only domesticates the 'harlot' Meerabai, he invents an Indian ideal of womanhood from within his own local tradition.

The traditional leitmotif of 'separation' associated with the discourse of Meerabai runs through Gandhi's correspondence with his Mira as well. In the absence of Gandhi, which is never very prolonged, the separation syndrome overtakes Mira. In his letter dated December 4, 1925, 'Bapu' underlines the disciplinary potential of separation: 'These three day's separation is good discipline' (ibid.: 3). In another letter, Bapu once again philosophizes separation thus: 'I know you were feeling the separation. You will get over it because it has got to be got over. The few days' separation is a preparation for the longer that death brings. In fact, the separation is only superficial. Death brings nearer' (ibid.: 4). Negotiating pangs of separation is the Gandhian prescription for attaining perfection: 'The parting today was sad, because I saw that I pained you. And yet it was inevitable. I want you to be a perfect woman. I want you to shed all angularities' (ibid.: 30). Gandhi insists on separation as penance: 'You must try to wean yourself from this longing for physical meeting. I hope the fever is off' (ibid.: 254).

If, for Meerabai, singing *padas* in honour of 'Girdhar Gopal' is a way of spiritual release, for Gandhi and Mira writing letters to each other, at times without a break of even a day, is a way of consolidating their platonic relationship. For Gandhi, 'Writing love letters [to Mira] is a recreation, not a task one would seek an excuse to shirk' (ibid.: 23). Writing letters to Mira embalms Gandhi's disturbed spirits: 'This is merely to tell you I can't dismiss you from my mind. Every surgeon has soothing ointment after a severe operation. This is my ointment . . .' (ibid.: 47). Each letter is part a sermon, part a prayer, part a love-message, and part a health-bulletin.

Gandhi's 'Mira' then performs so many cultural functions. She becomes an appropriate embodiment of non-masculine, effeminate (yet very much patriarchal) nationalism, championed and practiced by Gandhi. It is through the enabling metaphor of Meera that Gandhi bridges the civilizational differences between the East and the West. With Meera being the locus of both the self and the other within the same tradition, the whole postcolonial polemics of a civilizational 'other' is done away with.

III

Hindi poetry re-produced its Meera, predictably enough, during the high tide of *chhayavad*—a phase ripe enough for re-invoking the obtrusive mystical meanderings of the Bhakti period. As nationalism turned into a spiritual enterprise of self-recovery and inwardness during the latter phase (post-1920s) of the freedom struggle under the influence of Gandhi, Tagore, Aurobindo, etc., Hindi poetry delved deep into the recesses of the soul of the nation. The *chhayavadi* poets sought to go beyond the mere prosaic mapping of the nation done so rigorously by their predecessors from Maithilisharan Gupt to Dinkar; they tended to locate the nation in its abstract traditions, in its poetry and philosophy. While poets like Nirala and Prasad invoked the lofty Indian heritage of *advait, nishkam karma* and pantheism, Mahadevi Verma preferred to imbibe the mystical mould of Bhakti.

Just after the publication of her first two collections of poems *Nihar* (1930) and *Rashmi* (1932), Hindi literary critics and fellow poets immediately designated her as 'the modern Mira'. She figured in an anthology of poems written by women poets entitled *Stri-kavi-kaumudi* (Mishra 1931) which began with Meera's *padas* and ended with her poems. This prompted many critics to hail her as the modern descendent of the medieval princess-poet. Moreover, the language used by the reviewers of her early poetry was laced with Bhakti metaphors. Ramvilas Sharma, in his review of *Nihar* in 1934, discovered a Bhakti streak of *viraha* in her poetry:

> Just as the true *bhakta* (devotee) wants *bhakti* more than he does the Lord, and the *karma-yogi* (one who follows the way of detached action) abandons all hope for the fruit of his action and desires only the action itself, so [Mahadevi's] *virahini* ceases worrying about union and remains absorbed in separation. (quoted in Schomer 1983: 241)

It was not simply due to lack of critical language or due to an innate fancy for devotionalism that medieval Meerabai, the saint-poetess, was imposed on to the young Mahadevi. Even later critics invoked Meera as a critical yardstick to measure modern Mahadevi.[11] What led critics to brand Mahadevi as Meera, was the dominant streak of *viraha*-induced mysticism (often referred to in Hindi literary history as a phase of *rahasyavad*, as an offshoot of *chhayavad*) in her poetry.

Mahadevi's poem quoted here has a Meera sub-text, for in terms of its mood (of *viraha*) and imagery it is no different from her *padas*:

> Unseen, you make my pain
> infinitely sweet;
> unknown, you fill my eyes
> and overflow.
> Painter of golden dreams
> in the abode of sleep—
> who are you in my heart?
>
> My breaths
> constantly follow you out
> then return
> to kiss your feet.
> You who have made me captive
> in your victory—
> who are you in my heart?
>   (from *Niraja*, quoted in ibid.: 301)

The mood of separation only accentuates the sense of mystical union between the lover and the beloved. Both in the poetry of Mahadevi and Meera, the pain, despite differences in degree and type, is privileged over joy; rather it is a pre-condition to ultimate bliss.[12]

In another poem, Mahadevi seems to re-sing Meerabai; her idiom and articulation though is relatively more sophisticated and artistic:

> I don't know why some say
> that I am lost in shadows,
> in murky paths and bypaths,
> my weeping hid like lurking lightning
> With every atom of me, friend, I pour out tears of love
> for someone.
>   (from *Deep Shikha*, quoted in Rubin 1998: 179)

Meera also wonders as to why people describe her as a mad woman even though she is engaged in divine pursuits: 'I am mad with love/ And no one understands my plight/Only the wounded/Understand the agonies of the wounded' (Mirabai 1980: 62).

Though Mahadevi does not invoke Krishna as her lover-deity, yet her pleadings to the lover 'unknown' are quite similar to those of Meerabai's to her Girdhar Gopal:[13]

> Why strike the flesh with anxious trembling,
> or blight our smiles with pangs of grief?
> Giving us eternal thirst for life to drink,
> why have you played so cruel a game?
>   (from *Sandhya Git*, quoted in Rubin 1998: 174)

The saturnine and the ecstatic, the tragic and benevolent combine in one organic whole in the poetry of Mahadevi and Meera both. The complaints are more or less entreaties of a lover. If Miraji takes a fancy to Meerabai, the lover; Mahadevi is enamoured of her Bhakti aspect.

IV

By the 1970s, as nationalist fervour relents and poetic imagination seeks human explanations of events/icons rarefied beyond reason, the myth of Meera is re-staged with a humanist perspective. Such an exercise of humanizing the mythical woman—both the saintly and the sinful—becomes quite a literary trend in the mid-1960s. If, in Hindi, Dharamveer Bharati dares to re-present the sexuality of Radha as Kanupriya, in Punjabi, Shiv Kumar Batalavi redeems the condemned Loona of *Kissa Pooran Bhagat* as a vivacious young woman whose physical urges are humanly valid, if not culturally permissible.[14] As against the common perception of Meera being born a saint, Gurcharan Das, in his one-act play 'Mira', endeavours to trace the transformation of the saint-poetess from 'a human being into a love-obsessed *bhakti* saint' (2001: 'Introduction', 15).[15]

As the play opens, Mira as a young bride is shown seeking love from her husband Rana, but on the day of their honeymoon, she is asked to bow before goddess Kali—the family goddess of the Ranas. The dreadful Kali frightens Mira, and she refuses to worship her. The disenchantment set in, right in the beginning, multiplies and thus paves way for a plausible transformation of Mira into a saint. Since Rana and Mira do not consummate, the possibility of the birth of a mandatory son becomes impossible. She is accused of being barren, which she contests through a series of metaphors: 'A single lamp, no matter how bright, always casts a shadow. Put another one beside it and darkness of both disappears'; 'The chariot can't go anywhere on a single wheel' (ibid.: 107).

More than Mira's indifference to her husband's overtures; it is Rana who seems to be indifferent to her. He is obsessed with war and affairs of the state: The following sequence of dialogues between Mira (Actress 1) and her official maid Jhali (Actress 3) reveals the fundamental differences between the husband and the wife:

Actress 1: Mira is angry with the Rana
Actress 3: Marriage without quarrel is like food without spice.

Actress 1: Marriage without love is food at all.
Actress 3: He can't play with you forever. The Rana must rule the kingdom.
Actress 1: The Rana must also rule the Rani. He only thinks about the kingdom.
Actress 3: Mira only thinks of love.
Actress 1. He only thinks of war.
Actress 3: He is a conqueror.
Actress 1: The real conqueror first overcomes himself. (ibid.: 106)

Gurcharan Das tries to reason out the failure of Mira's marriage in terms of the usual middle-class post-marital acrimony between a non-working feminine housewife and a workaholic husband. The imperatives of modern corporate culture with its known internal family dissentions and marital feuds are thus transposed onto medieval Rajput culture.

In subsequent scenes, Mira's growing isolation is portrayed through a series of dramatic sequences. First she is shown caught between Kali—'holy goddess of million wars' (ibid.: 111), and Krishna—the eternal lover. As she is forced to make a 'humble offering of holy blood' before the goddess Kali, she faints. Then, Mira's warm embrace—'unorthodox welcome'—with her cousin Jai almost smacks of incest: 'She holds him in a spontaneous embrace. Let me look at you cousin. How handsome you've become!' (ibid.: 115). The palace women—the sisters-in-law, do make an issue of Mira's immodesty:

Actress 2 [Uda]: You don't go up and embrace a man like that. I almost died of shame. Think of your sacred husband. What must he have felt . . . and in front of everyone . . . if I had been the Rani . . . (ibid.: 117)

Mira's views on love-war, victory-defeat, sorrow-happiness accentuate the rupture. She feels constantly cornered among the war-hungry Rajputs of the palace. What was perceived to be a 'lover's quarrel' earlier by in-mates of the palace, turns into a full-scale dispute. Rana shuts the door on Mira's face.

In moments of utter seclusion Mira turns to Krishna. The playwright seems to suggest that Mira is driven to Krishna in sheer desperation. Krishna is a surrogate of husband:

Actress 1: Mira looking very hurt, goes and picks up Krishna. She then sprawls on the floor against the same door. She wants to cry but she

can't. She brings up her knees, crosses her arms on them, and puts her
face on her arms. (ibid.: 122)

Mira's sexuality—hitherto totally subsumed by her spirituality—is
also amply hinted, if not fully elaborated upon. She is very much con-
scious of her curves:

> Actress 1: Do my hair right. I am feeling hot. Here, take the comb. Feel
> how smooth my hair is. See how it falls on my shoulders. How it reaches
> down to my hips.
> Actress 3: The walls have ears.
> Actress 1: My long black hair on my round white hips. . . . (ibid.: 125)

This is indeed a bold depiction of a saint-woman. The playwright
retrieves the woman from Mira, the saint. Remarkably enough, it is
Mira who speaks of her sexuality in the face of espionage. She thus
comes out of her submissive feminine self and steps into the possible
feminist role.

What is merely hinted as an incestuous relationship between Jai
and Mira, takes on a concrete shape in the culminating scenes.

> Actor 2 [Jai]: I have missed you very much. Since you left Medta, I have
> been wasting away in the desert. Let's go away—tonight. We will ride
> through the forest, and no one will know. If they follow us, we can hide.
> I'll take care of you . . . keep you warm. (ibid.: 126)

The demand (as against the desire) for a son drives Mira to Jai, but
the encounter does not last. Mira's sex-life remains un-attended, un-
fulfilled. Krishna remains the only choice:

> Actress 1 [Mira]: Krishna, you are all I have left now. Even Jai is gone.
> I have nowhere to go. What shall I do? I think I'm going to cry. No I
> must be brave. Krishna, I never asked you for anything. Can you do
> something for me? Can you give me a son? I know it's asking a lot. But
> what are friends for—especially if they are gods. O please, my dear
> god . . . (ibid.: 127)

The sexuality of relationship becomes all the more evident, as Mira
without fear of backlash admits openly:

> Actress 1: Make him come to me. I remember it was dark. No one saw
> us. We went to a thicket and I was so shy. O he was flattering. My

couch was of leaves but his was my bosom. His lips were like nectar to mine. And I was drunk in his embrace. He held me tight, I could hardly breathe. And we together, I felt sweated and moist, hidden away. I thrilled him so. His half closed eyes became restless and he desired me again. (ibid.: 129)

The active participation of Mira in the sexual act brings about a sudden reversal of roles. Instead of Krishna thrilling her, it is she who thrills him. In such a sequence not only does Mira stand animated as a young lover; Krishna also is divested of his iconic stillness.

Mira's conversion into Mirabai is complete as the poison that she drinks for her unfaithful conduct as a wife, turns into nectar for her. To reinforce the process of transformation, the playwright shows Rana losing the battle, and his wife, both. The entire trajectory of Mirabai's life thus evolves from the quagmire of ordinary life. It is indeed questionable whether all women in the condition of Mira would have transformed into Meerabais. The playwright who undertakes the task of humanizing the divine diva, somehow succumbs to her spiritual aura. The process of transformation of poison into nectar remains unexplained. Is he not in a wishful manner equating suicide with spiritual release? Also, is madness a precondition to transcendence?

V

Though Indian English poets claim to be the descendents of medieval Bhakti poetry, Meerabai remained outside their creative purview for long. Except for a very sparse presence in women's poetry, Meerabai does not figure much in the mainstream Indian English poetry.[16] She comes back very late (as late as 2004) in a radically new incarnation in a long poem by Arun Kolatkar entitled 'Meera' (2004a: 26–33). In the poem, the spiritualized Meera of the Gandhian era casts off those rarefied nationalist hangovers that curtailed her activist potentials in the hierarchal social realm. She stands transformed into a downright dalit subaltern who, as a sweeper of the streets, dances like the traditional Meera, 'within the narrow compass/of the wicker bin' with 'a broomstick for a lute' (ibid.: 32). Unlike Gandhi's reflective Meera, this subaltern Meera is an untrained spasmodic dancer who breaks into action over 'the load of rubbish' in the sheer ecstasy of a devoted worker.

There is no lofty Mahatma to beckon her. Her only companion is a soulless 'footloose coconut frond'—'a dropout' from 'life at the top' in perfect harmony with another social outcaste. The ostracized duo forms a vivacious combination, the frond learns 'new tricks/at her bidding' (ibid.: 26), and she finds it 'more lively, more fun'. While the male sweepers prefer the regular, 'the fan-tail type' broomsticks, this Meera finds the coconut frond more 'effective/with its longer reach and wider sweep' (ibid.: 27). The frond–Meera camaraderie points towards the possible consolidation of the subaltern.

If, in the hands of the traditional Meera, the lute spells magical notes, in the hands of Kolatkar's sweepress Meera, the coconut frond is a perpetual 'clown' that performs like 'a bear, a green one'. The uncouth clownish frond through a subtle ideological reversal thus undoes the classical lute. The frond is a worker that actually works at the ground level: 'it lunges and takes sideswipes/at errant scraps of paper,/ chases the riffraff of dry leaves off the road' (ibid.: 27).

What lends joy to Kolatkar's Meera is not the epiphanic sight of Lord Krishna; rather it is the pile of garbage with all its contents and discontents that provides her a playful peep into the so-called high-life. As she clears after every fifteen minutes 'the modest piles of rubbish/ all along the kerb' made around Jahangir Art Gallery, she learns quite a few lessons of life. First, art has no audience, except for 'a few discerning crows and a kitten'. Second, the esoteric artistic installations simply ignore the rubbish of life they stand on. And the monotonous regularity with which new exhibitions take off, leaving behind the rubbish of the previous ones, suggests to her 'the essential impermanence of all art'. The 'scraps of paper, prawn shells, onion skins, potato peels, castoff condoms, dead flowers' thus yield to her insights into the tricky issues of permanence and impermanence, of eternity and transience, of beauty and truth.

Instead of the charismatic Girdhar, what enamours Kolatakar's Meera is the garbage trolley—'that rickety looking rattletrap', 'that honey cart' which even Euclid, the great mathematician, would have loved for its perfect yet simple geometrical design. Its jarring noise is all music for the subaltern Meera, for what matters more to her is its proximity to the ground:

> It stays close to the ground
> and trundles along
> as it moves like rolling thunder
> on two iron wheels with naked rims

> when pushed like a pram
> and has the decency to shudder
> at the noise it makes. (ibid.: 30)

The words 'thunder' and 'naked' complement well with the coarse and stark 'iron' realities of the subaltern. Only a devotee in trance can offer such an animated description of the instrument of his prayer.

Almost in mock-heroic style, the ancestry of the trolley is traced as though it is a solemn object of worship. The subaltern poetics, counter-canonical and anti-elitist as it is, entails parodic subversions:

> I won't be surprised
> if that tireless fossil belongs
> to the very first
>
> generation of trolleys
> that came to these shores way back
> in 1872 or some such date,
>
> with the noble mission
> of cleaning this city. (ibid.: 31)

The adjective 'tireless' adds to the activist credo of Kolatkar's Meera who too is a missionary of her kind—instead of cleansing souls, she cleans cities. The trolley and the coconut frond are Meera's instruments of subaltern participation in the tangible and concrete processes of nation-making.

Once on the top of the bin filled with garbage up to the brim, Kolatkar's Meera goes ecstatic. She pays 'obeisance to all the cardinal points', and dances like a woman possessed. 'Her free arm, raised/ in the air/is a flamingo in flight' (ibid.: 32). In the last section of the poem, the parodic refrain of the poem attains a higher pitch, as its Meera derives pleasure from the 'dirty' job she performs. The mythical Meera withdraws; Kolatkar's Meera participates. As 'she tramples it [the garbage]/like a vineyard wench/in a tub of grapes', its essence 'licks the soles/arches of her feet,/anoints/callouses,/ and rises/between her toes' (ibid.: 33). The leftovers of the high-metro—'eggshells and dead flowers,/dry leaves and melon rinds,/ breadcrumbs and condoms,/chicken bones and potato peels' (ibid.)—constitute the divine reality for the subaltern Meera. The unseen god, the intangible spirituality, the abstract reflection, constitute mere humbug of the elite.

VI

As creative imagination penetrates beyond the constructions of spiritualism, nationalism or ideology, it unfolds the politics of relationships. The hitherto obscure and camouflaged grammar of the inner domain, of the relations forged in its holy precincts, is laid bare without any attempt to reify them beyond human appreciation. Sudhir Kakkar, in his semi-fictional endeavour *Mira and the Mahatma*, reconstructs the relationship of Mirabehn and Gandhi in terms of bodily metaphors, physical approximations and suppressed desires, with the help of actual correspondence that takes place between the two. Not only does the novel bring out subtle differences between the two Meeras—Gandhi's Mirabehn and the mythical Meerabai—it also reflects on the ways the former eclipses the latter in terms of her understanding of love and relationship. The novel, written from the perspective of Mirabehn's Hindi teacher Navin, offers a peep into the Mira-Meera symbiosis.

First and foremost, Gandhi's Mira is tutored and trained to be passionless so as to approximate the Hindu ideal of *brahamacharya.* The traditional Meera by way of contrast has no such obligations; she is freer. In one of the entries in her diary, Mirabehn compares her destiny with her prototype and wonders as to why 'my [her] god forbids me [her] to dance with ankle bells on my [her] feet and with castanets in my [her] hands' (2004: 154). She questions as to why Gandhi re-christened her Mira 'if he did not want her passion?' (ibid.). Also, as compared to Meerabai's notional lover-god Krishna, Mirabehn's lover-god is a live 'animate' historical being. The pain of separation of the latter, therefore, is bound to be more intense and acute.

Unlike the traditional Meera, Gandhi's Mira has a deeply divided self. Her public persona and her private persona do not coincide. This is how she sums up her split predicament:

> In his presence and in my letters to him I will be the Mirabehn of Satyagraha Ashram, strong, sensible, loyal to his ideals and his vision. And in my diary, the Mirabai of longing and yearning, dedicated to his person. (ibid.: 161)

The distinct political and personal sides of Mirabehn, while lending an additional dimension to the character of the traditional Meerabai, also point towards the challenges of living up to mythical ideals.

In another significant way, Kakkar's fictionally recreated Mirabehn outdoes the original Meerabai. She comes out of her Bhakti vows and decides to have a relationship with Prithvi, a handsome inmate at Gandhi's ashram. Instead of looking at this development in her persona as a deviance, she describes it as her 'poorna swaraj', a process towards her completion. She confesses: 'O Prithvi, you do not know what you have been to me. I have strived to serve Bapu and his cause, but have been weak and wanting in all my endeavours, I have been but half a being. You have made me a whole . . .' (ibid.: 239). The mythical Meera never completes herself and remains throughout a wandering saint.

Mirabehn exceeds Meerabai in the sense that she combines love with faith and activist politics. As Prithvi spurns her offer of love, she writes back: 'You ask me to renounce my love, as if it were some sort of self-indulgence. You do not realize that *real love*, the love that rises from the depths of the soul, increases the power of service and is as sacred as religion' (ibid.: 256). Further, she adds: 'I seek your love and cooperation, not for my personal pleasure, but for greater strength in service for us both'. Also, as Mirabehn seeks to step out of her celibate self, her Krishna (i.e., Gandhi) also undergoes a shift in role; from a lover, he turns into 'an anxious father of a still unmarried daughter' (ibid.: 246).

In Sudhir Kakkar's account, Meera takes precedence over her Krishna. In one of her vulnerable moments with Gandhi, Mirabehn loses all control: 'Sobbing helplessly, she clutched his hand between hers. For a fleeting moment, she sensed a separate life in his hand' (ibid.: 147). Gandhi struggles to hold his feelings, innate responses; whereas Mirabehn opens out. Mirabehn wonders 'if Bapu envied her a little that she had become free of all restraint in his presence whilst he had to retain his self-control . . . could Krishna envy Mirabai? (ibid.: 147).

VII

In another text—*Dukh Dariya*, a Punjabi play written by Pakistani playwright Shahid Nadeem—the metaphor of Meera is deployed to delineate the pangs of partition and the turbulent history of the region thereafter.[17] In the play, beleaguered Kausar, the female Pakistani prisoner, becomes mother of a girl-child following her rape by the jailer in Jammu. As she desires to go to her home in Azaad Kashmir, her daughter, being Indian-born is denied permission to cross the border. As she waits to cross the *dariya* that flows alongside the border, she takes shelter at *dera*Meera Mai near the border at Amritsar during the night.

To her surprise, Kausar finds echoes of her predicament in Meera Mai's history. In the dark days of partition, Meera Mai could not make it to 'this [Indian] side of the border'. She consequently marries a Pakistani and conceives a daughter. Following the exchange of women from either side of the border, she is sent back to India. This results in what she terms as 'her second partition'. Her Indian parents also refuse to accept her; being a wife of a Pakistani Muslim she, they allege, is no longer pure. She expresses her anguish thus: 'The others separated me from my daughter, my own ones, separated me from myself' (Nadeem 2005). She is forced to live on the margins near the defunct *mazaar* of a peer Hazrat Gayab Ali Shah and converts the entire place into a *dera*. She takes on the role of a Sufi saint who gives *tabeez* to the newly born. In this kind of crossover the playwright Nadeem generates a Sufi Meera. As one of the constables in the play says: 'You are a *dervesh* and you are a woman too' (ibid.).

Kausar's character bears inter-textuality with that of the mythical Meerabai. Her in-laws condemn her for being infertile. She is driven to jump into the river, which finally takes her to Indian shores. She too breaks into frenzy in the *darbar* of Meera Mai.[18] She defies social conventions as she carries in her womb the child of her rapist. Her husband and her in-laws are proven wrong by her accidental pregnancy. Her daughter born out of wedlock is thus her Krishna, her idol, that she would never forsake even if it entails total annihilation of the self. Both Meerabai and Kausar celebrate the illegitimacy of their relationship with the same degree of defiance.

The playwright brings in yet another inter-text into the play to consolidate his theme of partition. The story of Sita parallels the stories of both Meera Mai and Kausar. Sita too was asked to live in exile. In the play, she is shown to live around the same area in which the present day *dera* Meera Mai is. Luv and Kush, the twin sons of Sita, as the legend goes, created the two Pakistani cities of Lahore and Kasur, while Sita was forced to roam around in the jungles near Amritsar. Mukhtar Nath, who happens to be the keeper of the *dera*, makes a cryptic observation thus: 'Sita's asharam is this side, her sons' kingdom on the other.' All the three female protagonists of the play thus undergo separation from their wards on account of the arbitrary boundaries drawn by political leaders. The myth of Sita flows into the story of Meera Mai and Kausar forming a continuum of experience.

In the Pakistani play, Meera's scope thus stands enlarged in three unique respects. One, it is lifted beyond its regional landscape of Rajasthan and Gujarat and is transplanted onto partitioned Punjab, a territory where otherwise powerful Sufi heroines like Heer, Sohni, Sundrara, etc., have hardly ever allowed any other female lover/ devotee to have much room in the Punjabi literary imagination.[19] In the play, instead of the *padas* of Meera, Sufi songs of Khusro and Bulle Shah, poems of Amrita Pritam and Shiv Kumar Batalavi provide the love-laced Bhakti backdrop. Meera's conversion into a Punjabi Heer or Sohni thus generates a mixed yet consolidated persona, which is not necessarily hybridized.

Two, the metaphor of Meera stands for 'the pain in separation' in general; it could be separation between the lover and beloved, or the separation between the mother and her daughter, or the separation forced on families displaced during partition. Mukhtar Nath, the male *jogi* in the play, introduces Meera Mai as the very personification of 'bicchore ka dookh'—the pain of separation. And three, it becomes the locus of the ancient as well as modern history of the region in the sense that Meera becomes a metaphorical link between the abandoned Sita on the one hand and the equally confused Kausar on the other. Nadeem's Meera is not simply a witness to multiple partitions; she herself is a victim of it as she is tossed around from this side of the border to the other.

VIII

One more text that bears the name of Meera in its title—*Meera Yagik ki Diary*—deserves to be mentioned here. Written originally in Gujarati in the form of a diary in 1992 and later translated into Hindi in 2006, this book deals with a university research scholar named Meera who enters into a lesbian relationship with Vrinda, which in Krishna-lore is another name for Radha. Though the writer Bindu Bhatt does not refer to the traditional Meera–Radha relationship in the text, yet it is difficult to ignore this larger cultural frame; more so when Bhatt's Meera is very much self-conscious of the medieval Meera she is named after:

> Vani Jayram is singing on the cassette player: *pran hamara vahan basat hai, yahan to khali khol* [my being lives there, here it is only

> an empty box]. Before this I had heard Meera's bhajan in Lata's voice. In the melody of Lata, Meera's devotion fliters ever so slowly. For the first time I was experiencing how a new voice and a new composition change the contours of the 'word'. In Vani's voice and Ravishankar's composition, there is an experience of Meera's singing and dancing both . . . *shyam mane chakar rakho ji* . . . a turbulent flow of surrender. (2006: 64)

Bhatt's Meera also intends to re-sing the old Meera in new composition. The naming of the two characters after Krishna's well-known beloveds—one mythical and another historical—therefore, has to do with the extraordinary subject matter of the text.

The Meera of Bindu Bhatt is deliberately shown to be not-so-beautiful; in fact, she has skin disorders—spots of leprosy marks. Right from her school days, she was addressed by her class-fellows as *chitkabri* (i.e., spotted). Her lover-friend Vrinda also addresses her as *kabri*, which instead of reminding her of her physical infirmity helps her get over any sense of complex. This is much against the pictorial representations of the saint-poetess in posters, in the paintings of Mahadevi Verma, in wall-portraits and in *Amar Chitra Katha*, wherein she is portrayed as a graceful tall lady with long flowing hair. Bhatt's Meera of course has long hair, which actually wins her first prize in a 'hair show', but beyond that the long hair only adds to her insecurities: 'a vacuity overwhelmed me as I received the first prize . . . who will be ensnared by these hip-long hair . . . who will ever reach me transcending this spotted touch' (ibid.: 9)? In modern rewritings of Meera, particularly by women writers, Meera's physical appearance is either underplayed or distorted so as to deny her any conventional femininity. In Rukmini Bhaya Nair's long poem 'Mirabai', Meera's face is 'pockmarked; she is a *bhootni*' (2004: 312).

Bhatt's Meera otherwise is also distinct and different in the sense that instead of the male Krishna, it is the female Vrinda who happens to be her intimate lover. And the intimacy between the two is explicitly sexual: 'She (Vrinda) surrendered her body to me. Eyes were shut but she was not asleep. I started stroking her hair . . . she fell over me, kissed the lobe of my ear . . .' (2006: 22). Meera looks at her body through the gaze of Vrinda: 'this morning as I sat down to bathe my body parts were speaking the language of Vrinda, "In the curve of your back there are streams of rivers in spate . . . between her breasts . . . my Taj Mahal . . ."' (ibid.: 40). Another entry in the diary suggests the full-bloodedness of the sexual encounter thus:

> I have drunk the depth of her naval . . . it pulls you deep, clutches every pore, clings like a wild creeper . . . running blind we are like the hunters riding the unbridled horse . . . one whirlwind, branches intertwined, lava begins to boil in the body, flowers bloom and crushed . . . soaking in full rain, enduring showers, lying down clinging onto each other . . . languid . . . kissing each other's breasts . . . we are like fish that come to the surface of the pond again and again from its bottom. (ibid.: 59)

The above lines constitute the new psalms of lesbian Meera. Her vocabulary is no longer shrouded in metaphysical camouflages. Bhatt's Meera retrieves the raw carnality of women that lurks underneath the divine songs of the traditional Meera.

Although, as this new Meera enters into a lesbian relationship, questions haunt her as to whether her encounter with Vrinda constitutes a new 'dimension' or a mere 'diversion'. Such self-reflexive pauses redeem Bhatt's Meera from being polemical. Also, in the latter half of the diary, as Vrinda leaves Meera in the lurch and settles for marriage with a divorcee Dr. Ajit, Meera asks another question: 'Then was I only an alternative arrangement for her? If yes, why do I chase after her? Am I also accepting it due to some lack?' (ibid.: 101). Bhatt's Meera, very much like her namesake traditional Meera, takes a plunge into an exceptional relationship, but she stops short of becoming a lesbian god/icon. Her diary is more a record of the evolution of a female self through the turbulences of sexual encounters—both hetero- and homo —than merely a one-sided conclusive statement on lesbian love.

IX

Thus, Meerabai, along with her poetic discourse, continues to enjoy a rich and varied post-life. While her own biographical journey still witnesses a keen historical-hagiographical divide and debate, the biography of the icon of Meera right from the nationalist period to the present-day post-nationalist subaltern politics and feverish feminist pitch appears to be more tangible than the historical persona. The successive writers and practitioners of different literary genres have deployed Meera as a metaphor of protest in all kinds of postcolonial situations right from the partition, subaltern poetics of participation from below, to the assertion of woman's sexuality. Poetry and the poet not only just survive in the so-called non-poetical times, rather, they invade other genres as well as time-zones as capable tropes of inter-textual re-writing.

Notes

1. Different latter-day writers have spelt Meera in a number of ways. In order to maintain a distinction between the original and her latter-day incarnations, in the text Meera or Meerabai stand for the medieval Bhakti-poetess; all other spellings such as Mira, Miraji, Mirabehn, Meera Mai, etc., are author specific and therefore placed in a comparative frame vis-à-vis the original Meera.

2. The 'original' Meera is as elusive as any other Bhakti saint is. In his extensive study of Meerabai, John Stratton Hawley comes to the conclusion that the six poems that are attributed to Meera—the poems that have clearly emerged from manuscripts dating to the middle of the seventeenth century or earlier—only the 'poem in the *rag maru* breathes the defiance of *kula-srnkhala* that is the keynote of much latter-day Mira poetry' (2005: 116).

3. The present attempt excludes 'filmy' as well as 'translated' Meeras, for both types require distinct studies beyond the scope of the present limited endeavour of mapping Meeras in the domain of creative literature only. For an extensive study of Meerabai in the comic *Amar Chitra Katha*, see Hawley (2005).

4. Miraji appeared on the literary scene in the 1930s when the Progressive Writers' Association (PWA) was gaining speed. Writers like Manto, Faiz, Rajinder Singh Bedi, Sajjad Zahir, Munshi Premchand, etc., wrote under Marxist influence. Miraji had a rather troublesome and uneasy association with the progressives. Neither he nor the PWA owned each other fully.

5. This is how Miraji designed the frontispiece of his book on translated Meera songs:

   > Miranjali
   > Mira's Offerings
   >
   > Mira ke git
   > Mira's Songs
   >
   > Hindi gujarati marwari
   > Hindi Gujarati Marwari
   >
   > *murattabah*
   > arranged by
   >
   > *Miraji*
   > (Patel 2005: 241–42)

6. 'In Rajasthan her name was often used as a term of abuse for promiscuous women. By abandoning her husband, she had defied male prerogative and upset Rajput Honour. The Rajputs in turn had retaliated and suppressed her name not only in written records but deep within society's memory as well. Her devotional songs so popular all over the country, were not sung in Rajasthan until recently' (Das 2002: 'Introduction', 13).

7. Kabir prefers to describe himself as *Ram ki bahuriya* ('wife of Rama'). In the Sufi poetry of Bulle Shah for instance, the saint poet projects himself as a 'madwoman in love with the divine' (*mein kamali yaar di*).

8. 'It was Mahatma Gandhi who resuscitated her [Meera] in the twentieth century when he entered the freedom movement in 1915. Through his writings, political speeches and his prayer meetings Mira entered the national consciousness. Gandhi had wisely tapped a reservoir of goodwill for Bhakti in the Indian psyche and secured for Mira a wide popular base amongst the Indian middle and lower classes and a place in the nationalist political culture. Following his example, Tagore named his daughter after Mira. So did many others' (Das 2002: 'Introduction, 13–14).

9. Gandhi is careful enough to avoid radical Bhakti poets like Kabir and Ravidas in favour of the not-so-radical Meera or Narsimh Mehta.

10. In many latter-day texts Gandhi is often projected as modern-day Krishna. In Dinkar's *Rashmirathi* (1960) or Bharati's *Andha Yug* (2005), Krishna is modelled after Gandhi. In Raja Rao's *Meaning of India* (1996), Gandhi is Krishna the master charioteer who takes Nehru as Arjuna through the ordeals of the *Mahabharata.*

11. Many latter-day Hindi critics also discovered in Mahadevi a potential Meera. Nanddulare Vajpayee not only placed Mahadevi in the lineage of Meera, but also believed that she would carry forward the unfinished poetic mission of the medieval mystic in modern times. This is what Vajpayee observes: 'I have to say that the basis of poetry in both Meera and Mahadevi, in many parts, is same, but both are creations of two epochs. Meera's poetry offers an example of innate overflow of emotions. . . . We do not get finesse of poetic art . . . Mahadevi's poetry has all the sophistication of poetic art' ('*Yama* ka Darshnik Adhar', Gurtu 1951: 222–23).

12. 'Mahadevi seems to adopt pain, for Meera pain is essential. Meera is helpless in her pain, and she is eager to get over it. She is thirsty and therefore there is a craving for water. Mahadevi seems to desire thirst only; she has not known thirstiness' (Jainendra Kumar 'Sushri Mahadevi Varma', in Gurtu 1951: 5).

13. The following song of Meerabai provides a perfect sub-text to Mahadevi's entreaties:

> Look how he wounds me
>   again
> He vowed to come, and the yard
>   is empty
>
> food flung away
>   like my senses
>
>   —tell me
> where to find them
>
> Why must you
> shame what you say?
>   You've wisped
> yourself away, lifter
> of the mountain

> left me here
>   to splinter
> (Meera 1997: 57)

14. The sexual assertion of Radha is amply expressed in the following lines taken from Bharati's *Kanupriya* written in the early 1960s:

    > and this my embrace is cruel
    > and blind, and frenzied, and my arms
    > tighten across your shoulders, arms and lips
    > like the coil of a nagavadhu (female-snake)
    > whose radiant toothline of blue signs have
    > just emerged on your body . . . (1996: 51)

15. The play was first performed at the La Mama Theatre, New York on May 20, 1970. It was directed by Martin Brenzell, with music by David Walker. The play has since been performed in Mexico City (1971), Bombay (1972), New Delhi (1973 and 1998), Ahmedabad (1973), Madras (1985), etc.

16. Among contemporary women writers, Draupadi continues to be the chosen female protagonist. From Mahasveta Devi (Bangla) to Pratibha Ray (Oriya), to Ajeet Kaur (Punjabi), a host of women writers across languages have re-written Draupadi as their central figure in their fictional forays. Meera's presence, in comparison to Draupadi, is negligible. Among modern women writers, only Rukmini Bhaya Nair seems to take some notice of her in the form of a poem entitled 'Meera' (Nair 1992).

17. The play is a production of Ajoka Theatre Group, Lahore, Pakistan. It was staged at Tagore Theatre, Chandigarh, on October 7, 2006 under the direction of Pakistani woman director Madeeha Gauhar. It had cast from both sides of the border.

18. Interestingly enough, Meera Mai in the play is at times invoked through metaphors and images that are often associated with the aggressive mainstream Hindu goddess Durga. Repeatedly, the *dera* of Meera Mai is described as *'darbar* of *jagat Maiyya,* of *jotan wali Ma'*—these are typical Durga invocations.

19. Meera is almost absent in contemporary Punjabi literature. The influence of local Sufi archetypes is so overwhelming that archetypes from other local cultures do not really register as much in the creative Punjabi unconscious. Even Punjabi woman writers, including Amrita Pritam, despite their Bhakti leanings, prefer to express through Sufi heroines. Except for a poem or two, that too either written from abroad (for instance, Ajmer Rode's 'Meeran de Hatthan Wich', 1999: 334) or from other non-Punjabi areas, Meera is apparently no match for a Sufi Heer or a Sohni.

5

Kissa as the Locus of Cultural History: *Kissa Pooran Bhagat* in Modern Punjabi Literature

I

Kissa Pooran Bhagat is 'a local Punjabi variant' of the 'original' Greek Oedipus. The two propositions made in the very opening sentence are contentious and demand some explanation. To say that this *kissa*, even in its deviant form, is patently Punjabi would be too jingoistic. In his very famous essay 'The Indian Oedipus' (1999), A. K. Ramanujan, for instance, recounts a Tamil story of Kulanan that runs strikingly parallel to the *kissa*. But let us first discuss the narrative outline of the *kissa*, as given by Kadaryar, believed to be the first Punjabi writer to have recorded the *kissa* in written form.

In the *kissa*, for those who are not aware of it, there is a local king, Salwan, whose wife Queen Icchran gives birth to a son named Pooran. Following a prophecy, the son is heralded as inauspicious for the king who confines him to a dungeon for twelve years. The king in his old age marries for the second time, a young low-caste woman named Loona. When Pooran comes out of the dungeon, young and handsome, Loona seeks love from him. Pooran spurns her advances. In order to teach Pooran a lesson, Loona tells the king that Pooran tried to outrage her modesty. The angry king orders that Pooran be thrown into a deep well with his hands and feet chopped off. The *kissa* is much longer, but for the purposes of this chapter, this part is self-sufficient and most of the later texts primarily configure around this part.

Now the Tamil tale, as Ramanujan recounts, goes like this: 'A stepmother desires her stepson who rejects her advances. She accuses him of making improper advances to her and his father punishes him by blinding his eyes' ('The Indian Oedipus', ibid.: 118). Many more such parallels can be culled from all across the globe, which prove beyond doubt that *Kissa Pooran Bhagat* is not purely Punjabi. Even some of the writers of the *kissa* hold it to be '*jagat prasiddha kissa*', which may be more out of their enthusiasm to prove 'local' as universal. But spatially the *kissa* does go beyond the Punjab region.

The issue of the Greek connection is pertinent in the context of the unmistakable cultural and political influence that Indo-Greeks had in the Sialkot region, the place from which King Salwan hails. 'The greatest of them [Indo-Greeks] Menander (Malind) of Sakla (Sialkot) struck against the powerful armies of Sunga kings in defence of Punjab' (1990: 5), informs Dr. Gurcharan Singh. He further adds, quoting W. W. Tarn, that it is unimaginable to think of streets and townships of Punjab modelled after Greek city-states without a culture of theatre. He says 'We have it on the authority of Tarn that the work of Sophocles (494–406 BC) reached India' and asserts 'that people in Gandhar were interested in Sophocles' (ibid.: 178).

Since temporally, the *kissa* is held to be an 'ancient' one, the question of its 'Greek lineage', therefore, may not be entirely speculative or ahistorical. Hellenic influence on Indian art, particularly the Gandhara school of art, is all too well-known, the debates of its being responsible for the beginning of art in India notwithstanding. Also, the image of Pooran that emerges from the *kissa* is that of a young charming boy with a spiritual halo around his face. It very much resembles the image of Buddha in Gandhara art. What Ananda Coomaraswamy says about Gandhara art in general is immensely applicable to the depiction of Pooran in the *kissa*: 'They [Greek Gods] are but grand beautiful men; sometimes, as in the case if many Apollos, it is uncertain even whether the representation is of a god or of an athlete' (1981: 93).

Another important qualification needs to be made to understand what really constitutes the 'original' Greek Oedipus in the context of the *kissa*. The *kissa* is not as much a variant of King Oedipus the Rex, believed to be the original Oedipal tale; rather 'it is modelled on the [another] Greek legend of Hippolytus and his stepmother Phaedra' (Singh 1990: 55). So the very term 'original' becomes quite problematic in the beginning itself. Throughout the chapter, the 'original' keeps on shifting. For each succeeding text, the preceding one acquires the halo of the 'original', thus unleashing a regime of hypersignifications till a point comes where originality as an issue exhausts itself.

Other foreign connections of the *kissa* are also speculated, adding to the intensity of the body-snatching game that is usually played around popular narratives/icons. Shiv Kumar Batalavi, for instance, relates the *kissa* with Huns who ruled north India around the third century A.D. While recounting the *kissa*, he observes that 'Salwan is a distortion of Shalivahan—a tribe that once ruled over India. "Atlana" Hun was their ancestor. Salwan was one of the castes of Huns' (1985: 42). There have been studies by historians that speculate about the Scythian origins of the Sikh-Jats. Writing extensively about this theory, a historian writes that 'chamar colony was an essential adjunct to the principal denizens of the village . . . interesting interactions of the Jat whose promiscuous proclivity towards chamar females has come to be told in village folklore of the Jat society' (Sara 1977: 260–61).

The Hindu antecedents of the *kissa* are also hard to ignore. It is significant to note that of all the *kissas* available in Punjabi, it is the only *kissa* which does not have an overt Persian or Arabic connection. This in itself is an indication of its pre-medieval genealogy. The fact that Punjab was the hub of Brahmanical culture, much before its subsequent invasion by Indo-Greeks and other foreign tribes, does in a way evoke the possibility of this *kissa* being Brahmanical, in its structural and philosophic thrusts. One way that the *kissa* could be read is that it is at bottom, a tale of colonization of the local tribes (represented by Loona) by the invading Aryans (represented by Salwan). Philosophically also, the very name 'Pooran' is highly sanskritic, and stands for the high Hindu ideal of 'wholeness' as the ultimate truth of life.

But there have been efforts to foregound the *kissa* in local medieval history too. Instead of the *kissa* being located in exclusive religious categories of Hinduism, Islam or Sikhism, it is attributed to *nath panthis.* It is believed that Pooran is modeled after the son of Guru Gorakhnath, named Chaurangi Nath. This shift from religious identity to a '*panthic*' one is very significant, and suggests a foregounding of the *kissa* in non-conventional region-specific categories.[1] In the cultural context of medieval Punjab, influenced as it was by Buddhism and Sufism, a multi-stranded *panthic* tradition emerged which displaced religion as the sole category of cultural identity. This *panthic* tradition cut across religious identities, and tended to be very composite in character and approach to the divine.

Historians, however, relate the *kissa* to the immediate political situation of Sikh politics, particularly the politics of Ranjit Singh and eternally feuding Sikh misls in north India. Kadaryar, in the history of Punjabi literature, is usually heralded as the poet of the 'Ranjit Singh Age'—the tendency of naming literary periods after the names of kings is equally pronounced in Punjabi literary historiography. Salwan's marriage with the low-caste hill woman Loona is seen as a political strategy used by the king to bring hill tribes in his fold. Such a trope is very much in consonance with Ranjit Singh's hegemonic design of expanding his empire beyond and across the hills. At another level, the marriage of a low-caste hill woman with a feudal lord is taken as a ploy on the part of the hill people to destabilize large kingdoms and tame big feudal lords.[2] M. Athir Tahir underlines the importance of the *kissa* in terms of its moral significance. By highlighting 'the virtues of piety, idealism and spiritualism' (1999: 64), Kadaryar possibly intended to show a way out to the corrupt and decadent Sikh politics.

There is yet another very interesting dimension to the *kissa*. It is seen as an 'autobiographical re-rendering' of the ancient legend.[3] It is said that the wife of Kadaryar's brother Razia fell in love with Kadaryar who refused to entertain her advances. She in turn defamed Kadaryar before the village elders, alleging that it was Kadaryar who wanted to molest her. Kadaryar redeemed himself by way of writing the *kissa* of Pooran Bhagat very much available in the oral folklore.

If all these claims and counter-claims over authenticity and 'original' authorship of the *kissa* are combined, it could be said that it is a *kissa* that is partly mythical, partly historical and even partly autobiographical. Maybe it is myth that is stretched to accommodate history, or it is history, personal or national, that is slotted in the mythical grid.[4] It is not only this conjunction of the mythical, the historical and the autobiographical that goes into the making of the *kissa*, the overriding moral and metaphysical imperatives are equally important.

It is pertinent to see how the 'original' *kissa* departs from the 'original' Greek Oedipal tale to accommodate local imperatives. In the *kissa*, instead of the mother it is the stepmother who yearns for her stepson. The king's second marriage to a much younger low-caste girl Loona in a way mitigates the immorality of the incestuous relationship implicit in the 'original' Oedipus. The one reason that such an 'incestuous' *kissa* gained wide acceptance in 'feudal and extremely patriarchal Punjab' could be that it avoided a direct depiction of the mother–son relationship, a relationship so thoroughly spiritualized by the mother-worshipping patriarchy. Also, it, in a way, not only legitimized the polygamous and even hypergamous practices among feudal Punjabis, it provided a perfect camouflage to their oedipal impulses as well.

In the *kissa*, Pooran does not turn out to be a warrior. In most of the Oedipal tales, the exiled son hits back as a prince or warrior of a border state; here, he is a 'jogi', a harmless ascetic. The abandoned infant Pooran, instead of being picked up by the army of the border kingdom, is looked after by the wandering mendicants led by Guru Gorakhnath. Young Pooran is sensuous, youthful and charming, yet his sensuality is underplayed. In the Oedipus myth the son even-tually kills the father and marries the mother. The *kissa*, however, stops short of such moral catastrophes, as Pooran takes recourse to a 'long route of progression' (H. S. Gill 1985: 152), namely renunciation. The overriding spiritual thrust of the *kissa* in a way tends to suppress the psychology of relationships.

The *kissa* in its received form, thus, combines the mythical, the historical and the autobiographical with the moral and the meta-physical to generate a discourse of 'expansive ambiguity' (Barthes 1998: 110) for the latter-day writers to play around with and re-inscribe new meanings. Combining so many strands in a narrative framework is always awesome and, therefore, at times structurally very unwieldy too; it always leaves a scope for its re-writing as a corrective measure for succeeding generations. H. S. Gill's observation in this context is very useful: '. . . its [*kissa*'s] contradictory strands lead to compositions whose ends are always loose and may be stretched in many directions. Several interpretations are possible, but each interpretation has serious consequences for our cultural development' (1985: 134). The present chapter is an extended endeavour to read various major creative re-writings of the *kissa* and the 'serious [cultural] consequences' they have on 'making/ mapping' history.

II

Though after Kadaryar a lot many writers wrote the *kissa* in different poetic forms, but from a critical perspective it is Sardar Pooran Singh's extended poetical narrative entitled 'Pooran Nath Jogi' which marks a perceptive shift, if not exactly a paradigmatic one, in the 'original' *kissa*.[5] The overtly moralistic *kissa* of Kadaryar is elevated to the level of a spiritual saga. Both Pooran and his mother Icchran bask under spiritual glory. Pooran Singh, in his terse prefatory remarks, holds Kadaryar's *kissa* to be 'divine inspiration' (1976: 130) which all of a sudden overtakes the consciousness of the poet and makes him re-write it. There is no intention to overturn or in any way challenge the basic configurations of the *kissa*. Pooran Singh re-writes only perhaps to consolidate the *kissa*, and renew it for contemporary readers with greater spiritual fervour.

The very opening metaphor of '*sooraj*', that is, the 'sun', for Pooran suggests a cosmic design of the poet with Pooran at the centre of it[6]. *Sooraj* is a significant symbol in Sikh mythos.[7] It stands for energy, both physical and divine. It is a symbol of *shakti* and *bhakti* both. Another sacred symbol, this time from the Hindu mythos, of the cow-calf is invoked almost in the same breath. Pooran's separation from his mother is seen in terms of the cow-calf separation. Sikh and Hindu metaphysics complement well in the mystical scheme of the poet.

In Pooran Singh's version, the emphasis shifts from King Salwan to Icchran, the mother of Pooran, whose sacrifice is eulogized in meta-physical terms. She is hailed as an incarnation of the divine itself: 'mother is some great impulse of divine' (ibid.: 137). In Kadaryar's *kissa*, she is totally marginalized, and is portrayed as a helpless mother bewailing the banishment of Pooran. Pooran Singh, however, spiritualizes the idea of motherhood: 'But mother's heart is ready always to offer its milk to every child/let every child, of every mother live, it prays/ . . . self-less, without personal motive, high and large is the heart of mother' (ibid.: 134). The exceptional stoicism with which she bears the banishment of Pooran is glorified in terms of '*sahaj-yoga*' (ibid.: 136). Queen Icchran is 'Devi, Bhavani, Durga, tapasvini, yogini, she is all' (ibid.: 137).

Icchran's sacrificing motherhood is juxtaposed with Loona's possessive craving for her stepson. The spiritualization of the former entails the demonization of the latter. Consequently, Loona is port-rayed as 'a virtual female ogre' (Pankaj Singh 2000: 115): 'statue of stone, lifeless, heartless' Loona can devour live human beings for her fulfilment" (Singh 1976: 138). The sudden elevation of Icchran to the level of goddess and Loona's demonization to the level of a nautch girl can be accounted for in terms of the re-construction of gender during the 1920s and 1930s in Punjab, in particular, and India in general. Two mutually exclusive constructs of womanhood were in circulation then—one was the construct of the 'new' woman and the other was the view of the 'common' woman. The former suggested a framework of motherhood which implied 'love, caring, suffering, sacrifice for children, moral strength and creative energy' (Mohan 1999: 187); the latter projected woman as 'coarse, vulgar, loud, quarrelsome, devoid of superior moral sense, sexually promiscuous, subjected to brutal physical oppression by males' (Chatterjee 1993: 127). The former included women of higher castes and feudal households, the latter covered prostitutes, nautch girls, street vendors, fisherwomen, washerwomen, etc.

If the text is placed in the context of nation as mother, the *kissa* becomes very much an allegory of the nation; its provincial or regional character does not stand in the way. In the allegorical scheme Icchran becomes India and Pooran becomes the son of Mother India. The spiritualization of Icchran is very much in consonance with the spiritualization of the nation as mother in the nationalist politics of the 1920s of which Punjab was very much the epicentre. Mother India in the nationalist rhetoric was portrayed as 'serene to the uttermost and possessed of great patience and grace' (Coomaraswamy 1981: 14). These are precisely the attributes of Queen Icchran as mother. Such 'glorification of motherhood, in the service of nationalism, tended to deflect the attention from the real woman' (Jain 2001: 23).

Pooran, as protagonist, is also very much cast in the image of Buddha or Boddhisatva in the state of becoming Buddha. Buddhism gains an intellectual ascendance among the new educated Indian nationalist elite as a paradigm of indigenous modernity (vis-à-vis Hindu orthodoxy on the one hand and Western existentialism, on the other). And Pooran Singh is no exception. In his *Spirit of the Sikh*, he endorses Buddhism as 'artistic, realistic, imaginative, rapturous, truly idealistic' while Hinduism or Brahmanism is dismissed as merely 'metaphysical and speculative' (1981: 64). The character of Pooran is indeed imaginative and rapturous: 'brilliance all around, . . ./ highest of them all . . ./ his flame of full youth lightens everyone' (ibid.: 140).

It is significant to note that Raja Rao, a noted Indo-English writer in spiritual nationalist mode, in his *The Meaning of India,* likens Nehru to Buddha.[8] Keeping in view the rarefied nationalist rhetoric of the times, it is very much possible that Pooran is Nehru in the Buddhist mould. Pooran is not an ascetic Mahatama, he is more like Nehru, immensely handsome and a committed son of Mother India, yet having some dalliance with Lady Mountbatten. Such a foregrounding of the 'local' *kissa* in the nationalist/Nehruvian context may not be entirely acceptable in the estranged phase of post-operation Blue Star, but in the pre-independence phase of history, Punjab was at the vanguard of Indian nationalism and Sikhism was not regarded as separatist.

III

In Shiv Kumar Batalavi's *Luna* (1985 [1965]) the focus shifts to the much-maligned Loona who is not condemned as an immoral promiscuous woman, but rather sympathized with as one who has been deprived of her rights as a young woman. Loona's sexuality is 'lyricized with a passion' that does away with all moral or mystical hangovers that have hitherto been created around the 'original' *kissa*.[9] In fact, the 'original' *kissa* had been patently so unjustified in condemning Loona as the lustful un-motherly female, that its re-writing from Loona's perspective was all a matter of time. Contesting her mythical construction, Loona sets forth her identity in plain biological terms: 'The fires of scorching summer/Blaze in my [her] breasts' (ibid.: 84).

Clearly, the credo of 'consecrated femininity' in the nationalist discourse did not enamour the writers of the postcolonial period, confronted as they were with problems of social injustice within the nation-space.[10] Yet it would be sweeping to term *Luna* as 'a discourse of social injustice' (Singh 2000: 130), for it romanticized the rebellion of Loona more as a woman than as woman of a low caste. Instead of challenging the notion of hers being a body of 'imperfect flesh', she seems to accept it: 'Give me of the impure flesh/A match, too, like impure' (1985: 89). Even Icchran, who also makes loud statements ('A land where woman suffers in hell/No more respected than footwear' [ibid.: 94]) about the subordinate position of the woman in a male universe, objects to Loona's entry as the second wife to her husband more on account of her low caste: 'I am traversing paths of shame/That the Raja should have brought as bride/A tanner's daughter' (ibid.).

Batalavi's re-writing of the *kissa* from Loona's perspective was mediated or even preceded by a host of discourses both within Punjabi poetry, and outside it. Amrita Pritam had already begun to assert the individuality of woman.[11] In the domain of art also, right from the 1940s onwards, Amrita Sher-Gil had denounced the Bengali school of painting for feminizing the female.[12] The icon of the sensual, earthy and feminine Didarganj Yakshi which was hailed by Indian historiography in the beginning as sublime and motherly, around the 1950s was re-recognized as a full-bodied female.[13] In Hindi poetry, texts like *Kanupriya* by Dharamveer Bharati had already made bold attempts to celebrate the sexuality of Radha in terms that are fairly modern and non-spiritual.[14] Published in 1959, *Kanupriya* had already paved way for Loona's outburst of self-assertion. In the arena of law and legislation, significant amendments in the Hindu Marriage Act, 1995 and Hindu Succession Act, 1956 aimed at ending women's subjugation on the subjects of marriage and divorce, and property rights had created quite a conducive climate for woman-centric discourses. On the whole, the sexuality of the woman was being retrieved from the earlier attempts of its sublimation into the ideals of motherhood. The point that needs be stressed while studying the poetics of the relationship between a myth and its re-writing is that many inter-textualities operate between the two and that at times the immediate provocation to re-write comes from sources away from and outside the original.

Luna as a text does constitute the first true attempt at the re-writing of the *kissa*, yet it fails to free the imagination from the mythical or the spiritual. In moments of stalemate, Loona's biological sexuality is expressed and realized through mythical paradigms only, thus defeating her own avowed enterprise of breaking free from the mythical. To bring home her state of sorrow to the not-so-receptive Pooran, she, for instance, takes recourse to the mythical story of Aindira, a fairy that King Indra loved, but could not marry. Also, to claim that spirituality as a cover up for sexuality was blown up, would be altogether too facile. Loona's gross sexual desires tend to culminate on a spiritual note: 'I am the fragrance of his limbs/I am the honey that drops from the words he speaks/I am light of the sun that shines in Puran's brow' (1985: 115). Second, unlike Dharamveer Bharati's Radha, Loona does not reveal any urgency of self-introspection and self-reflexivity.[15] Also, while celebrating women's sexuality, Batalavi's idiom degenerates into the idiom of the court poets of the seventeenth and eighteenth centuries: 'Men devour in the name of love/Our soft and sprouting stalks' (ibid.: 96). In such lines, re-writing tends to lapse into retrogression rather than progression.

IV

Atamjit, in his play *Pooran* (1991), re-writes the character of Pooran Bhagat in modern humanist terms to dramatize the existential dilemmas of contemporary Punjabi youth caught between the diametrically opposite pulls of inherited feudalism on the one hand and acquired modernity on the other. The feudal settings of the original *kissa* give way to an urban setting with Salwan instead of being a king, shown as an owner of a big estate. The estate in functional terms is a modern empire which comprises a textile mill, a rubber factory, agricultural farmhouses, dairy and poultry farms, a school for the workers of estate-keepers, a processing and a dyeing unit, a swimming pool, a motor garage, etc. Despite all the external trappings of modernity, the estate in terms of the attitude and social aspirations of its inhabitants is no different from an erstwhile feudal kingdom.

Salwan, as a true descendent of his archetype, behaves very much like an autocratic feudal patriarch. Not only does he marry twice, the second time he marries a woman of his son's age, the son from his first wife. He rears snakes in his estate, which is very much in consonance with the medieval tantric practice of worshipping snakes. Also, snakes reinforce his masculine virility. Loona, initially reluctant to come near the snakes, later on finds them utterly poison-less. Instead of destroying the regime of poison-less snakes, Loona aspires for a deadly cobra and thus continues to define her sexuality in medieval terms. Loona casts herself in the image of *vishkanya* so frequently invoked in folk stories. The appropriation of Loona's sexuality in the patriarchal scheme is thus complete and irrevocable. It is significant to note that this deployment of snakes as a metaphor of sensual desires figures in Batalavi's *Luna* with as much intensity.

To flaunt his richness, Salwan sends this son named Pooran to America for education. It is this departure from the 'original' *kissa* which lends a new twist to the tale. The possibility of Pooran's overt spiritualization, as it happens in the 'original' *kissa*, is pre-empted. Not only does such a creative trope befit well the diasporic tendencies among the Sikhs in general, at a philosophical level, the entire *kissa* undergoes a paradigmatic shift. Pooran, a U.S. returned graduate has no pretensions of being a *jogi*. Instead of being a part of Guru Gorakhnath's wandering mendicants, he is in the very throb of a very permissive and open culture. The *kissa* becomes Pooran-centric for the first time in the sense that Pooran refuses to be a tool or an easy medium for any moral/spiritual discourse.

Atamjit's *Pooran* could be seen as an attempt towards bestowing some measure of autonomy to the youth—a concern that seems to run through language literatures of the nation. One is immediately reminded of Ramesh Gaur's famous poem 'Pita Ke Naam Ek Patr', written in the 1970s in which the recalcitrant son refuses to tow the line of his father: 'O Father, why do you impose your cap on my head time and again/if forcing caps can extend your family tree, stamp of Nehru on the rupee coin, could have stopped the de-evaluation of currency' (1972: 182). Pooran's dialogues with his autocrat father border on the rhetoric of a novice. The way he chastises his father towards the end is utterly unconvincing, for nowhere does the dramatist show his process of maturing—so essential to lend authenticity to his claim for autonomy.

In order to create a live and dialogic relationship with tradition, Atamjit brings in Shiv and Kadaryar as characters of the play to justify their positions on the role of Pooran in their respective narratives. Such an explicit encounter with poet-predecessors is unwarranted as it in a way amounts to discounting the inherent dialogic/inter-textual potential of the very act of re-writing. Overall, the play is a rather feeble attempt at humanizing the ethical romance. Towards the end, the withdrawal of Pooran only justifies the tyranny of the mythical over the real or the human. Re-writing becomes more an act of re-inventing the archaic, rather than asserting the imperatives of the present. Pooran takes on the mantle of educating the parents, the lessons of marital life—a role not much different from his mythical incarnation of a *jogi*. Such a relapse into the mythical, both in *Luna* as well as in *Pooran*, points to the possibilities as well as limitations involved in the very act of re-writing.

V

The process of displacement of the *kissa* from its 'original' royal setting to the one that is more ordinary and local continues in Ajmer Singh Aulukh's play *Salwan* (1997). The playwright goes beyond the 'elitist' urban setting of Atamjit's *Pooran* as he happens to discover the operation of the *kissa* as an archetype of the feudal mindset at the micro-level day-to-day village life of post–Green Revolution Punjab. There is no conscious attempt to intellectualize the *kissa* as such, something so pronounced in Atamjit's version of the *kissa*. It is more a case of hitting upon a live situation in countryside Punjab that bears striking parallels to the events of the *kissa*. The playwright does not claim to have re-written the *kissa*, he very modestly puts it: 'I have not written this play to impart new meanings to the "myth" or "history" of Pooran, Loona and Salwan. Some time back I saw certain events in rural set up whose broad contours matched with the story of Pooran,

Loona and Salwan. I have taken a close look at these three characters' (1997: not paginated)'.

In this process of taking a close look at these characters in their rural incarnation, the playwright de/re-inscribes the characters of the *kissa* with subtle Marxist underpinnings. In the play, Salwan, to begin with, is no king but a disillusioned and angry ordinary peasant who aspires to acquire property and a house of his own, through guile, fraud and crime. Seen against the social fall-out of the Green Revolution, Salwan's desire for pelf and property, through means immoral and violent, is immensely understandable. The revolution had accentuated economic disparities to the extent that the small farmers were willy-nilly driven into the world of crime. Also, the quick economic successes which it brought about in the 1970s had made the peasantry impatient to wait for hard-earned success. Blinded by the desire for 'quick' wealth, no wonder Salwan forsakes his pregnant wife Icchran, and leads a life of a criminal on the run till he eventually manages to acquire some property with the help of local village touts, police officers and politicians. In her critical study of the Green Revolution, noted eco-feminist Vandana Shiva points out that the Green Revolution 'replaced traditional peasant values of co-operation with competition, of prudent living with conspicuous consumption' (1991: 184), 'increased the commercialization of social relations' (ibid.: 173) and 'led to an epidemic of social diseases like alcoholism, smoking, drug-addiction . . . violence against women' (ibid.: 185). Aulukh's *Salwan* in this context is the very site of the revolution's successes and excesses.

Kissa, a sordid tale of feudal tyranny and patriarchal authority, instead of being displaced and subverted, comes back with renewed vigour in modern Punjab. It enacts itself out pointing out the consolidation of an archaic feudal mindset in countryside Punjab of the post–Green Revolution phase. Instead of modernizing society, the revolution ends up in creating a revivalist environment. If one were to invoke Homi Bhabha's terminology, Salwan is a typical post-colonial 'mimic man' (1994: 125), an ambivalent subject who seeks progress by backsliding into past practices. The whole discourse of feudalism in modern Punjab in a way stands critically examined in the metamorphosis of Salwan from a petty peasant to a man with landed property.

Once a feudal of local stature, Salwan behaves much like his prototype. At a fairly old age he marries a very young low-caste woman Loona; such hypergamic practices become more pronounced in the post–Green Revolution Punjab. When grown up Pooran, an un-employed post-graduate son from Icchran goes to the house of his 'uncle' Salwan for financial help with which he could bribe someone for a job, both Loona and Pooran develop a liking for each other. Pooran, unlike his prototype, does not shy away and promises Loona's liberation. Salwan comes to know about this intimacy between Pooran and Loona, and arranges money for Pooran's placement abroad. Aulukh's Pooran is not as self-reflexive as Atamjit's Pooran is. He falls into the trap of clever Salwan.

Aulukh's *Salwan* (1997) does not overturn hierarchies, but it depicts how deep-rooted and wide-spread the tentacles of feudalism in contemporary countryside Punjab are. The playwright is aware of the compromise involved in this exercise of dovetailing the real with the mythical. Yet he holds that literary truth is not exactly the truth of the real. In the play, it so seems, that it is myth that bends back-ward to accommodate or even appropriate the real, ensuring in the process its seminal position of an archetype which no discourse of modernity, rationality, progress can possibly undo.

VI

The last text discussed in this chapter is a verse-drama, entitled *Palang Panghura* (Bed as Cradle [2000]) written by a diasporic Sikh, Iqbal Ramoowalia. As is evident from the subject position of the author, the thematic thrust of the text is to dramatize the cultural and emotional tensions of diaspora through a creative use of *Kissa Pooran Bhagat*. The drama begins with a dialogue between the father Paras who sings the *kissa* along conventional terms and son Bali (a short form of Iqbal) who intends to re-write the *kissa* in a different vein. When Paras recites his *kissa*, Bali replies:

> O father, yours is a story
> every age has to live,
> a sign it is, of every age!
> Your story has neither beginning nor end,
> in each age it changes its clothes
> to appear in different forms! (ibid.: 32–33)

Such meta-narrative comments ensure the dislocation of a patently local narrative from its immediate cultural moorings to a space that is spatially, as well as temporally, global and eternal. Predictably enough, in the first act, Salwan and Icchran are shown conversing with each other in their living room in England. Icchran has all praise for the glamorous life style of Salwan though Salwan is very much aware of the falsity of his outward glitter: 'This little garden blossoms/only on the cover of the book/of which every page is sick/through and through' (ibid.: 39).

Icchran too begins to realize the loss of intimacy: 'What was it that estranged/blood from the veins?' It is for twenty years that Salwan and Icchran have lived this life of utter meaninglessness. Icchran, having given birth to Pooran, does not require anyone else. She creates her own universe—complete and self-sufficient. Maternity overwhelms sexuality, or sexuality lapses into motherhood. Meanwhile, Salwan undergoes a bout of alienation and decides to come back. Towards the end of the first act, he repents over his sojourn to the cold West:

> Twenty years ago,
> abandoning a girl
> burning like hot coal
> young
> back home,
> I came here in the grip of
> this cold foreign land for shelter. (ibid.: 79)

He resolves: 'Now I shall return to homeland, I shall search for that hot burning river/I shall bask in heat of hot blooded Loona's/I shall get myself lost in her boiling body time and again' (ibid.: 79).

Loona thus becomes the signifier of Punjab, the 'imagined' homeland, warm and sensual. Icchran by implication stands for the cold-blooded West, Salwan is a diasporic Sikh, lost in two worlds—one the world of the material West and the other the world of the sensual East. Significantly, the native land often valourized in patriarchal nationalist discourse as 'motherland' undergoes a semantic shift, it is no longer spiritualized, rather it is approached in sensuous terms. Instead of the mother, the homeland is seen as the 'wife' yearning for a sexual encounter with her husband as exile. The Oedipal relationship often underplayed and even camouflaged between an exile and his homeland comes to the fore without moral dilemma through such a scheme of relationship.

In the second act, Loona is bubbling all over again with the anticipation of Salwan coming back to her. Iqbal invents two characters—Veero and Paro—as friends of Loona to portray her inner and outer emotions. For Iqbal also, more than Kadaryar, it is Shiv Kumar's *Luna* which serves the immediate reference point. Towards the end of this act, Loona, while standing before the picture of Salwan pleads for her rehabilitation. It is an irony of post-national times that it is Punjab that seeks its identity from the diasporic Sikh, and not the other way round: 'I seek your lyrical warmth for the rest of my life/A poem hanging mid-air I seek your title' (ibid.: 113). What surprises one all the more is that Punjab becomes an exile: 'I am a homeless boundary/in your map/grant me a home of nail's size!' (ibid.). In the post-national scenario, nations derive meanings and identities through their diasporas and other exiled communities, 'homeland exist[s] only in the imagination of the deterritorialized' (Appadurai 1997: 49).

Also, may be Punjab as province or nation may have lost its innate distinctness within the assimilative space called India, but in places like South Hall, Punjab is more recognizable as a distinct cultural space. The comments of another Indo-Canadian Sikh poet, Navtej Bharati, are pertinent here: 'Once I had become exile by going out of my village, today I have become exile on my arrival back to my village. One part of it had gone to London (England), one Toronto and one Vancouver. . . . Today to reach Rode, I have to travel through London, Toronto and Vancouver' (Rode and Bharati 1999: 784).

In the third act, Loona finally goes to England and lives in a multi-story apartment. This journey of Loona to the West signifies a large-scale migration of Sikhs and Punjabis to the First World. She undergoes moments of alienation: 'silent monologue is the only continuous/lesson of this place' (2000: 116). She asks herself: 'Tell me why have you come amidst these decorated graves? Have you come here to sentence someone or to undergo some sentence?' (ibid.: 123). Like all other texts, in this text also Loona questions earlier poets who portrayed her in immoral terms: 'Many poets came/sharpening their limping pencils/they went by . . . they . . . only filled most condemned notes in your every byte of sound' (ibid.: 123). Even Batalavi glorified her as an epitome of the sentiment of love-in-separation: 'then someone came with his ashen coloured lyricism of separation'. Iqbal, through Loona, laments that 'no one has come who could dig out the coldness implanted in your [her] boiling blood, who could explore the dying man in Salwan, who could explore the cause of iciness afflicting Iccharan's body' (ibid.: 125).

Once abroad, Loona remains unattended, till Pooran comes with a letter from Salwan to her. Loona smacks a lack of intimacy in the letter, she implores Pooran to spend more time with her: 'You are flower of a different vine/who will blossom my dry twigs/say something/hear something, O Pooran/sit, spend some time Pooran!' (ibid.: 134). Salwan comes and goes back all too sudden: 'After diving inside me/ and he goes back all too sudden.' This is a dig at the diaspora which comes to the native land once a while and goes back too soon. Pooran, first-generation diaspora, accounts for this attitude of Salwan who he believes is a committed nativist, but for his professional and business engagements. Out in England Loona is unable to make out,

> This my place of residence
> Is it my home or a hotel?
> Or a borrowed nest on
> a lost stem? (ibid.: 146)

Pooran empathizes with Loona's dilemmas in the land:

> How can fish swim
> in the milk pan?
> The forest which
> grow in pots
> how can deer run across?
> and how can by living under roofs
> clouds be wished? (ibid.: 148)

Finally Loona discovers in Pooran the image of a young Salwan. She drags Pooran to her bed. Thus, she reverses the trajectory of belonging traced by Icchran. Hers is a journey from cradle to bed, as against the journey of Icchran who travels from bed to cradle. In the case of Loona it is sensuality that overtakes the piety of maternity. Instead of looking at the mother as goddess, an object of worship, Pooran too gives in to the sensuous pull of Loona. He implores:

> From these swollen cloud like breasts
> offer your oozing lullabies
> from my body parts
> wake up the sleeping Salwan
> make them burning bedsheet
> and spread it over the bed
> this is how you can make
> bed and cradle
> sit in each other . . . (ibid.: 167)

Thus, Iqbal Ramoowalia engenders altogether new significations not only to the *kissa* as such but to the whole issue of the diaspora-homeland relationship.

VII

The *kissa* awaits its further re-writing in the context of the increasing dalitization of politics. Despite the fact that Punjab has the greatest intensity of dalit population in the entire nation, Punjabi dalit writings have not taken off in a noticeable way. Loona's sensuality in the light of her being a low-caste woman needs to be re-written to turn 'the comforting order' of the *kissa* upside down.

Notes

1. 'Panth [is] a body of people drawn together by their commitment to the teachings of a specific spiritual master, be he living or (more usually) dead' (Ballard 1999: 15).
2. Tejwant Singh Gill, while commenting on a Kangra painting showing a Sikh chief carousing with a dark woman, observes that 'the women from the Hill areas charmed the rulers with their startling beauty, endangering the very stability of the kingdom' ('Painters at the Sikh Court', 2001: 39).
3. This information is culled from Gulwant Singh's *Kadaryar: Jeevan te Rachana*, which refers to Surjit Singh Sethi's interviews with the third-generation relatives of Kadaryar (1980: 5–11). In these interviews the relatives suggest the immediate autobiographical foregrounding of the *kissa*.
4. According to Tejwant Singh Gill, *kissa* is a diachronic 'legend which imbibes elements of myth and chronicle without identifying itself to either' ('Nexus of Myth and Reality in *Luna*', 1985: 41).
5. From Kishan Singh Arif (1886) to Balak Ram Jogishwar (1921) as many as twelve writers had written the *kissa* of Pooran Bhagat. The information is culled from Tejwant Mann's *Daulat Ram Rachit Panjabi Kissa Kavi: Ek Adhiyan* (1991: 146–47).
6. It is significant to note that Shiv Kumar in his *Luna* and later on Sukhpalveer Singh Hasrat in his poem 'Loona da Yatharath' (1984: 74) in *Sooraj di Dosti* use the metaphor for the glory and youthful passion of King Salwan in his heydays.
7. Guru Gobind Singh also holds Surya as one of the incarnations of Vishnu.
8. 'If Mahatma Gandhi was a Vishvamitra, Pandit Jawaharlal was the Bodhisattva, Lord, mayst thou have a halo round thy auspicious face!' (Rao 1996: 32–33).
9. This phrase is being used here as synonymous of the Hindi phrase 'ragatamak sambandha' which Ajneya (2001: 320) employs to account for Radha's relationship with Krishna in Dharamveer Bharati's *Kanupriya* (1996 [1959])

in his small critical note on the poem entitled 'Raag-sambandhon ki Prishtha-bhoomi' included in *Dharmvir Bharati ki Sahitya-sadhana.*

10. According to Julia Kristeva, 'we live in a civilization where the consecrated (religious or secular) representation of femininity is absorbed by mother-hood' (1989: 186).

11. Amrita Pritam, right from her much-hyped poem, 'Akhan Waris Shah Nu' (1993: 22), to poems like 'Draupadi' (ibid.: 277) and 'Sundran' (ibid.: 278) brought in an unprecedented wave of feminism in Punjabi poetry.

12. This is how Amrita Sher-Gil demystifies the portrayal of the woman in Bengali paintings: 'At its best Bengali school produces little pictures that harmonize fairly well with the subdued tones of the modern interior—unassuming objects that create no lasting impressions on the mind of the onlooker and make no particular demands on the emotion or intellect' (1972: 140).

13. For an extended treatment of the kind of ideological appropriations Didarganj Yakshi has undergone since its excavation near Patna in 1917, see Tapati Guha-Thakurta's 'The Endangered Yakshi: Careers of an Ancient Art Object in Modern India' (2002: 71–107).

14. *Kanupriya* as a text contains a series of poems written by Dharamveer Bharati in which the poet tries to create a dialogue between Radha the mythical character and Radha the historical person. Radha is captured in moments of her 'intense self-brooding'—*bhavakul tanmayata* (1996: 7).

15. Kumar Vimal, in his analysis of *Kanupriya*, finds that Radha, despite being lovelorn and lyrical, evinces a high measure of self-anlaysis (*rasavanti aur premamayi hokar bhi antapragya hai*) (Vimal 2001: 374).

6

Translating Bhakti: Versions of Kabir in the Colonial/Early Nationalist Period

I

Right from the pre-independence nationalist period to the post-national globalized era, Kabir's poetry in English translation has appeared with such an uncanny regularity that today the translated Kabir rivals with, if not outgrows, the so-called 'original' in terms of its discourse value.[1] The saint-poet seems to survive more in the alien tongue than perhaps in his 'original one' as, with each new translation he bounces back as a poet resurrected all over again. Multiple translations of Kabir have not only taken the poet beyond the frontiers of his native domain to the global market, but have also ensured him an 'after-life' that borders on immortality.[2] What are the cultural imperatives that lend such a rich and resounding posterity to Kabir in his English incarnation? What is it that compels the translators, Indian as well as foreign, to re-write Kabir in or against the shifting cultural contexts? This chapter restricts itself to the comparative study of multiple translations of Kabir in English that took place during the colonial/early nationalist period with special emphasis on exploring the cultural politics and poetics that each translation is inevitably implicated in.[3]

Before Kabir was translated into English, missionaries who found his popularity, particularly in the northern parts of India, too conspicuous to be left unaddressed translated him into Italian outside 'the official Oriental project.'[4] What prompted them all the more was their assessment that his teachings were closer to Christianity in terms of their reformatory rhetoric. Thus, though the *desi* Kabir was not the chosen official subject of the *margi* orientalists, yet his translation into European languages begins as early as the latter half of the eighteenth century—a period hardly explored in the making of modern Hinduism—when an Italian Capuchin friar, Marco Della Tomba, undertook the translation of two important texts (the *Mulapanji* and the

Jnansagar) attributed to Kabir Panthis.[5] David Lorenzen observes that though Marco's translations are 'accurate', yet he seems to lend a 'decidedly Christian twist to the translation' (Lorenzen 2002: 39). For instance, as Lorenzen cites, *mukti*, a highly culture-specific term has been translated as *gloria permanente*—an expression patently Christian.

II

The early English translations of Kabir, in a way, begin by default. While introducing the credo of Kabir Panthis, H. H. Wilson cites a hundred *sakhi*s, two *ramaini*s (nos 1 and 6) and two *shabad*s (nos 56 and 69) of Kabir in his *A Sketch of the Religious Sects of the Hindus* in 1861. The obvious intent is to illustrate and exemplify. He writes, 'The *Sakhis of Kabir* deserve perhaps a more copious exemplification' (1977: 82), and that 'one hundred will be sufficient as a specimen of the whole' (ibid.: 83). The translated *sakhi*s are presented more as prose-sayings than rhythmic poetical utterances. A patently matter-of-fact tone knocks out the inherent musical strengths of the sayings of the wandering Bhakti saint. For instance, in the translated *sakhi*—'The offspring of the five elements is called man; if one element be withdrawn, the whole compound is destroyed' (1977: 22)—Wilson reduces the Bhakti-wisdom into a mechanical statement with scant regard for the aesthetics of Bhakti iconoclasm. At times the paradoxical textuality of Kabir's *sakhi*s is rendered in terms which are plainly moralistic: 'Put a check upon the tongue; speak not much; associate with the wise; investigate the words of the teacher' (ibid.: 75). The expression is not only formal but rather circumlocutory too. Instead of 'Put a check upon the tongue' a blunt and colloquial expression such as 'Shut your mouth' or quite simply 'Hold your tongue' would have lent a more forthright opening to the translated *sakhi*s. The dramatic violence built in the far-fetched yet homespun and striking conceits of Kabir is articulated in a cold-blooded tension-less expression such as this: 'In the concavity of the mirror the image is formed: the dog seeing this likeness barks at it till he dies' (ibid.: 83). The expression is no doubt modern and has thankfully no hangovers of the medieval archaisms, but it is not informal and direct. If one were to invoke famous French structuralist Roland Barthes, the translated expression of Wilson is more 'authorly' than 'writerly', it is more an expression of 'representation' than 'enfiguration'.[6] Wilson fails to register the dialogic dynamics of Kabir's utterances.

III

For quite a long period during the early colonial period, Kabir is translated more as one of the poets of the Sikh holy text *Adi Granth*, rather than as an independent poet in his own right. Dr. Ernst Trumpp (1828–85) translates some of the songs of Kabir as part of his translation of the *Adi Granth* in 1877. Trumpp—a German professor of oriental languages at the University of Munich—undertakes the translation in a 'literal grammatical way' using expression that is admittedly 'unidiomatic' in the hope that such an endeavour would yield a 'translation, which should be of any scientific value' (1978: vii).[7] The very purpose of being scientific in translation itself in a way forbids the translator from being creative and inventive enough within the thematic and structural grids of the original text. No wonder, the holy text is translated with the least empathy of a believer.

Kabir is translated quite literally and mechanically, to the extent that 'the original syntax' with all its punctuations, co-ordinates and sequence is retained rather fastidiously. The translator does not evince confidence to dovetail propositions that are conditional, contradictory or complementary; instead he separates them halfway by the strong *caesura*. For instance, he would write, 'Kabir is the barking dog, he runs after a carcass' (ibid.: 683) instead of 'Kabir is a barking dog that runs after carcass'. Similarly, in the utterance, 'sow such a seed, that is bearing fruit during the whole year!' (ibid.: 684), a single complex sentence would have been laconic: 'sow a seed that bears fruit throughout'. Sometimes this incapability of the translator to club clauses causes confusion: 'Kabir (says): at which gate the comers and goers nobody stops:/How should that gate, which is such a gate, be given up?' (ibid.: 674).

The frequent use of the conjunction 'and' in contexts that are so concomitant unnecessarily prolongs the final message. The use of 'and', for instance, in the expression 'Like as ripe fruits of a tree fall to the ground and do not stick back to the branch' (ibid.: 672), could have been totally dispensed away with in favour of a much more continuous and cohesive structure like this: 'Like as ripe fruits fallen, never return to their branch'. Trumpp employs parenthesis quite often to complete the syntax, otherwise left incomplete in Kabir's original structures. 'By coming in contact with it (people) have become most excellent, (like), the scentless iron (and) wood (is made fragrant by contact with sandal wood)' (ibid.: 675). There is an anxiety to use full grammatical structures, providing even utterly dispensable connectives, which are otherwise so well-anticipated or understood.

Rather rarely does Trumpp replace the literal with the idiomatic. He would retain 'idols of clay' (ibid.: 674), instead of the idiomatic 'puppets of clay' (ibid.: 288); 'bones wrapt in a skin' (ibid.: 672) instead of the colloquial 'bones in a bag of skin'; 'juice of the name' instead of the more Bhakti-specific usage 'the nectar of His name'; a literal expression like 'I remain in the wave of the lotus-foot at the end and at the beginning' (ibid.: 677) could have been translated idiomatically thus: 'I bask for ever in the joy of God's lotus feet' (ibid.: 297).

Instead of the active, Trumpp prefers to use the passive voice, toning down in the process the immediacy and the activist tenor of the saint-poetry. Instead of 'saints eat the butter', the translated expression is 'By the saints the butter is eaten' (ibid.: 672); instead of 'bones burn like wood, and hair like grass', we have 'bones are burnt like wood, the hair is burnt like grass' (ibid.: 762); instead of 'keep in mind', the chosen expression is 'this is to be kept in mind' (ibid.: 673); 'fisherman castes his net' is passivized thus: 'a net is laid out by the fisherman' (ibid.).

The purpose of Trumpp's translation was not to set an example of creative translation but to make the *Adi Granth* known—to make a text known was indeed one of the major concerns of nineteenth-century translators.[8] The enterprise is purely intellectual as the translator does not evince the requisite empathy with the sayings of the holy text. Ostensibly, he would ridicule Sikh Gurus and their sayings to denigrate Hinduism as a whole of which, he believed, Sikhism was an offshoot. Max Müller described Trumpp 'by no means a trustworthy translator' (quoted in Macauliffe 1909: xv). Though Kabir was not a part of the official oriental project, yet, a significant aspect of Trumpp's project was that it was supported by 'Her Majesty's Government for India which in due consideration of the importance of the work planned its execution and defrayed its expenses' (Trumpp 1978: viii).

IV

Max Arthur Macauliffe did another translation of the *Adi Granth* in 1909 in which Kabir's verses were translated in a different vein altogether. There is an intentional 'political' shift as, unlike Trumpp, he does not intend to portray Sikhism as a dwindling religion; rather his effort is to bring out the 'distinct' wisdom of Sikh Gurus and Bhakti saints. He refers to the 'novel plan' of his translation according to which, unlike most of the translations undertaken and accomplished under the orientalist project, the present work is thrown open to native criticism and its possible approval. He goes on to enlist the support he received on the authenticity of his translation from the Sikh clergy.

Macauliffe's plan suggests a subtle shift in colonial ways of negotiating/appropriating the East. Whereas Trumpp would not miss an opportunity to run down or ridicule Sikh Gurus and Bhakti saints, Macauliffe would rather appropriate Sikhism and native wisdom in terms that are overtly appreciative. Trumpp's effort was to underline that Sikhism (including Kabir) was a part of Hinduism; whereas Macauliffe championed the cause of Sikhism as separate from Hinduism and hence sought the support of native Sikh clergy. Though British colonial administrators sponsored both the translators, yet the shift in their stance marks the shift in the stance of colonial cultural policy. When Trumpp was commissioned to translate the *Adi Granth* and to look at Sikh scriptures, he was given the specific task of proving that Sikh theology and cosmology were different from those of the Vedas and the Upanishads. But he found nothing in them to support this view. He found Nanak a 'thorough Hindu', his religion 'a pantheism, derived directly from Hindu sources'. Unsatisfied with Trumpp's assimilative pro-Hindu findings, Macauliffe, a minister of culture himself, undertook the charge of re-translating the *Adi Granth* in terms of its distinctness from canonical Hindu texts. His effort was to create a cultural wedge between Hinduism and Sikhism.

Whereas in Trumpp's translation, there is no one 'God', in Macauliffe's translation, more often than not 'God' (or 'Lord') is the general term used for Hari, Vishnu, Rama and even Om. 'Maya' is translated various as 'worldly love' (1909: 279), 'the body' (ibid.: 281), illusion, etc. This is an obvious strategy of appropriation and assimilation.[9] The Hindu signifiers are translated in secular terms so that the Hindu forebearings of Sikhism could be played down or camouflaged. The attempt is to remove the cultural specific barriers, and if it is not easily achievable through easy one-to-one transference of secular lexicon, the translator would go for extended periphrasis. 'The whole world is dead' would be extended to 'The whole world is dead in *spiritual* ignorance' (ibid.: 288). At times such an extension becomes rather explicatory and banal 'I have seen and examined everything, and I find no one hath a friend' (ibid.: 295). Similarly, instead of saying 'khichri is good food, in which there is nectar like-salt' (ibid.: 681), he would use an extended expression 'an excellent dinner is khichari seasoned with sufficient salt to make it palatable' (ibid.: 307). Instead of leaving the expression open-ended as 'the name of God as water', he would add 'to *extinguish it* (fire)' (ibid.: 143). What is at times supplemented through the use of parenthesis in Trumpp's translation, is supplemented through the use of italicized expression in Macaullife's.

Macauliffe tends to be explicit in his translation thereby pre-empting or minimizing the needs of exegetical support from Hindu sources, and making his translation self-evident and autotelic. The authorial extensions are made in italics, pointing towards the translator's conscious attempt of being explicit and interpretative at the same time. Not only does this tendency to extend the phrase foreclose the semantic possibilities, it tends to generate 'unwieldy periphrasis' (ibid.: xxxi) of the pithy sayings. The enigma of the expression 'One day thou shall sleep stretched out at full length' is undone by the periphrastic addition of '*in the grave*' (ibid.: 298). The uncanny succinctness of Bhakti poetry has always been a challenge often unsuccessfully met by the English translator—foreign as much as native. To overcome the problem, he takes recourse to either long parenthesis or extensions through italics.

A very significant aspect of Macauliffe's explanatory additions is that they are selectively done as the translation targets the Sikh constituency mainly. Wherever longer explanations are required, Macauliffe would leave them un-explained or half-explained. For instance, in hymn XII (1909: 266), Kabir refers 'to twenty five categories' as worldly entrenchments; the translator would provide the canonical source namely Sankhya philosophy in the footnotes and then would hastily add, 'An enumeration of the categories here would not assist the Sikh student' (ibid.: 226).

Though Macauliffe's translation in its effort to combine the literal with the suggested tends to be explanatory and prosaic, yet at places it reveals his idiomatic and poetical prowess in definite measure: instead of the ordinary expression 'the blow of spear is easy', he would rather employ a more alliterative expression like this 'slight is the stroke of a lance' (ibid.: 306). Though Macauliffe avoids archaisms, yet he would often use the outdated subjunctive mood (ibid.: xxx) to retain the peculiar character of Bhakti poetry. In Bhakti poetry, the subjunctive mood is often used to engender some kind of literary deviance through the clever play of incompatible tenses in a single utterance. Overall, Trumpp's English is least poetical or literary; by way of comparison, Macauliffe has a greater control over diction. Trumpp's effort is at best a project of translation with no empathy for the text being translated; Macauliffe's translation is not as empirical as the anxiety of native approval always bothers him.

V

Meanwhile, Westcott's book, *Kabir and the Kabir Panth*, had come out in 1907. From the point of view of translation, the book may not be very important as the writer quotes the saint-poet mostly through translations already available (Trumpp's translation of Kabir in the *Adi Granth*, primarily), and occasionally though his own translations; yet being the first independent book in English on Kabir, it generated quite an interest in him, and could be taken as the first important venture towards the internationalization of the saint-poet. The orientalist hangover is clearly visible in Westcott's enterprise, for Kabir is seen as the Indian counterpart of the European Martin Luther. In fact, the book begins with a table that chronicles the rise of saint-reformers both in Hinduism and Christianity in close correspondence.[10] The syncretic character of Kabir Panth is acknowledged, but the underlying impulse is Christian. The very rhetoric of the question asked in the Preface points towards the Christian bias of the writer: 'If Christ had been an Indian, would not his Gospel have been welcomed by many who now, refuse to listen?' (Westcott 1986 [1907]: not paginated).

Westcott's translations are prosaic and at best can be described as of working nature only. More than the poetry, the emphasis is on its subject matter in terms of the secular approach of the saint-poet to issues pertaining to morality and metaphysics. Also very significantly, he divides different sayings of Kabir along thematic lines such as 'The World and Religion', 'Religion in Life', 'The Way to God', etc.—a practice which was later on followed by Vaudeville in her translations of the saint-poet. There is no attempt at versification, for the translated sayings are used for mere 'illustrations'. Unlike Trumpp and Macauliffe who stick to Kabir compiled in the *Adi Granth*, Westcott goes beyond the printed Kabir, and collects 'oral' sayings from the field. He is actually 'guided by the judgement of Kabir Panthis' (ibid.: 45) as much as his own in the selection of *sakhi*s included in the book.

In terms of its special attributes as a text of translation, Westcott's endeavour has two distinct features—first, the culture-specific terms are left untranslated, second, he gives an extended glossary of such terms towards the end of his book. The *desi* expressions are given extended treatment and their semantic nuances are explained in terms of their philosophical import. Kabir was pastmaster in employing words that have more than one meaning. While translating Kabir, Westcott does refer to the intended ambivalence of his couplets. Another peculiar feature of Westcott's book is that at times he would lift an equivalent Christian source or even a Sufi source, and would place it just after Kabir's *sakhi* to buttress his thesis that Kabir was as much an original thinker as a translator of 'old thoughts'.

VI

Tagore's *One Hundred Poems of Kabir* is the 'first major translation' of the saint-poet exclusively—a work that he accomplishes just three years after his world famous book of verses named *Gitanjali* appears in England in 1912.[11] It is major because it is the first exclusive endeavour of translating Kabir more as a poet than a mere religious reformer. It is also major in terms of its reception. Coming close on the heels of Tagore's Nobel Prize fame it received immediate international limelight. Different publishers, both in India and abroad, have reprinted it many times over and no subsequent translation of Kabir has received so much attention. The purpose of Tagore's translations in general was to internationalize Kabir as well his own writings. Sukanta Chaudhuri, a well-known Tagore scholar observes: 'Their surface [Tagore's translations] intent is to disseminate and institutionalize the poet's work abroad' (1999: 46).

Enamoured as he was by Indian mysticism, Tagore asked his friend Kshitimohan Sen to compile Kabir's songs as they are actually sung by itinerant sadhus all over Northern India (especially in Bengal). Out of the four volumes compiled, Tagore eventually selects a hundred songs of Kabir for his translation purposes. Unlike many later translations, Tagore uses the plain term 'poem' for any Kabir's verse, be it a *shabad*, a *ramaini* or a *sakhi*. Since the latter translators used written or printed texts as their source text(s), they naturally tend to be more fastidious about maintaining distinction of form; for Tagore, it is the unlettered 'oral' that constitutes the original. All subsequent translations rely singularly on the printed and the written. Tagore's fascination for the 'oral' over and above the written or the printed is very much evident as he quarrels with the publisher of a book of songs in Bangla thus: 'What we wanted was simple songs of genuine untutored hearts'.[12] Of course these remarks are made with reference to his love for Baul songs, but they hold true for his fascination for the 'oral Kabir' too.

No wonder, later researchers and translators question the very authenticity of the so-called Kabir's songs translated by Tagore. Rev. Ahmad Shah who had just compiled Kabir's *Bijak* in 1911, and was in the process of completing its English translation when Tagore's translation came out, in his observations questioned the authorship of the songs translated by Tagore, right then. According to Shah, out of the hundred poems translated by Tagore, there are 'only five which in a mutilated form can be safely attributed to Kabir' (quoted in Keay 1995: 62). Winand M. Callewaert, a well-known Kabir scholar writes: 'Having now prepared a critical edition of the songs of Kabir, based on the earliest available manuscript material, it is my guess that hardly any of the Tagore songs was composed by Kabir' (2000: vii). Further, he writes: 'I can understand that a translator of Kabir may look for a nice song without bothering about its authenticity. But let us not start writing commentaries on Kabir and fifteenth century Banaras quoting those songs' (ibid.: vii). Vaudeville, another Kabir scholar and translator has this to say on the authenticity of Kabir's songs in Tagore's collection: 'It was Tagore who suggested to his friend Kshit Mohan Sen the collection of the poems attributed to Kabir and sung by itinerant sadhus all over Northern India (especially in Bangal) and their translation into Bengali. The authenticity of these poems is very questionable; it appears that most of them were probably not composed by Kabir' (1974: 18). As a translator, even of his own works, Tagore seems to have less regard for the original. In at least twenty-six cases of his translations of his own works, as Sukanta Chaudhuri informs us, 'no original has been found, though a line or phrase here and there might recall some Bengali poem' (1999: 45).

In his selection of Kabir songs, Tagore reveals a conspicuous urge to choose those songs that are more mystical in content and message; the social side of Kabir is underplayed. What one encounters in the translations is an esoteric world where 'flame burns without lamp'; 'The lotus blossoms without a root' (1961: 58); 'a strange tree, which stands without roots and bears fruits without blossoming' (ibid.: 53). Tagore's Kabir is more or less a *vedantin*, his *lok-dharmi* aspect is underplayed if not knocked out altogether. Here, Linda Hess's observation is very pertinent: 'This Kabir is less caustic and more constantly ecstatic than the sharp-eyed observer of society who appears in older collections' (quoted in Callewaert 2000: 14). Tagore's propensity for the mystical Kabir is understandable, both in terms of his own strong personal inclinations for the metaphysical, and in terms of the cultural imperatives of the age in which he was writing.

The infinite is so ubiquitously present in Tagore's translations that one wonders if Kabir at all had any grasp of the tangible and the concrete:

> The infinite dwelling of the Infinite being is everywhere; in earth, water, sky, and air:
>
> Firm as the thunderbolt, the seat of the seeker is established, above the void.
>
> He who is within is without I see Him and none else.
>
> (Tagore 1961: 62)

The finite as the locus of Bhakti stands thoroughly compromised, if not erased altogether. Consequently, Tagore's Kabir in translation appears more as a refined and sophisticated Sankara, than a *desi* poet of the domain of the people. These are translations in what could be termed as a 'pseudo-oriental' (Chaudhuri 1999: 44) mould.

Tagore's own foregrounding in the art of versification, his control over English diction and cadences present before us an image of Kabir as one who is a poet of impeccable classical make-up. The directness of speech, its rough and blunt edges—the qualities that stand out as typically Kabiresque hardly emerge in the translation. The reader of Romantic and Edwardian English poetry as Tagore was, he engenders a rare literary touch to the otherwise earthy utterances of Kabir, almost compromising in the process the tone and tenor of his protest poetry. Vinay Dharwadkar would term it as 'opacity' (Kabir 2003: xi) in style.

The remarkable aspect of Tagore's translation, however, is that it redeems Kabir from the alien biblical mould; it approaches him more as a poet of the classical style and stature than just a social reformer. Again, by way of comparison, the translations of both Trumpp and Macauliffe were more in the nature of scholarly exercises; Tagore's endeavour is more poetic because it is a poet who translates another poet. Also, unlike Trumpp and Macauliffe, Tagore is not attempting an encyclopaedia; he is only presenting those chosen verses of the saint-poet which enamour him the most. Another distinct advantage that rests with Tagore's effort is that it comes from a *sahridya* insider, and not from the so-called 'objective' outsider. Tagore's Kabir is not a Martin Luther, but a wandering baul.

While reading Tagore's translation it becomes difficult to make out as to where Kabir ends and Tagore the poet takes over. One can read a verse of *Gitanjali* and a translated song of Kabir simultaneously as natural extensions of each other, without any sense of rupture or deviance of mood. Look at the first poem in *Gitanjali*; in imagery, message and paradoxical strain it is no different from a *sakhi* of Kabir:

> Thou hast made me endless, such is thy pleasure. This frail vessel thou emptiest again and again, and fillest it ever with fresh life.
>
> This little flute of a reed thou hast carried over hills and dales, and hast breathed through it melodies eternally new. (Tagore 1952: 1)

The imagery of a vessel being filled and emptied is conspicuously Kabiresque. Similarly, the songs of Kabir, particularly the ones translated by Tagore, can easily be read as poetic utterances of the poet Tagore himself. For instance, poem no. X is so Tagore-like:

> On this tree is a bird: it dances in the joy of life.
>
> None knows where it is: and who knows what the burden of its music may be? (ibid.: 37)

It is this poetic 'echo' which the translations of Trumpp and Macauliffe fail to invoke.[13] Kabir truly becomes the subject of poetic inspiration in the case of Tagore, and not an object of scholarly debates.

Inspired translations run the risk of deviating from the so-called sacrosanct original. Tagore's own poetical propensities, it can be argued, tamper with the original text, but they nevertheless enrich and enhance the open-ended dynamism of Kabir. Kabir would continue to be translated for the simple reason that his verses provide enough room to the creative translator for improvisations. The open-endedness and the eternal flexibility of Kabir's verses pose a major challenge to scholar-translators who want to contain the saint-poet in scholastic or reformatory frames; for the poet-translators they, however, constitute the right stuff for ontological transformations. Tagore's Kabir, as pointed out earlier, may be inauthentic but he is at his poetical best.

VII

Two years after Tagore's much-celebrated translation, another translation of Kabir by Rev. Ahmad Shah of Hamirpur (U.P.) appeared in 1917.[14] The translation remained more or less obscure, except that subsequent translators, while making a claim for their respective translations, referred to its 'poor' quality of translation.[15] The complex subjectivity of the translator of being an Indian Muslim converted to Christianity, however, adds an intriguing dimension to his very enterprise of translation. It is intriguing because Kabir for his anti-sanskritic stance and raw nativity was never on the official agenda of pro-brahminical orientalists—both native and the colonialist. It is well-known that the official orientalists were only concerned with the canonical and the classical. Rev. Ahmad Shah's translation, however, is not only financially supported by the then colonial government in U.P., he is amply assisted by two English Christian missionaries—Rev. E. W. Ormerod and Rev. Canon B. H. P. Fisher—of the Cawnpore Brotherhood as well. Should it be seen as an attempt of appropriation of Kabir into Christianity in the wake of his marginalization in *margi* Hinduism? Also, should it be seen as the beginning of the orientalization of the native and the folk, alongside that of the classical?

Interestingly enough, Ahmad Shah shows immense awareness of the body-snatching-game that was being played around the persona and poetry of Kabir. He would dismiss all attempts of his predecessors and contemporaries in projecting 'Kabir as Martin Luther' of Hinduism, or Kabir as a 'protestant' Bhakti saint. In fact, he does not approve of the appropriation of Kabir into any canonical religion. His introductory remarks are very informative indeed:

> In modern India, organized attempts, such as that of the Brahma Samaj, to correct the abuses in Hinduism tend to be branded as disguised Christianity. It may be noted that an interesting, if unconvincing attempt to connect the Kabir Panth with the teaching of the Jesuits has been made by Pt. Walji Bhai of the Irish Presbyterian Church. It seems probable that a similar tendency caused Kabir in his own day to be called a Moslem; while the Moslems on the whole welcome his efforts, as a help in combating the idol worship of India, and acknowledged him as a Pir for his self-denying and pious life (Kabir 1977: 40).

His approach towards Kabir is refreshingly new and unprecedented. He would treat Kabir as an 'original' preacher-poet—a stance which till date any of the scholars of Kabir have failed to accept and acknowledge. From present-day Dalit critic Dr. Dharmvir to Christian missionaries of the colonial period, Kabir has been placed in one religious discourse or the other, denying him autonomy of voice. Even in the introduction to Tagore's translation, what is highlighted is not Kabir's individuality, but his capacity to 'fuse' various strands of mysticism that run across various religions.[16] Ahmad Shah, on the other hand, would underline the 'enormous influence (that) he [Kabir] exercised upon subsequent religious thinking' (ibid.: 37) and not the other way round. The agency is granted to Kabir instead of to the various religions that supposedly shaped him.

Having advocated or asserted the 'originality' or 'agency' of Kabir, does Shah translate Kabir differently? In other words, do Kabir's verses in English translation look different from, say, the messages of the *Bible* or any other religious text? Despite the fact that Shah presumably translates Kabir not under any appropriating agenda, yet his translation has biblical tones in terms of its syntax, diction, tone and tenor. F. E. Keay, in his *Kabir and His Followers* quotes many passages from Kabir, which bear similarity with biblical messages. And interestingly, he deploys some of the verses translated by Ahmad Shah and also by Westcott for this purpose. While he does so, he makes a very pertinent comment on the limitations of translation, especially when the translator himself is foregrounded in the *Bible*, thus: 'With regard to such passages as these, it may be remarked that in translating them into English, a translator who is acquainted with the *Bible* tends to assimilate his language to the words of the *Bible*, and this often makes the connection seem closer than it really is' (Keay 1995: 169–70). Unlike Tagore, Ahmad Shah is neither a poet in his own right; nor does he reveal any understanding of contemporary English poetry anywhere. The *Bible* happens to be his only model.

As against Tagore's reliance on the 'oral' songs of Kabir, Shah's sources are written and printed. Also, in comparison to Tagore's very sophisticated and poetical translations, Ahmad Shah's translation never intended to be literary, for its purposes were more or less religious. It tends to be prosaic and message-oriented. There is no attempt at precision as structures are retained literally without even experimenting with the given punctuation: 'Renounce self and recite the name of Hari: efface defects from head to toe./Have no fear of any creature: this is the essence of *sadhu*'s faith' (Kabir 1977:138).

Unlike any other translation of Kabir, besides the customary Preface, Shah's translation contains a full five chapters dealing with the life of Kabir in legend, the design and layout of the original *Bijak*, the teachings of the *Bijak*, the cosmology of the *Bijak* and the principles of the Kabir Panth. These five chapters run into as many as forty-five pages. The extraordinary space given to prose essays in the book amply proves the fact that Shah's endeavour was not just contained to the translation of the saint-poet, it was to introduce Kabir and the Kabir Panth to the Western audience in a comprehensive way. Shah's book is, therefore, as much a translation of the *Bijak*, as it is a critical account of Kabir and the Kabir Panth.

Very much like Westcott, Ahmad Shah sticks to culture-specific vocabulary as native words like *ghat, mahavat, amrit, sadhu, pandit, ghi*, etc., are retained in italics. There is no extensive footnoting also. There is no such anxiety to forge an assimilationalist idiom—an idiom which Macauliffe aimed at. Even Tagore fails to show as much confidence in retaining the native words in his translation of Kabir. The unique feature of Shah's translation is that towards the end it contains a rather unusual glossary of proper names mentioned in the *Bijak*. Of course, most of the entries in the glossary have been lifted from Dowson's *Classical Dictionary of Hindu Mythology and Religion, Geography, History and Literature* (2003), yet what stands out is Shah's concern for specific details.

VIII

Translating Bhakti thus remains an endeavour that never receives the official support of the orientalists. It nevertheless flourishes on the margins of the project of oriental studies with no different motives. It rather extends and enlarges its scope and reach by way of appropriating the counter-canonical and native discourse of Bhakti in terms which are either patently Christian or brahminical. Not only is the discourse of Bhakti denied its autonomous character, it is also translated as a *desi* derivative of the lofty classical religions. Kabir is reduced to a countryside version of either a Martin Luther or a Sankara, and if at all he is granted originality, it is translated in terms which are so overtly classical and scriptural that the people-centric discourse of Bhakti remains under-expressed. It is so much lost in 'evangelical entanglements' and oriental imperatives that the entire enterprise of translating Kabir amounts to forging a vernacular form of Christianity.[17]

Notes

1. The binary of the 'original' versus the 'translated' becomes quite contentious and even untenable in the case of Kabir because the so-called original Kabir is itself elusive. Rev. G. H. Westcott puts the entire debate in perspective: 'We may safely credit Kabir with a considerable amount of originality and; even where originality seems unlikely, feel grateful to him for the genius with which he has given expression to old thoughts' (1986: 45). In other words, the 'original' Kabir is always already in some measure translated and, therefore, in this sense his subsequent translations could be seen not as versions of Kabir; they are rather extensions of Kabir in another tongue. Vinay Dharwadkar, employing postmodern terminology, would approach Kabir's corpus as 'collective experiments in the aesthetics of palimpsestic textuality' (2003: 65) thus enlarging Kabir beyond source-target dualism.

2. Walter Benjamin dwells on how, through multiple translations, a work transcends its organic corporeality: 'a translation issues from the original—not so much from its life as from its after-life. For a translation comes later than the original, and since important works of world literature never find their chosen translators at the time of their origin, their translation marks the stage of continued life. . . . In them [translations] the life of the originals attains its latest, continually renewed, and most complete unfolding' (1996: 254–55).

3. In the early phase of Third World nationalism, First World nationalism was perceived to be the modular form of nationalism, till it was challenged or at least theoretically questioned by the Gandhian ideal of *swaraj*. In the chapter, it will be maintained that nationalism remains very much the flip side of colonialism.

4. In fact, William Jones was very much aware of the verses of Kabir, but due to their heretical tenor, he chose to ignore them. Peter Gaeffke informs, 'When it was shown to William Jones, he read it but suppressed it because of the many heretical statements in it. In the times of Jones, it was not advisable to discuss Kabir in Muslim circles' (2002: 158).

5. David Lorenzen's observations in this context are pertinent: 'The lives and writings of the European missionaries who worked in India in the seventeenth and eighteenth centuries have still not been adequately studied. The best known of these missionaries is the Italian Jesuit Roberto de Nobili (1577–1656) who lived for many years in South India. Some of his works have been published and the modern Jesuit scholar S. Rajamanickam has written about him. The writings of four other early missionary intellectuals have also been at least partially published: the Portuguese Jesuit, Gonçalo Fernandes Trancoso (1541–1621), the British Jesuit Thomas Stephens (1549–1619), the Lutheran Bartholomäus Ægenbalg (1683–1719), and the Italian Franciscan monk, Marco della Tomba (1726–1803). One important unpublished text is a long dialogue between a Christian and a Hindu written in Hindi and Italian by another Italian Fransciscan, Giuseppe Maria da Gargnano, who was in North India from 1749 to 1761' (Lorenzen 1999: 638–39).

'The Italian Capuchin friar Marco Della Tomba, born in 1726 as Pietro Girolamo Agresti, arrived in Pondicherry in 1757. From there he travelled to Chandernagore and in 1758 set out for Patna and the small state of Bettiah on the border of Nepal. Apart from two years spent in Chatrapur and several short stays in Patna, he was mostly in Bettiah until his return to Italy in 1773. He returned to north India, and died at Bhagalpur on March 1803' (Lorenzen 2002: 33).

6. Roland Barthes makes a very pertinent distinction between 'representation' and 'enfiguration' in his *The Pleasure of the Text*. According to him, 'figuration is the way in which the erotic body appears . . . in the profile of the text. [T]he text itself, a diagrammatic and not an imitative structure, can reveal itself in the form of a body split into fetish objects, into erotic sites. . . . Representation, on the other hand, is embarrassed figuration, encumbered with other meanings than that of desire: a space of alibis (reality, likelihood, readability, truth etc.)' (1976: 57).

7. The German subjectivity of the translator is significant. Dorothy Matilda Figuira, in a study on the translations of Kalidas's *Shakuntala* mentions, 'For the most part [during the 19th century] German translations were characterized by an accurate and literal rendering of the original' (1991: 27). E. Trumpp explains his methodology: 'As I went on, I noted down all grammatical forms and obsolete words I met with, and thus I gradually drew up a grammar and a dictionary so that I could refer to every passage again, whenever I found it necessary for the sake of comparison' (1978: vii).

8. Trumpp explains: '. . . though I can hardly expect that the granth will not attract many readers, the less so, as Sikhism is a waning religion. . . . The Sikh Granth, which will always keep its place in the history of religion, lies now open before us, and we know authentically what their Gurus taught' (1978: vii–viii). Susan Bassnett argues that one of the purposes of translation in the nineteenth century was to it make the work known (1991: 69).

9. Assimilation prepares cultural background for conversion. John Assmann describes the dynamics of assimilation: 'Assimilation, the giving up of a traditional cultural identity in favour of a dominant culture, is necessarily accompanied by religious conversion' (1996: 28–29).

10. Westcott makes an interesting chronological table in which he places Hindu and Christian saints in corresponding time frames. Ramanand (1300–1400) is seen to be a contemporary of Wycliffe (1324–84), Gorakh Nath (1420–85) is placed against Erasmus (1467–1536), Kabir (1440–1518) is shown to be a contemporary of Luther (1483–1546), Nanak (1469–1538) is placed against Cranmer (1489–1555), etc.

11. It is significant to note that nowhere does Tagore use the word 'translation' in his *One Hundred Poems of Kabir* (1961). Clearly, the nobel-laureate did not intend to 'translate' Kabir as such.

12. Tagore, while reviewing a book entitled *Sangit Sangraha: Bauler Gatha*, takes exception to the inclusion of 'Brahmo songs and songs of modern English-wallahs into the book' (Tagore 2001b).

13. It is significant to note that Walter Benjamin uses the word 'echo' also: 'The task of the translator consists in finding that intended effect upon the language into which he is translating which produces in it the echo of the original' (1996: 255). A translator thus produces the echo of the original and not the originality of the original.

14. Shah finished the translation of *Bijak* in February 1916, which was subsequently revised and corrected by Rev. E. W. Ormerod. It was finally published in May 1917. The quotes from the book have not been given separate notes.

15. This is how one later translator refers to Shah's translation: 'Ahmad Shah's English translation of the *Bijak* was hailed by Grierson with enthusiasm, not so much for its literary achievement—which was rather poor—as for Kabir's extraordinary personality' (Vaudeville 2001: 135). Winand M. Callewaert, while acknowledging the non-selective nature of Shah's translation observes, 'Rev. Ahmad Shah's, *The Bijak of Kabir*, Hamirpur, India, 1917, while a very poor translation, remains the only complete English version of the *Bijak*' (Callewaert 2000: 'Introduction, 4). Linda Hess and Shukdeo Singh have this to say on the quality of Shah's translation: 'Ahmad Shah's 1917 translation of the Bijak is stiff and far from the original style of Kabir, and lacks notes on dubious points of translation' (Kabir 2002: xii).

16. Evelyn Underhill introduces Tagore's *One Hundred Poems of Kabir* in terms of their capacity to fuse various cultures: 'We may safely assert, however, that in their teaching two—perhaps three—apparently antagonistic streams of intense spiritual culture met, . . . and it is one of the outstanding characteristics of Kabir's genius that he was able in his poems to fuse them into one (1961: vii–viii).

17. Saurabh Dube's long essay 'Colonial Registers of a Vernacular Christianity' (2004: 161–71) explicates a great deal on 'questions of vernacular translation that lie embedded within the processes of evangelical entanglements between missionaries and "natives"'.

7

Anxieties of Native Descent/Dissent: Bhakti Sub-text of Indian English Verse

Can Indian English poetry claim to have its own innate native space/ lineage? This question is often raised by *bhasha* critics/poets primarily to run down Indian English poetry as mere 'plantation in the pot' *sans* any organic strength.[1] The younger generation of Indian English poets basking in the sunshine of the global capitalism of the post-1990s do not pay as much attention to this kind of cultural nativism.[2] But the urge for 'native housing' torments the poets of post-ndependence, caught as they are in the surcharged debate of linguistic nationalism of the late 1950s.[3] In fact, most of them, by way of critical rejoinders, are compelled to write poems exclusively on their relationship with the native landscape and English both.[4]

As criticism of modern Indian English poetry mounts and the allegations of its being elitist, twice-born, non-interventionist and alien begin to gather more support, the anxiety to forge/invent its credible native descent comes to the foreground. Among the different possible lines of descent that multi-layered Indian culture offers, Indian English poets, across their diverse ethnic/racial backgrounds seem to rally around medieval Bhakti poets at this decisive juncture of their cultural legitimacy.[5] Most of these poets, the Hindu poets in particular, overtly express their unequivocal allegiance to Bhakti poetry; the non-Hindu poets—Nissim Ezekiel, Keki Daruwalla, Jayanta Mahapatra, Agha Shahid Ali, etc.—also take to 'prayer-poetry' in ways that befit Bhakti paradigms of approaching the sacred.[6] The present chapter, while exploring the possibility of creative linkages between Indian English poetry and Bhakti poetry, unfolds the cultural politics of such a cross-connection.

I

Indian English poetry prior to the 1950s remains very much orientalist for it either invokes the glorious classical Hindu/Indian past or its poverty and squalor—both the positions gloss over the imperatives of ordinary human situations. From Derozio to Toru Dutt, the canonical Indian sacred literature is feverishly re-written with a *mantric* seriousness affording little room to day-to-day existential concerns of life. Among the shorter versions, prayer/invocation/ode to god(dess) is one of the preferred forms of early Indian English poetry. Derozio, for instance, in an ode to India, bewails the lost glory of the past thus:

> My country! In thy day of glory past
> A beauteous halo circled round thy brow,
> And worshipped as a deity thou wast.
> Where is that glory, where that reverence now!
> ('To India—My Native Land', de Souza 2005: 6)

The tropes of 'worship' and 'reverence' hardly concede any ground to human agency and volition; they rather reduce the poetry into either a prayer or a requiem. Much of the Indian English poetry during the early nationalist period is poetry of pleading. In the poem quoted here, England takes the merciful maternal position:

> Ev'n as a child, amid its sobs and frets,
> All fondly clingeth to its mother's breast
> So India clings to thee—her haven of rest, . . .
> Lo! crushed—all bleeding—prostrate there she lies!
> Oh, gently raise her—dry her weeping eyes!
> (Ram Sharma, 'To England', ibid.: 76)

The overwhelming sense of submission that these poets express virtually rules out the possibility of playfulness as well as protest in poetic pursuits. As the poetic imagination swings from the classical to the colonial, the medieval Bhakti movement suffers neglect.[7]

Even if occasionally the local/little traditions are invoked, they are transformed or appropriated into the classical sublime under the pressures of inventing lofty nationalism. Sarojini Naidu, for instance, in her collection, *The Feather of the Dawn* (1961), devotes an exclusive section to the Krishna–Radha romance—a patent theme of various cults of Krishna-*bhakti* that flourished in medieval India.[8] The accent, however, remains on the mystical aspects of the romance; the raw sensuality of the encounter, so profusely dealt with in the poems of medieval vernacular poets like Vidyapati and Bihari, remains unexplored:[9]

> Thou sadist, —O faithless one, self-slain with doubt,
> Why seekest thou my loveliness without,
>
> And askest wind or wave or flowering dell
> The secret that within thyself doth dwell?
>
> I am of thee, as thou of me, a part.
> Look for me in the mirror of thy heart.
> ('The Quest', 1961: 42–43)

The possibilities of sensual play, otherwise so characteristic of mythical romance, are undone by the total surrender of the poet as devotee. In a poem addressed to Ghanashyam, instead of the usual camaraderie between the archetypal lover and the beloved, what one comes across is a relationship of feudal hierarchy:

> And grantest to thy seekers and thy sages
> Mystic sanctuaries of transcendent calm.
> O take my yearning, soul for thine oblation,
> Life of all myriad lives that dwell in thee.
> Let me be lost, a lamp of adoration,
> In thine unfathomed waves of ecstasy.
> ('Ghanashyam', ibid.: 39)

In such passages, Krishna, the divine god, overtakes Krishna, the lover. The poet fails to harness the typical Bhakti aesthetics of 'double coding' that transforms desire for sex into love for god.[10] Also, the persona of Radha, her womanly desires, remain uncharted (something which Dharamveer Bharati later on accomplishes in *Kanupriya*).[11] Devotion in the case of Naidu is surrender rather than dialogue; it is unqualified oblation rather than argumentative acceptance.

II

After independence, as Indian English poets begin to address issues of nation-building in more concrete and practical terms, they emerge out of the intimidating aura of the classical past, its purple-adjectived 'soul-stuff'.[12] The poets take on the onerous responsibility of translating the native Bhakti poetry—something that the official oriental project strategically ignored or even underplayed in favour of Sanskrit and Arabic texts.[13] The desire (or anxiety) is to have a meaningful engagement with respective native traditions. While poets like P. Lal and

K. R. Srinivasa Iyengar continue to re-write the classical Hindu texts in rhymed English, all other major poets devote their creative energies as much to the task of translating native Bhakti poets as to the writing of their own poetry.[14]

Among the 'canonical first generation' (Hoskote 2002: 'Introduction', xv) poets of the post–Tagore-Aurobindo era, A. K. Ramanujan stands out as one major poet who derives his creative impetus from the South Indian Bhakti tradition. Not in terms of outer form alone, his poetry shares a lot with his translations of Bhakti poems at the level of theme also. As a father, he regrets the idea of giving birth to sons and daughters. He warns: 'Poverty is not easy to bear./The body is not easy to wear./So beware, I say to my children/unborn, lest they choose to be born' ('Warning', 1995: 42). In many of the Bhakti poems translated by the poet, the same issue of bequeathing a bonded future features frequently. In one of the *vacana*s of Basavanna, again translated by the poet, a son prays to the 'lord of the meeting rivers' never to be born again:

> Father, in my ignorance you brought me
> through mother's wombs,
> through unlikely worlds.
>
> Was it wrong just to be born
> O lord?
>
> Have mercy on me for being born
> once before
> I give you my word,
> lord of the meeting rivers,
> never to be born again.
>   (Ramanujan 1973: 68)

In a *vacana* by Devara Dasimayya, the idea of parents controlling or foreknowing the past and future of their children occurs but only in an interrogative sense:

> Can even begetter, father and mother,
> display for onlookers' eyes
> the future breast and flowing hair
> in the little girl
> about to be bride?
>   (ibid.: 109)

Ramanujan would have replied in the affirmative to such a question. It is not important whether Ramanujan as a poet endorses *vacana* poets with or without qualification; what is significant is his constant engagement with the issues raised by them. The poet operates very much within the Bhakti grid.

Ramanujan always doubts the very possibility of spirit without body, or spiritualism without desire. In 'A Hindu to His Body' (1995: 40), the poet seeks to enjoy the skyward journey of the spirit with all bodily sensuousness. Therefore, he prays his body 'not to leave him behind'. In one of his *vacanas*, Basavanna also ridicules the idea of spiritualism without desire:

> How can the slaves of the Bodiless God
> Desire,
>   know the way
>   our Lord's Men move
>   or the stance of their standing?
>   (Ramanujan 1973: 76)

Almost echoing Basavanna, Ramanujan, in an another poem, would say 'Desire, bodiless is endless' ('One or Two or may be Three, Arguments against Suicide', 1995: 72). One can easily notice the similarity of expression.

The translation of the Bhakti poetry of the deep south has remained one of the most passionate of academic pursuits of Ramanujan. The hymns of Nammalvar, one of the *alvars*—saint-poets devoted to Vishnu—have been translated by the poet-translator in his book entitled *Hymns for the Drowning* (1991). The book can be read as one of the main sub-texts to at least two poems by Ramanujan on Vishnu. It is very difficult to say whether these poems came 'before or after' the poet's translations of Nammalvar, but the dialectical dynamics of exchange between the two is visible beyond doubt.

The poem 'Mythology 2' (1995: 226) takes off from Nammalvar's hymn 'The Man-Lion' which reads:

> At the red hour of sunset,
> there was blood
> on the heavens and the eight directions
>
> Our lord
> plunged the demon into despair
> and slaughtered him:

a lion
tearing open
a mountain under his claws
     (Ramanujan 1991: 9)

The same myth of Vishnu's incarnation Narasimha destroying Hirnaya-kasipu, a king of antigods, forms the basic frame of Ramanujan's poem:

come now come soon,
Vishnu, man, lion, neither and both, to hold
him in your lap to disembowel his pride
with the steel glint of bare claws at twilight. (1995: 226)

The poem, of course, goes beyond the mere repetition of the translated version of the hymn to Lord Vishnu. Ramanujan's poetry, therefore, stems from the tension between the so-called original and the translated Bhakti poetry. It is a product of what Arvind Krishna Mehrotra prefers to describe as 'interlingual osmosis' ('The Emperor Has No Clothes', 2001: 470), whose exact matrices/topologies of exchange are difficult to map out.

The Bombay school of poetry led by Nissim Ezekiel adopts a humanistic stance and addresses secular concerns of life; there is no ambition to acquire the equipoise of a classic yogi.

I do not want the yogi's concentration,
I do not want the perfect charity
Of saints nor the tyrant's endless power.
I want a human balance humanly.
    ('A Poem of Dedication', Ezekiel 1989: 40)

The tendency is to avoid the spiritual extravagance of the preceding generation of Indian English poets. Ezekiel professedly learns his lessons in democratic humanism from M. N. Roy, but he is open enough to gain wisdom from traditions other than his own Judaic one, provided they are not dogmatic. He does mention Sufism in this regard: 'Sufism captivates me as completely as the Cabala does. . . . It doesn't do justice to the poetry to go with dogmatic expectations' (de Souza 1999: 11).

Ezekiel's 'Latter-Day Psalms' has all the trappings of Bhakti poetry as the poet subverts the wishful religious prayers *a la* Kabir or a

Tukaram. The last psalm is re-written with a boldness and brazenness of an iconoclast of the Bhakti mould:

> All that fuss about faith,
> all those decisions to praise
> God, the repeated appeals,
> denunciations, laments and hopes,
> the division of men into virtuous
> and wicked! (1989: 260)

Ezekiel, identified often as a Brahmin Jew, is not an orthodox devotee; his 'brahminism' lies in his being critical of religious orthodoxy of any kind. In his *Hymns of Darkness*, his brashness comes forth with equal candour as he describes God as 'The absentee landlord/the official of all officials' (ibid.: 222). 'The Egoist's Prayers' simply overturns the relationship between the deity and the devotee. The poet is ready to carry the burden of his 'brahminism' provided it serves his personal interests, first and foremost: 'I'll do your [god's] will/Please try to make it coincide with mine' (ibid.: 213).

Other first-generation poets like Jayant Mahapatra and Keki Daruwalla, irrespective of their distinct religious backgrounds, take on the roles of medieval Bhakti poets in exposing the politics of religion. Mahapatra, in his poem, 'Total Solar Eclipse', compares a brahmin with a crocodile thus:

> And cautiously the crocodile
> pushes its long snout from the deep water
> like the fearsome Brahmin priest in the temple,
> secure by shadowy layers of sleep,
> so out of date, in alleviative belief,
> using darkness to be a portent of gods . . .
> (1987: 54)

Both brahmins and crocodiles take advantage of the divine darkness to trap their victims. The poverty outside the holy temples of Puri often invites Mahapatra's uncanny attention:

> Outside, in the bright sun,
> the screams of five children crying
> for slices of watermelon pierce his ears;
> he sees a tree of ten hands

> scoffing the atrocious innocence of Jagannath
> in his sheltered shrine.
>> ('A Summer Afternoon', ibid.: 72)

The innocence of the divine not only borders on cynical smugness but it also suggests its impotence. Modern Indian English poets fail to reconcile with the all-powerful divine's lack of ability to positively intervene in human affairs.[15]

Daruwalla, in his *Crossing of Rivers*, draws vignettes of the holy city of Benaras in terms of a modern-day confused pilgrim. As he reaches the Ganga *ghats* he wonders: 'What plane of destiny have I arrived at/where corpse-fires and cooking fires/burn side by side?' ('Boatride Along the Ganga', 2006: 98). Another uneasy question that the poet asks has clear Bhakti undertones: 'Why, installing a mistress/ is like installing a deity in the home?' ('Crossing of Rivers-2', ibid.: 114) Both the questions, raised towards the end of the poems, stylistically speaking, remind us of the Bhakti way of unsettling the affirmations of conventional wisdom. Also, the juxtaposition of the sacred with the profane, the existential with the essential, the sensual with the spiritual, lends an intended double-edgedness to the poetic utterance.

III

As Indian English poetry matures and gathers confidence, its claim to the Bhakti heritage grows subtle. The latter poets of the Ezekiel era— like Arun Kolatkar, Dilip Chitre, Arvind Mehrotra, etc.—foreground their poetic discourse in the Bhakti lore in a manner which is markedly eclectic and experimental. English, despite being a non-vernacular language, loses whatever colonial stigma it presumably suffered as these bilingual poets neither entered into nor entertained any debate on the choice of their preferred poetic language.

Arun Kolatkar's poetry, as the poet himself acknowledges, gets its naughty irreverence from the equally abrasive Bhakti poetry.[16] In *Jejuri*, smoking cigarettes turns out to be a better form of release than performing *pooja* inside the temple. The mood of defiance is conveyed thus: 'I will be out in the courtyard [of the temple]/where no one will mind/if I smoke' ('Makarand', 2001: 39). The iconolatory of orthodox religion is subverted as the poet describes 'every other stone' in the holy town as either 'a god or his cousin' ('A Scratch', ibid.: 28). The poet is at his ironical best as he looks inside a door in search of a god but only finds 'a wide eyed calf/looking back at him' ('Manohar', ibid.: 20).

In his later collection, *Kala Ghoda Poems*, Kolatkar's humour turns black. From being naughty and sarcastic, the poet becomes nasty and blunt. In a poem 'The Shit Sermon' (2004a: 115–19) he accepts the greatness of god for 'He has given all his creatures,/ great or small,/ two holes:/a feedhole and a shithole'. Thereafter, the poet takes recourse to the vernacular slang: '*Usne sabko diyela hai/ – khaneko muh,/ hugneko gaand.*' Rubbish, instead of a holy temple, becomes the site of worship. The sweeper-woman pounding her feet on the pile of garbage to fill the wicker bin to its maximum capacity is no less than a Meera:

> and [she] begins to dance
> within the narrow compass
> of the wicker bin
>
> like a Meera before her Lord,
> a Meera
> with a broomstick for a lute
>   ('Meera', ibid: 32)

Excrement is transformed into a matter of sublime attention; sheer waste is a site of epiphanic revelations. An old bicycle tyre lends the vision of 'a wobbly zero/a spastic shunya' ('An Old Bicycle Tyre', ibid.: 52). The body of a street dog traces the map of seventeenth-century Bombay, 'with Old Woman's Island on my forehead,/ Mahim on my croup/and the others distributed/casually along/brisket, withers, saddle and loin' ('Pi-dog', ibid.: 16).

Dilip Chitre's poetry dwells in seemingly two disparate zones of avant-garde experimentalism and Bhakti eclecticism, with a clear slant towards the latter. The poet places his poetry in the context of the 'integrated vision' of Bhakti poetry that entails a fusion of the ethical with the aesthetic.[17] To the poet, language is a deterrent towards self-realization if it does not stem from within; in a self-mocking tone, he questions his own credo of a player of words thus: 'Words. More and more words. Clear as a city street/At midday. I will leave behind a more garbled version/Of the same word. The richer for my own noise' ('Travelling in a Cage 2', Mehrotra 1992: 107). The feeling of being linguistically imprisoned constantly runs down the poet:

> . . . . or language
> Exposed and caged by my own condition
> What doors can I open in this fear
> What windows look out
> And will I ever find my own face out there?
>
> (ibid.: 109)

To the poet, poetry is nothing more than incest if it does not free us from the tyrannies of language: 'Poetry is the strangest form of incest/People making love to the same idea . . .' ('In Limbo', ibid.: 110).

Chitre's poetic endeavour is not to sound prophetic like Whitman, rather it is to be inclusive like Tukaram or Kabir—the two poets that influence him the most.[18] The ordinary existence and the high essence emanate from the same metaphors. The poetic metaphors, therefore, have an earthiness and a deliberate pungency:

> Praise the garlic for its tight
> Integration of cloves and its white
> Concealment of unbearable astringence.
>
> Praise the onion for keeping
> Its eye-opening secret
> Under so many identical skins.
>
> ('Of Garlic and Such', ibid.: 111)

The profundity of life is discovered and articulated not through sophisticated metaphysics, but though the creative deployment of images from ordinary life. Garlic and onion emerge as revelatory icons of the subaltern.[19]

Beneath the veneer of Arvind Mehrota's avowedly Ezraesque poetry, the Bhakti-tropes of subversion operate in consonance with his modernist fragmentary vision. Writing after Ghagha, a local visionary, the poet writes 'Bhojpuri Descant' in which he re-writes the native wisdom in its characteristic laconic style thus: 'If landlords are saints/ Pestles are bowstrings' (1984: 39), or 'Three oxen, two wives:/Death's at your door step' (ibid.: 40). In the 'Book of Common Places', the poet overturns the rare with the common, the exceptional with the everyday, and the special with the ordinary:

> I depend on the rag-and-bone-man
> And know nothing
> About architecture

> Yesterday
> All the rare lines
> In the book
> Were traded
> For common ones.
>   (ibid.: 11)

A translator of Kabir, Mehrotra relies more on common sense and observation than puerile erudition or theoretical explanation.

Mehrotra's poems—long or short—have the typical paradoxical Kabiresque sub-structure wherein an image and its counter-image are locked together in a single whole: 'The book lies open on two-voiced/ Summer: hawk-cuckoo's/Grey and white liners through hazeless/ Air . . .' ('Scenes from a Revolving Chair', 1998: 20). This doubleness recurs throughout his poetry. The birds flying above and the leaden boats below create a landscape of tension:

> Without lifting their wings
> The prey birds climb
> And fill the sky's dyed ground,
> Throwing quilled shadows
> Even as they move
> Away from the eddying
> River of consonants, the vowels that drown
> Before leaden boats can reach them.
>   (ibid.: 20–21).

The poem reminds one of Kabir's binary of the 'lonely swan' (*hans akela*) pitted against or caught in the circus of the world (*jagdarshan ka mela*).

Agha Shahid Ali, a Kashmiri Muslim poet, invokes the local Sufi as well as Bhakti traditions as he bemoans the bloody present of his motherland. While on a flight to Srinagar, the poet hears the voices of Begum Akhtar, Lal Ded and Shiekh Noor-ud-Din in quick succession. As the *ghazal* of Begum Akhtar comes to an end, the plane nears the mountains of his burning Kashmir:

> . . . Below us,
> the mountains quicken cremation's shades,
>
> and up there the sky rainbows itself. Was it thus
> that Lal Ded—robed in the brilliant green
> of Paradise—rose from ashes, fabulous

with *My body blazed?*
('I Dream I Am the Only passenger on Flight 493 to
Srinagar', 2000: 19)

The songs of Lal Ded, a Bhakti poet, also referred to as Lalla or
Lalleshwari, reverberate the Kashmiri troposphere. Her songs as well
as blessings to Sufi-saint Noor-ud-Din echo in the dreaded valleys. The
voice of the saint warns about the burning of the sacred Sufi shrine
Chrar-e-Sahrif: 'I hear his voice: "Fire moves on its quick knees –/
through Chrar-e-Sahrif – towards my shrine."' The Sufi voices implore
the poet to rush back to his motherland 'before ash filigrees/roses
carved in the wood of weeping trees' (Ali 2000: 19). The attitude of
Shahid Ali towards his Sufi heritage is that of tragic acceptance.

In an introductory prose poem entitled, 'The Blessed Word: A
Prologue', Shahid Ali locates the present-day agony of Kashmir in
the tragedy of Habba Khatun, a sixteenth-century woman poet of the
valley. The poet wonders whether the Kashmiri women will continue
to sing the songs of Habba Khatun as the chinar leaves they used to
gather have been reduced to ashes: 'And will the blessed women rub
the ashes together?' (2000: 4). While recounting the tale of Habba's
grief on her husband's exile forced upon him by the then Moghul
king Akbar, the poet discovers that her grief is 'alive to this day'. It
is from the days of the Moghuls that 'Kashmir has never been free'.
Shahid Ali's poetry—mostly *ghazals*—bears a clear imprint of lyrical
and quasi-spiritual Indo-Islamic Sufi poetic traditions. The underlying
impulse is to foreground his poetry in the cultural continuum that he
discovers from Lal Ded to Begum Akhtar.

IV

By the time Indian English poetry enters the era of globalization or
post-nationalism, it overcomes the anxiety of striking a sustained
genealogical relationship with Bhakti poetry for native acceptance.[20]
As an obsessive undercurrent, the Bhakti influence subsides, but it
continues to add on to the increasing multicultural portfolio of the new
poets. Bhakti poets are resurrected for the sake of poetic metaphors
of the un-classical kind, and the endeavour always is to transpose
them to new landscapes/situations. In the new contexts of the market-
economy, for instance, Tabish Khair wonders:

Who will follow you now, Kabir,
From the marketplace of deceits

> Through the song of protest
> To that hut where a king of kings
> Came without his crown?
>   ('The Other Half of Kabir's Doha', 2000: 96)

The appropriation of Kabir by different vested groups having totally dissimilar ideologies and principles has distanced the Bhakti saint from the common people. He is itemized into textbooks as any other poet to be debated and counter-debated by puerile academics for their petty promotional gains. As the poet Khair struggles to free Kabir from the prison of a book, he hears 'grandfather's wordless cook/ Casually complete your [Kabir's] couplet' (ibid.: 97). The illiterate cook, ironically enough, completes the half-sung couplet of the saint poet.

It is through Surdas that Leela Gandhi discovers poetry's regenerative potential in completing its own handicaps. She invokes the visually handicapped Bhakti poet for poetic inspiration. Poetry, a handicap in itself, she argues, 'hangs on a limb/Severed by the world's misgivings' ('Sur: Surdas', Gandhi 2000: 39), but then through a process of pain and suffering, it completes the whole. In a poem entitled 'Sur: Surdas', the blind, the handicapped and the have-nots are projected as potential poets, for it is through their acute sense of incompletion that they strive for the whole:

> Poetry attempts the air on crutches, inchoate
> And accidental, gives pause, takes pain,
> Lives, on the sharp edges of absences,
> In the rough silence of speaking things
> Stammers its dissent, complains,
> Makes whole again, compensates; . . .
>   (ibid.: 39)

Surdas becomes the very locus of poetic process for the poet, its take off and its finale: 'It takes a blind poet, scrabbling in the dark,/ To letter the night with words, insight' (ibid.: 39). Vikram Seth, the most multicultural of the new poets, while thinking of doomsday, also remembers Surdas along with other artists of the world thus: 'We are the last generations. Surdas, Bach,/ Rembrandt, Du Fu, all life, love, work and worth/Will end in the particular rain' ('Close of Play', 1999a: 41). The poet thus registers the role of Bhakti wisdom in the making of 'the extinct consciousness', 'the radiance we attained' which he conjectures would fascinate even the aliens as they take over.

Kabir's songs were cautionary warnings against the excesses of institutionalized religion. Ranjit Hoskote's 'Cautionary Tales', as the poet himself adds in the subtitle, take after Kabir's verses with the difference that instead of institutionalized religion, his tales are directed against the excesses of the state. The nation-state befools its own people by waging protracted battles against the neighbouring countries. First, it does not let its own people know its internal games of plunder; the poet, *a la* Kabir cautions:

> Beware, my sons, of towns founded by gold miners,
> now abandoned in the saddle of a valley.
> Before long, parting ways with your muleteers,
> you'll stumble on routes
> no caravan has used for decades.
>   ('Cautionary Tales; After Kabir', 2006: 126)

Those who are led by official signboards, milestones, take 'the wrong direction'; rather, as the poet emphasizes, 'have been taken for a ride'. The pastures are 'flecked with ash' not as much due to the enemy's fire as it is due to the excessive mining of the area below. The rhetoric of external threat is exposed: 'Who *talks* of that other country/misses the point'.

In another 'cautionary tale', Hoskote warns the daughters of the village about those who pretend to have forgotten their rural roots, and come back to village-rocks to mine them:

> Beware, my daughters, of men who say:
> I've forgotten the name of my village,
> I've forgotten the way back
> tomorrow, I'll cross the river
> in an iron canoe
> with rocks for ballast. (ibid.: 126–27)

The poet takes a dig at the mining mafia that ransacks the countryside in the name of development. The reference to Kabir in the subtitle of the poem underscores the increasing relevance of Bhakti poetry in present-day debates on alternative models of development. In another poem, Kabir survives the existential scare—expressed through the images of 'parrot's gossip' and 'hawk cry'—as he manages to ascent despite scepticism all around. The vultures of the lower sky tend to ensnare him, yet wrapped in the torn (but not tainted) fabric of the sky he goes upward towards a new level of awareness: 'Wrapping himself in the torn fabric of sky,/ Kabir climbs on' ('Landscapes with Saints', ibid.: 174).

Kabir beacons Meena Alexander in times of siege. In a poem written in response to 9/11, the poet reminds us of the porous fabric the human body is made of. No amount of insulation/evasion from external threats can redeem us from the fact of our being ordinary earthly mortals:

> What a shame
> they scared you so
> you plucked your sari off,
> crushed it into a ball
> then spread it
> on the toilet floor.
> Sparks from the towers
> fled through the weave of silk.
> ('Kabir Sings in a City of Burning Towers', 2004: 14)

The terror cannot be wished away; it seeps through the weave of human fabric. The poem ends on a note of irony, typical of Bhakti wisdom: 'Kabir the weaver sings/*O men and dogs/in times of grief/ our rolling earth/grows small*'.

In a poem entitled 'Indian April', the gap between Meena (Alexander) and Meera virtually collapses. Allen Ginsberg, the poet of the Beat Generation who drew heavily from oriental sources, becomes Meena's Krishna: 'Allen Ginsberg your flesh is indigo/the color of Krishna's face, Mira's bitter grace' (Alexander 2002a: 57). In the poem, as he sits down on the banks of the Ganga, he hears the *padas* of Mirabai:

> Watched Mira approach, her hair a black mass
> so taut it could knock over a lamppost,
> skin on her fists raw from rubbing chipped honeypots.
>
> in the middle distance
> like a common bridegroom
> Lord Krishna rides a pianted swing. (ibid.: 54)

In the second section of the poem, the poet recounts her birth at 'the Ganga's edge' (ibid.: 55), fashioning herself to be a Ginsberg's Mira. She learns from Ginsberg that 'the tabernacles of grace/are lodged in the prickly pear' (ibid.: 56).

Meerabai re-appears in the poetry of some of the women poets of the post-1990s with a greater urgency, not just as an indigenous icon of feminism, but also as a fierce nationalist who seeks freedom of the spirit. While passing through the 'snowy' deserts of Kutcch, Rukmini Bhaya Nair encounters a ferocious Meera rising from 'the scorched salt' as a tigress in search of total freedom. Standing alone near a salt-pit, she personifies the 'spirit of Dandi'. The poet deliberately disfigures her so that more than her sensuality her spirit should come forth. Therefore, as this Meera lifts her veil, her face turns out to be 'pockmarked', she is a '*bhootni*', 'a laughing ghost'. Nair's Meera does not surrender in a one-sided feminine manner; she demands total surrender from 'you' as well:

> Meera, *bhootani*
> Does not ask for your manhood,
> Since when does freedom lie in the tick of the penis?
> She wants you to believe in the colours of the desert
> In promises, poems, marches, the gentleness of tigers
> She wants you to trust your soul, her body . . .
> (Meerabai, 2004: 112)

Nair's Meera combines 'poetry, marches and gentleness of tigers'; she is a rare embodiment of aesthetics, politics and bestial instincts.

Another young poet, Archana Sahni, transforms Meera from being a devotee into a goddess in her own right. Instead of Krishna bestowing his graces on his devotee, it is the devotee who lends voice to the dumb deity: 'His flute is in your voice/. . .' ('Meerabai, My *Amar Chitra Katha* Heroine', 2005: 51). The reversal in roles does not subvert the Bhakti-credo, rather it stands extended and enhanced:

> Meerabai, I am writing
> a new *amar chitra katha,*
> in which you are Krishna—
> woman with blue lotus face,
> feathers and flute—
> and I am Meerabai. (ibid.: 52)

The poet clamours to take on the role of Meera, but her god is not a male Krishna, but Meera herself. Meerabai does not suffer a crisis of relevance; rather she bounces back as 'a heroine' for the new budding seekers of love.

V

Some of the new poets do not invoke Bhakti poets directly but in matters pertaining to divinity, religion and spirituality, their attitude is quite in consonance with that of Bhakti poets. The familiar Bhakti tropes—such as conditional devotion, informal invocation, naughty caricaturization of the divine, the assertion of ego in prayer, protest against institutionalized religion, etc.—provide a structural sub-text to their poetry. As these poets visit sacred Hindu temples, they evince the characteristic Bhakti attitude of reverence and ridicule, of prayer and parody, of devotion and defiance.

The unholy nexus between commerce and religion invites Sudeep Sen's attention. As he walks inside the famous Puri temple, he steps on 'petals, piss, potholes and prayer'; 'the commerce and claustrophobia of the inside' does not let his prayers reach as the mediating priests are perhaps more eager 'to erase the unholy, from their own selves' ('Jagannath Temple, Puri', 1997: 57). Another poet, Bibhu Padhi, also undergoes the same forbidding experience of chaos inside the temple that virtually denies him access to the goddess:

> The polished floors, slippery
> and deceitful, wouldn't hold my feet.
> Does the goddess know that
> I could hardly stand upright
> in her archaic territory.
> > ('In the Temple', 1999: 6)

The poet, unlike Sudeep Sen, stops short of being mischievously irreverent or playful. In the end, he takes his inability to reach the goddess possibly as a sign of his own weakness: 'my willingness to accept defeat' (ibid.).

Jeet Thayil, in his poem 'Pashupatinath', comes across a play of opposites both inside and outside the holy temple. Outside the sacred temple, there is trade and traffic of drugs ('marijuana fields'); inside, the priests look for hefty offerings:

> With hands full of money,
> flowers and prayers,
>
> our unruly lines
> mobbed the priest
> who slapped each supplicant

> across the head,
> the smaller the donation
> the louder the slap.
>   (2003: 74)

In another poem, the poet seeks the simplicity of a leaf. The asceticism implied in the following lines only suggests inward meditation *sans* external claptrap:

> Hold your breath until
> you are God's green thoughts.
> Stop eating,
> air will suffice for food.
> Water is another matter:
>   ('How to Be a Leaf', ibid.: 20)

In Bhakti poetry, nature is the eternal theatre of the divine; culture, on the other hand is man-made. Instead of observing the extensive rituals and rites of institutionalized culture, the poet would plead for inner organic growth: 'limbs grow inward./Conjugate patience./Worship women and trees' (ibid.). The trees emerge as perfect devotees, and the endeavour is to become one with the green vegetation.

Vijay Nambisam, almost echoing Kolatkar's experiences at Jejuri, draws a very inhospitable, if not utterly hostile image of a cave that does not house its deity any longer:

> The god is gone. His cave is bare.
> In shadow from the sun
> The clotted bats hang from the roof.
> Below, the scorpions run
> And pious folk no longer come
> Lest evil should be done.
> ('The Deserted Temple', see www.openspaceindia.org/7_vijay.htm)

The poem describes one of the caves at the holy town of Sravana-belagula. Kolatkar's animals—cows, monkeys and birds—are far less vicious than bats and scorpions that run across what was once the holy sanctum sanctorum of the temple in Nambisam's poem. The disappearance of the god paves way for evil forces to occupy the vacant slot. The deserted temple is visited only in times of utter crisis.

Imtiaz Dharker's poetry also negotiates with the intricate issues of fundamentalism, honour killings, terrorism, *purdah*, etc., in ways which are patently unconventional and even heretical. Her god is no more than 'a tourist in this world', a mere 'visitor' walking 'around battered streets,/distinctly lost/looking for landmarks/from another, promised past' ('Postcards from God-1', 1994: 3). In her 'Postcard-poems', instead of the devotee pleading for his redemption, it is god who speaks and struggles for its existence:

> Who am I speaking to?
> I think, I may have misplaced the address,
> but still, I feel the need
> to write to you;
> not so much for your sake
> as for mine. (ibid.: 5)

The god is no more than a battered dhobi 'bow-legged', carrying 'a bundle/that has always been big for me [him]'. Each day he takes the count, 'separate[s] the dusters from the sheets, . . ,/ till each one is ready to be thrown free/laid across the ground' ('Taking the Count', ibid.: 8). The echoes of Kabir, the weaver poet, defining life in terms of a spotless fine sheet (*jhini jhini bini chadriya*) reverberate in such lines. The fundamentalists are not true worshippers of the divine: 'Everywhere you scream my words,/but you forget my name'. Dharker's beleaguered god asks his devotees:

> Did I create you
> in my image
>
> or did you create me
> In yours?
>   ('Question 2', ibid.: 32)

What makes him uneasy is his invocation for fundamentalist battle-cries to petty consumerist ends. His name looms at unexpected places: 'On the wall of a mosque, my name/confronts me,/blazed in a passionate calligraphy' ('Face', ibid.: 37). He is all the more embarrassed when a plastic doll planted on the dashboard of a taxi 'opens my [his] mouth and speaks'. In the shops, he is 'squashed between/detergents and boiled sweets,/my [his] face is painted an unlikely blue . . .' (ibid.). Dharker thus subtly extrapolates Bhakti arguments to take on the growing spectre of fundamentalism.

Part-time poets like Anurag Mathur and Anita Nair also enter into a dialogue with the divine in terms that puncture the obligations of conventional devotionalism. Both the devotee and the deity are rather tentative in the poetry of Mathur. As the poet seeks 'him' 'in the hallway of stars,/where suns blossom/in citrus fire', he is reminded of his decaying physical self:

> But the straitjacket
> skin squeezes
> its acid colour permeates,
> dissolving uncertain bones.
> ('Seeker', 2005: 4)

The mystical ideal of being a singer and the song is difficult to realize, as the divine itself is lost and lonely in 'A world full of mirrors'. The poet praises 'him', but 'partly':

> Born gifted, born damned
> stalked by his talent
> he hid himself
> in remote corners.
> of himself.
> In a chameleon world
> at once Arctic,
> at once Saharan,
> both creature and Christ
> in a vast and hidden land.
> ('In Praise, Partly', ibid.: 6)

The god is as much a creature as he is a creator. He is everywhere, but is hidden in the remote corners of the chameleon world.

In the opening poem of Anita Nair's collection *Malabar Mind*, Lord Muthappan seeks to de-rarefy himself as he craves to have physical relations with his woman-devotee. In the poetry of new poets, it is the dumb divine who is forced to speak and plead in terms that humanize both the players involved in the praying-act. Lord Muthappan is eager to 'match my [his] longing with yours [the woman-devotee]':

> Let me sear your lips with mine.
> Let me burn your flesh with my hunger.
> Why then do you evade me now?
> Is it that you smell the savage?

> Is it that you fear who I was?
> Woman listen,
>
> I am a man;
> Only sometimes a god.
>> ('Mostly a Man. Sometimes a God', Nair 2003: 11–12)

The body of the divine becomes the locus of the savage and the sacred, the lustful and the lofty simultaneously. Being godly is a part-time duty; the main occupation of the divine is to be as much a human being as his worshippers are.

Thus, in the Indian English poetry of the post-1990s, Bhakti poetry continues to operate at a sub-textual level, but the relationship is more dialogic than unilateral or one-sided. The new poets at times do derive their poetic arguments from Bhakti poets, extrapolating them to latest situations across cultures. The unorthodox deployment of Bhakti metaphors/poets in situations that range from 9/11 to the fictional possibility of 'the end of the world' generates a poetics more of exchange than of mere descent. The new Indian English poets lend a new lease of life to Bhakti poets as much as they receive cultural strength from them. A cultural continuum is thus forged that amalgamates the medieval with the (post)modern, the local with the global, the sacred with the secular.

Notes

1. While expressing doubts about the survival of Indian English writings in post-independence India, Naresh Mehta, a Jnanpeeth award winning Hindi poet, uses this metaphor of 'plantation in the pot' (1983: 15). The cultural ambivalence built in the very term 'Indian English' invited other strange metaphors; Gordon Bottomley described Indian poetry in English as 'Matthew Arnold in a saree'; V. K. Gokak reversed the metaphor to 'Shakuntala in skirts' (quoted in Naik 1980: 27).
2. 'These poets are not apologetic about the fact that they write in English; their poetry is refreshingly free of the excess ideological baggage of Indianness that encumbered the earlier generation of post-colonial Indian poets in English. They feel no obligation to prove their Indianness to nativist detractors . . .' (Hoskote 2002: 'Introduction', xiv).
3. Leela Gandhi refers to the anxiety of what she terms as 'nationalist housing' (Ezekiel 1989: 'Preface', xvi) among Indian English poets.
4. The attitude of the Indian English poets towards English or the native landscape is never that of unqualified possession. Keki Daruwalla, for instance, assigns

English the role of a mistress that has a complex genealogical inheritance. Its distinctness from the colonial English is asserted:

> No, it is not Anglo-Indian. The Demellos would
> bugger me if they got scent of this,
> and half of my body would turn into a bruise.
> She is not Goan, not Syrian Christian.
> She is Indian English, the language that I use.
>
> ('The Mistress', 2006: 161)

In another poem, the allegation of Indian English poetry being non-native, simply exasperates the poet. Invoking the Tagorean god, 'The Endless One', he writes:

> Tell us which doctor
> will plant the gland of nativism
> in our benighted souls
> Teach us how to distinguish between night and day.
> Show us the way!
>
> ('Invocation', ibid.: 32–33)

Jayanta Mahaptra lapses into a long poem to express his relationship with his native Oriya culture:

> I know I can never come alive
> if I refuse to consecrate at the altar of my origins
> where the hollow horn blows every morning
> and its suburban sound picks its way
> through the tangled moonlight of your lazy sleep.
>
> ('Relationship', 1987: 43)

Nissim Ezekiel also underlines the distinctness of 'Indian English' in his oft-quoted 'Very Indian Poems in Indian English' in a manner which is comic if not utterly burlesque. Jeet Thayil also refers to the possible rift between English language and Indian silence: 'I would be ruined still by syntax, the risk/and worry of word committed to stone/English fills my right hand, silence my left' ('English', 2003: 39). Vikram Seth portrays English as a god which empowers as well as isolates its speaker in the native context:

> English! Six-armed god,
> Key to a job, to power,
> Snobbery, the good life,
> This separateness, this fear.
>
> ('Divali', 1999a: 66)

5. There could be many genealogies or lines of descent of Indian English poetry. Buddhism is one of the major presences in Indian English poetry and it can as well be established as the fountain-source of the non-canonical, syllogistic poetry of modern Indian English poets. Keeping in view the overt religious/

mythic inter-textuality of this poetry, one can locate Indian English poetry in mainstream *upanishadic* heritage as well. Arvind K. Mehrotra does refer to the 'pact' that post-independence poets make in their own backyard 'with Kapilar, Paranar, Basavanna, Allama Prabhu, Tukaram, Nirala, Faiz' (1992: 'Introduction, 2).

6. Bhakti, in this chapter, does not refer to its classical baggage as is explicated in canonical Hindu texts, particularly *Srimadbhagavat* in which it is ranked as the fifth *purushartha*, even above *moksha*. Here it is employed as the prime signifier of medieval Bhakti discourse wherein it is no longer just mysticism, but also a criticism of life. Here the observations of Ramesh Chandra Shah, a noted Hindi critic, on the meaning of Bhakti as it was understood by medieval Bhakti poets, are pertinent: 'Bhakti is not necessarily mysticism: most of these Bhakti poets offer solid "social" and existentially defined stuff which includes criticism of life as well as Revelation of a Hidden Life. They consciously and unconsciously reveal the self-contradictions as well as the self-transcending possibilities of a society which is no longer in confident and creative possession of its own achieved ideals; and which is, therefore, threatened with disintegration from within and without. And it is something more than revelation; the saint poets perform a curative function too' (1989: 69).

7. G. N. Devy, in his *After Amensia: Tradition and Changes in Indian Literary Criticism* (1993), underlines the complicity of brhamanical discourse with the colonial one. To him, both the Sanskritic and the colonial (western) have systematically displaced the *desi* or the *bhasha* literatures into obscurity.

8. During the medieval period, many Radha-centric Bhakti cults such as the Radha-Vallabh, Nimbarka, Gaudiya, Chiatanya *sampradaya*s had raised Radha from being a passive consort to an active deity in herself. She appears in different moods. The Gaudiya *sampradaya* worships Sri Radha Govinda in *parakiya* (paramour) mood, in *manjari bhava*. The Nimbarka *sampradaya* worships Radha Krsna also but in *swakiya* (wedded) mood, in *sakhi bhava*. They have *sambhoga rasa* (union) and Sri Chaitanya Mahaprabhu has *vipralamba rasa* (separation).

9. Medieval poets Jayadeva, Vidyapati and Bihari describe the beauty of Radha in erotic terms, and her devotion to Krishna borders on a suggested illicit sexual encounter in their poetry. Jayadeva's *Gitagovinda* is full of erotic exuberance in which young Hari plays like an erotic mood incarnate: 'He hugs one, he kisses another, he caresses another dark beauty./He stares at one's suggestive smiles, he mimics a willful girl . . .' (1977: 77). To Vidyapati, Radha is a 'virgin maid, nectar-faced,/ Of wondrous beauty, for the love god to enjoy' (1999: 423). Bihari is more explicit and audacious of the two:

> Exchanging clothes
> Radha and Krsna
> came to the rendezvous
> for love-making.
> She was on top
> but dressed as a man,

> so they got the thrill
> of novelty
> even while
> seeming
> to make love
> in the normal way
>   ('Love Making', 1990: 119)

10. 'This principle of double coding', as Vijay Mishra explains, 'is an attempt on the part of the Brahmins to ensure that the text's rampant sexuality is re-channelled into a religious fervo[u]r so that desire for sex becomes love of God' (1998: 121–22).

11. Dharamveer Bharati, in his *Kanupriya*, also highlights the aggressive sensual persona of Radha:

    > and this my embrace is merciless
    > and blind, frenzied; and my arms
    > like the coil of a snake-woman
    > become tighter
    > as the blue marks of a bright teeth-line
    > of the snake-woman emerge
    > on your shoulders, arms, lips . . .
    >   ('Kelisakhi', 1996: 51)

12. P. Lal, in his 'Introduction' to *Modern Indian Poetry in English: An Anthology and Credo*, refers to pre-independence Indian English poetry—with particular reference to Aurobindo's *Savitri*—as 'slushy verse' in which words like '"soul", "spiritual", "subtle", "deeps" and "deathless" enjoy a private tea party . . . there is nothing to hang on to. When the eyes are focused to catch a glimpse of so obviously an entrancing image as "soul stuff" or "soul-ground", the picture blurs and slithers off like some theosophical apparition' (1969: vi).

13. Dilip Chitre and Arun Kolatkar translate the Marathi Bhakti poets Tukaram and Jnaneshwar, Ramanujan translates Tamil Sangam poets as well as South Indian Bhakti poets, Jayanta Mahapatra and Niranjan Mohanty translate Oriya Bhakti poets. The non-Hindu poets like Ezekiel, Dom Moraes and Keki Daurwalla, of course did not translate Bhakti poets, but they did write prayer-poetry in which they challenged the dogmatic aspects of their respective religions in much the same direct and even burlesque manner in which Bhakti poets did.

14. P. Lal, besides being a publisher and anthologizer of new Indian English poetry, is also known for his transcreation of classical texts such as *Mahabharata*, *Upanishads*, Sanskrit plays, etc. K. R. Srinivasa Iyengar is the author of the semi-epical *Sitayana*, *Satisaptakam*, *Krishna-geetam*, etc.

15. In Ramanujan's 'The Watchers', the eternally mute deities are denied their divine glory and are debunked as indifferent watchers, 'Unwitting witnesses', 'Mere seer[s] with impotence their supreme virtue' (1995: 137). In Dom Moraes's 'Prophet', the divine is once again portrayed as an ageing deity too

helpless to intervene: 'The known desolate land/Kisses my bare feet/ . . ./ I have aged' (2004: 92).

16. Arun Kolatkar wrote a series of poems in Marathi about Balwant Buwa, a bhajan singer in the *varkari* tradition of Bhakti singers. On being asked as to what interests him about the Bhakti cult, Kolatkar replies, 'The poetry essentially. When I went to Pandharpur, I didn't enter the temple or bribe anyone to help me break the queue. . . .' (quoted in de Souza 1989: 17). Bruce King, a noted critic of Indian English also equates Kolatkar's scepticism with that of Bhakti saints: 'We might see the emotional withdrawal, scepticism and humour [of Kolatkar] as a kind of modern equivalent of the medieval Bhakti saint who could ignore rituals and address his God directly, conversationally, even sceptically' (2001: 170).

17. In an interview to E. V. Ramakrishnan, Chitre says: 'In Bhakthi poetry the very idea of beauty or sensuous apprehensions of life is not excluded at all if you look at their lyrical outpourings. They had an integrated vision. The kind of either/or question the Western culture posed regarding the ethical and aesthetic components of life, does not arise here. I place my own poetry in this context' (1995: 230).

18. Chitre acknowledges the influence of Tukaram on his poetic make-up thus: 'I have been rediscovering at various stages in my life, the significance of Tukaram's view of poetry as a confessional mode which is all inclusive, which is a poet's way of recording his own life and the life around' (quoted in Ramakrishnan 1995: 227–28). In the same interview, he hails Kabir as his favourite poet.

19. Garlic, despite its not-so-friendly odour, attracts the imagination of modern poets. Amarjit Chandan, an expatriate Punjabi poet settled in U.K., discovers in garlic the smell of native familiarity: 'In a far-flung corner of California/ . . ./ *Lasan* was like/A sugar lump on my tongue' ('*Lasan* Garlic', 1993: 11). To Arun Kamal, the onion is the very structure of the struggling rural peasantry:

> Onion is a structure like
> our people around the fire
> like farm-labour taking
> its mid-day meal
> in a group
> sharing roti and salt.
> Onion is a structure of
> fist held tight in anger and resolve . . .
> ('Pyaaz Ek Sarnchana Hai', 2002: 52)

20. 'There is, I believe, a noticeable difference in the attitude of the post 1980s poets. These poets are more comfortable, more at ease with their surroundings, whether they live here or elsewhere. This does not mean that they are insensitive to what is happening around them, but only that they do not agonize that much over their identities. These poets are not over-anxious about trying to ascertain who they are' (Paranjape 2001: 145).

Section 3
Disseminating Dissent

Section 3: Introduction

What could be the genre of postcolonial protest or resistance, particularly when it is derivative and oppositional at the same time? From a pamphlet to a short passionate poem, there could be various genres for the articulation and dissemination of pure non-self-reflexive political protest. But the poetics of postcolonial resistance and collaboration demands a discovery of a new genre—a genre that can inhere the complexities of postcolonial reality. Any genre with conspicuous colonial pedigree should ideally be rejected forthwith for it would pre-empt protest before it is articulated. But strangely enough, postcolonial theorists and practitioners zero in on 'the novel' as the genre of the postcolonial. And this is despite its apparent fore-grounding in the colonial past and its capitalistic credo. The logic advanced in favour of the novel is that 'postcolonial writers have wrested the novel from itself' (Hitchcock 2003: 303). To Rushdie, the novel is already a 'hybrid form' most suitable for new postcolonial imperatives of rupture and displacement.[1]

Instead of positing a general genric implosion/collapse, this singular interest towards the novel, to the exclusion of poetry, is hard to understand. The reservation against poetry stems primarily from the fact that it has an intimidating and unrelenting epic ancestry that allows little room for negotiation with the predicaments of postcolonial situation(s). The fact that poetic imagination has travelled from the so-called cosmic to the comic, from the sublime to the mundane and the quotidian, and from the eternal to the everyday, is often overlooked by the votaries of postcolonial fiction. If 'postcolonial writers have wrested the novel from itself', the postcolonial poets too have gone beyond the epic exaltations. Postcolonial poetry is as much a discourse of negotiated reality as postcolonial fiction is.

Given the ambivalent nature of postcolonial protest, poetry—particularly the non-epic, secular poetry with its play of juxtapositions as its structural requirement—should ideally be the natural genre of such a protest. When Walcott writes with the lancing nib of his pen, 'Happines sparkles on the sea like soda' (1984: 39) to negotiate native historylessness, or Yeats discovers 'terrible beauty' (1957: 392) in 'Easter 1916', or when Faiz writes, 'There are other sorrows in this world/comforts other than love' ('Don't Ask for that Love Again', 1991: 5), none of these postcolonial poets just sloganeer; rather they invoke the inherent 'dialogic/oxymoronic' strengths of poetry. Poetry has the capacity to fuse disparate elements/attitudes/emotions into a whole. If postcolonial fiction claims 'hybridity' as its core principle, double-edgedness is the hallmark of poetic textuality. Each postcolonial poem is ordained to be a mini-dialogue—between the self and the other—unto itself.

Despite the fact that postcolonial societies have produced poets like Tagore, Walcott, Yeats, Neruda, Faiz, Darwish and others, poetry is wishfully dismissed almost as a genre frozen in time. It needs to be stressed here that these poets do not just write poems; they are also hailed as intellectual spokesmen of their respective civilizations in the embattled international arena. Poetry, politics and culture thus go into the making of postcolonial poetic imagination and it is this synthesis which leads to the critical re-discovery of poetry as a genre itself. Postcolonial poetry is as much a continuation of poetry as a genre in general as it is a critique of it. Postcolonial poetry is not an escape from reality; rather it is an intervention into it. And this intervention is not only its responsibility; it is its very *dharma*, its inevitable destiny and duty.

The four chapters in this section bring out the intrinsic relationship between the political and the poetical. The first one dwells on the relation of prison with poetry—a relation not seriously explored yet, despite the fact that many Indian languages have a rich reservoir of prison-poetry. It deals at length with Punjabi prison-poetry, right from the days of the Ghadar movement to the emergency and beyond. The poets studied include famous Congress leaders, such as Sardar Gurmukh Singh Musafir, who later became chief minister of Punjab, Hira Singh Dard, Avtar Sandhu Pash, Sant Ram 'Udasi', Harbhajan Hundal and Santokh Singh Dheer. These poets actually wrote poetry from inside the prison. Incarceration leads to poetic output. Congress leaders who approached prison as *swaraj ashram* wrote poetry that was spiritual in its intent and tone, while the naxalite who approached prison as a structure of state and class oppression wrote poetry that was rank political and ideologized.

The second chapter is devoted to the study of contemporary Indian English poetry in terms of its participation in the political and social processes of the nation. Because of the overt concerns of this poetry with subtleties of prosody, it is denied any political sense. Much against the general critical estimate, the chapter brings out the political consciousness of mainstream Indian English poets such as Nissim Ezekiel, A. K. Ramanujan, Keki Daruwalla and Arun Kolatkar. Beneath the veneer of their poetic sophistication, these poets challenge the structures of oppression through their ironic subversion and double-edged parodic reversals. Even in times of siege, Indian English poets have risen to the demands of time and have taken an intellectual lead in confronting communal politics of the times. The chapter is entitled 'From Participation to Protest: Political Consciousness of Modern Indian English Poetry'.

The penultimate chapter of the book explores the regional nuances of Dalit poetry from the 1970s to 1990s through a comparative analysis of Marathi, Hindi and Punjabi dalit poetry. To begin with, the poetics of counter-aesthetics is varied and heterogeneous, and is suggestive of the multivalent textuality built in the discourse of the dalit as such. Dalit poetry provides an excellent example of the poetry–politics conflation for most of the dalit poets happen to be frontline activists as well. As dalit poetry enters the post-Mandalization phase of Indian politics, it begins to consolidate itself as a pan-Indian poetic discourse in which there is a deliberate attempt to postpone ideological dissensions and regional differences within. Dalit poets turn self-conscious, and instead of expressing their autobiographical experience in the first person pronoun, they begin to speak for the entire community in an ostensibly essentialized way.

The last chapter of the book makes an attempt to trace various sojourns of Indian feminism through its poetry in Indian English, Hindi and Punjabi from pre-1947 to post-9/11. While woman poets of the late 1940s—Sarojini Naidu, Amrita Pritam and Mahadevi Verma—operate within the rubric of patriarchal nationalism, the poets of the 1970s onwards evince varying degrees of radicalism. Not only do they bring into open the gender politics of the domestic (nation) space as they march ahead in time, they dare to speak against overt attempts of re-masculinizing the public sphere through the resurgence reactionary right all over the globe. The phallic and the fascist collaborate to push women back into the insularity of the backyard. The chapter highlights the political awareness of young woman poets of the post-1990s in times of siege.

Note

1. According to Rushdie, the novel 'is part social enquiry, part fantasy, part confessional. It crosses frontiers of knowledge as well as topographical boundaries'. He argues, 'There is a room for all of us in here [in the novel]' (2002: 58).

8

Poetry of Incarceration:
Punjabi Prison Poetry from
Ghadar to Emergency and Beyond

I

From the Kuka movement just after the 1857 struggle for independence to the more recent movement for Khalistan, a series of protest movements have rocked the history of Punjab with such regularity that 'each such movement can be taken as a stepping stone' in the making of a rather chequered Punjabi identity.[1] Most of these movements, people-centric as they were, relied on horizontal affiliations such as 'the traditional organization of kinship and territoriality or on class associations, depending on the level of the consciousness of the people involved' (Guha 1982: 4). Led more often by peasants, (ex-)army men and religious clergy, these movements were against the domination of the elite—colonial as well as nationalist. Given their subalternist nature, these movements tended to be extremely violent and militant, as revolutionaries often resorted to guerrilla warfare, banditry and acts of loot and terrorism. Most of the revolutionaries were either killed by the state in encounters, or arrested and hanged; some languished in jails for years as terrorists; some chose self-exile. Those who followed a 'legalistic and constitutionalist' (ibid.) means of protest, particularly the leaders of the Congress during the freedom struggle, however, were privileged enough to be designated as 'political prisoners'.[2]

Prison as an institution of resistance-containment, state oppression and also as a terrain of nationalist politics, therefore, becomes quite a theatrical site of power-politics in Punjab, both in the colonial and postcolonial periods of Indian history. Hitherto, the investigation of the discourse of prison has remained more or less confined to the study of penal sanctions and the nature of the legal-political processes available to the state and prisoners both. Normally, jail manuals and reports of various committees on jail reforms constitute the primary material for this kind of research. In the construction of the nationalist discourse, however, memoirs, autobiographies, diaries or interviews of political prisoners written from prison often receive primary importance, but creative literature in the form of novels, short stories or poems goes unnoticed for reasons not very difficult to figure out. Most of the writings from prison are by activists and political leaders who prefer writing diaries, memoirs and pamphlets rather than short stories or poems. Only when the poets or writers as such, become political leaders could there be a possibility of creative 'prison' literature. Whether such a literature in itself can constitute a distinct genre or not in the hierarchy of literary genres is debatable.

This chapter focuses on Punjabi prison poetry exclusively available to us in its fragmentary form from the days of the Ghadar movement of 1913–20 to the period of the emergency and after. The accent is on poetry because 'the literature produced, as a result of these protest movements, was mostly in the form of poetry' (Singh 1988: 1). Poetry served both the mundane purpose of passionate sloganeering and intense inner reflection for the poet-prisoner or the prisoner-poet. Given the oral character of Punjabi folk culture, poems as songs had greater reach and penetration among the non-literate masses than propaganda through other mediums and forms. The chapter is divided into four sections that deal with the changing poetics of prison poetry written during four distinct periods/movements of modern Punjab—the Ghadar movement, the national freedom struggle under Congress leadership, the naxalite movement of the 1970s and the Emergency. The chapter in no way intends to survey all that was written from prisons in Punjabi.

II

The Ghadar movement, although it peaked during 1913 to 1920, yet in terms of its origin, it is traced back to the sepoy mutiny of 1857. Most ghadarites went abroad in sheer desperation as the domestic conditions were extremely harsh on account of three dreadful diseases—'famine, plague and poverty'—caused by the exploitative economic policies of the colonizers.[3] Around 1915, just after the beginning of World War I, when some of the ghadarites came back home to launch an armed struggle against the British, they were killed, arrested and hanged to death. According to one source '64 ghadarites were hanged to death, 101 were killed in encounters, 316 underwent life imprisonment' (Kapoor 2001: 90).

Bhagwan Singh, Harman Singh Toondilat, Munsha Singh Dookhi, Sant Visakha Singh and Hari Singh Usman were leading poets of the movements. Most of these poets wrote their poetry anonymously or under pseudonyms to escape the backlash of colonial administration, and also to lend an impersonal character to their poetic output. Harman Singh Toondilat used to write under the pseudonym of either 'Ek Punjabi Singh' or simply 'Punjabi Singh'; and 'Fakir' was the pseudonym of Hari Singh Usman. 'Pritam' and 'Dookhi' or 'Dookhiya' were other two common fictitious names used by Bhagwan Singh and Munsha Singh respectively. Most of the revolutionary poet-prisoners were addressed as 'Baba' ('Babe' in the plural sense) singing the 'baani' (sacred songs of gurus) of patriotism and radical social reforms.[4] The 'secular' poetry thus produced by the protest-poets enjoyed the prestige of holy 'baani' sung by the erstwhile Gurus in the sacred domain. The vulnerability of such a co-option and appropriation of the secular and the political by the religious and the sacred has been a regular feature of Punjab politics.

Out of the available corpus of Ghadar poetry, it is very difficult to ascertain as to how much of it is actually written from prison, how much of it came from abroad, but keeping in view 'the life-details of some of the poets of Ghadar', it can be safely surmised that some partial chunk of it must have been written from prison—which in most cases happens to be the infamous Cellular Jail of Andaman islands.[5] Sant Vishkha Singh, a poet-prisoner of the Ghadar movement, for instance, gives a graphic description, of course, in verse form of the barbarous torture that his fellow prisoner Parmanand underwent in the Cellular Jail, right before his eyes: '[They] started lashing cane-stick, peeling flesh off his body/his beautiful physique soldered, beating him blue to bleed/supervising it Berry asked them to rain lashes nonstop/a stream of blood flowed, . . .' (quoted in Jas 1975: 176). In any case, both abroad and prison happen to be two complementary sites of Ghadar poetry, in the sense that both marked the painful exile from home. It needs to be stressed that the first-generation Sikh diaspora had to undergo 'trying circumstances in the West', and their transition from being 'farmers to daily-wages labourers' in the indifferent West was not a lesser ordeal.[6]

At a time when Punjabi poetry was all set to be overtaken by some vague romantic and mystical outpourings of Bhai Veer Singh and his other contemporaries, the credit of inaugurating political poetry in Punjabi goes to the Ghadar poets. In terms of its ideological thrust

Ghadar poetry is partly fired by Marxism and partly by the militant discourse of Khalsa as preached by Guru Gobind Singh in particular, in ways that are highly complementary. While describing the political unconscious of Ghadar poetry, Kesar Singh Kesar in his introductory remarks observes, 'in its every pore, the character of the militant, tireless, freedom-loving farmer-tribe of Punjab is deep-seated' (1995: 26). Despite being overtly political, Ghadar poetry is never bland or plainly prosaic for it combines fierce nationalism with a high degree of self-criticism. While there is an uncanny understanding of the colonial ways of exploitation, there is an unrelenting criticism of Indians for their being passive or backward looking.[7] A poem entitled 'Baint: Sara Jagat Bhagwan da Jagda Aye', written by a ghadarite reads: 'The whole world, even god knows, you my fellow Indians have fallen into a stupor/by their sweet tongue whites have destroyed you, while merrily with your arrogance you just keep sitting/the enemy challenges you day in and day out, meet him eye to eye/why like shameless beings suffer, where have you lost your sense of pride?' (ibid.: 148). Also, unlike most of the nationalistic discourses, it seeks to project a vision of the future, instead of the usual retrogressive nostalgia for the so-called golden past. The latent thrust of secularism and dalit emancipation in the Ghadar discourse is a marker of its progressive outlook.[8]

In terms of its tone and tenor, three distinct moods—'of anger, excitement, and hope'—emerge in the poetry of Ghadar.[9] Despite its not being aesthetically very sophisticated, Ghadar poetry, whether written from inside the prison or from abroad (exile), cannot be dismissed as mere rhetoric or stage poetry. In terms of its inter-textuality, one can hear echoes of Guru Gobind Singh's poetry, Sufi *kissa* poetry and other folk and classical texts. It employs some of the standard prevalent metres/stanzas in Punjabi tradition which include *baint, korda, barahmasa, doha, kafi, cchand*, etc. No wonder then, collectively Ghadar poetry is considered as the 'epic poetry' of nationalism.

III

For all intents and purposes, Ghadar poetry dwells in the twin domains of diaspora and prison, and therefore, it is not exclusively prison poetry as such. If Ghadar poetry marks the beginning of political poetry in Punjabi literature, poetry written by Congress leaders undergoing imprisonment as political prisoners—Gurmukh Singh Musafir and Hira Singh Dard in particular—herald the arrival of what is termed in Punjabi as 'bandi-kavya' (Singh 1999: 325), a native equivalent of prison poetry in the proper sense of the term.[10] Two collections of Musafir—*Musafirian* and *Toote Khand*—contain poems which are actually written in prison, and the full-time writer as he was, he furnishes us information about the name of the jail from which a particular poem (along with its date) has been written from. At least three poems of Dard, namely 'Adhurian Sadhran', 'Bandiwan Kavi da Ek Geet' and 'Shreenh de Cchavan', as reported by the author himself, have been written from the Shahpur and Miyanwali jails where the poet was interned from 1941 to 1944.[11]

There is a perceptible shift in the prison poetry written by the leaders of the Congress who escaped hard prison punishments due to their status of political prisoners. Musafir's poetry is personal and autobiographical as against the 'collective' or public poetry of the ghadarites. The 'home' in Ghadar poetry is more a trope of nation or *kaum*; in the poetry of Musafir it attains a more vertical dimension as the poet is often reminded of his close family relations left behind. On the death of his father, he writes from Shahpur prison:

> The heritage, as though, is snatched
> how to repay the debt?
> The parapet has crumbled,
> how to rescue my small dwelling?
> One brick of the foundation has fallen off,
> how to support the walls?
> ('Pita Ji di Yaad', in *Musafirian*, 1999: 332)

In the same poem, he expresses the dilemma of a prisoner caught between the pulls of familial past on the one hand and the sordid reality of the solitary present on the other. The image of the father 'unforgettable to the heart/and invisible to eyes' (ibid.: 335) comes to him in its full vivacity in his dreams, only to ditch him on being woken up.

Prison is a potential site of love poetry for it augments the sense of separation. The journey that begins from the lover's street ends in prison with no stopover in between.[12] The poet as prisoner simply lapses into love poetry, which finally culminates, rather dramatically, into a statement for the love of the motherland. At times, Musafir is overwhelmed by the memories of his wife. More than a beloved, she is recognized as the mother of his children:

> Whose heart is a treasure of love
> holding Musafir's household intact,
> I pray for her well being
>> Let the mother of my children live long
>> ('Jindi Rahe Mare Bachiyan de Maan', *Toote Khand*, 1999: 394)

In the same poem, the poet gives credit for his undivided loyalties to the cause of the nation to his wife's sacrifices:

> Sitting here I sing the song of nation
> I play tunes, tension-free
> Be I am out or in he jail
>> Let the mother of my children live long . . . (ibid.: 393)

From a contemporary critical perspective, Musafir can of course be pilloried for spiritualizing his wife as a mother looking after 'the inner' domestic front, as he himself is free to be the hero of the external domain.[13] But given the times in which Musafir was writing, this kind of division of labour was accepted rather uncritically.

Dard also implores his wife to forget and forgive him for his inabilities to fulfil her demands and desires:

> You better stop waiting for me
> enchained as I am amidst the stream of blood.
> Your wait has been washed away in many waves:
> some of it petered out in my imprisonment, some in the field.
> The storm of injustice,
> has thrown me from your gardens
> to the hotbed of prison
> I am helpless
> I am not destined to
> honour in the soothing shades of your gardens of love and beauty
>> ('Adhurian Sadhran', 1944: 86)

Musafir's wife also withholds her 'desires hidden in her bosom' ('Ek Geet', *Toote Khand*, 1999: 339), as her 'dhola' (lover in Sufi poetry) decides to leave her behind for a higher cause. The inner domain is cleverly dovetailed in the external. The simultaneous play of love for the wife and love for the nation is a peculiar feature of prison poetry. What makes this kind of juxtaposition so inevitable in the contest of Punjabi poetry is its heritage of Sufi *kissa* poetry. In the context of lovelorn Sufi narratives as major cultural paradigms of Bhakti, an erasure of love poetry from the purview of nationalist prison poetry is culturally unthinkable.

Ghadar poets, obsessed singularly as they were to the cause of Ghadar, hardly invoke nature as a signifier of freedom and organicity. Instead of religion, or *panth*, in the poetry of Musafir, the springboard of sustained struggle against the Raj happens to be nature in all its macro as well as micro manifestations. Nature's unbound bounties offer a befitting binary to the sense of enclosure that the poet suffers in prison:

> It is evening:
> after a sand storm
> clouds cover the sky,
> the arrows of rain drop pierce through heart.
> Unrest profound
> as the windows of the barrack open
> mind soars skywards
> ('Visri Yaad', *Toote Khand*, 1999: 399)

In another poem, even while the poet-prisoner cherishes the unbridled flight of the migratory birds, he rues his own confinement in the prison cell. The migratory bird, as it keeps soaring in the high skies, takes a hard prick at those who are 'encaged,/imprisoned/ trapped in worldly bondages/and are confined to palaces' ('Tupri Vaas', *Toote Khand*, 1999: 404). Such a shift from religion to nature is quite significant as Punjabi prison poetry of the Gandhi period veers away from the martial or *shakti*-centric Guru Gobind's discourse of Khalsa, towards a more serene and mystical discourse of Bhakti of the earlier gurus, particularly of Guru Nanak.[14]

Often the poet-prisoner is besieged by the mirth and colourfulness of nature. Birds, drops of rain or breeze that occasionally blow across his dark prison cell mark the festivity of freedom outside. This is how the poet-prisoner describes the early morning scene inside the jail:

> Branches, leaves, flowers
> all fresh after the shower
> waiting for the winds
> to dry them up.

> Some flowers have the red eye
> some, yellow, blue or black
> some have the pinkish hue
> while some white like sunshine,
> but none
> without tears
>   ('Vatan Piyar', *Toote Khand*, 1999: 438)

Even as nature unfolds its organic and resplendent charms, it is soon engulfed in the grey sombre shades of the prison.

Instead of the imagery of the ferocious 'lions', the poet-prisoner is rather bemused by the micro-mini insects that intrude into the privacy of his prison cell now and then.[15] The poem on 'ants' written from the Amritsar jail is remarkable for its thematic richness; the industrious ants stand for collective strength and perpetual dynamism:

> Crazy to the core, yet patient.
> Never stop, never hasty either.
> Rivers run ever so seriously,
> for to stop is to die.
> Stagnating waters stink.
> They keep walking, walking
> holding each others hand.
> One comes from this side, other from that,
> never do they collide.
> Just keep moving ahead.
>   ('Kidi', *Toote Khand*, 1999: 395)

From the stifling confinement of the prison cell, not only does the poetic gaze become very responsive and penetrating; any moving object, be it an ant or a straw, also attains an unprecedented signification of freedom and dynamism.

In another poem, a lifeless straw dangling on the turbulent waves of the sea happens to be the rallying point of the poet in his fight against the mighty Raj:

> In whose belly sank
> thousand ships overloaded
> and whose depth to fathom
> divers plunged
> but never came back,
> and hearing its roar from a distance
> even brave men shudder.

> On its bosom, this straw
> marches on arrogantly
> ('Tila', *Toote Khand*, 1999: 409)

It is remarkable that the poet-prisoner while being confined inside his cell is able to imagine the straw-sea dual outside. In prison poetry this kind of extrapolation of imagination is understandable for physical confinement often leads to the expansion of horizons.

The personal sublimates in the national almost with a teleological swiftness. The dark clouds accentuate the longing for the wife, which in turn triggers off a longing for the nation: 'memories of the home/pleadings of the poor nation/merge with the dark clouds/that hang above/overtake the mind' ('Visri Yaad-2', *Toote Khand*, 1999: 413). In another poem, while suffering a mild bout of fever inside the prison, the poet, almost in a flashback, is reminded of the care he used to get from his wife back home: 'My mind/flies off/to the outer world/today some string is making frenetic sounds / those hands come to mind/those which are expert in feeling my pulse/in whose touch there is the flow of amrit/today my chest/bustles with unrest/what good/it is to live for a slave/today my whole nation is helpless/let this fever never go/till my nation is ill/let this pain be continuous' ('Nikka Nikka Bukhar', *Toote Khand*, 1999: 407). The 'sublimation of the imprisoned self' from being an individual to a nationalist, and finally to a spiritualist is in keeping with the elite nationalist style of Congress politics—which under the spell of Tagore, Aurobindo and Gandhi gravitated towards metaphysics and cosmopolitanism.[16] The individual becomes the locus of the national and then the cosmic as 'the imprisoned self divests itself of physical trappings'.[17]

As against the sufferings inflicted by the jail officials, the poet, very much in Gandhian footsteps, would opt for self-suffering. Instead of the graphic description of the brutalities of *kala pani* as recounted by ghadarites, what one encounters in the poetry of Musafir is an urge for self-denial. Outer punishment is underplayed in favour of inner penance. While re-writing a prayer of Tagore, Musafir discovers 'the destination of freedom' in the capacity and 'desire for braving miseries' ('Tagore de Prarthana', *Toote Khand*, 1999: 421–22). Instead of swords and kirpans, tears are the instruments of change. But these tears have their own dialectics of tension:

> These brave young children
> do not cascade down

as sentinels
unleash
arrows from their
stretched bows ('Hanjhu', *Toote Khand*, 1999: 428)

In another poem entitled 'Do Hanjhu', the poet-prisoner extends the imagery of tears as sentinels:

Two sentinels, on both sides of the gate
with arrows many but bows two

On the dire commands of a general
the two have taken position on both sides

One emotion, one matter, one thought
one article, one title but meanings two . . .
                        (*Toote Khand*, 1999: 430)

Instead of armed combat or militant struggle, Musafir believes in the poetics of surrender and self-sacrifice. Therefore, it is the credo of 'tears [that] will/bring spring' ('Vatan Pyar', *Toote Khand*, 1999: 440) in Musafir's world-view. Dard's fellow prisoners also 'shed tears/ as they mourn the tragedy of the nation' ('Shreehn de Cchavan', 1944: 97), but these tears 'keep jolting the entire nation' (ibid.). These are the tears that keep 'nurturing the tree/sitting under the thick shadows' (ibid.: 94) where prisoners assemble and confabulate.

Dard's prison poems strategically deploy bird-imagery to put into contradistinction the plight of the prisoners incarcerated in their dark cells. Birds that perch on the 'tree' bring messages to the prisoners of their dear ones: 'Sitting under the shadow of those trees/ each day of our imprisonment passes by/a bunch of parrots and crows flocks/brings messages of brothers and sisters' ('Shreenh de Cchavan', 1944: 92). In the same poem, the poet-prisoner writes: 'as we watched/free and happy birds soaring in the sky/the pleadings of slaves/swelled in our bosoms/. . .' (ibid.: 93). For Musafir, birds stand for tireless striving:

On the wings of total confidence
in the skies of faith
a tireless flight it takes

Before the dawn break
against the pitch dark backdrop
it welcomes the milky white light of the day

> This faith is a bird
> sitting on the top of self-belief
> it never gets tired, nor bored.
> ('Shardha', *Musafirian,* 1999: 343)

The poet is enamoured of the brave flight of a nest-less sparrow which, perching for a while on the edge of his cell's ventilator, takes flight in the full face of heavy rains thus:

> One little sparrow
> robbed of her nest
> all wet
> comes flying
> settles on the edge of a ventilator
> while the rain outside becomes heavier.
> It arranges her feathers
> flies off
> beyond all thresholds
> the prison-locks remain mute
> and the sentries are stunned into helplessness.
> ('Visri Yaad', *Toote Khnad,* 1999: 400)

In another poem, the metaphor of the bird takes a different turn. The parrot, imprisoned for so long in the cage, has lost all sense of freedom; the cage, ironically, is its free space:

> Bonded for so long
> born slave
> has forgotten how to fly.
> All desire is dead,
> its vision is its cage
> its experience is cage.
> Fears and frights are the bars of its cell
>
> . . .
>
> a veritable prisoner.
> ('Bansi Lal da Tota', *Toote Khand,* 1999: 420)

The parrot is different from the little sparrow in that it fears freedom. The commanding sounds of the masters are its best security.

While most of the prison writings, particularly by the political elite, remain silent on the interactions among prisoners (especially non-political ones) inside the jail, Musafir's writings are an exception. In fact, his collection of short stories entitled *Vakhari Duniya* (1999) contains many stories that deal with the lives of fellow prisoners inside the jail. Some of the poems also speak about the predicaments of prisoner-criminals as such. The poem 'Bhagora' (ibid.: 433–35) is really poignant as it recounts the story of a poor prisoner who escapes from custody a month before his formal release only to be caught again. Why should he do it?

> Not even a speck of grain
> what shall I eat
> if I go back?
> Not even a patch of cloth
> what shall I wear?
> Let me have easy
> food here
> for few more days.
> This escape
> I thought
> would extend my imprisonment
> (*Toote Khand*, 1999: 435).

There are a number of references to the interactions among prisoners. In a poem entitled 'Kaidi Valon Kaidi Nun', the poet-prisoner underlines the necessity of harmony among prisoners of different backgrounds in the jail:

> Dear friend where we live, let us know each other.
> Those who depart, meet again in the flowing waters.
> Across the bars of cell, let us connect the wires of heart.
> Let us get over the differences of here and there.
> (*Toote Khand*, 1999: 396)

More than what Foucault terms as the perpetual gaze of 'panopticon', what really controls the prisoner-poets is the Gandhian principle of 'swaraj'.[18] The prison which is a signifier of exile and penal excesses becomes 'swaraj ashram'—a site of self-suffering, self-purification, and self-discipline—in post-Ghadar prison poetry.[19] Dard would herald jail as university: 'Brothers, life of imprisonment/is one holy book of new realizations/prison today is a university/of ghadars and battles' ('Shreehn de Cchavan', 1944: 98). Both Musafir and Dard repeatedly stress the need of 'flow' in life, and prison, paradoxically enough, is not seen as a deterrent in this flow, rather it emerges as the very condition of it. Dard would approach prison as 'safri dera'

('Bandiwan Kavi da Ek Geet', ibid.: 89)—a halt where co-travellers meet and assemble for a breather.

IV

After independence, the most cataclysmic event in the history of Punjab was the arrival of the Green Revolution. It brought sudden prosperity to the region, but also brought naxalite violence in its wake.[20] The capitalist mode of the agricultural economy reduced the self-cultivating small farmer into an agricultural labourer.[21] Young peasants, partly inspired by Maoist ideology and partly by local traditions and socio-economic conditions, adopted the militant way of taking on the capitalistic state. The naxalite movement flourished in the 1970s and a whole breed of naxalite poets, mostly belonging to the small peasantry, arrived on the horizons of Punjabi poetry, lending it an unprecedented activist edge. The salient feature of this movement was that the poets were its leaders too.[22] Consequently, a comparatively rich reservoir of naxalite prison-poetry is available. In this chapter, however, only the poems of two major naxalite poets— Avtar Singh Sandhu Pash and Sant Ram 'Udasi'—are discussed and analyzed.[23] While Pash was arrested prior to the promulgation of the emergency, 'Udasi' was jailed during the Emergency. The distinction between naxalite prison-poetry and Emergency poetry therefore is very tenuous, for most of the naxalite poets continued to languish in jails during the Emergency as well. However, still, I have included one poet—Harbhajan Hundal—under a separate section which deals with the poetics of Punjabi prison-poetry during the Emergency.

The naxalites perceived the state power in independent India no different from the colonial one for it continued to be governed by the forces of 'feudalism, compradore-bureaucrat capitalism, imperialism and social imperialism' (Mohanty 1986: 253). Consequently, jail is seen as 'an arena of class struggle' (Singh 1998: 225) with the state as the same old jailor. 'Udasi' writes:

> How shameless sons we are
> of you,
> dear nation
> who like rebels, taking shelter in your lap
> kept filing cases against you
> under section 212/216!
> And for these long 29 years we could not get verdict

> as you remained till date
> the same old jailer.
>   ('Bedawa', 1996: 183)

The poem offers a peep into the mindset of a naxalite who quite candidly looks upon himself as a rebel from within, challenging his own nation-state, questioning its capabilities of responses and dispensing justice timely.

Prison, in naxalite poetry, is not a sacred place. Neither Pash nor 'Udasi' mystify prison as the site of self-purification, they take digs at its capacities to contain revolutions or changes from below. The efficacy of prison as an institution of control is questioned by Pash:

> They had the illusion
> To put behind bars
> Rude moment's disembodied existence
> And raise walls on the road's chest,
> So many years has light
> Kept the company of clouds
> None could withhold seasons
> Coming in each other's trail,
> Only roofs have suffered
> The pangs of moments
> Flourishing on arrow's sharp edges.
>   ('Jail', 1999: 38)

Jail does deprive the poet prisoners of mundane day-to-day comforts, yet it cannot, as Pash puts it, 'Draw out breath from life?/And from "We" decant "I"?' ('With Me', ibid.: 40).

In naxalite prison poetry the bird imagery attains a political pitch as birds clamour not for a perch inside the prison but on trees that grow in the localities of the untouchables:

> I envy the freedom of those birds
> Who feel affronted
> Singing on the trees of jail
> And fly far away
> To the taste the
> Fruits of the trees
> Grown in the
> Courtyards of the
> Untouchables
>   ('Emptiness and Envy', ibid.: 185)

The indifference of birds is an indictment of the politics of prison so ardently followed by Congress leaders. In fact, the whole practice of political prisonhood is distrusted and debunked by the naxalite poets for they smacked its definite complicity with establishment. Jail is no occasion for peace songs.

There are no parrots or sparrows to bemuse the poet-prisoner in his cell; instead, vultures with their hooked beaks and sharp talons hover above. Pash writes, 'There is nothing here looking/Like doves of peace hovering around,/Song-bearing tree don't grow/For swings to hand from their branches' ('Let It be So', ibid.: 44). Pash would rather prefer to chase eagles as the very collection of poems that contain his prison poetry is entitled *Ud de Baajan Magar* (*In Pursuit of Flying Eagles*) (1974). It is quite remarkable to note that the imagery of eagles as a signifier of violent anti-hegemonic struggle recurs in Punjabi poetry from the times of Baba Farid (twelfth century) onwards. Baba Farid writes:

> The crane, perched on the river bank enjoys (his hunt)
> But, lo, while enjoying this, he is pounced upon by the hawks Unawares!
>
> Yea, when the hawks of God pounce upon him, all revelry goes
> And that what was never in his mind come to pass
> O, such are the doings of God. (*Sri Guru Granth Sahib* 1984: 1314)

Later, in the seventeenth century, Guru Gobind Singh in a small composition juxtaposes sparrows with eagles: 'Unless I raise one to stand against many/cause sparrows to spurn hawks, I shall not deserve to be called Gobind Singh.'[24] Shiv Kumar Batalvi employs eagle imagery to underline the carnivorous character of his beloved thus: 'O mother! I have chosen eagle as my friend/ . . . /mashed crumbs/he does not take/I have fed him/with the flesh of my heart/ . . .' (Batalvi 1999: 199–200). While in prison, Pash is overtaken by this whole legacy of eagle-imagery.

Journey as a trope of mobility appears quite regularly in naxalite poetry as well, but it is far more risky and death-defying. Pash as a traveller is ready to undertake journey beyond death and destination, but without fetishizing it in quasi-spiritual terms:

> For I am just a brute traveller
> Who has only this to say:
> No word stands for farewell

> Journey is not a tale of pain
> Death is not a stop on the way
> Destination has no meaning at all.
>
>   ('Journey', 1999: 46)

Naxalites refused the status of political prisoners, and in fact they staged many jailbreaks. While in jail, political freedom looks facile. Instead of romanticizing freedom in abstract semi-philosophical terms, the naxalite poets look forward to economic freedom. 'Udasi' writes:

> Tomorrow in the jail itself
> the decision on the difference
> between Santo the sweeper, and Rukhsana of Delhi
> will become clear.
> Tomorrow we shall understand
> the meaning of economic slavery in Freedom . . .
>
>   ('Shugal', 1996: 191)

In the same poem, instead of exalting jail either as 'university' or 'ashram', 'Udasi' looks upon it as a site that induces sickness both mental and physical:

> Tomorrow then shall leave behind
> a whole lot of good impression!
> Many nights of the prisoners
> would pass well in amusement
> chatting about the cheeks, breasts, eyes, and limbs
> of the wives of officers.
> Day after tomorrow
> the joy of being pinched
> would go as usual in the name of lice and bed-bugs.
>
>   (ibid.)

The idiom and tenor of 'Udasi''s poetry is quite noticeably down-right rustic and, therefore, frank and without make-up. As a dalit naxalite, 'Udasi' is far more vitriolic and abusive than Pash or any other naxalite poet.

If in Musafir's poetry a light drizzle is enough to inspire songs of freedom, the naxalite poets would demand no less than a heavy downpour:

> . . . the colourful clouds
> are not dark heavy clouds—

> clouds that can rain with thunder and lightening.
> The colourful clouds
> do not dare wink at the palaces of the enemies
> because they want to kill them
> with paper swords studded with diamonds
> and keep playing with me the game of hide and seek.
>> ('Jadon Varkha Hundi Hai', 1996: 196)

Further, the poet 'Udasi' spells out:

> Dark heavy clouds visit me like a wedding procession
> lightening winks
> and lays bare the faces of golden domes.
> The contours of faces obscured by the sacred scriptures
> emerge clearly
> and I come to know that
> gentlemen of my village are not gatekeepers of the divine
> they are stinking insects surviving on the rites of religion.
>> (ibid.)

The lightening of the cloud affords an opportunity to 'see' the underside of reality. Dark clouds are not romantic messengers of love; rather they are the harbingers of violence and bloodshed.

In protest poetry written from the prison in particular, all festivity is a bane, a luxury of the powerful. If Musafir bemoaned the celebration of Diwali 'Udasi' would smack of some capitalist conspiracy in Dussehra celebrations:[25]

> Come what may
> we shall not let rishis take shelter under Birla Mandir.
> Come what may
> on the pretext of cremating
> the paper effigy of Ravana
> we shall not let you burn
> the newspaper pictures of Bhagat Singh, Banda Bahadur
> and Guru Gobind Singh
>> ('Jail vich Dushira', 1996: 203)

Naxalites do not mind siding with Ravana, for the simple reason that Rama has failed them. This element of the vehement subversion of the holy hierarchies is far more pronounced in naxalite prison-poetry than any other poetry written in Punjabi hitherto.

High morality, which the poet-prisoners of the Gandhian era declaim, is done away with. In moments of possible victory, they do not intend to be sagacious and all-forgiving. Quite cold-bloodedly, 'Udasi' would say:

> Whenever our day of victory would come
> O my brave people
>
> while punishing the class-enemies
> do not show any pity
> just keep reminding yourself
> the atmosphere of interrogation centres
>
> On that day
> we shall be left with nothing to
> offer in the name of
> mercy
> for by that time
> we would have distributed it all.
>   ('Asin Taras Nahin Karna', ibid.: 192)

The naxalite poets, die-hard revolutionaries as they were, never relented. There is no compassion; it is only anger unplugged. Hardships of prison-life engender unyielding bitterness in these highly ideology-driven prisoners. One is reminded of Faiz Ahmad Faiz who, writing from prison, spurns all offers of reproach: 'If your reproaches seemed out of place, it was our fault, surely/ . . . /It's bitterness of life that's on our lips, Faiz/For we were not at all inclined towards acrimony' ('Wasokht', 2002: 247).

V

As mentioned earlier, many poets, particularly the naxalite ones, were detained during the Emergency, and Punjabi prison poetry during the emergency is more or less naxalite prison poetry. In this section, the poetry of Harbhajan Singh Hundal, who was more a moderate protest poet than a naxalite one, is taken up and therefore, his collection *Kale Din* (1978) cannot be discussed along with Pash and 'Udasi'.[26] *Kale Din* contains about thirty-two poems (from fourteen to forty-five) that were written from Kapurthala jail during the poet's detention from September 16, 1976 to January 27, 1977. 'These poems', as the poet writes, 'bear the stamp of the black shadows of high prison walls . . . [and] . . . contain novel experiences which could only be realized from that obscure island which lies behind the prison walls' (1978: 7).

Though working within the stock imagery/tropes of prison poetry which includes birds, trees, flowers, rain, sky, journey, etc., Hundal in his poetry tones down the high rhetoric of naxalite poetry. Once again, we are transported back to the world of encaged nightingales: 'Like fragrance, the song spread out in the skies/the cage-owner, standing at a distance, near the door/was taken aback/as warm waves were oozing out from his eyes' ('Bulbul', ibid.: 72–73). In his poem, 'Barrack Lagla Pipal', the poet-prisoner observes the seasonal arrival of birds, and their sudden disappearance in the autumn: 'Inside the barrack, alone/he watches the colour of the seasons/pondering/as to when shall new pipal leaves shoot/as to when shall new birds would perch over it again/singing their rosy song' (ibid.: 89). If the arrival of the birds is a very common trope in the prison poetry of the Gandhian period, their disappearance is more pronounced in naxalite poetry. Hundal stands at the cross-roads of two legacies and, therefore, is a witness to both the seasonal arrival and departure of birds from the trees planted in the prison precincts.

The freedom of the outer world inspires Hundal to take up the pen, but not the sword which is quite exceptional, keeping in view the martial propensities of the region and religion both:

> This music, this moon, this grey pigeon
> and the fragrance from the fields
> re-connect me back to relations
> snapped with the outer world
> and to capture these wonderful moments
> in rich vibrant images
> my hands stretch out to the pen.
> ('Relationship with Pen', ibid.: 47)

To Hundal, prison is the very space of poetry. Both the existential hardships and emotional ruptures that the poet-prisoner undergoes inside the prison ferment a poetic outburst:

> This poetry is a strange thing:
> when I am at home, it stays away
> but when I am here
> like some spell—it weighs on my nerves
> that aspires to be penned down.

> In fact in every moment of challenge
> it stands by me.
> ('Tapoo de Sair', ibid.: 53)

The difference between Emergency poetry and the preceding naxalite one is that while the former provided some kind of mental stay to the jail-exiled activist, the former created unrest, and inspired armed action.

In fact, in many of his prison poems, Hundal seems to be closer to 'the non-violent' poetry of Musafir and Dard than to his immediate predecessors—the naxalite poets. In one of his ghazals, Hundal strikes a note that is typically Gandhian:

> They had intended to intimidate us.
> Having suffered, we have grown stronger
>
> the wait of your letter boosts our morale.
> Your memories make us richer.
>
> They levelled allegations against us.
> We became more popular among the public
> ('Ghazal', ibid.: 38)

A stay in prison is a way to fame. Prison is not seen as a space for the unwanted immoral criminals; it becomes a kind of 'rough passage' that makes the 'political prisoner' more people-centric. Instead of rupturing relations with people, prison becomes the very instrument of popular politics. It is also a passage to divinity. A journey to jail is more than a pilgrimage: 'No pilgrimage is more sacred than going to jail' ('Prikhiya', ibid.: 48). And imprisonment is a form of penance: 'We have been sent to this island for penance' ('Nazarbund', ibid.: 51).

Paradoxically enough, prison poetry is poetry of flow, of eternal movement within and without. Hundal would advise: 'instead of holding like kids/the flood waters behind the make-shift embankments,/it is necessary to understand/that flowing water can never be stopped,/ and time is not the fiefdom of anyone' ('Asal Gal', ibid.: 66). The river, instead of receding, swells and flows all the more. Earlier, he used to imagine the river as a serpent wading though the mountains and valleys, spreading out in the plains before it finally dies out. But now 'when you have broken away/from all worldly attachments/ you have embarked upon a new journey/the image of dying river/ looks stale . . .' ('Failia Hoya Aapa', ibid.: 62–63). But in Hundal's poetry this flow is not very momentous, nor is it radical, for change of the old with the new is an acknowledged fact of life: 'Those characters who were dominating the stage/we shall have to change their roles/ see the new act is being set/in another time, each one shall say the same' ('Rangmanch', ibid.: 45).

VI

During the post-Emergency period, as police atrocities on farmers, unemployed youth, teachers and dalits continued unabated, many writer-activists found it difficult to act neutral. Though there was neither any ideology-inspired movement like that of naxalism, nor a sustained state oppression in the form of Emergency, these writer-activists, on their individual levels, jumped headlong almost compulsively into local demonstrations by different sections of society. Santokh Singh Dheer, a noted short-story writer, is one such writer-activist. While watching police atrocities on the unarmed teachers demonstrating peacefully at Chandigarh he breaks into shouting 'Shame! Shame!!' and is taken to prison for charges of sedition. From the infamous Burail jail during his short stay of about two months, he writes a collection of poems entitled *Aaun Wala Suraj* (1985). The collection is significant because it was written not as much to defend or to propagate a particular ideology from the potentially propagandist site of prison, as it was to speak for human dignity and freedom in general. Hitherto, most of the prison literature was written for narrow ideological/nationalist ends.

Since Dheer's collection has a broader perspective, his metaphors are therefore rather bold and magnificent. Jail is transformed into the very site of cosmic support for the struggle against oppression. Instead of the poet-prisoner looking outside for respite, it is the outside that comes inside for its own liberation. The sun, sea and the Himalayas pay a visit to meet the poet-prisoner in the jail, and instead of blessing him, they feel blessed. This is how the sun redeems itself:

> Friends! The whole world
> bows before me
> particularly in the morning
> as I ascend the horizon
> Friends! To the contrary
> it is you who

> I have been bowing before
> since ages'
> you—the revolutionaries,
> the ones who have been taking
> this world forward
> since ages.
>> ('Sadhi Jail Val Takda Sooraj', 1985: 13)

The seas also seek to lend their 'thunder', 'rage', 'fire' and 'anger' to the prisoners for their struggle for human freedom. Instead of a site of exclusion, jail becomes a site of inclusion where 'dreams' are nurtured and protected. The sea addresses the prisoners:

> Warriors! You
> are fighting for our dreams
> for mountains
> for oceans
> for green plains
> vast deserts
> Warriors! You are fighting for
> our self-esteem
> our protection.
>> ('Samunder da Suneha', ibid.: 29)

Instead of prisoners invoking the natural powers in moments of siege, it is the natural powers that invoke the prisoners. Since Dheer's prison poems stem from a larger conviction that does not have any immediate political agenda, the poet is able to bring about this enabling reversal of roles. While the sublimation of the poet-prisoner into a divine persona commanding respect from the entire cosmos is patently Gandhian, the anger and contempt which fires his poetic outbursts remains fundamentally naxalite. Gandhian renunciation and naxalite activism supplement each other, as one becomes the necessary condition for the other.

Dheer's collection does not have poetic sophistication in the sense that it swings between bouts of naxalite anger and spiritual strides of an emancipated persona in a manner that is too arbitrary and wishful. Only rarely does Dheer go beyond nature-imagery, whose repetitive use makes the latter poems of the collection too predictable. The poet's over-use of macro-level objects of nature instead of its smaller manifestations only points towards his lack of appreciation for the finer subtleties of life. Instead of reflective poetry, what Dheer offers is enlightened rhetoric—passionate sloganeering coupled with the metaphysics of total liberation.

VII

The last major militant movement that jolted the history of Punjab was the separatist movement of Khalistan in the 1980s. Quite significantly, though this movement lasted for about three to four years, and many terrorists were sentenced to life imprisonment as well, none produced poetry from prison. Of course, a lot of inflammatory literature and songs were written, distributed and sung in the countryside, but nothing literary was produced from inside the prisons. The absence of prison-poetry in a way explains the lack of cultural support and imagination that the Khalistan movement eventually suffered from.

Notes

1. Gurcharan Singh, in his edited book *Babbar-Kav Sangreh* (Punjabi), makes a very pertinent observation: 'From a particular perspective, many twentieth century movements such as ghadar-movement, akali-movement, babbar-akali-movement, national freedom struggle, peasant-movement and naxalite-movement could be seen as distinct phases of history of protest in Punjab' (1988: 1).
2. These nationalists as political prisoners, observes Ujjwal Kumar Singh, 'distanced themselves from ordinary prisoners by invoking their superior position in the social hierarchy' (1998: 19)
3. According to Hira Singh Dard, from 1906 to 1913 around 5,000 farmers went to Canada and the same number went to America (1944: 15). These three factors are identified by 'A Punjabi Singh' in his poem 'Ghadar Karan Noon Jhutt Taiyyar Ho Joyo' ('Get Ready for Ghadar Immediately'). The poem is anthologized in Kesar Singh Kesar's *Ghadar Lahar de Kavita* (1995: 121–22). The work contains Ghadar literature published in various Ghadar journals and papers. The literature was compiled by Kesar Singh Novelist, and was subsequently edited by Kesar Singh Kesar. It is the seminal work on the subject as it anthologizes all the available poetry of the movement. All the quotes of Ghadar poetry used in this chapter have been taken from this book.
4. One of the books of the Ghadarites was even named *Desh Bhagatan de Bani*. It was published by Desh Bhagat Yaadgar Committee, Jallandhar with the efforts of a Ghadar poet and activist Baba Bhagat Singh Bilga and others.
5. In a book entitled *Ghadar Lahar de Kahani: Ghadari Babian de Jubani* there is a self-account of as many as eighteen ghadarites wherein they describe their stories of *kala pani* and stay in other prisons.

'According to official records, in 1916, 263 ghadarites were sentenced to the dreadful "kale pani", out of which only 173 were actually sent there' (Singh 2002: 47).

6. Ghadar poets repeatedly refer to the inhuman working conditions and various kinds of discrimination they had to undergo in the West. Here are some examples: 'We are pushed out from everywhere, there is no support,/ English call us coolie, everyone slights us' (Kesar 1995: 140); 'The entire world calls us coolie, when shall we redeem as sardars' (ibid.: 219).

   Joginder Singh Nehru explains: 'While in abroad, he was compelled to be a labourer so that he could meet the ends he came there looking for. He accepted all kind of jobs—inferior, menial or otherwise. To become a labourer from one who had enjoyed the background of a proud farmer once, was one big psychological blow. The psychology of farmer is that of an owner of land, howsoever small it may be. Therefore this degradation from being a farmer to labourer was indeed unbearable, a pain which he kept to himself' (1998: 25).

7. This is how 'Sewak' laments the 'divide and rule policy' of the British: 'By creating dissensions among us/[they] divided us into many segments/ tearing apart the heart of India, they roasted it on the bars' (Kesar 1995: 295). Another poet, 'Punjabi Singh', complains about the drain of wealth thus: '[They] imposed high *mamla* tax on us, and drained off the wealth to England' (ibid.: 122).

8. One 'Premi Singh of Ghadar' asks all Indians to rise above communal distinctions: 'Let Hindu take the oath of Veda, Sikh of Granth, and Muslim of Koran/throw the thief out of the house/establish your own insignia' (Kesar 1995: 127). Another poet pleads against untouchability: 'We are all brothers born of the same mother, the clever British divided us/O brave sons come together; untouchability has destroyed us all' ('Ek Dookhiya Singh', Kesar 1995: 103).

9. Pyara Singh Bhagal in his essay 'Punjabi ki Upakeshit par Chamatkari Ghadar Kavita' finds three emotions—of *rosh* (anger), *josh* (excitement) and *asha* (hope) —that dominate it (2001: 57–62).

10. Musafir was in and out of jail from 1921 to 1946. 'In June 1921, Hira Singh Dard had to go to jail when he and Sardar Partap Singh refused to give evidence with regard to an article written by Sardool Singh on Nankana Sahib . . . then in December 1922 he was sent to Lahore jail for editing 'Akali' and . . . was sentenced to six months of imprisonment . . . in 1924, he came back from jail . . . in 1942 he was arrested for three years for his participation in Quit India movement' (Sidhu 1982: 18–22).

11. Shreehn is a name of a tree commonly found in Punjab. It is a scriptural tree whose shadows are supposed to becalm the wandering traveller. In the translation, only 'tree' is used as an equivalent of 'shreehn'.

12. Faiz Ahmad Faiz—the celebrated Urdu poet who was jailed from 1951 to 1955, and escaped death sentence—in one of his prison poems would say: 'Faiz, no spot appealed to us anywhere on the way, / When we left the loved one's street, we turned to the gallows' (2002: 249).

13. Partha Chatterjee, explaining the division of domains into inner and outer in the nationalistic discourse during the freedom struggle, mentions that while the former belonged exclusively to the father/husband, the latter was taken to be the insular zone of the mother/wife. If women participated in the outer sphere, they were deemed to be 'coarse, vulgar, loud, quarrelsome, devoid of moral value, sexually promiscuous' (1993: 127).

14. Guru Gobind Singh brings about a distinct turn in Sikhism. He invokes the 'sword' instead of the deities of nature or religion. In his 'Bachitra Natak', the opening lines read: 'invocations to the sword, help me concentrate; help me in completing the granth' (1998: 96). Dr. Jodh Singh, a well-known Sikh scholar, while commenting on the *shakti*-centric discourse of Khalsa explains it in terms of the juxtaposition of the *saastra* (the holy book) and the *sastra* (the weapon). He adds, '[I]t can be said that the steel of humility, good conduct and rocklike composure was supplied by Guru Nanak and other Gurus, of which sword of the Khalsa was made by Guru Gobind Singh' (1999: 226–234).

15. In Ghadar poetry, the Sikhs are repeatedly reminded of their being 'Singhs' which is the native equivalent of lions. In some of the poems the imagery of the jackal-lion is used rather explicitly. For instance, an anonymous poet in *Ghadar Lahar de Kavita* writes: 'Pounce upon them like roaring lions; what lions will get by turning away from battle/You lions, why act as jackals/why should you fear, o ghadarites! . . .' (Kesar 1995: 107).

16. Ranajit Guha describes this collation of the national and the spiritual: 'The history of Indian nationalism is thus written up as a sort of spiritual biography of the Indian elite' (1982: 2).

17. The prison-poetry of Sachchidananda Vatsyayan Ajneya, a famous Hindi poet, also offers clear clues on the cosmic or spiritual longings of the imprisoned self: 'Wholeness I seek, even if am battered/by being dirt, I want to overwhelm the skies of someone' (1986: 18); 'Liberating me from myself, I am looking back at my life with detachment' (ibid.: 50); 'Having crossed the life-ocean, I have reached at a place of rest' (ibid.: 62). All these quotes, translated by myself, have been taken from Ajneya, *Sadanira: Sampoorna Kavitain.* These quotes are from the poems which Ajneya wrote from prison in the early 1930s in his collection *Vishvpriya.*

18. Foucault, in his *Discipline and Punish*, dwells on the concept of panopticon as a centrally located tower from which each cell is 'perfectly individualized and constantly visible' (1985: 200). This structure is used to monitor the conduct of prisoners inside the jail. Foucault, in fact, derives his idea of the panopticon from Bentham who describes the advantage of a panopticon in terms of 'the *apparent omnipresence* of the inspector combined with the facility of his *real presence*' (1995: 45). Gandhi's idea of *swaraj*—'self-rule through self-discipline'—in a way subverted the very idea of institutional surveillance.

19. Gandhi refers to the usage of the phrase by an Assamese leader: 'Babu Tarun Ram Phooken calls his jail "Sawaraj Ashram". Sjt. Phooken is an Assam leader.

I may inform the reader that he is first class shot and a fine sportsman. But he has learnt the secret of suffering' (1996: 245).

20. Vandana Shiva writes about the violent outcome of the Green Revolution: 'Instead of abundance, Punjab has been left with diseased soils, pest-infested crops, water-logged deserts, and indebted and discontented farmers . . . conflicts . . . reflect cultural and social breakdown and tensions between a disillusioned farming community and a centralizing state which controls agricultural policy, finance, credit, inputs and prices of agricultural commodities. . .' (1991: 12).

21. Pritam Singh terms the 'small farmer as the stepson of Green Revolution' (1995: 435).

22. Amarjit Chandan, who himself was a naxalite and a poet-prisoner too for some time, now settled in U.K. dilates upon this feature: 'This movement of Punjab has its own peculiarity, which cannot be found elsewhere in the protest poetry of the world. People used to know more the poets of its movement than its [political] leaders' (1992: 2).

23. Pash's *Ud de Baajan Magar* (1974) contains as many as nine poems that have been written from jail. Sant Ram 'Udasi''s *Jeewani Ate Smuchee Rachna* consists of sixteen poems which the poet has written from January 1, 1975 to August 5, 1976, from jail. All the quotes of his poems included in this chapter have been taken from this source.

24. This is a translation of the well-known couplet—*sava lakh se ek ladaun/ chidiyaon se mien baaj taruon/tabhe Gobind Singh naam kahaun*—attributed to Guru Gobind Singh.

25. Musafir, in his poem, 'Diwali of 1942' ('1942 de Diwali') laments the darkness within: 'Darkness all around/my heart is devoid of light/what is this night of lamps? How to celebrate diwali,/ where even in the day light there is no light/the earthen lamps are lit/my heart sinks all the more' (*Musafarian,* 1999: 329–32).

26. For instance, Dr. Guriqbal Singh, in his book *Naxali Punjabi Kavita: Alochnatmak Adhiyan,* refers to Hundal only in the margins for the simple reason that his poetic output was more or less non-committal. 'Neither did he resort to experimental poetry for its rather impersonal expression of man's unsatiated desires, nor did he make revolutionary sloganeering a part of his poetic experience' (1999: 61–62).

9

From Participation to Protest: Political Consciousness of Modern Indian English Poetry

The deployment of terms such as 'participation', 'protest' and 'politics' in 'the context of modern Indian English poetry' might appear misplaced, if not far-fetched, because even its passionate votaries would hesitate to assign any significant interventionist role to this primarily metro-dominated poetic discourse.[1] Much against this general impression, this chapter ventures to explore the hitherto under-stated political dynamics of the much-maligned 'passive' poetry. Given the complex position of English in India—colonial, yet at the same time a language of the postcolonial urban elite deemed necessary for growth and progress—there can never be room for an unadulterated Fanonian brand of militant postcolonial protest in Indian English poetry; nor would any other stereotypical oppositional paradigms of protest be critically enabling enough to measure its political involvement.[2]

While it is true that Indian English poetry may not have any overt revolutionary agenda to take on the oppressive power structures in any combative and militant way, but it would be naïve to presume that it is a discourse of utter status quoism *sans* any social commitment. The mainstream Indian English poets, right from Nissim Ezekiel to Arun Kolatkar adopt different strategies—as varied as those of critical participation, parodic subversion and subaltern defiance—to come to terms with the post-1947 historical reality of which they are players and participants in a very limited but significant manner. These strategies are discernibly different from those of the overtly ideological *janvadi* Hindi poetry or the militant 'naxalite' Punjabi poetry. The volatility of Indian English poetry might be low, but its political vision is sharp and well-defined. Among the Indian English poets, the political consciousness of as many as four major poets—Ezekiel, Ramanujan, Daruwalla and Kolatkar—is discussed in this chapter to bring forth the distinct dynamics of participation as well as protest in

Indian English poetry as a whole. These poets—different as they are in their tone, temper and style—reveal a range of possibilities within the aesthetics of protest.

I

Immediately after independence, as the post-independence national ruling elite sits down to negotiate its priorities in terms of its policies towards minorities, languages, economic models, etc., Indian English poets, led by Nissim Ezekiel, participate in this process of transition in their own subtle ways. These poets, engaged as they are in the process of nation-building in their own small ways, bring about a much-needed this-worldliness to their poetic expression. As against the intimidating quasi-spiritual concerns of their nationalist poet-predecessors of the stature of Tagore and Aurobindo, they seek to forge a poetic voice which is intimately human and pragmatic.

Nissim Ezekiel's poetry participates very much in the predicaments of post-independence India at every conceivable level. The issue of secularism and of racial identity in multicultural India forms one of the major concerns of Ezekiel's poetry. His racial identity of being a Jew is one very potent site of politics that is played upon quite regularly in a double-edged manner. He makes an issue of his Jewish background, and yet he is critical of it. The exceptional humanist zeal with which he disclaims any special ethnic status or cultural identity on account of his being a Jew has its own deep-seated cultural sub-text. At one level, it could be symptomatic of the poet's anxiety to assimilate into the predominantly Hindu society. In his 'Background Casually' (1989: 179), this insecurity comes forth without any camouflage:

> I went to Roman Catholic school,
> A mugging Jew among the wolves.
> They told me I had killed the Christ,
> That year I won the scripture prize.
> A Muslim sportsman boxed my ears.
>
> I grew in terror of the strong
> But undernourished Hindu lads,
> Their prepositions always wrong,
> Repelled me by passivity. . . .

At another level, it is an indirect assertion of the consciousness of his being a Jew. The poet is acutely aware of his distinct ethnic identity, more so when he is pitted against other ethnic groups or people. He may be 'mugging', but he is a Jew nevertheless.

In an another prayer, the poet's rather combative and arrogant dialogue with the divine not only underlines his cultural compulsions and academic obligations, but more importantly, his co-option in the so-called 'secular-humanism' of the post-1947 ruling elite:

> Do not choose me, O Lord,
> to carry out thy purposes.
> I'm quite worthy, of course,
> but I have my own purposes.
> You have plenty of volunteers
> to choose from, Lord.
> Why pick on me, the selfish one?
>
> O well, if you insist,
> I'll do your will.
> Please try to make it coincide with mine.
> ('The Egoist's Prayers', ibid.: 213)

The poet is not ready to relinquish his special racial status, and at the same time his attitude is that of stark pagan defiance. The posture of humanism can hardly masquerade the strong Jewish urge of being a chosen volunteer of God.

In fact, in his 'Latter-day Psalms' also, the poet undertakes an overtly heathen act of humanizing the divine gospel. Perhaps he is out to prove his being a critical Jew. The 'Concluding Latter-day Psalm' is intensely critical, if not totally dismissive of the holy text:

> All that fuss about faith,
> All those decisions to praise
> God, the repeated appeals,
> Denunciations, laments and hopes,
> The division of men into virtuous
> and wicked!
>
> How boring and pathetic, but
> Also how elemental, how spiritual
> The language, how fiery and human
> In the folly of its feelings! (ibid.: 261)

Only an agnostic with strong foregrounding in the western discourse of secularism can subvert the scriptural texts with so much of intellectual distancing. The playful preference for the secular over the sacred has a fine academic balance and a clever syllogistic frame. But the very use of a sacred Semitic text itself is indication enough of his being a conscious Jew.

Ezekiel takes the position of an atheist to condemn Hitler and the Holocaust—the Jewish nightmare. In the poem 'An Atheist Speaks', the poet targets the divine for being a silent schemer in the naked onslaught of Jews by Hitler:

> He
> made Hitler and Stalin
>
> He
> made the Inquisition.
>
> He
> made the Holocaust. (1989: 287–88)

The poet's atheism is his convenience, and as such it is co-extensive with his secular humanism. The injustices of the divine look more pronounced when it comes to Hitler and the Holocaust. Though being a Bene-Israeli Jew, Ezekiel or his parents never experienced the Holocaust, yet he chooses the metaphor of the Holocaust as the supreme metaphor of God's indifference or injustice. Maybe, through such larger catastrophic anti-Semitic tropes, the poet is seeking some kind of acceptance of his 'low' community among other later Jews who came to India along with British traders in the earliest phase of colonialism. Baghdadi Jews and Cochin Jews considered Bene-Israelis as the 'lowest among the low' (Rao 2000: 10).

'Jewish Wedding in Bombay' is strategically self-critical. It hits hard at orthodox Jews:

> Even the most orthodox, it was said, ate beef because it
> Was cheaper, and some even risked their souls by relishing pork.
> The Sabbath was for betting and swearing and drinking.
>
> (Ezekiel 1989: 235)

Not only does he lampoon Jewish rituals, he even seems to suggest his agnosticism towards Mosaic Law. He is not an easy believer: 'who knows how much belief we had?' (ibid.). But behind the apparently self-caricaturizing stance there is a strong Judiac presence. Why should the secular poet choose the frame of the Jewish wedding only to problematize or lament marriage and the rituals associated with it?

Gieve Patel is right when he observes, 'Judaic presence is strong in the tone of lament in many of the poems' (Ezekiel 1989: 'Introduction', xvii). More than simply the metaphysics of the self, it is the politics of identity that informs Ezekiel's 'Jew-poems'.

Thus, Ezekiel consciously tries to distance himself from his ethnic identity of a Jew through his modernized improvisations of Jewish beliefs and sacred texts. But more important than his rationalizations are his overt statements of his commitment to India. In a number of poems he asserts his loyalty towards India as a nation:

> I cannot leave the island,
> I was born here and belong.
> ('Island', 1989: 182)
>
> x x x x
>
> I have made my commitments now.
> This is one: to stay where I am,
> As others choose to give themselves
> In some remote and backward place.
> My backward place is where I am.
>   ('Background Casually', ibid.: 181)

But this commitment is in no way a traditional emotional response of a heady patriot. It is a calculated and measured response of an urban-educated non-Hindu Indian. The critical acceptance of India befits his predicament, or rather his 'status' of an alien-insider or insider-alienated. R. Raj Rao sums up the cultural predicament of Ezekiel:

> He would advocate Indianness (or Hinduness) in poetry, and self-consciously employ it in his own verse, in an attempt to overcome his cultural and spiritual alienation from mainstream India. It wouldn't be far-fetched to suggest that, on the whole, he would want the world to see him as a Brahmin Jew. (2000: 10)

Ezekiel's humanism, politically speaking, is nothing but a strategy of upward social mobility. In the contemporary context of secular politics, ironically enough, humanism overtakes sanskritization as a trope of this mobility.[3]

In his 'Very Indian Poems in Indian English', Nissim Ezekiel shifts his focus from 'race' to 'language'—another equally potent site of cultural politics. The poems retain the double-edgedness of his 'Jewish poems', as English is projected as the language of subjugation and redemption both; it is alien and intimate at the same time. At one level the poems smack of the poet's colonial arrogance, at another level, they reflect his critical awareness of what English has done to us. In the poem 'Patriot', for instance, the poet caricaturizes the enthusiastic and sentimental Indian native who overstates:

> I am standing for peace and non-violence.
> Why world is fighting fighting,
> Why all people of world
> Are not following Mahatma Gandhi,
> I am simply not understanding. (1989: 237)

If seen from a postcolonial angle, the poet is also perhaps subtly underlining the distortions English has engendered in the Indian character. The verbalization of such an innate and intense a feeling as patriotism in an alien medium, with all the concomitant risks of being linguistically incorrect and even improper, reveals the predicament of the postcolonial Indian native. The attitude towards Gandhi is mischievously ambivalent.

In another 'Very Indian poem', 'The Professor', Ezekiel portrays the typical middle-class hangovers of a retired Indian professor through the dialogic poetics of parody—a parody implicit in the mixed culture that the professor inherits as a result of his colonial past. The image of prosperity—'One is Sales Manager,/One is Bank Manager,/Both have cars'—are images of cultural deprivation too. Life is defined in terms of the settlement of sons, marriages of daughters, grandchildren, 'no diabetes, no blood pressure, no heart attack', etc. This in a way is a counter-discourse to high values of dispossession, disinterestedness and *vairagya* that are normally associated with old age in the canonical Indian thought. The poem is self-deprecating as perhaps Nissim Ezekiel, the professor as poet, caricaturizes his own lot.

In 'Goodbye Party for Miss Pushpa T.S.', English formalism and Indian mannerisms combine to generate a discourse of cultural aberrations that postcolonial Indians are condemned to live with. The helplessness of a colonized native once again becomes the chosen site of poetical politics of the poet. On the occasion of the farewell of a woman colleague, she is addressed as 'our dear sister'—a common Indian honorific. The farewell speech is full of platitudes and overstatements: 'Pushpa Miss is never saying no./Whatever I or anybody is asking/she is always saying yes,/ . . .' (1989: 191). The poet is lampooning Indian sentimentalism as also its anglicization. A genuine sentiment turns grotesque if it is conveyed in an alien medium.

The rationalizing impulse of Ezekiel's poetry springs from a very important dimension of his subjectivity. As a professor, that too of English, Ezekiel knows how to 'negotiate' and strike a balance with a cultural environment that is very alien from his own: 'The wise survive and serve—to play/The fool, to cash in on/The inner and the outer storms' (ibid.: 181). In the following poem, for instance, this propensity to negotiate becomes all too clear:

> The price of wisdom
> is too high,
> but folly is expensive too.
> Strike a bargain with me, Lord
> I'm not a man of ample means. (ibid.: 213)

In poem after poem, one discovers a clever but clear syllogistic frame. There is a crisis of imagery, as the professorial instinct to theorize overtakes the poet in him. Perhaps it is easier for an 'alien outsider' to negotiate with India on the level of abstraction, than on the solid ground of actual living. While commenting on the poetry of Ezekiel, G. N. Devy also observes that it 'has denied itself . . . possibility of greatness by making a sterile intellectuality a kind of poetic value' (1995: 61).

The cultural politics of Ezekiel's poetry needs to be seen against the post-1947 political scenario as well. In postcolonial India, as Partha Chatterjee informs us, 'the dominant elements of [its] self-definition, . . . were drawn from the ideology of the modern liberal-democratic state' (1993: 10). Indian English poetry as a discourse of the ruling urban elite too operates within the frame of the same 'national' ideological imperatives. In its search for alternatives, Indian leadership chose the overtly modernist path of democracy, secularism and non-alignment. Ezekiel's poetic prescriptions—

> Whenever you worship
> the Absolute,
> may you remember
> all its Relatives.
>   ('Blessings', 1989: 281)

> Salvation belongeth unto the
> Lord. It is not through
> One or other Church.
> Thy blessing is upon
> All the people of the earth.
>   ('Latter-Day Psalms', ibid.: 254)

—fit in the agenda of the post-1947 ruling comprador intelligentsia. The pragmatic undercurrent of Ezekiel can be traced back to the Nehruvian oft-repeated argument that Indian metaphysics is alright, but that is not enough to fill the bellies of poor Indians. It is quite significant that the subtle pragmatic undertones that Ezekiel's poetry evinces fall short of Marxism towards which he is gravitated in his youth. Does in some measure the graph of Ezekiel's ideological leanings, from being an M. N. Roy radicalist to a modern humanist, not resemble the graph of Nehru, a staunch socialist-turned-modern humanist?

The Nehruvian brand of politics suited most of the English-educated Indian intellectuals of the post-independence phase. It is very difficult to conclude whether it was the ruling elite which dictated terms to poets or the poets themselves were eager to join the power bandwagon, but a cursory look at Ezekiel's poetic discourse is enough to discover the complicity between the two discourses. This alignment even dropped Gandhi from its discourse. Either Gandhi does not figure at all in Ezekiel's poetry, and if he does indirectly, he is always at the receiving end. For instance, in yet another prayer poem, the Gandhi–Nehru conflict forms the sub-text. The poem quoted here could as well be taken as Nehru's plea to his tough master Gandhi:

> No, Lord,
> not the fruit of action
> is my motive.
> but do you really mind
> half a bite of it?
> It tastes so sweet
> and I'm so hungry.
>   ('The Egoist's Prayers', ibid.: 212)

Perhaps, the idealist Gandhi is being told the need of being practical and worldly-wise by the pragmatic Nehru.

As an assimilationist universal humanist, he invariably underplays or seeks to resolve the inherent ambivalences and ambiguities of his colonized self in favour of 'a plainer view' ('Background Casually', ibid.: 181)—a view which befits his ordinary common self. He seeks 'recognition/of dilemma/and the quickest means of resolving it/ within my limits' ('Transparently', ibid.: 150). Far from being plainer, this is a view deeply entrenched in the politics of survival, which a Bombay-based Jew Indian English poet-cum-professor advances forth as poetry of human balance. Ezekiel's poetry is the poetry of a literate urbanite who is interested neither in vague metaphysics, nor radical Marxism. In the nation's political discourse, this poetry fits in the Nehruvian paradigm of a secular society, mixed economy and a measured distance from bloc-politics.

II

A. K. Ramanujan as a person and a poet presumably shows little interest in politics. In his 'Preface' to *A. K. Ramanujan: Uncollected Poems and Prose*, Kieth Harrison observes:

> 'Raman, as his friends called him, had never seemed to me a deeply political person in the sense that I could very easily have defined his place on the political spectrum; the day-to-day business of political events held little interest for him and he rarely spoke about them' (2001: xi).

In a haiku entitled 'Tarantulas' (1995: 260), the poet reveals his unease with politics: 'Why do tarantulas crawl/through my stomach skin/ when I think of politics?' Tarantulas, large hairy spiders, clearly do not tickle a sense of humour in the poet-persona. They are known for their highly painful bite that sends the victim into a maniac dizzy called tarantism. Even though the poem ends on an interrogative note, the tone of outright disapproval of politics is unmistakable. Apparently, politics is anathema to Ramanujan and therefore, his poetry supposedly should not have any well-defined overt political agenda or programme to support it. But this does not mean that the poet is neutral to political choices or that he accepts the oppression of power structures without evincing any measure of discontent or unrest. If protest is taken as a way of expressing discontent or intellectual disagreement, or even apprehensions, his poetry does offer a counter-perspective—a perspective that definitely unsettles the power structures of society. It could be described as poetry of subdued or inverted anger. The poetry does have a subtle socio-political consciousness, but since it is not high-pitched, it usually goes unnoticed.

Ramanujan, despite being not-so-political, is not happy with poetry being just a discourse of innocuous and harmless aesthetics either. In 'Any Cow's Horn Can Do It' (ibid.: 93–94), the activist urge of the poet comes to the fore as he laments the uselessness of poetry in so many words:

> . . . Poems aren't even words
> enough to rankle, infect
> or make the smallest incisions . . .

The deployment of disease-imagery, in the context of the efficacy of the poet's own poetic pursuits is indeed intriguing and even perverse. But such is the level of the poet's exasperation that he does not mind even if poetry causes some harm, there is the consolation that it (poetry) is at least capable of doing something, albeit negatively. The inefficacy of poetry is pitted against the panic that a cow's horn can cause. A cow's horn tilted at a child in the street can cause quite a flutter, but poems 'cannot flay like eyes or hurt/like a fall on a sidewalk'.

Poetry as a genre proves to be utterly toothless against the charms of petty sensationalism or saucy rumours that float across society as 'real happenings'. For instance:

> . . . a suspicion
> of pregnancy is enough
> to make wife, sister, or girl friend
> walk silent from room to room
> smouldering with no care for burned
> rice, . . . (ibid.: 93)

Frivolous gossip circulates more than the sublime truths of poetry. Women, especially, take a fancy to scandalous stuff. The trajectory of women's fancy is deliberately overstated:

> Any number of things
> can make a woman lie awake
> and watch window-squares crawl out,
> grow oblong and vanish
> all night long with every car
> in the street till morning's small
> shadowless hour (ibid.: 94)

Although, in the poem, the poet seems to hit at the low poetical aptitude of women as a whole, yet at the back of his mind is the larger question of poetry's (in)efficacy in engineering social changes. The interventionist urge to make things happen, therefore, constitutes an important subterranean aspect of Ramanujan's poetic mission. In the morning's 'small shadowless hour', as the quoted lines suggest, nothing slanderous can sustain us. The latent belief of the poet is that in the full glare of sunlight only truths espoused and vindicated by poetry or high literature would stand by us. Modern Indian English, as a whole, despite its measured responses, no longer shies away from political participation as it endeavours to break free from the self-imposed aesthetics of sophistication. To read modern Indian English poetry apolitically would mean denying this poetry a sense of historicity and its share of participation in life on the whole.

Ramanujan, despite his deep Hindu forbearings, does not endorse the metaphysical attitude of disinterestedness towards issues and concerns that threaten human existence. In his poem, 'The Hindoo: The Only Risk' (1995: 90), he takes a dig at middle-class modern Hindus who do not evince any social or activist concern in the face of grave provocation. The attitude of playing safe, 'Not to be caught/ dead at sea, battle, riot, adultery or hate' is detested in no uncertain terms: 'At the bottom of all this bottomless/enterprise to keep simple the heart's given beat,/the only risk is heartlessness' (ibid.). Clearly, 'heartlessness' is not the choice of the participatory poet; a risk-free life is nothing more than a sham, 'a bottomless enterprise', no enterprise at all. Any ideology or religion which prevents an indi-vidual to express 'that itch to take a peek at the dead street-/dog before the scavengers come'—does not constitute Ramanujan's way of life. The poet, at the cost of 'heart's simple given beat', would like to express his anguish and protest at the 'neighbour's striptease or a friend's suicide' (ibid.).

To stay away from the flow of life under the pretext of any so-called superior ideology or transcendental belief is a social sin that Ramanujan, despite his not-so-loud activist proclivities, disapproves forthright. In his 'The Watchers' (ibid.: 137), he takes god and the godly to task for their royal abstinence from the active and challenging domain of the human and the existential. It requires the credo of an activist to dismiss the divine as 'Mere seers', 'Unwitting witnesses, [with] impotence/[as] their supreme virtue'. The poet privileges his pursuit of 'living' with their luxury of 'watching': 'they watch . . . , as I live/over and over'. The act of living is an act of affirmation; it is the necessary condition of activist leanings later on. Ramanujan, through his subtle inversions and rather subdued reversals, may not sound a full-fledged confrontationist, anti-establishment poet, but his desire to participate, intervene, and act in the discourse of life is un-equivocal, it is measure enough of his type of 'sober' activism.

Broadly, Ramanujan's poetry can be divided into two separate domains—'one the outer (*puram*), and other the inner (*akam*)'.[4] This is in keeping with his Tamil heritage. Most of the poems of the poet are poems of the interior landscape—that is, the landscape of his home, relations, self, etc. The rest few belong to the public domain of politics and war. While dealing with the political consciousness of the poet it is the poet's *puram* poetry—the poetry of the out-of-the-house world—that usually comes into focus. These are a set of poems that deal exclusively with the world outside, 'the deserted street blazing with sunshine' ('Returning', 2001: 14). Of course, this does not mean that the so-called private poems of the poet are totally bereft of political consciousness or larger social concerns. Each poem, howsoever private it may sound, constitutes an 'ideologeme'.[5]

The secular domain of power politics is very much a subject of creative reflection in the poetry of Ramanujan. Cannibalism is a mild metaphor of modern polity. The poet re-works upon this metaphor to reveal further the petulant and murky nature of contemporary politics. 'A Chinese fancy-dish/of fish/that rots/till it comes alive [with] . . . worms' ('An Image for Politics', 1995: 46) comes to him as an allegorical trope for the 'rotten' politics in which the bigger worm devours the smaller one:

> Cannibal
> Devouring smaller cannibal
> Giants are left to struggle,
> Entwined,
> Like wrestlers on a cliff

The game of politics is no less a wrestling match, that too at the top of a cliff. The underwater power-politics of one-upmanship comes above the surface to full public glare, on a platform as high as the mountain top. The bloody tussle for power continues till 'at last/only One/omnipotent/maggot/ceasar' emerges as a lone victorious survivor from the mob of worms. 'Maggot ceasar' is Ramanujan's chosen epithet for modern-day despots and also perhaps for the unassailable divine.

The arrogance of the despot is conveyed: 'his fat and lonely body stiff/ and blind with meat,/ his wrings without a wriggle'. It is a caricature of present-day pot-bellied stiff-necked politicians.

It is through 'the anti-establishment intent of parody' that Ramanujan punctures and deflates the totalizing and tyrannical impulse of power politics. Parodying the concept of the 'kitchen cabinet', the poet exposes the mundane and even non-professional character of modern polity:

> Governing the country from a kitchen sink
> she brandishes ladles as the goddess her sword
>
> puts ministers to work like daughters-in-law
> sorting lentils and votes, slicing the gourd
>
> the big white house is hushed when she takes nap
> but caterpillars and mice gnaw holes in the map.
> ('A Ruler', 1995: 252)

The kitchen as the very hub of contemporary Third World politics subverts the much-hyped myth of parliamentary democracy. Sorting lentils and garnering votes are in no way very different exercises, one informs the other. Slicing the gourd is the ultimate execution of power.

On the whole, the poem could be taken as a subtle indirect statement against the dictatorial mode of governance of the late Mrs. Indira Gandhi who treated her cabinet colleagues as her daughters-in-law. The female politician, in the poem, is raised to the level of goddess with a sword in her hand. Mrs. Gandhi, for her bold and daring acts, in the form of a nuclear test at Pokharan and the intervention in Bangaldesh's struggle for freedom, was often hailed by even her arch-rivals as a fierce Durga mounted on a tiger. But the reference to 'the big white house' towards the end suggests that the operation of power structures is not very different in the U.S. as well. The might of the modern dictators is surreptitiously humbled by 'caterpillars and mice [who] gnaw holes in the map' (ibid.). The suggestion is that contemporary caterpillars and mice with all their gnawing skills could well be the rulers of the future.

In fact, many strange and grisly insects crowd Ramanujan's poetic landscape to belittle the power of political as well as theological despots. In 'From Where?', inchworms remind the poet of Hitler and his army: 'green inchworms arching/their backs in "39 from peapod/ to desolate peapod when I" just heard/of the World and Hitler's pack' (ibid.: 271). In 'Lac into Seals: On a Kind of Politics' (ibid.: 50), the poet likens the seals of state to the shapes that insects' excreta leaves behind. In the armpits of trees, the poet discovers 'whole rows of bead-eyed beetles/laying for days their bowel's designs'. And as these beetles 'dream endlessly/of futures' they leave behind 'seals of state/and signatures of brass/on their most casual turd'.

'A Report' (ibid.: 248) is a running commentary on twentieth-century politics, and the very range of references to the so-called world leaders and their polity proves beyond doubt Ramanujan's uncanny perception of the grossly political that is happening around him. All the major international political events of twentieth century, viz., the rise of Nazis in Germany, the Marxist dictatorship in Russia, the colonization of the Third World, the phenomenon of Gandhi, the U.S.–Vietnam War, etc., figure in the poem as images running in quick succession in a peep-show. In the first six–seven lines the travesty of politics is amply displayed:

> Hitler, housepainter who painted Warsaw
> red, rumoured alive in Argentina,
>
> is dead; Stalin defaced; Lenin is a name
> for a telephone museum. Vietnam
>
> is a box office hit. Gandhi and King
> are black and white photographs smiling
>
> away in bidi shops . . .

The lines quoted here reinforce the fact that despite the poet's avowed indifference to politics, he is sensitive and responsible enough to respond to, if not react against, the politics of oppression all around him. Yesterday's icons are playthings today. Bloody wars are filmed for box-office gains. To ensure a memorable posterity, the ruling political elite stoops to absurd limits of naming even telephone exchanges after the names of its leaders. Gandhi, the Mahatama and the King, the Crown of the Empire, in the postcolonial phase of exhaustion and disillusionment are good enough to languish in still photo frames displayed at local *bidi* shops. In Ramanujan's poetry all greatness languishes in dingy places like *bidi* shops.

In 'As Eichman Said, My Brother Said' (ibid.: 250), Ramanujan, through the recollections of Eichman, a German Nazi official who was later on executed for war crimes, reconstructs the operation of the mass killing of Jews in concentration camps:

> as he herded people like himself
> into cattle cars, children like his own
>
> into ovens not unlike the ones
> in your kitchen, only larger, dying men
> making pyramids of tangled hands
> and feet, fingers in another's eye,
> towards the airhole, the chimney
> through which they went up in the smoke.

The way Ramanujan offers us a graphic account of the genocide during the Holocaust, reveals beyond doubt his strong sense of disapproval of the acts of ethnic cleansing that are frequently pursued in the name of nationalist politics. In 'Surviving' (2001: 32), another poem exclusively on Nazi atrocities, each bout of ethnic purgation in the camps is compared with the periodic menstrual flow of blood and mucosal tissue from the uterus: 'In Auschwitz time stopped/ like menstrual cycles'. The poet brings out poignant images of the absurdities that the fear of imminent death or surviving it, had engendered in the inmates of concentration camps in Nazi Germany: 'One man lived for a bowl/of bean soup with a fish head/looking at him almost with affection.'

The images of violence, bloodshed and atrocities from all across the globe 'terrorize' the poet, making him vulnerable even to slightest knock at the door past midnight. The dreaded images of 'Wounded museums/of Hiroshima' ('Fear', 1995: 132–33) or 'that well known child/in napalm flames/with X-ray bones' instill insecurity or fearpsychosis to the extent that 'small fears' such as 'a certain knock/on the backdoor/a minute/after midnight' are enough to unsettle him. In 'Bosnia' (ibid.: 247), only the atrocities that begin with B—'Bosnia/ Biafra, Bangladesh'—are alphabetized to underline the essentially violent and traumatized world that the poet finds himself in. The violent ironies of postcolonial civil strife are well arrested in the following image of Bosnian mothers:

> . . . , or Bosnia mothers
>
> who lift their babies to strangers
> squabbling for a foothold in lorries fleeting
> to the borders where only death waits
>
> gun and milk in hand, . . .

The irony of mothers handing over their babies to strangers and fleeing from one place of insecurity to sure death at another brings to the fore the cruel absurdity of internecine ethnic battles. The political participation of the poet as a citizen of civil society is unmistakable. It goes on to prove that politics in the case of Ramanujan is not an excuse for propaganda, it is very much fore-grounded in the civic-humanist perspective, espoused so fiercely by Hannah Arendt.[6]

The colonized past is too difficult to be erased from memory; it comes back in processed forms, belying any hope of emancipation and freedom. Ramanujan, in his oft-anthologized poem, 'Small-Scale Reflections on a Great House', unfolds the perpetuity of colonial practices:

> And also, anything that goes out
> will come back, processed and often
> with long bills attached,
>
> like the hopped bales of cotton
> shipped off to invisible Manchesters
> and brought back milled and folded
>
> for a price (1995: 97)

The 'Great House' as nation receives its own things at a higher price provided they carry a colonial tag. The ruling elite flaunts its liking for fine and costly Manchester cotton, little realizing that it is made up of the raw material produced in its own backyard. The drain of wealth involved in such a deal is conveniently overlooked by the comprador elite.

The politics of communalism/secularism is one such dimension of the volatile Indian subcontinent that no creative writer can afford to overlook. In 'Time and Time Again' (1995: 64), Ramanujan takes a dig at 'the perennial feuds and seasonal alliances' between different religious communities forged for the sake of electoral advantages. The relationship between communities is extremely vulnerable to rumours and propaganda. 'A change of wind,/a change of mind or a siren/ between the pieces of a backstreet quarrel' can flare up communal divide. In 'Any Cow's Horn Can Do It' (ibid.: 93–94), the death of a cousin is no ordinary event, for it takes place in 'the walled red-fort city'—an area normally believed to be vulnerable to communal violence.

Ramanujan understands the psychology of the extremists. They dive headlong into a project, forsaking comforts. 'They have only themselves/for bricks, knees for hinges; heads/for the plinths of their rain- /soaked Corinths' ('Army Ants', ibid.: 70). There is an unmistakable streak of appreciation and approval of the ways in which the extremists dedicate themselves headlong into a mission. But very significantly in Ramanujan's poetry, the small is insurrectionary; only ants have the potential to be *fidayeen.*

Despite a lack of class-consciousness, Ramanujan is intensely aware of the economic disparities in India and the entire Third World. Poverty as a theme features very regularly in his poetry. During the night, the poet is haunted by the images of poverty: 'The rummaging poor/in the garbage alley/even in distant Salvador/come close' ('Suddenly', 2001: 31). The poet realizes the uselessness of hoarding money in banks: 'money festers in the bank,/a sore dipped in a septic tank'. Poverty belies the notion of a golden past. It takes the sheen away: 'A poor man's history will brown the gold/of day as mere air browns a cut apple' ('If Eyes Can See', 1995: 264). Both 'gold' and 'apple' stand for the promise of pleasure and wealth.

The helplessness of a beggar in the face of pilgrims passing him by without dropping a coin in his empty 'soup-can' forms the theme of Ramanujan's poem significantly entitled 'Poverty' (ibid.: 253). Poverty in its familiar form no longer catches the attention. Therefore, very succinctly, the poet observes: 'Poverty is a stranger now.' In order to evoke a sympathetic response from passers by, the beggar would inflict pain on his dog:

> After watching pilgrims
> pass him by, poverty blinds
> his eyes so his status as a beggar
> rises. He breaks the dog's
> front legs to raise the pitch
>
> of pity . . .

The passers by are not ordinary people, they are pilgrims—supposed to be the repository of piety and selflessness. They, ironically enough, do not part with a simple coin to help the poor beggar. The indifference of the rich makes the poor all the more wretched and selfish.

'To change the colours/of poverty' ('A Poor Man's Riches-1', 1995: 141), Third World labour seeks to migrate to the West. Acquiring a passport and a visa is their lifetime ambition, or what Ramanujan would like to term as 'the poor man's riches'. The absurdity of the whole exercise is graphically reported:

> for the hundred muscles you move
> to stand perfectly still; in offices
> of immigration
>
> for coloured and discoloured aliens, brown
> eyes, father's name, five moles
> classified
>
> in each oblong of visa and passport.

Despite the humiliation that the poor migrating aliens suffer on account of their brown skin colour, they scramble for passports and visas. Ironically, they lend 'under the sweating boiler pipes' as cheap labour. In a sequel poem entitled 'A Poor Man's Riches 2' (ibid.: 143), Ramanujan, with his characteristic wry humour, sums up what ultimately constitutes happiness or 'riches' for these poor migrants: 'committing grand/larceny under the boiler pipes'. 'Poverty' as a condition of economic impoverishment, thus, is a recurrent theme in the poetry of Ramanujan. Nowhere does the poet spiritualize poverty as a necessary attribute of abstinence from worldly desires.

Thus, Ramanujan's poetry carefully avoids high-pitched activism in favour of subdued but intelligent response to the complex post-colonial situation of which he is a part and parcel. He is not a status quoist or an easy assimilationist who treads the non-productive middle-path of least disturbance. A famous Hindi poet, Sudama Pandey Dhoomil, himself very belligerent, in his oft-quoted poem 'Mochiram', while underlining the importance of slogan shouting in any revolutionary movement, also mentions the subtle role that intelligent silence can play in engendering change:

> In the shaping of future
> a scream of vehement 'no'
> and
> an intelligent silence
> both play roles
> of similar nature

in their distinct ways.
(Dhoomil 1980: 41)

Ramanujan is a poet of subtle, subversive and cunning silences. He may not create stirs of revolutionary magnitudes, but he is definitely a poet of change. His inversions are too unfriendly and antagonizing to be dismissed as mere 'cosmetic dissenting'.[7]

III

As compared to the two poets discussed in the previous sections, Keki Daruwalla tends to be more open, forthright and courageous when it comes to the articulation of social protest for reasons not so difficult to explore.[8] As the poet himself puts it in his poem, 'The Poem', written in protest against Stalinist Russia, poetry as a whole, comes of age to take on an activist tenor:

> It has slept that long, this
> embryo, for half an eternity,
> and suddenly it can wait no longer,
> Now it is outward bound,
> precipitous in its longing,
> looking for a soul, a body
> through which to find utterance.

The embryonic phase of poetry is over, and now it is all set for its outward journey into the domain of public life. The next lines of the poem elaborate on Daruwalla's idea of poetry's outward 'utterance':

> There are blood poems that take you to the knife,
> and death poems that give you
> a vulture's eye-view of what the vulture sees;
> and poems that marks themselves out
> for a particular locale;
> grey wall behind you and guns in front.
>
> Such poems descend perilously
> on the imperilled (2006: 306)

The sudden shift in the locale of poetry and its encounter with violence engenders the unprecedented drive to Indian English poetry. It comes perilously close to death by violence. The gap between reflection and action, utterance and event, victim and poet closes down. The poetry no longer remains an evasive act of saturnine brooding over the quagmire of existential life; rather there is restlessness and agitation to confront the political violence.

Both Ezekiel and Ramanujan as professors in the academia do not have as much exposure to the outer politics of knives and guns as Daruwalla, being a police officer (now retired), has. 'The experience he has acquired in a long professional career as a senior police officer, reinforced by a robust temperament, gives his poems a wide access both to the turbulence, and to the stiller impulse that is life of India in the metropolis, the provinces and the hinterland' (Patke 2006: 260). The poet himself explains his credo thus:

> There is little that is urbane or sophisticated about my poetry. I avoid a well-groomed appearance and strive for a sort of earthy poetry . . . I tend to make my verse as condensed and harsh as possible. . . . Significant incidents I turn into what I call 'incident poems' . . . (quoted in ibid.: 261)

The incident then leads to poetic outburst, a mental action, if not a call for action or direct and immediate intervention as such. Unlike his other fellow academician-poets, Daruwalla does not derive poetic strength from close-door readings or classroom verbal jugglery, but from live human situations being staged and enacted in the outer field perennially. Curfew, riot, genocide and incidents pertaining to violence, death, terror and carnage are transmuted into poetry not for reflection, or for mere representation, but for urgent human intervention. Each poem is part a succinct reportage, part a critical observation and part an urgent call for action.

In his very first collection, *Under Orion*, Daruwalla takes the reader straight into a riot-torn city, into its barren streets seething with fear. The graphic description is no ordinary journalese, it is a call for the restoration of the ordinary human self:

> Blood and fog
> are over half the town
> and curfew stamps across the empty street.
>
> A thinning drizzle
> has smeared the walls,
> giving moss and fungus a membrane of bile . . .
> ('Curfew in a Riot-torn City', 2006: 41)

More nightmarish images of 'carting headless bodies in a burning van' (ibid.: 42) begin to flow as 'They [rioters] get down/one pins the rickshaw-puller's arms behind him,/the other takes brick/and excavates his brain' (ibid.: 43). The violence is endless as it spirals out, the poet as police officer wonders: 'What the hell is it, you wonder;/curfew or contagion?' (ibid.). The poet complements as well as contradicts the policeman in him.

Curfew is a metaphor of violence locked in us. The poet understands the limitations of curfew-controlled violence:

> Plug all the cracks,
> Fear, love and hate must crumple where they are.
> Nerves exposed upon the tarmac must be hacked.
>
> Between the outrage without and the pain
> within there should be no discourse. Passions must be
> held in the disordered geometry of lanes
> ('Curfew 2', ibid.: 137)

In lines such as these, the vocational and the a-vocational self of the poet argue with each other and thus retain the necessary poetic tension. The terse commands only suggest the impossibility of their being ever met.

The incidents of communal violence invariably propel Daruwalla into poetry for a response to such situations entails the larger question of responsibility of the intelligentsia to pressing social issues. From the partition to the recent Gujarat riots, nothing escapes the uncanny poetical/political attention of the poet. Being himself a victim of the partition trauma, the poet recalls the fate of his brothers:

> They went through hell, that is, Punjab, Sindh, Rajputana:
> showing sacred threads each time to prove a different case;
> not Hindu first, not Muslim later. One took shelter
> in a brothel—lucky guy I wish I were in his place!
> ('Childhood Poem', ibid.: 254)

The brothel is probably Daruwalla's 'Toba Tek Singh', a no-man's land.[9] The identity of being a Parsi makes the poet doubly insecure as well as safe in the crossfire of the two major subcontinental communities of Hindus and Muslims.

In 'Partition Ghazal', Daruwalla looks at partition as a continuous, perennially recurring political project that keeps revisiting the subcontinent regularly. The sudden eruption of violence at the stroke of independence baffles the poet: 'Suddenly broke rank and fled, we don't know where./How could freedom's flame spark off such a blast?' (ibid.: 278). The poet caricaturizes the political leadership for its helplessness: 'Gandhi's egg-shell head, round as a shrunken sun,/ Has it set for ever into a black-hole past?'; Jinnah too is lampooned: 'His classic suit replaced by bone-hugging achakans,/Which made him look tall, though he was shrivelling fast'. The protest of the poet takes a tone of deliberate and intended sarcasm, which is not very difficult to decipher. The division of the subcontinent first into two parts and then later on into three causes apprehensions of its future splintering: 'And let's pray friends, our ship of state, some day,/Are not sold as scrap metal in American yards.' The demolition of the Babri mosque in Ayodhya brings back memories of the partition:

> Then brick by brick, three mossy domes went down—
> The world got a glimpse, of *kar sevaks* power.
>
> Across the Wagah, a hundred temples broke,
> Icon noses slashed, stone goddesses deflowered. (ibid.: 278)

Daruwalla bemoans the uncanny capacity of the divisive past to re-stage itself back into the present without respite. The poetic laser penetrates the political miasma often generated by religious national-ism, and is thus able to see through the grammar of divisive politics.

The post-Godhara communal riots of 2000 in Gujarat once again bring into focus the poet's apparent disapproval of communal politics in terms which are rather unequivocal for poetry, more so for sophi-sticated Indian English poetry:

> Gujarat is not just the corruption of an absolute,
> It has manufactured its own corrupt absolutes:
>
> 'If night fell on Godhara, we are within our rights
> to unload night on innocence elsewhere'
> ('Gujarat 2002', ibid.: 24–25)

The poem, written in times of communal siege, literally takes on the state-backed rightists. In Daruwalla's poetic credo, the indirections never blur or tone down the message; rather they accentuate them. Indirection becomes a strategy of augmentation. The political never eclipses the poetical; rather both sustain each other. Poetry unsettles the communal absolutes.

If in Ezekiel's poetry, the study is the site of happening, in Daruwalla's it is life in the streets and along the ghats and in the ravines that matters most. Not only is Daruwalla a poet of incidents, he is equally a poet of outer landscapes. But never does he allow his landscapes to be non-participatory, still, passive and frozen sites/ sights marked by human absence. His landscapes are animate sites of politics and power-play. From curfew-clamped towns, the poet takes the Indian English reader through the hitherto uncharted terrain of the dreaded Chambal valley known to be a sanctuary of bandits and brigands. Ezekiel does venture into 'deserted lanes and where the rivers flow/ in silence near the source, or by the shore' ('Poet, Lover, Birdwatcher', 1989: 135), but it is Daruwalla who treads into the risky zones:

> In this fissured valley everything cracks;
> The heart through minor skin-burns, the skull
> When the sun tramps on it long enough
> And friendships crack at the tug of a cross-pull.
> ('Monologue in the Chambal Valley', 2006: 49)

But the poet is not a mere reporter, as he deciphers with his poetical prowess the strange tensions of the valley. The informer outsmarts the bandit in the game of power; the bandit admits: 'you're better bandit/ than I: your blood is colder/you have more of a instinct, more of guts' (ibid.: 49). As the poetic eye zooms in, it brings out the paradoxes of banditry: 'The desire to kill and the fear of being killed/are aspects of the same passion' (ibid.: 50). There is a reversal in the definitions as to who is a better bandit; the loud and strident bandit or the sly informer. According to the poet, both are gainers in the game of power:

> They pay you your percentages, I am told,
> Cattle-thieves and brothel-owners
> And rice-smugglers, lest you have them caught.
> Yes, we both have made our way up
> I as bandit, you as informer. (ibid.: 50)

Chambal valley thus emerges as a metaphor of a vicious power-game that is played in the macro-world outside. The so-called corridors of power are modern sophisticated tropes of the Chambal ravines.

In Daruwalla's dynamic vision, the ghat becomes the 'amphitheatre [that] unfolds like a nocturnal flower in a dream' ('Boat-ride Along the

Ganga', ibid.: 97). While taking a boat ride along the Ganga ghats, the poet encounters strange contradictions of life that demystify, if not totally puncture, Ganga's paradisiacal holiness:

> The concept of the goddess baffles you—
> Ganga as mother, daughter, bride.
> What plane of destiny have I arrived at
> where corpse-fires and cooking fires
> burn side by side? (ibid.: 98)

The open-endedness of the poetic response unsettles the granted purity of the space. The politics of faith is undone with the candour of a mischievous Bhakti poet in another poem, towards the end of which the poet poses an almost similar question that borders on blasphemy: 'Why, installing a mistress/is like installing a deity in the house!' ('Crossing of Rivers', ibid.: 114). The pithy poetic observation is like an arrow that the poet unleashes on power-structures within the rarefied discourse of religion and outside.

Daruwalla's poetry, outwardly as it grows, does not shy away from taking a definite stance on tricky international political events ranging from Cold War politics to global terrorism. On the West Asian crisis, the poet identifies more with the displaced Jews than with the incarcerated Arabs; in a rare sermonizing tone the poet pleads:

> Let's have less of blood,
> both in poetry and on the ground.
> Let peace descend on you and your neighbouring people.
> They too have had a two-thousand-year-old exile.
> I pray that they never drive your children into the desert
> and may your children drive them into the sea
> ('To a Palestinian Poet', ibid.: 23)

The poet also goes on to establish similarity between a 'Yahudi' and a 'Parsi' (the poet himself): 'I can understand what it is to be a Yahudi./ We have affinities—The same long nose,/ a skull-cap vaguely similar, velvet-black; . . .' ('Yahudi', ibid.). The experience of diaspora that Jews have undergone for centuries evokes sympathy in the poet:

> But to be a Yahudi was to be terminally ill,
> scraped into ghettoes and out of ghettoes at will
> driven from Portugal
> slaughtered in Spain
> burnt in city square or ghetto lane . . . (ibid.: 24)

The images of the mass butchering of the Jews in concentration camps during the peak of Nazism keep haunting the poet.

As a poet Daruwalla explores, and even rehabilitates, absences more than presences, but in the context of social exclusions only. In his poem 'History', the poet questions the elitist/nationalist constructions perpetuated in the name of authentic history:

> History always came from the north.
> It generally had an aquiline nose
> And browner hair
> And a lighter tone of a skin.
> I have forgotten the colour of its eyes.
> History always came on the horseback
> Clad in britches, stinking of unwashed bodies, holding
> Stronger-thewed bows
> And spark and power and matchlock. (ibid.: 239)

The violent ways with which the so-called superior race of the fair-skinned Aryans subjugated the ordinary dark-skinned people tend to occupy the centre stage in nationalist histories. With a subalternist zeal, the poet refers to a series of small events—such as that of 'the drummer boy who fought with the landlord/and ran away to become a bandit' (ibid.: 241), of 'the pretty village girl who eloped/and was found in a city brothel' (ibid.)—that often go unnoticed in larger official historical narratives. Quite succinctly he concludes: 'This too was history/though no one ever wrote it' (ibid.).

It is difficult to surmise whether poetry precedes theory or theory follows poetry, or they occur concurrently. But in some of the poems, Daruwalla becomes a precursor to latter-day theoretical insights pertaining to the politics of culture. Much before Said's sensational *Orientalism*, Daruwalla writes a poem back in 1964 to fellow writers of Europe in which he lampoons their tendency to de-humanize the orient. The cultural politics of reducing the Third World into either an exotica or a veritable hell is brought forth without much poetic camouflage:

> Would you care to photograph
> those urchins lost in their laughter?
> . . . the space-clad sadhu
> the lunatic in hessian
> or the beggar with the running sore.
> It sure feels good, Sir

> discussing pus-pockets
> with disinfected pen
> on sterilized paper.
>   ('To Writers Abroad', ibid. 90)

The excessive sense of hygiene of the western writers, bordering on contempt, indifference and arrogance is juxtaposed with the over-played poverty, disease and pestilence of the so-condemned tribal orient.

IV

The stinking subaltern takes over the poetic landscape in Arun Kolatkar's later poetry. In his *Kala Ghoda Poems*, the Bombay poet, in his familiar burlesque style, sings sermons of shit, garbage and rubbish that characterize the underside of the big metropolis. Poetry no longer remains an act of aesthetic evasion; it becomes an exercise of exposure and resistance. The obscured, the obliterated, and the oppressed India, hitherto presumed to be unfit for poetry, suddenly appears to be the very hub of life-from-below bubbling with a poetic energy that the poet taps with a rare degree of involvement. The entire tenor of Indian English poetry undergoes a radical shift, as its idiom turns bold, brusque and belligerent. A new aesthetics is invented in the process—aesthetics of the ugly and the uncouth. The poetry bristles with the potential of activist intervention for it comes out in the open, at the very crossroads of ordinary life, on the pavements, without camouflaging its filth and grime.

The celebration of the excremental is overwhelmingly obsessive; the ironies, if any, are kept in suspended animation. Rubbish 'ovulates', releases 'scent', and 'copulates with the winner' ('A Note on the Reproductive Cycle of Rubbish', 2004a: 35)—one who makes the highest bid for its/her recycling. The garbage is not without its intoxicating essence:

> dry leaves and melon rinds,
> breadcrumbs and condoms,
> chicken bones and potato peels
>
> start giving of their essence,
> exude the wine
> of worthlessness, express

> an attar of thankfulness
> that floods . . .
>> ('Meera', ibid.: 33)

There is not an iota of repulsion or disgust; rather there is a carnival-esque buoyancy in Kolatkar's attitude towards the rubbish. Such exuberance is missing even in the most passionate of dalit poetic descriptions.

Even as the poet draws the vignette of a female street urchin running 'her fairy fingers' through the hair of her 'lousy lover', 'producing arpeggios of lice/and harmonics of nits', there is not a hint of revulsion in the poetic description. In the hands of the beloved, the lover's head is a harp, which she plays with her swift fingers. The lover on the other hand has his own moments of dream and fantasy—romantic as well as dreadful:

> as bangles softly tinkle over him,
> he drifts off and dreams
> that he's holed up in a mossy cave
>
> behind a story-telling waterfall
> booby-trapped with rainbows,
> and hear the distant bark of police dogs.
>> ('Lice', ibid.: 58)

Kolatkar, in such passages, no longer remains a voyeuristic gazer for the magical fantasy his characters break into suggests the involvement of the poet in the characters.

Kolatkar's poetry is the poetry of the pavement; its characters/situations/metaphors are therefore not very sophisticated; rather they are 'uncivilized' as much as they are un-covered and un-mannered. The poetry gathers activist edge as it dares to represent the subalterns of the street without those condescending elitist hangovers that are often associated with Indian English poetry in general. The caricature of the street 'baby-bather-in-chief' is more intimate than mere lurid:

> The one-eyed ogress
> of Rope Walk Lane
> (one breast removed,
>
> hysterectomised,
> a crown of close-cropped
> in a scarecrow sari)

> has always been a kind
> of an auxiliary mother,
> semi-official nanny . . .
>> ('The Ogress', ibid.: 39)

'The dirtier the better' and 'the naughtier the better' (ibid.: 40)—are the twin underlying principles of Kolatkar's poetics. Defecation in the open is an act of public defiance in the face of the growing menace of skyscrapers, 'the honking world' around:

> He points his little
> water cannon
> at the world in general
>
> and (Right!
> Piss on it, boy)
> shoots a perfect arc of piss,
>> ('The Ogress', ibid.: 44)

In Kolatkar's topsy-turvy world, the piss is 'lusty/and luminous/in the morning sun' (ibid.: 40). The rubbish glitters with hope.

The agility, the swiftness and the precision of a teenaged female pavement drug-peddler playing with knucklebones invites the eclectic poet's admiration. The low-caste girl offers a range of images that are too overwhelming to invite facile moral indictment. Her legs are a 'matched pair of clasp-knives/the left one folded at the knee/and the right one that, blade out, shows its steel' ('Knucklebones', ibid.: 67). Not only does the body itself become a sharp-edged weapon; its precise posture sets the clock for the bourgeoisie Bombay as well: 'Lawyers, bankers, painters, shop assistants—/everyone passing by—can set his watch/according to your [her] legs (it's ten past ten)' (ibid.: 67). The space within her wide-angled legs becomes 'a playing field', a whole expanse of universe itself where the knucklebones fall into starry patterns: 'Every time you throw the seven pebbles,/ a new constellation is formed' (ibid.: 68). Even the formation of the ominous Little Bear does not terrorize her for, as the poet guesses, she is a 'born bear-slayer' (ibid.: 68). It is through a series of transformations that Kolatkar induces activist energy into his subalterns as well as into his poetry.

The subalterns of the sideways are Kolatkar's everyday heroes for they smile in the face of adversity. The poet's smiling (and sometimes giggling) Buddha is not the suave Gandhara Buddha beaming with a mystic smile, but a 'turnip-headed woman's body' who 'wisely goes about/wrapped in what looks suspiciously like a bedsheet/and a baggy choli' ('Breakfast Time at Kala Ghoda', ibid.: 98). The discourse of high spirituality is thus turned upside down. The shoeshine boy 'fancies himself/as the funkiest kid on the block' who 'hasn't lost a minute either/to start flirting with the girls' (ibid.: 100). The poet discovers fullness of life among pavement dwellers. As 'the barefoot queen of the crossroads' dries her wet hair in the sun: 'She scatters spitfire droplets of water/all around her;/ they dart about like rainbow-tailed moths' ('The Barefoot Queen of the Crossroads', ibid.: 77). The whole voyeuristic world revolves around her.

The open space of the street serves the purposes of a drawing-room, a theatre, a 'pop-up cafeteria' and a cricket pitch for Kolatkar's ebullient have-nots. The economic deprivation is not necessarily a condition of emotional attrition. The blocks of concrete planted on the roads as dividers are useful items of furniture:

> A most useful piece of street furniture,
> I must say.
> Make great road dividers,
>
> great traffic-island markers
> and more to the point, great settees.
> By the way,
>
> they make great pillows too
> in case you feel like a snooze afterwards . . .
> ('Breakfast Time at Kala Ghoda', ibid.: 108)

The rat that comes out of the safety of a hole in search of food on to the pavement proves to be a loose ball that a street urchin hits with his bat to the 'extra-cover boundary'. The big jumbo-size box of *idlis* that everyone waits for at breakfast on the pavement is the makeshift cafeteria that very soon disappears along with 'the king and the queen [of the street]/the courtiers,/ the court jester and the banqueting hall' (ibid.: 113).

The leftovers turn into playthings as well as instruments and agents of change. An old bicycle tyre refuses to hang on treetops as a passive site of breeding insects or as a harmless big zero:

> a wobbly zero,
> a spastic shunya—

> but that doesn't mean
> I'm ready
>
> to hang myself
> up on a finial yet,
> or rot
> on a mossy rooftop
>> ('An Old Bicycle Tyre', ibid.: 52)

As long as there is 'mileage/left', the tyre is ready 'to give/a slap-happy boy/a good run/for his money' (ibid.: 55). The drop-outs seek to participate in the circus of life. The coconut frond 'with nothing to do up there' and 'bored with life at the top' descends to 'clown around, jump and dance'; it 'lunges and takes sideswipes/at errant scraps of paper' ('Meera', ibid.: 27). Kolatkar is the redeemer of the marginal, the borderline and the small.

Dogs, lice, rats, crows and other such stray and smutty animals of the Bombay footpaths replace the temple rats and monkeys which Kolatkar had written about a great deal in his *Jejuri*. These animals of the pavement may not have the ferocity or vitality of the elite forest animals, but they do have their own histories and mythologies to sustain them. The dog squatting right at the 'exact centre of this traffic island [Bombay]' becomes its very embodiment:

> with Old Woman's Island
> on my forehead,
> Mahim on my croup,
>
> and the other distributed
> casually among
> brisket, withers, saddle and loin..
>> ('Pi-dog', ibid.: 2)

After sufficiently de-glamorizing the glittering metro by comparing its contours with those of the body of a dog, Kolatkar, in his characteristic style, traces its pedigree first matrilineally to 'the only [surviving] bitch' that was 'imported all the way from England' in 1864 and then from the father's side to Yudhishthira's dog that followed him to the Himalayas on his last journey. Kolatkar's (under)-dogs are not stray animals without any sense and sensibility. Not only do the dogs happen to be the 'only sign/of intelligent life on the planet', the crows are discrete as well. Before pouncing upon the half-dead rat as their prey, they thoroughly scan it: 'Is it too rotten, too brittle, too limp, too heavy, too light?' ('To a Crow', ibid.: 38). The poet gives a graphic description of their air-devilry thus: 'executing/a perfect hyperbolic curve/with throwaway ease' (ibid.: 36).

Thus, Kolatkar's *Kala Ghoda Poems* in a way extends his activist credo set forth in *Jejuri* with the difference that, while in the latter he seeks to combine modern scepticism with Bhakti iconoclasm, in the former, postcolonial subalternism combines with postmodern celebration of the small and the petite. The subaltern in his poetry is amazingly happy and positive, yet never complacent and contented.

Notes

1. It is significant to mention that there was never so much distrust against the Indian English novel or even Indian English journalism when it came to expressing anti-colonial nationalism. Indian English poetry, however, 'never qualified *qua* genre for the realist work of narrating the nation; a handicap only exacerbated when the verse was executed in the language of the conqueror' (Gandhi 1999: xv). Jayant Mahapatra, a leading Indian English poet, has serious reservations about the activist potentials of Indian English poetry as a whole: 'Most English poetry in this country fails because our poets are simply unaware of the society from which the poetry emerges; because being city poets they deal with the basically uninspiring middle-class, and their poetry turns out to be equally uninspiring; they produce a kind of "willed poetry" that is forced out of their selves and which ignores the rural psyche' (1980b: 34).
2. Frantz Fanon, an Algerian revolutionary, in his seminal essay, 'On National Culture' (1990: 167–99), works out three phases of protest in postcolonial liter-ature; these are the phases of assimilation, pre-combat and armed militant combat. The given 'Indian' paradigms of protest could be divided into three broad categories—i. paradigms of radical socialist protest, ii. paradigms of defining identity in terms of the cultural Hindu past, and iii. paradigms of complicity and co-option. The first category covers the protest-discourses of Bhagat Singh, Ram Manohar Lohia, Jai Prakash Narayan, etc.; Ambedkar too falls into this category with a difference that his protest is not so much against white colonialism as against the brahmanical order. The second category includes the critical traditionalists like Aurobindo, Tilak, Dayanand, Gandhi, etc.; the critical modernists like Rammohan Roy, Tagore, Nehru, etc. constitute the third category. In terms of ideology, the first category has direct Marxist bearings; the second category has rightist underpinnings of cultural nationalism, both of the extreme and moderate type; the third category derives strength from western humanism and empiricism.
3. M. N. Srinivas, in his *Social Change in Modern India*, defines Sanskritization as 'a process by which a "low" Hindu caste, or tribal or other group, changes its customs, ritual, ideology and way of life in the direction of a high, and frequently, "twice-born" caste' (1998: 6).

4. *Akam* is the poetry of the interior landscape, *puram* is the poetry of the exterior domain. Ramanujan, in his 'Afterword' to *Poems of Love and War*, distinguishes between the two ancient Tamil poetic forms: 'In classical poetry, as we have seen, *akam* poems are love poems; *puram* are all other kinds of poems, usually about war, values, community; it is the "public" poetry of the ancient Tamils . . .' (1996: 235).

5. Ideologeme is defined as 'the smallest intelligible unit of the essentially antagonistic collective discourses of the social classes' (Jameson 2000b: 37).

6. Hannah Arendt in her 'What is Freedom?' (1961: 149) argues that 'Without a politically guaranteed public realm, freedom lacks the worldly space to make its appearance', and therefore all desire of freedom gains meaning only within the realm of citizenship.

7. Ashis Nandy's term for postcolonial comprador intelligentsia is 'ornamental dissenter' (1993: xiv). Ramanujan, of course, is not an ornamental dissenter.

8. Ezekiel, in his comments in *The Illustrated Weekly* writes: 'He [Daruwalla] has a desperately independent air, as if he was born full-grown from the head of some hitherto unrecognised goddess of poetry . . . Daruwalla has the energy of the lion, Ramanujan has the cunning of the fox' (quoted on the cover of Daruwalla 2006).

9. Toba Tek Singh is the name of a lunatic character in Manto's short story of the same name. In the story, Tek Singh refuses to accept the politics of partition. He creates his own small space ('toba') on the border of the two nations.

10

From Confusion to Consolidation: Politics of Counter-aesthetics in Dalit Poetry

The corpus of dalit poetry has expanded enough to merit a close region-/language-wise analysis of its evolving aesthetics. The rhetoric of 'counter-' or 'alternative aesthetics' employed initially to understand it, is too overarching to account for its inner conflicts, ideological rifts, structural shifts and multiple registers. Dalit poetic experience as well as expression is not a one-time invention, nor is it as homogenous and predictable as is generally assumed. This chapter is divided into two parts—the first part makes a comparative analysis of Marathi, Punjabi and Hindi dalit poetry from the early 1970s to the mid-1980s in terms of their markedly different and localized inter-textual constitution; the second part probes into the changing configurations of latter-day dalit poetry (of the late 1990s and beyond) in the context of its emergence as a pan-Indian poetic discourse wherein a medley of regional dalit voices collaborate and inseminate each other towards a political consolidation of dalit identity.

I

The regional nuances of the dalit poetry of the 1970s—a defining period in 'post-Ambedkarite' dalit history—often go unnoticed as well as unmarked for in our critical practices we are yet to appreciate the discursive formations of sub-national identities.[1] If at one level these nuances seem to create fissures in the making of a presumably unified dalit discourse, at another they redeem it from lapsing into banal binary-driven polemics of 'counter-aesthetics'. Across the general tenor of pain, hunger, deprivation, poverty and social injustice, there are regional sub-texts and inter-texts that continually buttress the dalit poetic imagination from below. Beneath the veneer of the seemingly abusive and even pornographic idiom of dalit poetry, there are local traditions and con-/counter-texts specific to each language. The wide and markedly specific array of inter-texts in each language stream of dalit poetry points towards the challenges of approaching 'dalit' as a uniformly defined pan-Indian category of social identification/stratification. The multivalent inter-textuality of dalit poetry comes into sharp focus once its regional variations are mapped in a juxtapositional frame. Marathi dalit poetry of the 1970s happens to be the baseline, or the seminal critical context, for it not only heralds in a very emphatic way the arrival of 'exclusive dalit literature', but inspires poet-activists from other languages as well.[2]

i

Marathi dalit poetry, which becomes prolific in the wake of the Dalit Panthers (named after the Black Panthers) movement in 1972, has its well-marked inter-textual constituents that collectively lend it a distinct character. Written primarily in a critical response to the legacy of Ambedkar, Marathi dalit poets invoke the violent and militant tone of Black American poetry. The erstwhile mild native protest-poetics of the Bhakti poetry of Chokha, Tukaram, Jnanshewar, Namdev and other saint-poets of the local *varkari* tradition, which once provided a fulcrum to dalit unrest, is forsaken with a lot of disgust and venom.[3] God or even his divinity in the sufficiently mediated version of Bhakti poetry is nothing more than a perpetual abuse to be cursed vehemently by the Dalit Panther poets. Some of the neo-Buddhists (also referred to as Ambedkarite-Buddhists) among the young educated dalits also re-write Buddhist tropes/metaphors in ways that engender a sufficient element of activism in them. Some of the earlier readers of Marathi dalit poetry also tend to contextualize it in the 'avant-garde movements' and 'the little magazine movements' in Marathi literature and in other Indian language literatures written in the 1960s and 1970s as such.[4] These rather disparate, if not conflicting, frames, one of the constitutionalist Ambedkar, another of the non-casteist and non-violent Buddhist world-view, another of combative Black poetry, and yet another of avant-garde literary expression, thus go into the making of the Marathi dalit poetry of the 1970s. Its aesthetics, consequently, is an enigmatic mix of aggression and withdrawal, of resistance and renunciation, of invasion and evasion, of participation and secession, of politics and philosophy, of direct statement and surreal subversion—the twin principles of post-parliamentary poetic expression.

The legacy of Ambedkar, a Maharashtrian Mahar as he is, is immediate and direct in the case of Marathi dalit poetry. It is invariably the most compelling take-off point for Marathi dalit imagination. But by the 1970s, when the democratic nation-state, on whose agency or instrumentality Ambedkar had reposed some degree of confidence fails to bring about much-needed social change, restlessness sets in among the neo-literate lower-caste unemployed youth.[5] The attitude of the new dalit poets, led by Namdeo Dhasal and Daya Pawar, towards Ambedkar is not unquestioningly salutary. A love-hate relationship with Ambedkar is evident in the following poem of Namdeo Dhasal, one of the founder poet-activists of the Dalit Panthers movement:

> I've cursed you too, but
> you gave us the tongue to curse
> I've even sunk you in the water, but
> you gave us the water
> We've done things to you, even so
> anything can be done to you
> But the question of my loyalty,
> my honesty
> still remains
> Who are you?
> Who were you?
> Whose are you?
> ('Ambedkar: 1980', Paswan and Jaideva 2002: 131)

By the revolutionary standards of the Dalit Panthers, Ambedkar's reasoned and scholarly ways to assert dalit emancipation appear too decent to cut much ice with the orthodox Hindu order.[6] The poets of this movement, while acknowledging his contribution towards the making of dalit consciousness, at times turn sceptical about retaining his parliamentary ways of advancing the dalit cause. The lines quoted here are not as much an accusation against Ambedkar from within the dalit discourse as they are an indication of the restlessness within this discourse of going beyond mere empowerment through state-intervention in the form of reservations and other concessionary legislations.

To Dhasal, the parliament is nothing more than a 'brothel' where 'This country we call Mother/sleeps with the god of wealth' ('Ambedkar: 1979', ibid.: 130).[7] Ambedkar, who had shown a preference for parliament as against Gandhian decentralized Panchayati Raj, is thus turned upside down in a single stroke. In the same poem, Dhasal blames Ambedkarites for engendering passivity among dalit masses: 'Your followers act like false gurus/They use a loincloth for a tie and babble/Their heritage is mother-fucking'. In the post-Ambedkarite dalit poetry, the very commitment of Ambedkar towards radical dalit amelioration is challenged within the frame of reasonable disagreement.

Some poets do not name Ambedkar as such, but they do target his scholarly ways of advocating dalit emancipation. J. V. Pawar, for instance, urges dalits to abandon reason:

> No more reasoning now;
>> unreason helps a lot
>> Once the horizon is red
> What's wrong with keeping the door open?
>> ('It's Reddening on the Horizon', ibid.: 126)

Ambedkar's legacy is cherished, but it needs to be transformed into an activist credo. Jyoti Lanjewar, remembering her mother's last words, underlines the central position of Ambedkar in dalit imagination: '"Live in unity . . . fight for Baba . . .don't forget him . . ."/and with your very last breath/ "Jai Bhim"'(ibid.: 103). The same poet, however, realizes the inadequacies of Ambedkar's legacy in the face of unrelenting caste-oppression: 'Wrapping yourself in smoke from a dead fire won't work./ You have to plant the cinder of revolt in your own body' (ibid.: 99). Ambedkar, obliquely speaking, is thus reduced to 'a dead fire'; in Dhasal's much quoted poem 'Hunger', he is projected as a 'light' that 'turned false'.[8] The poet says, 'We wanted more from light/ than mere life/But light turned false' (ibid.: 128).

Unlike their constitutionalist predecessors, Dalit Panthers as poets do not seek state-doled alms, the state is too weak to empower them. Hunger is their birthright and they shall have it—with this degree of black humour they approach the issue of dalit deprivation:

> Hunger; your fashion's unique.
> You're the last whore
> We can make love to.
> If we can't get laid with you,
> If we can't get you pregnant,
> Our entire tribe would have to kill itself
>> ('Hunger', Dhasal 2007: 79–80)

Hunger is neither metaphysicalized under some Buddhist hang-over, nor raked up to garner sympathy. In lines such as these, not only does Dhasal take on the elite politics of fasting-feasting, he also disassociates himself from the pre-Pantherite dalit politics of pleading and petitioning. Dalit idiom transgresses even the complexities of so-called double-edged irony for it is the poetry of offensive realism, of post-ironic combats. Irony blunts anger, sublimates it into sophisticated poetics of containment; the dalit experience of the 1970s refuses even the graces of irony, for it has understood its subtleties.

In fact, as dalit poetry enters a militant phase, Buddhist metaphors/narratives, which are otherwise too reflective and meditative, undergo contestatory revisions that transform Buddha into a political god. They are impregnated with violent energy, keeping in view the radical urgencies of dalit movements in the post-1970s. Dalit poets refer to a possible elitist conspiracy in iconizing Buddha as a passive and pessimistic brooder:[9]

> Tathagata
> I do not want you in your yogic postures as in the pictures
> Before whom I could place my offerings of flowers and prayers
> Pardon the slaves of fetishism
> Who created idols in your name and festivals
> (Bhagwan Sawai, 'Tathagata: Two Poems', Paswan and Jaideva 2002: 115)

The act of conversion into Buddhism is not a sign of renunciation or of easy escape into spirituality; it is as much an act of rediscovering Buddhism from a subaltern perspective. Buddhist ideals inspire dalit intelligentsia as much as it retrieves the religion from obscurity.

Buddha stands for political radicalism too difficult to be arrested in the static frames either of the Ajanta and Ellora cave-paintings or of Gandhara statues.[10] Daya Pawar locates his Buddha in the outer domain:

> I see you
> walking, talking,
> breathing softly, healingly,
> on the sorrow of the poor, the weak;
> going from hut to hut
> in the life-destroying darkness
> torch in hand,
> giving the sorrow
> that drains the blood
> like a contagious disease
> a new meaning
>   ('Buddha', ibid.: 104)

Pawar's Buddha, very much like the pro-active protagonist of Ambedkar's Navayana Buddhism, thus, is a doer, and not a frozen marble statue decorating the shelves of the upper-caste elite.[11] He runs frenetically from one hut to another to assuage the sorrow of the poor.

In one poem on Buddha's wife Yashodhara, a dalit woman poet, Hira Bansode, focuses on her total erasure from public memory, while Sita and Savitri continue to attract major attention. There is hardly any trace of Yashodhara even in Buddhist *viharas*. The poet brings out the dark underside of Buddha's 'enlightenment' enterprise:

> We were brightened by Buddha's light,
> but you absorbed the dark
> until your life was mottled blue and black,
> a fragmented life, burned out,
> O Yashodhara!
>
> ('Yashodhara', ibid.: 115).

The responses towards Buddhism are not only at times critical, but they are self-contradictory too. In one poem, Daya Pawar looks upon Angulimal as 'the symbol of fierce society towards him' (ibid.: 37):

> O Siddhartha
> You made a tyrant like Angulimal
> Tremble
> We are your humble followers.
>
> How should we confront
> The ferocious Angulimal.
>   ('Siddhartha Nagar', ibid.: 109)

In another poem entitled 'Angulimal', Tryambak Sapkale himself takes on the *avatar* of Angulimal who wears a garland of the fingers of those who laugh at him:

> Those fingers that point at me
> will become fingers dangling
> in the garland around neck.
>
> Angulimal.
> I am Angulimal . . .
> I am Angulimal . . . (ibid.: 81)

Thus, in a paradoxical manner, both the dreaded Angulimal and his redeemer Buddha become rallying archetypes of dalit emancipation. The poets of the Dalit Panthers—caught as they are within relatively non-violent discourses of Ambedkar and Buddhism on the one hand, and violent unrest within, due to unrelenting caste-oppression—thus respond to hitherto available strategies of emancipation with a critical, if not utterly sceptical bent of mind.

While Ambedkar, probably in his anxiety to work within the frame of indigenous nationalism, chose to convert to Buddhism (as against Christianity or Islam), the dalit poets of the 1970s do not suffer from any such nationalist hangovers.[12] Not only do they derive their critical energies from Black movements in America and Africa, they do not shy away from seeking secession from the nation as well.[13] B. Rangarao would like to be the invisible man of Ralph Ellison: 'Or else I too would be here invisible/like Ralph Ellison's invisible man./ Trying to shake off heritage of want . . .' ('On a Desolate Night Like This', Paswan and Jaideva 2002: 143). Daya Pawar derives pleasure when upper-caste Indians are discriminated as 'niggers' or 'blacks' in the West; he would write back to his friend: 'Now you've had a taste of what we've suffered/in this country from generation to generation' ('You Wrote from Los Angles', ibid.: 107). In moments of utter despair, Marathi dalit poets would prefer to sail abroad. As the motherland alienates them, they seek to secede from it. Baburao Bagul would declare openly: 'You have made the mistake of being born in this country/must now rectify it; either leave the country/or make war!' ('You Who have Made the Mistake', ibid.: 155). Pralhad Chandwankar asks the nation as to why he should evince loyalty to it:

> This country which demands
> A pot of blood
> For a swallow of water
> How can I call it mine
> Though it gives the world
> The (empty) advice of peace.
> (quoted in Zelliot 1992: 306)

What is merely an understated sentiment in Ambedkar takes a full-fledged shape of a demand for secession. In the post-independence phase of history, patriotism could not be fed on anti-colonial rhetoric.

Since Marathi dalit poetry of the 1970s literally erupts like a volcano against the dominant literary traditions in non-dalit Marathi and other Indian literatures, it tends to attain a very eclectic poetic character, particularly in its textual presentation. Some of the poems, particularly of the metro-based, educated dalits like Dhasal, are almost surreal in their poetic arrangement:

> A leaking sun
> Went burning out
> Into the night's embrace
> When I was born
> On a pavement
> In crumpled rags—
> ('On the Way to the Dargah', Dhasal 2007: 55)

The image of the 'leaking sun', signifying a dwindling Ambedkar, yokes together Salvador Dali's surreal 'The Persistence of Memory' with Vincent Van Gogh's 'Sunflowers'. In his latter poetry, Dhasal becomes all the more absurdist, and ostensibly anti-poetic: 'The creeping plant of my penis is about to flower/Ibsen's Doll is about to get married'.[14] In the following excerpt taken from one of the earliest poems of Dhasal, there is an overwhelming element of nihilism:

> One should open the manholes of sewers and throw into them
> Plato, Einstein, Archimedes, Socrates,
> Marx, Ashoka, Hitler, Camus, Sartre, Kafka,
> Baudelaire, Rimbaud, Ezra Pound, Hopkins, Goethe,
> Dostoevsky, Mayakovsky, Maxim Gorky,
> Edison, Madison, Kalidasa, Tukaram, Vyasa, Shakespeare, Jnaneshvar
> And keep them rooting there with all their words.
> ('Man: You Should Explode', ibid.: 35)

Not only is the entire literary tradition disowned in one stroke, even the much-hyped Bhakti legacy is not spared. The poem has a large canvas and depth too. The poet deliberately avoids any chronological sequencing of names, the mixing of cultures/spaces and the haphazard temporal arrangement generates a montage-like texture. While commenting on a poem from Dhasal's *Golpitha* (Dhasal 2007 [1972]), Vinay Dharwadkar observes: '. . . the poems of Namdeo Dhasal . . . achieve a great deal of density, verbal polish and playfulness, and even wilful obscurity of the Western high-modernist and surreal kind' (1994: 321). While the influence of avant-garde movements within

Indian literatures on Marathi dalit poetry cannot be ruled out, it cannot be stretched beyond a point either. Dalit experience continues to be its primary input, and it is a matter of sheer coincidence and idiomatic compatibility that in its textual form it comes closer to modern 'existentialist' literature. It is also true that some Marathi dalit poets do not turn to modernist experimentalism, and continue to write in traditional folk forms. Aniket Jaaware would even go to the extent of describing Marathi dalit poetry as a field of aesthetic differentiation, in which a group of poets like Vamanrav Kardak and Pralhad Chandvankar continue to be traditional.[15]

ii

Punjabi dalit poetry of the post-1970s is equally volatile and combative, but its imagination is animated by a different set of discourses—religious as well as ideological. Historically speaking, the dalit movement in Punjab has its own autonomous past starting from Master Mangu Ram's Ad-Dharam that loses its hold around 1946 as other popular religious-reform movements—such as 'Nirankari', 'Udasi', 'Radhaswami' and now 'Dera Saccha Sauda'—operating within the broad frame of Bhakti and Sikhism make their headway, and spiritualize movements for social justice.[16] Even the most radical of Punjabi dalit poets would seek to express his protest through the Bhakti frames. Sant Ram 'Udasi', a naxalite-dalit poet of the 1970s, in his poetic invocations, transforms Sikh Gurus and martyrs into champions of social justice. In one of his poems, Guru Gobind Singh is actually made to pronounce that he did 'the exercise of forging a common *panth*/to safeguard the lower castes from the clutches of exploitation' ('Guru Gobind Singh Ji da Lokan de Naam Antim Suneha', 2004: 11). Sikh Gurus emerge as protectors of the have-nots, the lower castes and the workers. Gobind Singh is extrapolated to different time zones as an eternal warrior fighting against oppression of any kind:

> This is the feat of a true Singh
> he brings death to the cruel, and is a shield to the poor
> Your Singh always fights for true rights
> even though he fights in Vietnam.
>
> (ibid.: 23)

Guru Nanak is invoked but he is asked to come in a radically new *avatar*. 'Udasi' requests the Guru, 'if at all you decide to come back/come now with a sword in your hand/mere re-iteration of the divine would not do' (ibid.: 41). The poet warns the Guru of police atrocities: 'if you summoned truth/you will be killed by the police as naxalite' ('Guru Nanak te Aj', ibid.). The poet would even dare to defy the Guru

> if atrocities keep happening in your name
> I shall challenge you openly
> if you remained smug in your showoffs
> I shall turn a rebel against your divinity. (ibid.)

If Marathi dalit poets infuse rare political activism in the persona of Buddha, Punjabi dalits do the same to the persona of Guru Nanak. What is Buddha to Marathi dalit poets, Guru Nanak is to Punjabi dalit poets.

Even local Bhakti poets are re-worked more from the class perspective than from the caste one. In a poem on Ravidas, the low-caste saint poet of Punjab, 'Udasi' very explicitly writes: 'labourers form one class, not caste/all these caste-differences are mere tricks of the madmen' ('Bhagat Ravidas Nu', ibid.: 34). In another poem on the saint-poet, 'Udasi' accepts him as the poet of the untouchables: 'It so appears that in your divine light, there burns the fire of untouchable castes', yet in the very next couplet his approach turns overtly Marxist: 'it is not as much a matter of touchable-untouchable, all fight is between the rich and the poor' (ibid.: 64).

What is remarkable to observe in Punjabi dalit poetry of the 1970s is the near absence of Buddhism even though, historically speaking, Punjab had once been the hub of Buddhist culture. The image of the world-famous Gandhara Buddha comes from the erstwhile region of pre-partition Punjab. In one of the poems by Lal Singh 'Dil', 'the face of comrade looks like that of a Christ/exhorting waves and tempests to go higher and higher' ('Vishwas', 1997: 40).[17] Christ figures over and above Ram and Gautam put together. The mainstream Punjabi poetry/literature has all along been influenced by Buddhist ideals of existentialism and renunciation. From Pooran Singh to Dilip Kaur Tiwana, there are a number of mainstream writers who openly acknowledge the Buddhist underpinnings of their creative imagination.[18] Sikhism, strangely enough, combines with an extreme form of communism during the colonial and postcolonial Punjab, and the combination thus forged seems to knock out Buddhism from the activist imagination of poets like 'Udasi' and 'Dil'. Even in Marathi dalit poetry,

Buddhism comes *via* Ambedkar, otherwise, it seems to have little organic relationship with the dalit past.[19]

One of the most virulent inputs in Punjabi dalit discourse happens to be the ideology of naxalism, of which Punjab has always been a nursery of a kind right from the days of Ghadar and Bhagat Singh's Hindustan Socialist Republican Association. Communism does inspire Marathi dalit poets (Dhasal is one prime example), but it is eclipsed by patently casteist Ambedkarism; in Punjabi dalit discourse, its extreme form—naxalism—operates in the foreground, so much so that it becomes more a militant discourse of the landless versus the landed, than simply of caste-oppression. The economic disparities and cultural distortions that the Green Revolution brought about only postponed pure dalit resurgence in the region in many ways.[20] Dalit discourse, therefore, flourishes on the margins of naxalism, which in terms of its class and caste character was largely dominated by middle-level rural Jatt peasantry. Punjabi naxalite poetry merges into Punjabi dalit poetry and vice versa without any significant gap in thrust, ideology and tenor. According to one partial view, dalit poetry in Punjab is not as much a by-product of the purity–pollution dichotomy, as it stems primarily in response to the lop-sided landownership in the region.[21]

In his introductory note to a special issue on dalit literature of a Punjabi journal *Shabad*, Gurmeet Kallarmajri, a new dalit poet, observes that 'till today, the debate whether the fundamental basis of Punjabi dalit literature is economics or caste-experience remains unresolved' (2007: 8). The title poem of the very first collection of Lal Singh 'Dil', one of the major poets of Punjabi dalit discourse of the post-1970s, offers direct evidence of its naxalite intent:

> hopping over my shoulders
> I feel
> that you [the river Satluj] are like
> a gun placed over them
> call it a madness of my vision
> that all trees look
> like warriors on horse back
> with leaves tied on their heads . . .
> ('Satluj de Hawa', 1997: 2)

The local agrarian economy and the martial discourse within Sikhism seem to galvanize the poet-activist into a revolutionary mould:

'farmers have started off/on the paths have emerged the footprints of/Gobind Singh's horses . . .' ('Paid', ibid.: 38).[22]

If Marathi poets question Gandhi's rather diplomatic upstaging of Ambedkar in the signing of the Poona Pact, Punjabi dalit poets also question him for his non-interventionist, if not fully complicit, role in the matter pertaining to the death sentence of Bhagat Singh. Dil would write: 'Here Gandhis do not have that much of freedom/That in the name of negotiations on Bhagat Singh's death sentence/They join hands with the enemy camp' ('Vietnam', ibid.: 41). It is once again critically very interesting to observe that Ambedkar hardly figures in the Punjabi dalit poetry of the post-1970s. It is only in the poetry of the late 1980s and 1990s that Ambedkar seems to make some headway as the protagonist of dalit consciousness. Gobind Singh, Banda Bahadur, Bhagat Singh and other local warriors/gurus emerge as able icons/symbols of revolutionary surge.

But history in general is never as much the staple source of dalit metaphors, as it is the credo of hard manual labour that provides dalits poetic imagination. Since most of the low castes in Punjab are involved in agriculture mostly as tillers, the activism in dalit poetry stems from the soil: 'As soil has everything/Wheat, sweat, iron and dynamite/The people also have everything/Waves, flood, tempest' ('Vishwas', Dil 1997: 40). 'Udasi' also exhorts his 'pair of bulls to plough vigourously/as [he] is to sow the weapons' ('Haaliyan-Paaliyan da Geet', 2004: 87). Besides the typical Marxist symbols of hammer and sickle, other tools used in agriculture attain a revolutionary edge:

> the hand that remained
> a companion of grass-weeding tool
> in the hot season,
> this hand with its swollen veins
> appears to be the forehead of a warrior.
> ('Nadeen', Dil 1997: 35)[23]

Even things/objects which do not have revolutionary potential stand suddenly transformed into instruments of change, weapons of a bloody second coming:

> where lighting the fire
> the lands walk as naxalbaris
> where without those high forests

the tiny hands of tea leaves are weapons
probably there you are going my friend . . .
   ('Fauji Gade Vich Baithe Dost', ibid.: 78)

Even radium that radiates its radioactive rays to fight against the hegemony of darkness fires the dalit imaignation:

Darkness concentrates
its colour
fills it bit-by-bit with blackness . . .
Without bowing to any sun
radium continue to sing its song.
Never does it turn back
the innocent on its threshold .
   ('Radium da Geet', ibid.: 55)

Metaphors of such radiance, which may not have the glare of sunlight, but have the energy of inspiring human resistance and resilience, redeem Punjabi dalit poetry from propaganda.

Another distinctive feature of Punjabi dalit poetry is the masterly deployment of folk tropes, rhythms and songs. The use of *tappe*, *boliyan*, *heer* and other folk forms suggests the proximity of Punjabi dalit poetry with the naive milieu—which otherwise is not as much evident in Marathi dalit poetry. 'Udasi', for instance, uses familiar folk refrains of 'bajre da sitta' (2004: 45) 'mavaan thandiyan cchavaan' (ibid.: 49), 'kaliye kavaan ve' (ibid.: 50); he also employs folk forms of *shikva* and *boliyan*. In Marathi dalit poetry, particularly of the Dalit Panthers, the oral/folk dalit culture stands relegated in the wake of the emergence of printed literary culture. There is so much of anti-traditionalism in this poetry that not only is the canonical sanskritic past debunked, even the native dalit past is rejected. Gopal Guru refers to this growing chasm between local dalit performers as in-formal grass-root level cultural activists and dalit literary writers as new privileged spokesmen of dalit consciousness: '[T]he dalit writers who seem to have arrogated to themselves from Dalit literary persons of the oral tradition by attributing symbolically higher literary value to their own literary creation. . . . This strategy involves condemnation of the symbolic forms produced by the popular literary tradition as brash, gauche, vulgar, immature and unrefined' (2001: 188). Punjabi dalit poetry operates from within the local traditions of Sufism and

Sikhism, and other folk narratives; the imposition of sanskritic culture, however, is vehemently resented.

iii

The Hindi heartland fails to produce a conspicuous dalit poetic discourse during the 1970s, or due to historiographical biases it does not come into as much eminence. For purely academic purposes, a very small number of dalit poems, short stories or reformatory prose pieces can be mentioned—right from Heera Dom's poem 'Acchoot ki Shikayat', published in Mahavir Prasad Dwivedi's *Saraswati* in 1914, believed to be the first dalit poem in Hindi (Bhojpuri), to Biharilal 'Harit''s *Bhimayana*, presumably the first ever book-length dalit poetic discourse in Hindi published in 1973—but the fact remains that even dalit critics and literary historians, while attempting an evolutionary account of dalit poetry in Hindi, tend to start from the 1980s as the potential take-off decade.[24] And the reasons for this absence or slow arrival are not difficult to surmise. This has directly to do with the rather late arrival of dalit politics in north India. Sudha Pai, in her analysis of the caste-politics of Uttar Pradesh very pertinently observes: 'The absence of anti-caste social movements and the moderating effects of Gandhi upon the anti-colonial struggle, shape[s] the identity of SCs as "Harijans"' (2001: 284). Such a quasi-spiritual categorization or what Gopal Guru terms 'philanthropic naming' (2001: 261), only 'inculcates an element of resigned fate in the subject' (ibid.), and thus postpones the rise of radical dalit consciousness.

Besides Gandhism, other ideologies and reform movements also contribute towards the late resurgence of dalit discourse in the cowbelt. Kanwal Bharati, in an informative article, 'Dalit Kavita: Pratikranti ke Swar' published in *Dalit Sahitya* (2005) informs how two dalit Jatavs—Swami Shankaranand and Ayodhyanath Brahmchari of Aligarh, once members of Ambedkar's Scheduled Caste Federation—turn into fierce Arya Samajis, and try to nullify the tempo set for revolution by the Adi-Hindu movement leader, Swami Acchutanand, through their bhajans and religious discourses in as early as 1954.[25] Under the impact of Arya Samaj, they endorse the institution of varnashram: 'see everyone, all of us are tied by four varnas/Brahman, Kshatri, Vaishya, Shudra, so says Yajurveda' (1945: 14). They not only try establish the brahamnical forbearings of their dalit caste 'Jatav', but also try to cause a rift among dalits by suggesting caste-hierarchies among them.[26]

The rise of the progressive school within Hindi literature around the mid-1930s also in a way pre-empts the rise of an autonomous dalit discourse. Mainstream progressive Hindi writers of the pre-independence era, from Nirala to Premchand, in their own partial ways also dwell so rigorously on dalit issues and metaphors that the neo-literate dalits are left with no option except to be overawed by their 'sympathetic' intervention.[27] Even after independence the upper-caste Hindu poets continue to write epic-length poems on mythical dalit characters. Dr. Ramkumar Verma's *Eklavya* (1973), Ramdhari Singh Dinkar's *Rashmirathi* (1960), Jagdish Gupt's *Shambook* (1977), etc., are some of the prominent ones. Such is the volume and intensity of non-dalit writings on dalits that even today, despite doubts expressed about the authenticity of their once-removed experience, they tend to form a complementary well as competitive context of dalit writings.

Hindi dalit poets of the 1970s and 1980s, taking inspiration from mainstream upper-caste Hindi writers, model their long poems on B. R. Ambedkar along the lines of medieval narratives. Biharilal 'Harit''s *Bhimayana* (1973) is a 426-page-long epic composed in various *kaands* (cantos)—'Parivaar Kaand', 'Shiksha Kaand', 'Baroda Kaand', 'America Kaand', 'Ghrina Kaand', etc.—which map out the evolution of Ambedkar along the lines of Lord Rama's evolution in *Ramcharitmanas*. 'Harit' employs the same poetic stanzas—of *doha, chaupai* and *kavitt*—that Tulsi uses in his grand epic. Lakshmi Narayan 'Sudhakar' writes *Bhimsagar*, a *prabhandhakavya*, in 1984; Shri 'Rajavaidya' Mata Prasad and Shri Gokaran Ram 'Karunakar' co-author *Bhim-Charitmanas* in 1989 (quoted in Prasad 1993: 196–97); Babulal 'Suman' composes an epic in eleven cantos entitled 'Ambedkar' (quoted in ibid.: 186–87). Ramdas Nimesh writes the 416-page-long *Bhimkathamritam* in 1990 which is divided into nine sections, and is composed in *dohas* and *chaupais*.

Early Hindi dalit poetry does not sound as belligerent and scathing as Marathi or Punjabi dalit poetry. In terms of its inter-textuality, it takes its form, metaphors and idiom from Hindu scriptures and other canonical texts. The forms—*sagar, shatak* and *charit*—that the dalit poets choose to write in have traditionally been upper-caste literary forms/sub-genres in which the protagonist is deified or eulogized by the poet-as-devotee in terms of surrender and supplication. Such is the constraint of these forms that the very scope of radical social protest goes a begging. While it elevates Ambedkar into a 'mahamanav', 'vishva-guru', 'yug-purusha', 'prakash-stambha', etc., it denies him an active social role at the level of the grass-roots. The protest, if any, is expressed more in the form of a mild-mannered complaint, than in the form of an aggressive call for action. Look at the following two couplets from Sudhakar's *Bhimsagar*:

> Constitution is the sole basis of our freedom
> Future of India stands enshrined in it
>> (quoted in Prasad 1993: 185)

> If your mission is to address all as Harijans,
> We don't have objection, if that is what you aim.
>> (quoted in ibid.: 186)

The prosaic messages only point towards a rather non-confrontationist stance of early Hindi dalit poetry. It oscillates between Gandhian passivity and Ambedkar's constitutionalism, with no intention of taking on the structures of oppression in a radical way.

II

By the time dalit poetry enters the late 1990s, across and above the gamut of regional differences, internal hierarchies (shudra versus *ati*-shudras), ideological dissensions (Ambedkarism versus Marxism) and representational predicaments, it goes through a process of consolidation at the national level.[28] Debates on its multiple performative sites, its colonial recastings, its proximity and dualism with Marxism, are consciously put on hold in favour of an essentialized dalit identity that refuses to buckle under any pressure/inducement/critical intervention from outside.[29] As anthologies of dalit poetry as well as special issues on dalit literature of leading journals from *Indian Literature* (Sahitya Akademi) to *Shabad* (a Punjabi journal) begin to surface from all over India in various languages and in English translation, dalit discourse no longer remains the monopoly of Marathi Mahars. In fact, dalit journals/anthologies in one language bring out issues/supplements on dalit poetry published in other languages, generating a space for dialogue and exchange among the dalit poets of Punjabi, Hindi, Marathi and other languages. Thus, the late 1990s mark the arrival of an all-India dalit discourse—a rare development in the sense that 'poetry' is defined exclusively in terms of the caste of its writers; the language/region in which it is written no longer constitutes even its secondary address.

i

As 'caste' overtakes 'language' as its predominant structure of feeling, dalit poetry in different languages undergoes significant changes configurationally from the late 1990s onwards. Most noticeably, the intimate regional metaphors, images and folk tropes slowly begin to give way to the non-provincial—national, natural and philosophical (Buddhist)—frames of poetic articulation. Ambedkar, already a very strong presence in Marathi poetry, emerges as 'a national icon'[30] competing with other mainstream icons such as those of Gandhi, Lord Ram or Bhagat Singh. Under the imperatives of consolidation, dalit poets of the post-1990s rally around Ambedkar with the least scepticism about the inadequacies of his constitutionalist credo. Even Namdeo Dhasal, in his collection *Tujhe Bot Dharooon Chalalo Ahe Mee*, published as late as 2006, accepts the sin of idolizing Ambedkar—something which Ambedkar detested most:

> Babasaheb—
> Forgive me!
> You detested idolatry.
> You didn't allow your followers to hero worship you.
> I've committed this crime after you were gone.
> I couldn't do without writing
> The poetry of your achievement.
>
> ('Dedication', Dhasal 2007: 134)

In dalit poetry of the post-1990s, Ambedkar receives singular attention and he is projected as a demi-god across regions and languages. It is interesting to observe that while in mainstream politics as well as in literature, Gandhi's myth of mahatma undergoes a very uncharitable, if not hostile, dismantling; in dalit-domain, Ambedkar, after momentarily losing ground to the Panthers, not only regains ground, he stands resurrected literally as a Christ reborn.[31] The post-Ambedkarite phase of dalit poetics is more a confirmation and continuation of Ambedkarite poetics than its negation or critical rejection.

In Hindi dalit poetry, as suggested earlier, right from the mid-1970s, Ambedkar is elevated to an epic hero. In the 1990s, the trend continues, but instead of trying longer narratives, the poets choose shorter poems in free verse, marking in a way their liberation from the metrical bondages of classical poetry. An *Ambedkar-shatak* is attempted at in the year of Babasaheb's birth centenary, 1992, with the difference that this time it is not written by one author, rather it comes in the form of a hundred poets contributing to a volume edited by Dr. Sohanpal Sumanakshar. The very presence of hundred poets not only suggests the expanding base of Hindi dalit discourse, but also the steady nationalization of the Marathi hero. The collection opens with two poems; 'Vandana' having the opening refrain 'vande Ambedkaram', and 'Gaurav Gaan' modelled after the national anthem: '*pad dalit ke bhagya vidhata/bhimrao jaye he . . .*' (Acharya Guru Prasad, in Sumanakshar 1992: 9).

Not only does Ambedkar become the poetic subject, he is transformed into a poet as well. Kanwal Bharati, a leading Hindi dalit poet, in a daring experiment, re-writes Ambedkar's prose-messages into poetic form to assert the underlying poetic prowess of the scholar-politician. The poet 'search[es] these poetic spaces in "Ambedkar's contemplation" and give[s] them the form of poetry' (Bharati 2004: 217). Badri Narayan and A. R. Misra, in their anthology of dalit writings entitled *Multiple Marginalities*(2004), publish the English translation of Bharati's *Dr. Ambedkar Kee Kavitayein*, originally published in Hindi by Boddhisattva Prakashan in 1996. Here is a 'poetic excerpt' from Ambedkar's 'Hindus and Want of Public Conscience', reproduced in verse from by Bharati:

> A slave is not
> Legally a free man;
> An untouchable
> Is legally a free man;
> Yet, a slave has the social freedom
> To progress
> Which is not available
> To an untouchable.
>   ('Achoot Aur Azadee', ibid.: 225–26)

The appropriation of Ambedkar into the very community of poets suggests two things—one, in dalit discourse there is never a gap between poetry and politics, and two, dalit aesthetics is dissimilar, its lyricism lies in its experience of exclusion and not as much in sophisticated craft and diction.

Even in Punjabi dalit poetry, the local poets see a 'failure of regional reform-movements towards the rise of revolutionary dalit conscious'; the erstwhile gurus and Bhakti saints appear impotent, if not dubious.[32]

Instead of receiving solace, Dwarka Bharati undergoes bouts of shame at the so-called holy sites of spiritual freedom and release:

> Why it so happens
> that as I pass through a
> religious place of worship
> my head bows
> not in reverence
> but in shame?
> ('Sharm', Bharati 2006: 297)

Another poet, Mohan Tyagi, expresses his total disenchantment with the local religious frames/institutions of social emancipation:

> How come your hub is so desolate?
> Probably your devotees have turned rebel
> Excuse me, I also beg your leave
> I go in search for another Gorakh
> I am Pooran, condemned son of destiny
> My mother Icchran must be waiting for me back home.
> ('Guru Ji', Kallarmajri and Singh 2002: 70)

Ambedkar emerges as a potential new Gorakh. He is indeed seen in the lineage of great Indian spiritualists. In his title poem, 'Jai Bharat, Jai Bhim', Iqbal Gharu, for instance, places Ambedkar in the lineage of great spiritualists—'Mahatma Buddha, divine Nanak, Dashmesh Guru, *bhakta* Kabir, Tulsi Das, and Bhim Rao' (2002: 11)—that India has produced. Dr. Inderjeet Singh Vasu, employing the folk form of 'var' writes, 'Dr. Ambedkar di Var' which in a way marks the assimilation/ appropriation of Ambedkar in Punjabi dalit folk imagination:[33]

> He was a form of fierce fire, a stream of progress,
> Whose one slogan was, let the revolution be total.
> . . . .
> Who taught us the way to walk upright.
> Who kindled the rebel dormant within us.
> (Virdi 1994: 88)

Chanan Lal Manak, a disciple of the folklore poet Nand Lal Noorpuri, invokes folk metaphors while recounting the life-history of Ambedkar thus: 'So that one might not walk with uncovered head, while the other walks with embroidered scarf,/ By going to London, this hero raised the banner of the backwards' ('Dr. Ambedkar Ji', ibid.: 91). In Punjab, women observe this practice of covering their heads with *dupatta*, as a mark of respect for the elderly and self-integrity both. Jagdish Kallar, another poet, heralds Ambedkar as a crusader of women's rights: 'Pir, godmen, gurus none took note of her plight/It was Bhim who assigned women the place of crowning glory' ('Bhim te Bharati Nari', ibid.: 89). Ambedkar, thus, enters the Punjabi landscape, though he does not invade it as much.[34]

ii

At a rather subsidiary level vis-à-vis Ambedkar, Buddhism also gains ground among Hindi dalit poets and to a very minor extent among Punjabi poets, who till the 1970s had operated either largely within local Bhakti movements or under the Marxist rubric for social emancipation. As anti-caste movements gather force in the 1980s, Buddhism is invoked in dalit literatures across Indian languages more regularly as the earliest discourseof social and political justice than an alternative theology or philosophy.[35] Hindi poets do feel gravitated towards Buddhism, but they realize the ordeal is too arduous to be wishfully negotiated through conversion to Buddhism:

> That time and again
> the blue sky will echo
> from one end to another
> from infinity to infinity
> sangham sharanam gachcchami
> sangham sharanam gachcchami
> sangham sharanam gachcchami
> but the night is too dark, long and dense.
> (Ajay Navaria in *Dalit Sahitya* 2004: 177)

Buddhism is one of the paths of upward social mobility, it is not the climax or the finale of dalit struggle. It is not an official religion of dalits as such. This is how Illaiah would explain the relevance of Buddhism in dalit imagination: 'The contemporary Dalit Movement (the neo-Buddhist movement) is not so much a movement to revive Buddhism as to challenge the caste-system' (2001: 1). Sohanpal Sumanakshar urges *bhikshuks* to come out of their *viharas* to join the combative struggle against the upper caste:

> Leave your sanctimonious-ness.
> First make your soul pure, fearless.

> come out of temples/ Buddha *viharas*.
> Go to the houses of dalits,
> make them brave, enterprising . . .
>> ('O Mere Bhikshuo!', 1990: 13)

The activist credo of dalit poetry comes in conflict with the sense of resignation built in the discourse of Buddhism. And, therefore, dalit Buddhists, as the poet urges, are not supposed to settle into secluded monasteries. 'The Dalits today appear to be moving towards a socially more engaged Buddhism, but not really in the direction of liberation theology' (Zelliot, see http://frontierweekly.googlepages.com/dalits-38-49.pdf).

iii

Betrayed by culture and its discriminatory constructions, dalit imagination goes back to the very state of nature—non-casteist ground zero of culture, a pre-civilizational site bereft of artificial distortions. Dalit poets of the 1990s discover the so-called *jungle-raj* to be more egalitarian and just than the so-called man-made culture:

> There is this law in the
> world of jungle:
> lion and jackal
> elephant and deer
> small-big
> weak-mighty—
> all drink water from the same river-bank.
> (Satnam Singh, in *Dalit Sahitya* 2005: 355)

Nature offers a landscape of primitive communism, of refulgent pre-historical co-existence, of non-institutionalized and non-hierarchized humanity. The brutish state of nature is far less nastier than the miseries that the caste-divided brahmanical society imposes on its men. Nature in dalit poetry is more a site of social justice and a level play field of participation than romantic escape or social evasion.

Dalit poetry, very much like women's poetry, makes a serious ecological intervention for it forewarns against the intimidation of nature by the repositories of culture.[36] Nature sucked dry and dead is the potential zone of forest-fires.

> No body torched the jungle
> Sir,

> The wind was brisk and the bamboos were dried
> They just messed up
> And the jungle was all aflame
> No body really torched the jungle.
> ('Jungle de Ag', Shudarak 2002: 21)

The dalits, reduced to the status of denuded trees, are bound to blaze with anger; there is no need of any outer provocation now. Valmiki, therefore, highlights the importance of 'leaves' for the 'tree':

> Tree,
> you are tree
> till these leaves
> are with you.
> The moment they fall
> you would not be called a tree, but a stump only
> you will die a living death.
>
>   (1997: 11)

The tree stands for tradition, rootedness and depth of vision; leaves signify its richness, its civilizational expanse and, more importantly, its nourishing machinery. Any snag or hierarchy in the organic relationship would destroy the whole eco-balance.

Dead trees, bruised birds, dried rivers, autumnal leaves, thorny cacti, therefore, emerge on the dalit landscape as symbols of the socially abused, incapacitated, caged and exploited innocent and raw dalit masses. Dalit poetry is, therefore, the poetry 'of a wingless bird/ . . . a *dastan* (a narrative) of leaves/falling from the trees' ('Kavita', Madhopuri 1998: 13).[37] Even as caged birds, dalit poets of the 1990s refuse to sit quiet:

> Birds have drunk deep
> Of winds of equality
> Oh, do not enslave them!
> They'll soar aloft
> Bearing your prison along.
> Do not underrate them.
>   (J. V. Pawar, in Dangle 1994: 41)

Birds in the dalit poetry of the post-1990s are no longer easy to contain for they have known what freedom is. It gives a slogan: 'Nature is the Great God/And we are all restless birds . . .' (Bhjang Meshram in Indian

Literature 1996: 68). The urge is to hark back the rivers that have dried due to the excesses of the brahmanical elite:

> Come back rivers
> I want to show you
> the river inside me, all dried up
> which used to flow once,
> I want to show that leafless tree
> which koel once used to perch
> singing her song.
> ('Nadiyo! Vapas Parat Aao', Kallarmajri 2002: 92–93)

Dalit poets effect such a reversal of aesthetics that now even cacti attain social prestige, if not precedence: 'Grew on a barren land/without any care/ . . . /it is better to be cactus/than rose' (Sharad Narayan Khare in *Dalit Sahitya* 2004: 187).[38]

However, while setting up a contrast between nature and culture, dalit poets of the 1990s do realize the mounting rigidity of the latter in the face of the growing backlash by the former. Writing in response to the reports about how during the post-tsunami relief operations high-caste Hindus refused to share tents with low-caste dalits, Madhopuri says:

> And those tsunami waves
> which had walloped the rocky edges
> could not over-ride
> high tides
> of hatred in our minds,
> the barriers of caste.
> ('Tsunami Lahiran', *Shabad* 2007: 190)

It is not that dalit poets revel in natural disasters, but they do discover a poetics of backlash in them. Nature is cherished as an ab initio site of human existence, which has been usurped by the votaries of culture irretrievably.

iv

As dalits attain focus and become single-minded towards their emancipation, dalit poetry of the post-1990s spurns its appropriation by the spiritual and the sanskritic nationalists as well as the communists and the socialists. Neither ideology, nor religion can override 'caste' of this poetry. The slogan of socialism, which the post-independence comprador intelligentsia raised to lull the teeming low-caste poor into obedience, fails to enamour the new dalit poets. The latter-day disillusioned Lal Singh 'Dil', a committed communist dalit till his death, in his collection *Satthar* published in 1997, would take a dig at loud-mouthed fellow comrades:

> We the comrades
> deliver endless speeches
> But when it comes to
> Staking life, we just bow out
> We the comrades
> why should we raise
> the slogans of Inquilab?
> It demands self-sacrifice
> Listen you
> Hungry and naked,
> Bereft of all prudence,
> We the comrades
> mean you well!
>   ('Kamreddan da Geet', 1997: 130)

Another Punjabi poet, Madan Veera, addressing his poem to a fellow comrade, points towards the elitist tendencies of modern socialists:

> Let you enjoy
> The fragrance of paper-flowers
> Ours is a relation with the aroma of the soil
> Ours is a relation with the smoke of the chimney
>   ('Tuhanu Hi Mubarak Hon', Veera 2001: 17)

The image of paper-flowers suggests the kind of disconnection which the modern-day comrade has developed with the grass-roots, the very constituency of his ideological credo. A Hindi poet refers rather explicitly to the nexus between Marxism and Manuvaad thus: 'The "left" of class-struggle,/ has nurtured the ideology of/Manuvaad over Marxism' (Premshankar, 'Ambedkariye Kavita', in Gupta 1996: 123).

   Dalit poetry, which initially drew strength from the Bhakti credo of the medieval period, turns wary of its relapse into any spiritual mould all over again. This is what Dhasal would say in response to the enticements of spiritualism: 'I don't wish to entomb myself here in a trance/As for me I still have to worry/About tomorrow's bread'

('Worry', 2007: 107). To Valmiki also, spiritualism is no consolation to bruised souls. He finds 'spiritualism's window forever closed/in the dead of winter' as 'numb limbs/and fingers groping in the dark/dash hard against it/bleeding/on the threshold of morning' ('Himsa ka Arth', 1997: 37). God, his divinity, benevolence and justice are vehemently rejected: 'we are not fans of your justice/we do not accept your world as just/because in your balance there are aberrations' ('Karvat', Madan Veera, in Bharati 2006: 309.)

V

Another major shift that dalit poetry undergoes in the late 1990s is that, instead of writing as much about little but significant auto-biographical failures, frustrations and struggles, dalit writers/poets tend to speak for the community in general in an overtly political way. The personal pronoun 'I' paves ways for the collective 'We', suggesting its social expansion with the passage of time. Suresh Chander, a Hindi poet writes: 'They are reciting vedic mantras,/ to allure *us*' (*Dalit Sahitya* 2004: 184, italics mine); Sushila Takbhaure, a dalit woman poet, inscribes dalit consolidation: ' . . .*we* shall/discover *our* own morning/ we *have* learnt to fill sun in *our* eyes/to hold moon in *our* fists . . .' ('Peera ki Faslein', Gupta 1996: 63, italics mine); a Punjabi poet, Madan Veera, asserts the new-found 'us-ness' among dalits: '[They] kept *us* deprived of *our* rights for generations together/threw us into animal farms . . .' ('Nimane', Kallarmajri and Singh 2002: 48, italics mine). This is poetry of exhortation that seeks to bring dalits out of their maudlin mode into the public sphere with a clear-cut agenda of their political galvanization.

One of the possible factors of the collectivization of dalits divided hitherto into sub-castes and hierarchies within (shudras and *ati-*shudras) has been their clubbing under the constitutional category of 'Scheduled Caste'. Surajpal Chauhan thanks urban India for fostering in them a sense of unity:

> In the villages
> I used to be
> divided into isolated fragments
> in different forms of
> of dalit *samaj*.
> In cities
> we are only

> 'Scheduled Caste'!
> Thank you city—
> You
> have transformed 'me' into 'us'.
>   (*Dalit Sahitya* 2005: 354)

The poetry of the collective dalit self does border on sloganeering, but what lends credence to it is the sustained autobiographical experience and expression that goes into the making of it. Sloganeering in the dalit poetry of the 1990s is post-poetic, and not pre-poetic.

Dalit poetry undergoes a process of consolidation at the level of gender also. While Marathi dalit women's poetry continues to flourish due to the sustained efforts of poet's like Hira Bansode and Meena Gajabhiye, Hindi poetry produces its dalit women's poetry in a visible manner only in the 1990s.[39] Kusum Viyogi questions the double standards of morality that brahmanical culture imposes on dalit women. While dalit women paraded naked by dalit landlords for their lust are branded loose and immoral, the upper-caste women flaunting their naked bodies in fashion shows and cabaret dances hardly invite as much moral censure:

> But they [dalit women]
> do not sell their womanhood
> to wolfs like you.
> On the other hand
> your mother, daughter and sisters
> donning make up of fairies
> dance in five stars hotel
> as call-girls and cabaret dancers
>   ('Anyaye ke Viruddha', in Gupta 1996: 190)

Another Hindi dalit poet, Rajni Tilak, brings into contrast the predicament of the lower-caste women vis-à-vis those of the upper caste through a series of juxtapositions:

> Doubtlessly both grill all day long
> One in the fields,
> Other in the four walls of house
> In the evening one sleeps on the bed
> Other on thorns
>
> Doubtlessly both are teased
> One in cars, cinema houses, and on roads,

> Other in fields, townships, mines
>
> . . . .
>
> Both suffer the same labour pains
> One delivers near the drain
> Other in a hospital . . .
>   ('Aurat-Aurat Mien Antar', Bharati 2006: 145)

Any attempt to forge a 'sisterhood of women' across communities is thus seriously challenged by the young breed of dalit woman poets.[40] Writing about dalit women's poetry from Andhra Pradesh, M. Sridhar also observes that 'They resist being subsumed under the banner of some universal woman experience' (2004: 106). Very strategically, the focus of dalit women's poetry is on the differential between a dalit woman and a non-dalit one; gender discrimination within dalit community is underplayed.

Kusum Meghwal, another dalit woman poet, seeks her revenge against those *thakur*s who impregnate dalit women forcibly and get away with it:

> Choose each and every *thakur*,
> give birth to their children
> and then
> send the fair-skinned children
> with a broom
> in each hand
> to the houses of their fathers
> to collect their excreta.
>   ('Mehtrani Ki Kos', Gupta 1996: 88)

The body of a dalit woman thus becomes the locus of her victimization and her revenge, exploitation and retaliation, both. What, however, is missing in dalit women's poetry is the articulation of the auto-biographical; dalit woman poets of the 1990s, very much like their male-counterparts, tend to speak for the entire community.[41]

Instead of poeticizing their own travails, dalit woman poets take on larger roles of drawing intimate poetic-portraits of fellow women highlighting their social neglect and sexual abuse. However, in the process, the thrust of self-presentation—the most significant aspect of dalit writing—is once again forfeited in favour of representation, with a difference that now it is done by a fellow caste-woman, that is, from within the community and not outside it. Charanjeet Kaur Jot, one among the very few emerging dalit female voices from Punjab, draws a vignette of an old maid:

> In the evening of her life
> that woman
> with a piece of bread in her hand
> half-winking, dazed
> searches for moonlight.
> With hands hard as rock
> and face heavily wrinkled
> she suffers the agony of cleaning utensils
> of others . .
>   ('Bhande Manjdi Aurat', *Shabad* 2007: 193)

Unlike Kusum Meghwal's women, Charanjeet Kaur's old maid does not even have the wherewithal of vengeance. The poetry of protest need not always be combative, it could as well be a poetry of description sans the rhetoric of revolution.

Not only do dalit woman poets write about their own gender, even male dalit poets, partly due to the pressures of consolidation and partly due to gender-sensitization in general, increasingly step out of their male universe and speak out for the still very much silent/ silenced dalit woman. If the poets of the 1970s dwell largely on the relation of the mother, dalit poets of the 1990s write in general about dalit women not from a possessive and protective male position, but as fellow exploited beings.[42] Young Marathi poet Ketan Piplapure shares the agonies of *devdasis*:[43]

> My dream consists of silent torments
> of the laments of undressed devdasi
> whose feet tradition have tied a string of bells
> and are asked to dance under its poisonous gaze
> I would roll out a green turf of affection
> under her burning feet.
>   (Bharati 2006: 369)

Both Sadhu Singh Shudarak and Valmiki present a graphic image of the female street-sweeper/scavenger of the roads as she toils hard to manage her container of filth:

> As long as
> there is a rickety iron trolley

> in the hands of Ramesri,
> making noise while being pushed
> on the road,
> the democracy of my country
> is an abuse!
>   ('Jharoo Wali', Valmiki in Bharati 2006: 59)

Male dalit poets, despite their empathetic intervention, fail to locate the problems of dalit women beyond the limited frame of democratic emancipation. Mere political equality is not adequate for gender empowerment.

vi

Dalit poetry of the post-1990s turns increasingly self-conscious; mere experiential veracity is inadequate to account for its shifting dynamics.[44] While the poets of the 1970s, even as they enter into a dialogue of difference with the existing poets and poetics, sound tentative, open-ended and even confused about the language of their expression and its aesthetic sophistication, the poets of the 1990s are post-dialogic in the sense that now they are in the process of, what Jaaware terms as 'in-folding' (1998: 273).[45] To them, dialogue is the methodology of appropriation. They do not want to get into the quagmire of devious semantics. Mohandas Namishrai would prefer to relapse even into a pre-word culture, because words, once scribbled, do impose meanings:

> It were words only
> which were scripted in Manusmriti,
> Ramrajya has gone
> But the echo of a begging Shambook is still there
> Words do not sigh.
> They speak
> They hit . . .
>   ('Shabd', Gupta 1996: 45)

Dalit poets, therefore, protest against the very culture of words that acquire arbitrary meanings.

Though the questions of language, diction and aesthetics continue to preoccupy dalit poetry, yet, as it grows, it declaims defiantly about its commitment to pre-cultural aesthetics of words *sans* their enlightened semantics of transcendence. Omprakash Valmiki, a formidable voice in contemporary dalit literature, looks forward to the primordial earthiness of words, rather their sublimation into other-worldly abstractions. He writes:

> Yet there is this belief
> That words would descend in
> Public, displaying their
> Primitive form.
>   ('Adimroop', 1997: 28)

Dalit poets seek 'words [to] descend on earth like sunshine' (ibid.: 29) without discrimination, piercing through the dark designs of culture. Excluded by history, tradition and civilization as such, dalit poets of the 1990s invoke metaphors/words of pre-society-state without the baggage of meanings subsequently imposed on them by vested power groups: 'Words never tell lie/their meanings do/—meanings which change/according to the fee you pay to the priest' ('Pandit ka Chehra', ibid.: 32). The nakedness of words torments the Punjabi poet Gurmeet Kallarmajri, for it reminds him of 'the nomadic voice of his ancestors', 'the terror of the jungle inside' ('Shabdan de Dahshat', Kallarmajri and Singh 2002: 61).

The meta-poetical interventions of dalit poets engender an element of self-reflexivity in their poetry. The dialogue which the early dalit poets of the 1970s engage in with regard to their different poetic aesthetic is now internalized, and the counter-voice is negotiated in the poem itself. New dalit poetry is aware of its critique, its aesthetic deviance, and therefore, the questions of alternative- or counter-aesthetics are now answered within the scope of the poem:

> This is alleged
> That the colour of your poetry is black
> Features dull
> Alliteration worn out
> Rhyme a patch-work only
> Melody un-rhythmic
> Sorrows precede happiness
> Pains speaks before peace
> Tell me now
> If I don't write poem of this type . . . what should I do?
>   ('Kavita', Manmohan, in Kallarmajri and Singh 2002: 43)

Such meta-poetical fortifications also point towards the underlying urgency of consolidation from within. A Marathi dalit poet, Keshav Meshram, would also raise a meta-question in a way that it becomes its own answer: 'Do I possess at least the freedom/of abuses of my own choice?' (*Indian Literature* 1996: 83).

As dalit imagination ossifies into a distinct credo and as the tide of the Dalit Panthers ebbs down, dalit poetry redefines its role. Consolidation, normally understood as a process of horizontal alignment and proliferation, acquires a vertical dimension too. Some poets explore this axis of consolidation and suggest a path different from mere sloganeering. Balbir Madhopuri, in the opening poem of his collection *Bhakhda Pataal*, underlines the role of poetry in the late 1990s:

> Poem, don't become slogan,
> Be a voice.
> Poem, don't be an ember
> Be the warm wings of a hen
> Shielding shivering chickens under it.
>   ('Kavita', 1998: 14)

Another poet, Dr. Chandra Kumar Varthe, would assign the same role of engendering warmth instead of dissipating fury in the minds of the agitated:

> The child is shivering
> Take this poem, wrap around him
> Like a blanket
> And in the warmth
> let him have dreams
> of the coming morning . . . .
>   ('Yeh Kavita Tumhare hi Naam', Gupta 1996: 139)

This is poetry of post-protest, of turbulence recollected in tranquillity, of positive participation. It seeks to go beyond mere rhetoric, towards a well-meaning intervention:

> No, poetry is not synonymous
> with inflammatory slogans
> . . . .

> My poetry is a challenge
> to both the rhetoric and the rule
> in the worry of redeeming
> man and earth.
> (Ramesh Panwar 'Tanha', *Atm-bodh* 1995: 24)

The endeavour of some of the post-1990s dalit poets is to address larger civilizational concerns in their crusade against caste-oppression, so as to reach beyond dalit ghettoes, and to strike alignments with deprived sections of humanity at large. After necessary 'in-folding', some of the dalit poets do seek to detonate into the larger expanse of the sky.

vii

While early dalit poets re-write archetypal dalit heroes such as Eklavya, Shambook, Angulimal, Karan, Valmiki and others, subverting the over-arching brahmanical intent of the so-called grand narratives, dalit poets of the 1990s add a new rigour into this process of re-writing. Not only are the old heroes re-written with newer significations, new ones are also invented with deconstructionist finesse.[46] From the deconstruction of mythology, religion and culture, dalit poetry of the 1990s enters a phase of deconstruction of the so-called secular history. The poets are aware of the new debates of historiography and politics of representation and the play of power in the so-called objective accounts of the past:

> While scripting
> autobiography
> and pronouncing the end of history
> I should read Foucault
>
> and should forget
> the geography of
> my childhood.
> ('Sva-Jeevani Likhan Vele', Kallarmajri 2002: 40)

Ashok Bharati questions the erasure of millions of low-caste labourers, who were actual players/makers of history/historical monuments: 'who raised/fort after fort/*diwan-e-aam, diwan-e-khas*/tomb of love Tajmahal' ('Kaun The Ve', Bharati 2006: 190). Neera Parmar refers to the obliteration of grass-roots people from official or canonical chronicles: 'time takes no notice/of those steps which inscribe/a

primitive script/on the tracks of passes, jungles, and river-banks'
('Samanantar Itihas', Gupta 1996: 143).

Of the most significant dalit historical characters that are retrieved
from the obscurity of the elitist nationalist discourse, Jhalkari Bai, a low-
caste warrior, guarding the main gate at the fort of Rani Lakshmibai at
Jhansi, receives repeated attention from dalit biographers and poets.[47]
In his poem, 'Virangana Jhalkari Bai', Rameshchandra Changosiya
projects the dalit heroine almost on the same pedestal on which Rani
Jhansi is often placed:

> Surrounded as Maharani was
> by the English
> Jhalkari plunged in
> for the sake of Rani and Jhansi
> blazing as she was
> in the form of fierce war-goddess—
> that destroyer.
>
> (1995: 13)

A woman poet, Kumari Archana Verma, has the same level of admir-
ation for Jhalkari Bai, but she also brings in the fact of her being
widowed in the battlefield: 'Lost husband, she remained unnerved,
fought hard in the battle/though manuvad is discriminated/an
untouchable as she was' (quoted in Prasad 1993: 101).

Besides rehabilitating dalit heroes of history, there is an underlying
bold attempt—though very tentative and provisional to begin with—
to genealogically trace a parallel history/tradition of dalits with the
Indus Valley civilization, the pre-Vedic culture, as the starting point.[48]
Dr. Sohanpal Sumanakshar goes on to write a full collection of poems
entitled *Sindhu Ghati Bol Uthi* (1990). Kamal Dev Pal, a Punjabi
dalit poet, claims: '. . . but our relationship with flowers/is as old as
Harappa-Mohanjo-daro civilization is/therefore by stuffing soil on
the bottom/of a broken bowl, we raise roses' ('Din Parat Aunge',
Kallarmajri and Singh 2002: 73). S. R. Dharnikar discovers his ancestry
from the buried Indus Valley skeletons:

> From the broken bones of buried skeletons
> at Mohanjo-daro
> to the paper-flowerpot of your room,
> on the shoulders of my long life
> burning in my own ashes
> I give rebirth to my-self
>
> (quoted in Prasad 1993: 274)

In a sweep, Ashok Bharati includes scheduled tribes within the fold of the anti-brahmanical discourse: 'It is I only/[who is] excluded from your culture/always a target of your *ashvmegh/bhil, munda, kol, santhal*—scheduled tribe' ('Brahmanvad ka Vinashak', Bharati 2006: 191). This genealogical/anthropological mapping of the dalits suggests the wide-ranging ramifications of their process of consolidation.

III

Dalit poetry of the 1990s and beyond, thus, veers towards an exclusive Ambedkarvad/Ambedkarism, with little room for Marxism and Gandhism. It consolidates the discourse of dalit identity both horizontally as well as vertically in the sense that more poets, both female and male, now contribute to its upward march. No longer an adjunct or sub-school of Marathi literature, it has an all-India presence and visibility. It strategically avoids debate on the marginalization of *ati-*shudras among the shudras for the essentialization of dalit as caste seems to be its pressing concern at the moment. It still operates within the binary frame of upper versus lower castes, by-passing the role of middle castes in the perpetuation of caste-discrimination. It remains more or less silent on the role of British colonialism in augmenting caste-feuds/wars. It continues to foreground the purity-pollution dichotomy; the economic ramifications and other discursive domains and performative sites of dalit identity are put on hold. In terms of its aesthetics, from autobiographical experience and expression, dalit poetry of the 1990s moves towards a polemical politicization of its tone and tenor as the poets speak on behalf of the community; the poetics of self-presentation, the high point in dalit writing, seems to give way once again to the poetics of representation, though with the difference that this time it is from within the community, and not outside.

Notes

1. The term 'post-Ambedkarite dalit discourse' primarily refers to the rise of dalit writings in the late 1960s and early 1970s in which Ambedkar's contribution to the making of dalit consciousness is accepted but is critiqued as well for being not radical enough to challenge the hegemony of the upper castes. So the term stands for a critical resurrection of Ambedkar after his death in1956.
2. There is no easy consensus as to what really constitutes dalit literature. But most of the pantherites tend to give it an exclusivist orientation. Arjun

Dangle would acknowledge the contribution of non-dalits, yet he finds a lack of aggression in their writing: '. . . Dalit and non-Dalit writers have acknowledged the different nature of Dalit literature and justified it, there is a minute but very sharp distinction between their two ways of thinking. The aggressiveness seen in the writing of Dr. M. N. Wankhade or Baburao Bagul is not to be seen in that of Prof. R. G. Jhadav or Sharatchandra Muktibodh' (Dangle 1994: 'Introduction', xii–xiii). Limbale would categorically declare that 'By Dalit Literature I mean writing about Dalits by Dalit writers with a Dalit consciousness' (2004: 19). Aniket Jaaware, however, cautions against the growing intransitive nature of dalit literature as propagated by the Dalit Panthers: 'When dalit readers consume these products [dalit literature] there is an in-folding of readership which allows another reflexive-reflective assertion of marginality, and the community-formation, which is equally intransitive as far as society at large is concerned' (1998: 273).

3. While mapping the rise of dalit consciousness, the poetic discourse of low-caste Bhakti saints is often sited as the most defining one. The poets of the 1970s, however, find it too fatalistic. In the following *abhang* of Chokha, for instance, the saint poet accepted his low status as his *karma*, the result of bad action in a previous life:

> Pure Chokamela, always chanting the name.
> I am a Mahar without a caste, Nila in a previous birth.
> He showed disrespect to Krishna; so my birth as a Mahar.
> Chokha says: this impurity is the fruit of our past.
>
> (quoted in Zelliot 1992: 7)

4. E. V. Ramakrishnan, for instance, while underlining the essential dialogic imagination of dalit poetry, right at the outset advises his readers to study this poetry 'in the context of the avant-garde movements that arose in several literatures of Indian languages during the sixties and the seventies' (1995: 97). Vinay Dharwadkar, in his article, 'Dalit Poetry in Marathi' (1994), and Aniket Jaaware in his 'Eating, and Eating with, the Dalit' (1998), also tend to agree that Marathi dalit poetry takes on the existentialist hues of modernist literature. The term 'avant-garde' is commonly used in French, English and German for those works of art and literature that are radically innovative. Influenced by modern western art, in India a lot of avant-garde schools within literature such as *akavita, absurd theatre, akahani*, etc. took off in the 1970s in various languages. The late 1960s saw an efflorescence of the little magazines in Maharashtra; their main task was to struggle against 'polite' modes of writing. *Asmitadrash* was founded by Prof. Pantawane at Milind College in Aurangabad, *Satyakatha* was published by a group called Angry Young Men, Baburao Bagul launched *Amhi*. A number of periodicals were published in the 1970s with titles such as *Kala, Sooraj, Garud, Dalit Bandhu, Nayamarg, Disha, Akrosh*, etc.

5. Ambedkar was a votary of democratic liberalism provided it meets the principles of social justice: 'The way out seems to be to retain Parliamentary Democracy and to prescribe State Socialism by the Law of the Constitution so

that it will be beyond the reach of a Parliamentary majority to suspend, amend or abrogate it. It is only by this that one can achieve the triple object, namely to establish socialism, retain Parliamentary Democracy and avoid Dictatorship' (1979a: 412).

6. In the Manifesto, the word revolution occurs with a frequency never felt before: 'When we gather revolutionary mass, rouse the people, out of the struggle of this giant mass will come the tidal wave of revolutions. Legalistic appeals, requests, demands for concessions, elections, *satyagraha*—out of these, society will never change. Our ideas of social revolution and rebellion will be too strong for such paper-made vehicles of protest' (quoted in Murugkar 1991: 238).

7. Interestingly, Gandhi in his *Hind Swaraj*, described the British parliament as a 'brothel', 'a talking shop' that in the name of representation denies people their direct participation in decision-making: 'That which you consider to be the Mother of Parliament is like a sterile woman and a prostitute. Both these are harsh terms but exactly fit the case . . . . The natural condition of that Parliament is such that without pressure, it can do nothing. It is like a prostitute because it is under the control of ministers who change from time to time' (1997: 30).

8. The imagery of 'light' and 'sun' occurs quite regularly in relation to the persona of Ambedkar in dalit writings. One dalit song reads:

> The sun of self-respect has burst into flame—
> let it burn up these castes!
> Smash, break, destroy
> these walls of hatred.
> Crush to smithereens this eons-old school of blindness,
> Rise, O people! (quoted in Omvedt 2001: 143)

In a poem by Namdeo Dhasal, Ambedkar is compared with the sun:

> You are that Sun, our only charioteer,
> Who descends into us from a vision of sovereign victory,
> And accompanies us in fields, in crowds, in processions,
> and in struggles:
> And saves us from being exploited.
> You are that Sun
> You are that one—
> Who belongs to us ('Ode to Dr Ambedkar', 2007: 42)

9. According to Ambedkar, Buddhism is not just about sorrow or *dukkha*, it is about its removal: 'No doubt my Dhamma recognizes the existence of suffering but forget not that it also lays equal stress on the removal of suffering. My Dhamma has in it both hope and purpose. Its purpose is to remove Avijja, by which I mean ignorance of the existence of suffering. There is hope in it because it shows the way to put an end to human sufferings' (Ambedkar 1979b: 130–31).

10. Buddhism in the contemporary dalit discourse is not invoked for philo-sophical purposes to understand the complexities of existence and

spiritualism. It is invoked for patently political purposes. Kancha Illaiah, in his 'Introduction' to *God as Political Philosopher*, very candidly writes: 'The contemporary Dalit movement (the neo-Buddhist movement) is not so much a movement to revive Buddhism as to challenge the caste-system—to give a political identity to the Dalitbahujans (the Scheduled Castes, Scheduled Tribes and Other backward Classes), the subalterns—in their struggle for survival, assertion and power' (2002: 1–2).

11. Ambedkar approaches Buddha in a different light. Far from being an ahistorical, spiritualistic, cosmological persona, 'Buddha to Ambedkar is a man, though definitely an unusual and compelling one, and the goal of the teachings is oriented to social reconstruction and individual advance in this life' (Omvedt 2003: 8).

12. For Ambedkar, as Eleanor Zelliot observes, 'Buddhism had become not only an intellectual passion but a more viable new religious home for those who found sanction within Hinduism for their new role and function. In Buddhism, Ambedkar had found an Indian, not a foreign, religion which could legitimate the claims of the Mahar' (1992: 208). Jaffrelot also tends to concur with Ielliot thus: 'The simple fact that Ambedkar saw conversion to Islam and to Christianity as a factor to denationalisation and one likely to attenuate the freedom struggle, is evidence that still he had not completely embraced the separatist discourse . . .' (Jaffrelot 2004: 22).

13. Dalit Panthers seek to strike international brotherhood. This is how their manifesto opens: 'Due to this hideous plot of American imperialism, the Third Dalit World, that is, oppressed nations, and dalit people are suffering. Even in America, a handful or reactionary whites are exploiting blacks. To meet the force of reaction and remove this exploitation, the Black Panther movement grew. From the Black Panthers black power emerged. The fire of the struggles has thrown out sparks into the country. We claim a close relationship with this struggle. We have before our eyes the examples of Vietnam, Cambodia, Africa and the like' (quoted in Murugkar 1991: 237).

14. During the 1970s, in Hindi poetry, for instance, a school of anti-poetry called *akavita* or *nishedh kavita* employed the same kind of language. Here is one example:

> . . . and from the debris
> I choose a half-burnt girl
> Who could be prepared for producing offsprings
>
> Excuse me, my times
> I cannot be of any use to you right now
> Because I . . .
> am undergoing treatment for my impotence.
> ('Mukhbir' 1972: 64)

15. Comments of Aniket Jaaware on the use of folk forms in Marathi dalit poetry point towards not only the differentiation of dalit poetics within Marathi poetry, but also the constant erasure of folk from it: 'A quick comparison

of these types of poems by Kardak and the more recent poems by Dhasal is sufficient to give some idea of the internal differentiation of city and country, of modernity and tradition within the field of dalit poetry. If in *Golpitha* Dhasal writes in free verse of the depravity of existence . . . Kardak writes in traditional forms of the greatness of the great leader B.R. Ambedkar' (1998: 275).

16. A well-known Punjabi critic, Sarabjit Singh, provides information about Mangu Ram: 'Mangu Ram was born in a rich [*chamaar*] family. This family used to supply shoes to British army. Despite being rich, it suffered on account of caste discrimination. Mangu Ram spent his initial years in England and America. There he associated himself with Ghadar movement. Confiscated documents suggest that Lala Hardayal had deputed him on the dalit front of Ghadar movement. . . . He was the main functionary of Ad-dharam Mandal. This Ad-dharam later came into contact with 'Purification movement' within Arya Samaj, and which later got submerged into Ambedkar's Scheduled Caste Federation. It was this Federation which later on took the form of political party called Republican Party of India' (2002: 60–61).

17. 'Dil was born into the low-caste *chamar* [tanner] community, and he dared to be a poet. The first of his clan to finish school and go to college, he could have been a teacher, but Naxalbari intervened. Police torture, imprisonment and rejection forced him to leave Samarala. He moved to Uttar Pradesh, where no one knew his caste. His conversion to Islam was yet another way of changing his life' (Dutt 2000: 52)

18. Pooran Singh, during his short stint as a student of pharmaceutical sciences, comes close to Japanese culture and life. In his *On Paths of Life* he writes, 'Buddha and Guru Gobind Singh both are the sacred inspirers of Japanese womanhood and manhood' (n.d.: 129). Buddhism provides the essential intellectual stimulus to Dilip Kaur Tiwana's *Katha Kaho Urvashi* (1999).

19. Here, observations of Dr. Dharmvir, a leading dalit critic are very pertinent: 'If Baba Saheb is not Buddhist, then for dalits Buddhism is not worth a straw of grass. . . . It is a fact that in the heart of a dalit, place of Baba is higher than Buddha . . . ; Baba Saheb is the real king of dalit-heart, by addressing him Boddhisatava, the glory of his name is jarred. Dalit asks; who is this Boddhisatava in comparison to Baba' (2000: 47–48).

20. The Green Revolution postponed dalit resurrection because it generated 'three kinds of conflicts' (Shiva 1991: 174)—(i) class conflict due to the pauperization of lower peasantry, (ii) religious conflict in the form of movement for emergence of separatist Sikh identity and (iii) the state-centre conflict over sharing of economic and political power. These conflicts did not allow caste to come in the foreground of Punjab politics.

21. Ronki Ram is of the view that 'Caste discrimination in the Sikh community is different from that in the Brahmanical social order, because relations are not framed through the purity/pollution dichotomy. Rather, power in Punjab is based on land ownership. Much of the land is owned by the Jat-Sikhs.

Although SCs in Punjab constitute a higher proportion of the population (28.3%) than the India average of 16.32% (1991 census) their share in ownership is negligible. . . . Since cultivation involves Dalits in its various operations, it was not feasible to strictly follow the system of untouchability based on the principle of purity/pollution, as in many parts of India. Nevertheless, Dalits are discriminated against in Punjab, and the asymmetrical structure of agrarian rural economy has made them subordinate to the landowning upper castes' (2004: 898).

22. In its first edition, published by Trishul Prakashan Jallundhar in 1971 instead of 'kisan', the word used is 'guriley' (guerrilla). Amarjit Chandan, using his editorial prerogative, tones down some of Dil's other words also. For instance, a loaded word like 'Jutt' is replaced by a fairly secular word like 'kisan' in Chandan's edition of Dil's first collection.

23. The reference is to a local manual agricultural instrument, which in Khari Boli is called *khurpa* or *khurpi*; in Punjabi it is called *ramba*.

24. The English translation of a section of Heera Dom's forty-line-long poem 'Achoot ke Shikayat' quoted in the 'Introduction' to *Multiple Marginalities* reads:

> We shall not go to beg for the sake of Brahmins
> We shall not take up arms for the sale of Thakurs
> We shall not manipulate in weighing for the sake of Banias
> We shall nit take the cows for grazing for the sake of Ahirs
> We shall not compose poems for the sake of Bhats
> We shall not go to courts putting turbans on our head
> We shall earn by the labour of our sweat
> And eat with the members of our family distributing whatever there is
> They fear to even touch us we are doms (Narayan and Misra 2004: 16)

There is a slight difference of opinion on the publishing details of Heera Dom's poem. Rajat Rani 'Meenu', in her book, *Navein Dashak ki Hindi Dalit Kavita*, refers to this difference: 'On deeper probing about the poems and the brief comments written along with it, there is no proper information about the author's life and address. Quite possibly, this was sent to Saraswati by some unknown individual who must have heard it somewhere. According to Dr. Manager Pande, it was published by Mahavir Prasad Dwivedi, but S.R. Vidrohi believes that its was Diamond Jubliee issue of *Sarasvati* and it was edited by Narayan Chaturvedi, and not Mahavir Prasad Dwivedi' (1996: 15–16). Both Rajat Rani 'Meenu' and Mata Prasad hold the 1980s as the potential take-off decade of Hindi dalit poetry. 'Meenu' writes: 'Hindi dalit poetry is available in sparse form in the dalit magazines/journals published from 1980 to 1985. Therefore we shall study the initial phase of the journey of dalit poetry from these sources only' (ibid.: 19). Mata Prasad, in his book *Hindi Kavya mein Dalit Kavyadhara*, though, avoids giving cut-off dates/years/decades for the rise of exclusive Hindi dalit poetry, yet he cites poetry primarily of poets published in different journals of the early 1980s. In his survey, he also includes poems of non-dalit writers writing on dalit issues/symbols/icons, etc.

25. In the footnotes, Sudha Pai distinguishes Adi-Dharma from Ad-Dharm: 'The Adi-Hindu movement of the United Provinces must be distinguished from the Ad-Dharm by Mangoo Ram and his followers in Punjab. While both shared the notion of the depressed classes forming the original inhabitants of the sub-continent, in Punjab this ideology was forcefully developed into an alternative religion under which the depressed classes themselves as a great "quam" distinct from and superior to the Hindu "quam" which came from outside. This provided the impetus to action which was missing in the United Provinces. Moreover the Ad-Dharm was sharply opposed to the Arya Samaj, which rejected it as a Hindu offshoot' (2002: 47). Sudha Pai also provides some details on the life of Achhutanand: 'Born as Hiralal, Swami Achhutanand belonged to Farukhabad, but spent most of his childhood in the Devlali Cantonment, where he received his education. Initially he joined the Arya Samaj and was named Swami Hariharanand. However he realized that the Samaj was interested only in minor reforms in Hinduism and not in radical change, especially where the depressed classes were concerned. He particularly did not like the *shuddi* movement of the Samaj. Hence in the 1920s he left the Samaj and started Adi-Hindu movement, changing his name to Swami Achhutanand' (ibid.). In 1954, Swami Shankranand's *Shankranand Bhajanavali* was pub-lished from Mainpuri, U.P. Though, presumably, it was influenced by Swami Acchuotanand's ideas, it did try to co-opt dalits in the Hindu order.

26. To Shankaranand, 'Jatav' is Yaduvanshi, and not *chamar*. This is how he justifies it: When Bhrigupati Parsuram was killing kshtriyas en masse, at that point of time the Yaudvanshis, dropped 'Jadav' and changed it to Jatav: 'When twenty-one times all Yaduvanshis were destroyed/ then to rescue themselves, one method came to mind/ "y" alphabet was replaced by "j" and "d" with "t"' (Shankaranand and Brahmchari 1945: 9).

27. Nirala, under the impact of the progressive movement, writes poems like 'Bhikshuk' (1949), 'Todti Patthar' (1988b) and 'Kukurmutta' (1980b) in which he tried to privilege the oppressed and the exploited. Premchand, one of the leading luminaries of the Progressive Writers Association, writes fiction rooted in the casteist sociology of the nation. His stories like 'Kafan', 'Thakur ka Kuaan', 'Sadgati', 'Mandir', 'Ghaaswali', 'Mantra', 'Dhoodh ka Daam', etc. presented a chilling account of caste discrimination in North India. Non-dalit writers, including Premchand and Nirala, are critiqued by latter-day dalit ideologues and critics like Shyoraj Singh 'Bechain' (2004: 9–14), Kanwal Bharati (2006), Omprakash Valmiki (2005: 30–38) for being partial to the dalit cause. In their writings they find dalits to be pathetic characters, devoid of any agency and volition to participate.

28. Early dalit poetry suffers a crisis on account of the language of self-presentation. Since the so-called language is not just appropriated by the upper caste, it is invented by it, how much of protest can actually be expressed in the language of the oppressor? This question always bothers both subaltern theorists as well as poets of the Dalit Panthers movement. Arun Kamble, caught between grandpa's half-vituperative lingo and the sophisticated Sanskrit of his Brahmin teacher asks: 'Which Language should I Speak?' (Dangle 1994: 54).

29. Dalit politics/poetry of the 1990s tends to essentialize caste so as to consolidate itself. Debjani Ganguly reads 'caste as a series of articulations at sites of overlapping discursive domains, and not an essence that is responsible for South Asia's backwardness'. She argues that caste can be comprehended 'in terms of performance, enunciation or practice rather than in terms of an imperial/nationalist pedagogy that would contain it in the discourse of progress and rationality. . . . It simply suggests that the discourse of policy, amelioration, even modernity, cannot exhaust the multiple performative sites at which caste intersects with other cultural practices and produces complex and efficacious modes of subjectivity' (2000: 45). A colonial census conducted along caste lines lent a new dimension to caste-politics in India. In his study on caste, Nicholas B. Dirks observes that 'the emphasis on caste in the decennial census had given rise to increasing agitation over caste denomination and the assignment of social status by caste groups. The colonial census might have re-inscribed a Brahmanic ideal of caste but, ironically, in doing so it gave rise to a competitive politics that began to make caste the basis for political mobilization on a new scale' (2002: 235–36). Caste, after colonial intervention, is disembedded from its traditional system of agrarian distribution at the village level; it also stands more regimented and fixed.

30. According to Gail Omvedt, 'By the beginning of the new millennium, when Dalits took their campaign against casteism to a world arena and tried to focus world attention at the World Conference against Racism, held in August September 2001 at Durban, an international interest in Ambedkar himself could be seen' (2003: 266).

31. Recent plays on Gandhi, for instance, Feroze Khan's *Gandhi, My Father* (subsequently transformed into a film) and Pratap Sharma's *Sammy*, demythify the mahatmaization of Gandhi as he has been shown as a failed father. Ambedkar conversely has often been invoked as 'Daliton ka Masiha' (Christ of dalits), but never as 'Daliton ka Gandhi' or 'Daliton ka Ram'.

32. Gian Singh Bal, a Punjabi dalit critic, expresses his deep scepticism on the revolutionary potential of the Bhakti movement in Punjab: 'According to my study, they [*bhakti* saints] never launched any movement against untouchability. Their social concerns were not as much directed towards struggle among people, as they had their concern towards the relationship between man and god' (2007: 59).

33. 'Var' is a Punjabi folk form of heroic poetry in which the warrior, his acts of bravery, his ancestry and his large-heartedness are eulogized in verse form.
34. There are many collections such as Balbir Madhopuri's *Bhakhda Pataal* (1998), Madan Veera's *Bhakhiya* (2001), Gurmeet Kallarmajri's *Nadiyo Vapas Parat Aao* (2002) and Sadhu Singh Shudarak's *Nav Manthan* (2002), where there is not a single direct reference to Ambedkar.
35. According to Gail Omvedt, Buddhism makes the earliest mention of a dalit in any Indian literature:

> Birth does not make an outcaste, birth does not a Brahman make:
> action makes a person low, action makes him great.
> To prove my case I give just one example here—
> the Sopaka Matanga, Candala's son of fame.
> This Matanga attained renown so high and rare
> that masses of brahmans and Khattiyas to serve him were drawn near.
> He ascended, so they say, in a chariot divine,
> defeating lust and hatred, from passion freed, so high
> nor did his birth or caste bar him from paradise!
> But born brahmans are there, kin to the mantra-knowers
> whose evil deeds expose them again and again,
> scorned by the faithful and virtuous, facing a future doom
> their brahman birth does not prevent scorn now or later doom
>
> (*Sutta Nipata*, 136–41, quoted in Omvedt 2003)

36. There is a movement within feminism named 'ecofeminism' that seeks to establish a connection between gender theories and environmental thinking. Ecofeminists such as M. Mies and Vandana Shiva (1994) argue that women and nature are intimately related.
37. Balbir Madhopuri's autobiography also bears a similar title, *Chhangiya Rukh*, which means 'a leafless tree'.
38. Nirala also eulogizes *kukurmutta* (mushroom): 'Aye! rose listen/the fragrance, and colour that you have/you, the uncivilized, have sucked the blood of fertilizer/a capitalist flaunts on the bough' (1980b: 145).
39. Here is an example of Meena Gajabhiye's poetry:

> Crows in flocks and flocks
>   in every corner
>   caw shrilly
> Souls fed on funeral feats cry
>   the revolution has come
>   the revolution has come
> There was a cuckoo in the crow's nest
> so she started calling too
> and an arrow came straight and hit her
>   Even the air vibrated
>   with her song of pain

> The revolution went somewhere else
> taking the song of my cuckoo—
>> (quoted in Zelliot 1996: 67–68)

40. Chandra Talpade Mohanty contests the notions of forging 'feminism without borders' (2003: 9) as she seeks to decolonize feminism from western feminist discourses. Stretching the logic of Mohanty further on the domestic plane, it can as well be surmised that dalit women also tend to contest any essentialized notion of Indian feminism, for there are caste boundaries within the nation.

41. Not many dalit women have written autobiographies. Bama's *Karukki* (2000), Viramma's *Viramma* (1998), Mukta Sarvagoda's *Mitaleli Kavade* (Closed Doors) (1983), Kumad Pawade's *Antasphota* (Inner Explosion) (1995), Baby Kamble's *Jina Amucha* (The Prisons We Broke) (2008) and Shantabai Kamble's *Mhasya Jalmachi Chittaskatha* (The Disjointed Story of My Life) (1998) are some of them.

42. Marathi poet L. S. Rokade, for instance, refers to his mother's misery at the time of his birth:

> Your body covered
> With generations of poverty
> Your head pillowed
> On constant need
> You slept at night
> And in the day you writhed
> With empty fists tied to your breasts!
>> ('To be or Not to be Born', Dangle 1994: 1)

Waman Nimabalkar also writes a poem on the tragic death of his mother who, while collecting firewood in the jungle, is bit by a snake: 'Mother is gone. We, her brood, thrown to the winds./ Even now my eyes search for mother. My sadness grows' ('Mother', ibid.: 36). And, most significantly, Dhasal's very famous poem 'So that my mother may be convinced . . .', in which the poet, while recounting the days of his mother's post-marriage ordeals, seeks her support for his radical credo thus: 'Mother be the support for my weapon/O mother of poverty, make me free for the new world . . .' (Omvedt 1980: 177).

43. The term 'Devadasi' stands for those temple dancers who are 'married' to a deity. With the passage of time, following degeneration in Hinduism, the temple priests used them for prostitution. The practice of dedicating devadasis was declared illegal by the Government of Karnataka in 1982 and the Government of Andhra Pradesh in 1988.

44. The conscious political shift in dalit aesthetics is suggested by Santosh Bhoomkar in his 'Translator's Note' to Saran Kumar Limbale's much discussed autobiography *Akkarmashi* (*The Outcaste*) (2003): '. . . Then recently again the author sent the third and entirely new version of

Akkarmashi under the new title *Akkarmashi Again* (*Poona Akkarmashi*, 1999). This time too the author suggested I follow the new text. As I read and compared it with the original one I found it impossible to follow the author's suggestion to incorporate the changes. It was written in an entirely different manner. The original text was a dialect of Marathi whereas the new version is in standard Marathi. In the new version the original flavour appeared to be missing. The narrator was now a mature man with firm convictions. The tone was also rather polemical and he consciously made a noise as against the boyishly naive narrator of the 1984 original' (2003: xi).

45. Arun Kamble's poem, 'Which Language should I Speak', refers to how a dalit is preempted at the level of language itself. The poet is caught between two linguistic registers. On the one hand, the father would insist 'You whore-son, talk like we do', on the other, his Brahmin teacher tells the poet: 'You idiot, use the language correctly!' (Dangle 1994: 55).

46. Almost without exception, every dalit poet has re-written the myth of Eklavya and Shambook, lending dalit discourse a structural unity and cohesion right from the 1970s till date in terms of its chosen arch-characters.

47. Many biographies of Jhalkari Bai have appeared of late. Bhavani Shankar Visharad's *Veerangna Jhalkaribai*, was published in 1988 by Anand Sahitya Sadan, Aligarh, and is also anthologized in its English translation in *Multiple Marginalities* (Narayan and Mishra 2004). Mohan Das Namishrai wrote a biographical novel, *Veerangna Jhalkari Bai*, published by Radhakrishan Press, Delhi in 2003. Earlier, an attempt of the similar type was made by Naresh Chandra Saxena 'Sainik' who wrote *Amar Balidani Jhalkaribai* in 2002.

48. G. B. Prashant writes a prose tract entitled *Mool Vansh Katha*, in which he holds Mohejo-daro as the original land of the dalits: 'In the Valley of Sindhu, in the ruins of Harappa is located Mohenjo-Daro. It is a word in Sindhi language and its Hindi translation is "the mound of the dead": from the unique ruins of this city of the period of Satyug, a melodious voice can be heard Disciples! Take your old inheritance and deposits. Your history has been demolished . . .' (Narayan and Mishra 2004: 75).

11

On the Frontiers of the Public Sphere: Indian Women's Poetry from Pre-1947 to Post-9/11

Strange for someone as secretive
as me, I don't mind.
I'm opening up the public spaces.
There are no intruders.
They own this place as much as you,
as much as me.

My arms are more relaxed now,
no tension in the neck.
Lately, I've fallen into a new habit,

leaving my life unlocked.
('Open', Dharker 2007: 50)

From the erstwhile 'interior landscape' or 'inner courtyard' hitherto identified as the insular arena of innate postcolonial cultural nationalism, Indian woman poets of the 1990s step into the outer domain of contemporary politics marred by the rhetoric of civilizational clash, global terrorism, retrogressive nationalism and communal genocides.[1] These poets refuse to be intimidated by the violence and destruction of the outer world of which women continue to be the prime targets. Transgressing the gendered polarity of '*ghar* versus *bahir*', Indian woman poetic imagination marches out of its assigned domestic ghettoes into the open contaminated spaces of national and international politics, staking its claim for participation and agency in the making of the new world order.[2] As woman poets plunge into the very vortex of current turbulent political history, their invasion into the public sphere takes them much beyond the protest-poetry of their poet-predecessors. The first section of the chapter, therefore, deals with some of the overarching nationalist frames within which Indian woman poets during the freedom struggle and immediately after 1947 tend to operate in their struggle against the colonial power. The second section maps out the simmering of discontent and dissension among the 'new woman poets' from the 1970s onwards as they speak out against the patently patriarchal nation-state. The third section dwells rather extensively on the growing political consciousness of Indian women's poetry through an exclusive focus on its responses to national as well as international events that have happened from the days of terrorism in Punjab in the 1980s to the recent 9/11 and beyond. Indian women's poetry of the 1990s goes beyond the 'room of its own' in its efforts to challenge the vehement re-assertion of the phallic/fascist in the public realm.

I

During the freedom movement, a whole range of woman poets in Indian English, Hindi and Punjabi appear on the literary horizon but more as subsidiary nationalist voices than as literateurs talented enough to be a part of the mainstream literary canon. Among Indian English female poets, Toru Dutt and Sarojini Naidu receive limited recognition; in Hindi Subhadra Kumari Chauhan and Mahadevi Verma emerge as potent female voices, but they only form the second rung of literary leadership in their respected time-frames.[3] In Punjabi poetry, young Amrita Pritam suffers a lot of male ridicule because of her ostensibly bohemian ways that do not fit in with the traditional frame of femininity.[4] The pre-textual or the extra-textual (enumerated through endnotes) in case of each of the woman poets mentioned here is as important as their textual output, for it suggests the larger underpinnings of the Indian women's poetic discourse in its early phase. These woman poets, in their own distinct ways, lay the foundations of a modern feminist poetic discourse in India, though their protest, circumscribed as it is within the imperatives of 'patriarchal Indian nationalism', may not match the radical rebellion of latter-day woman poets of the 1990s and beyond. For purposes of precision and focus, a short poem representative of Sarojini Naidu, Mahadevi Verma and Amrita Pritam is discussed here.

i

Sarojini Naidu's 'To India' (1943: 58), written as an ode (of twelve lines) to the motherland, offers us a direct instance of the possible conflation of nationalism and feminism during the nationalist period. But this possibility is belied, as the writer's gender does not seem to play any instrumental role in the re-imagining of the nation. Far from any new feminist re-inscription of the nation, the poet re-iterates the patriarchal/sanskritic notion of nation as mother.[5] Even contemporary male Indian English poetry approaches the nation in the same motherly terms.[6] S. H. Jhabvala, for instance, while recounting 'The Tale of India's Sacrifice', addresses India thus: '. . . ; Mother! Thou did'st keep/Even these marauders 'neath thy sheltering arm . . .' (de Souza 2005: 171). Even when India is not elevated into a mother, its gender is always that of a female, that too very weak and passive.

Sarojini's 'Mother' in terms of her attributes is no different from the orientalized sanskritic mother. She is not only 'young through all thy immortal years', she has an 'ageless womb' to regenerate India. Her prime and sacred duty is to beget children: 'And, like a bride high-mated with the spheres,/ Beget new glories from thine ageless womb' ('To India', 1943: 58). The relapse of 'Mother' into a 'bride high-mated' does hint towards the restoration of sexuality in the de-sexed 'Mother', but it proves too ephemeral, as she mates not with men, but with 'the spheres'. Such a mating suggests deification of the mother beyond human recovery. Motherhood not only overtakes womanhood, it becomes its very aim.

The image of 'womb' as a site of the possible new glories is patently feminist for two reasons—one, it brings woman's biology into the foreground, and two, more than male insemination, there is an implicit precedence given to female gestation.[7] But instead of retaining the 'womb' as a female organ over which she exercises her personal volition, the poet tends to reduce it into a sacred site, *sanctum sanctorum* or *garbha griha* of the temple called 'nation'. The womb is the 'embryonic nation' (Sarkar 2001: 43) of which women are 'true patriotic' repositories. The agelessness of the 'womb' de-womanizes the female image. 'Mother' becomes the site of eternal 'male' exploitation. By lionizing her capacities of permanent fertility, the poet portrays 'Mother' as an eternal giver without demanding anything in return. She becomes a symbol of 'the fecundity of the nation and vessel for its reproduction' that requires 'the defence and protection of patriotic sons' (Ivekovic and Mostov 2003: 10). She gathers her identity by virtue of her children. She is to rise from her slumber for 'thy children sake'.

Sarojini's 'Mother' is less a woman, more a goddess or a nation's spirit personified or 'an empress of [its] sovereign past'. In her poetry, goddess, mother and nation are so alterable with each other that a prayer to Goddess Kali and an ode to India bear hardly any semantic incongruity. The extract quoted here

> O terrible and tender and divine!
> O mystic mother of all sacrifice,
> We deck the somber altars of thy shrine
> With sacred basil leaves and saffron rice;
> All gifts of life and death we bring to thee
>   ('Kali The Mother', 1943: 177)

can be sung as song divine in the glory of any goddess or India as motherland; the real physical mother stands dispersed or even lost in the high discourse of spiritualism on the one hand and equally lofty ideals of nationalism on the other. 'Mother' in Sarojini's poetry is hoisted on a pedestal as an object of veneration, silent and static, without a personal volition or sense of participation in the flow of life.

Sarojini's eternally young 'slumbering Mother' is utterly passive and saturnine—a damsel in distress. The fact that a woman poet exhorts her 'Mother' to 'Rise', 'Waken', 'Answer' generates the possibilities of a woman-to-woman dialogue towards empowerment. But once again the poem stops short of such a dialogue. Not only is 'Mother' silent, the woman (the poet) in dialogue with her has no positive methods of empowerment to suggest. Sarojini's idea of motherly/womanly sacrifice is shockingly medieval by modern standards. By way of cross-reference, let us look at two other poems of the poet—'Suttee' and 'The Pardah Nashin'—addressed to fellow women.

Despite a whole range of discourse of woman-reform to beacon her, Sarojini Naidu, in her poem 'Suttee' (1943: 18) continues to portray Sati almost as a sacrificial deity: 'Life of my life, Death's bitter sword/Hath severed us like a broken word,/ Rent us in twain who are but one . . ./ Shall the flesh survive when the soul is gone?' (ibid.: 18). Similarly, instead of holding *pardah* to be a constraint and an impediment in women's liberation, the poet romanticizes it:

> From thieving light of eyes impure,
> From coveting sun or wind's cress,
> Her days are guarded and secure
> Behind her carven lattices,
> Like jewels in a turbaned crest,
> Like secrets in a lover's breast.
>   ('The Pardah Nashin', 1943: 53)

The poet that implores 'Mother India' to look towards the 'Future' is, ironically enough, herself mired in the conservative past.

The reformist agenda of the native as well colonial elite in the nineteenth century seems to make little headway in bringing about a fundamental change in the perspective of the nationalist poet. Clearly, Sarojini is no Pandita Ramabai for instead of retrieving India from the orientalists, she 'nativizes the Orientalist project' (Paranjape 1993: 12).[8] 'To India' remains more backward looking than a leap into the modern future. The womanly presence in the poem is too feminine, conditioned and informed by patriarchal constructions of womanhood and motherhood.

ii

During the formidable *chhayavadi* period of Hindi poetry, amidst the colossal presence of poets like 'Nirala', 'Prasad' and 'Pant', Mahadevi Verma lights her own flickering flame of poetry (*deep-shikha*) foregrounding the pain, the anguish and the sorrow of contemporary women in it.[9] Her songs, prose-portraits as well as paintings delve deep into the women of her times, exploring their aspirations as well as frustrations in terms of their subtle emotions of love and surrender. Her *geet* 'Main Neer Bhari Dhookh ke Badli' measures out delicately the travails of a woman as she travels with all her grace, elegance and innocence into the patriarchal sphere. The elegiac lyricism of the poem suggests the stronghold of medieval orality on Mahadevi's creative unconscious, with the difference, however, that its authorship is well-defined.[10]

In the poem, the 'cloud', which otherwise is constructed as an aggressive and volatile male in *chhayavad*, stands transformed into a young vivacious female, and hence it is termed 'badli' instead of 'badal'.[11] 'Cloud' in the translated version of the poem, used here for analysis, therefore, has a female gender. The cloud as female-protagonist, though weighed down by the burden of sorrow, enlivens the surroundings by virtue of its dynamic tension:

> A continuous stillness resides in its trembling.
> World laughs in the roar of its cries,
> which like lamps light up in the eyes.
> A cascade swells beneath the eyelids. (1970: 329)

The woman in Mahadevi Verma is a redeemer of humanity for she brings music, dreams, colours and soft breeze even to the indifferent patriarchal society:

> My each step exudes music
> Breath flows with dream-pollen
> New colours of the sky weave tapestry
> In my shadow, a fragrant breeze thrives (ibid.)

The romantic tropes do bring the woman out of the closet into the firmament. She has the sensuousness bordering on sensuality of a dark cloud dancing in the sky, and is all set to burst into rain: 'On the dust particles, it sprinkle watery ones/new life, springing sprouts come forth' (ibid.). The restraint that Mahadevi Verma exercises in depicting the physicality of her woman-protagonist probably has more to do with the impositions of patriarchy and its poetics of gaze. On hindsight, the poet, while lending the openness of the sky to her woman-protagonist ends up making her too feminine—oozing with sensuality, yet very pious, cool, caring and careful.

More than defiance, the overwhelming impulse is to surrender and self-sacrifice—the supreme virtue of impeccable womanhood as imagined by patriarchy. As she goes and comes out of existence, she leaves hardly any trace of her memory: 'never does she defile her path, nor does she leave a sign behind'. Her ordinariness is denied to her. She may not be a goddess like Sarojini's Mother, but she appears to be a perfect devotee, too ready to submit:

> The world is spread out
> Yet not a corner belongs to me
> This is me, my history
> I rose yesterday, shall vanish today. (ibid.)

The cloud (as woman) is not just transient, it is forgettable, silent and utterly tearful too. It appears on the horizon either to carry the burden of humanity's sorrow, or to pour forth so as to sprout new vegetation. The woman in the process becomes a willing tragic heroine, too reluctant to stamp her presence in any emphatic way. She evaporates after a momentary flicker.

Mahadevi tends to liquefy women, thereby postponing or even diffusing their female identity in the very moment of their assertion. The consistent refrain in her poetry is to sublimate the woman into a cloud which would merge into the larger expanse of either the sky or the rivers or the oceans below: 'The clouds . . ./ go swiftly to the dark horizon, as/rivers in its splendour to the sea, breast overflowing' (Rubin 1998: 177). In another poem from *Nirja*, the poet seeks to flow like a 'wet languorous dark and silent' cloud 'forever streaming' (ibid.: 167). The cloud/woman attains freedom in its/her self-annihilation or dissipation—this is its/her right to surrender, right to self-effacement. The drift in Mahadevi is always from finite to infinite, from tangible to intangible, and from material to metaphysical. Archana Verma reads this drift in feminist terms thus: '[T]hat there are so many rigid and unrelenting limits in the life of woman . . . that their very burden is so direct and their oppressiveness so dense and impermeable that in the language of woman the very desire of freedom from them could relatively be expressed more emphatically through the idiom of the infinite only' (2007: 149).

iii

Amrita Pritam's oft-quoted poem 'Aakhan Waris Shah Noo' consti-tutes an important female intervention during the dark days of par-tition violence.[12] The poem is an invocation to Baba Waris Shah, the medieval Sufi saint-poet of Punjab who presumably rendered the tragic version of the famous Sufi *kissa* Heer-Ranjha.[13] It is pertinent to observe that like Sarojini Naidu and Mahadevi Verma, Amrita too harks back on indigenous cultural frames for her poetic idiom and expression. While Sarojini Naidu reiterates the mantric past, Mahadevi invokes the tradition of mysticism as it travels from the Vedic age down to Meerabai in the medieval period; Amrita relies on local Sufi-lore. Indian women's poetry during the nationalist period remains more or less rooted in the indigenous frames of emancipation, howsoever limited or circumscribed they might appear from the contemporary radical feminist perspectives of the West.

In the poem, Amrita speaks for thousands of the female victims who were silenced in the communal frenzy that the partition brought in its wake.[14] Besides being the land of five rivers, Punjab is seen as a land of daughters, which is ravaged by male violence, no matter which community it emanated from. The daughters as Heers represent love, harmony and beauty. More than a communal divide, the partition is approached as a tragedy of these Heers forever separated from their Ranjhas from across the border. Against the spectre of divisive violence, Amrita opens a page from Waris Shah's book of love, and implores him to re-appear from his grave to console the bewailing daughters:

> To Waris Shah I turn today!
> Speak up from the graves midst which you lie!
> In our book of love, turn the next leaf.

> When one daughter of Punjab did cry
> You filled pages with songs of lamentation,
> Today a hundred daughters cry
> O Waris to speak to you (1982: 93)

The engendering of Punjab, hitherto imagined in bold masculine terms, as a daughter, and that too a lover, is indeed audacious. Instead of approaching daughters as dutiful, obedient carriers of the 'lofty' traditions of patriarchy, Amrita looks upon them as rebellious lovers.

As compared to the motherified India of Sarojini Naidu, Amrita Pritam's Punjab is not as much spiritualized or deified. The Sufi image of a lamenting Heer, as a correlative for the bleeding Punjab, is far more secular, tangible and locally accessible. The anguish of violated Heers is articulated through the devastated and poisoned landscape of Punjab which is fairly romanticized through the deployment of feminine symbols of rivers, flutes, songs, spinning wheels and swings. Amrita's poem is a dirge over the loss of this feminine Punjab:

> Song was crushed in every throat;
> Every spinning wheel's thread was snapped;
> Friends parted from one another;
> The hum of spinning wheels fell silent. (ibid.)

The foregrounding of partitioned Punjab in the laments of Heer, however, serves the purposes of feminism only half-way for Amrita's Heers are projected only as helpless daughters of a communally divided nation/civilization. Once again, women become easy sites of cultural/communal warfare, of bloody nationalist aspirations; they need a male voice, howsoever enlightened it may be, to soothe their psychic/physical ruptures.

The roles that these Heers perform—from spinning on the *charkha* to swinging on swings and singing songs—are typically feminine, with not even a hint of any reversal of roles. Moreover, bemoaning Heers only consolidate the image of the woman as the weak sex. The assertion of love against violence, though an enabling sentiment, does not raise the poem beyond the level of delicate feminine outcry. Since Amrita's 'love' tends to be more platonic or devotional than sensual or corporal, it ends up de-historicizing the experience/event. The symbol of *charkha* is as much metaphysical as it is feminine.

Sarojini Naidu's enchained 'Mother', Mahadevi Verma's tearful 'cloud' and Amrita Pritam's bewailing 'Heer', despite regional/language-specific shades, are cast in a tragic or melancholic frame. This is not an innocent coincidence. Smarting under the pressures of serious and sublime nationalism, the woman poets of the 1940s tend to opt for a very solemn representation of their fellow women. Even they seem to address only women as their readers. Playfulness, laughter and sex continue to remain 'almost censored' for the nationalist woman.[15] Even as they protest, awaken and cry, they work more towards larger national goals than gender-specific missions. The gender in their poetry, therefore, never comes in the foreground; though it does provide an additional dimension to the background. More than the distinction of languages which the three woman poets write in, what matters in their poetry is the preponderance of essentialized nationalism, and not its differences and discontents.

II

From the 1970s onwards, as movements of liberation of women gather strength nationally as well as internationally, the number of women poets writing and publishing in Indian languages increases drastically manifold, pointing towards the arrival of an unyielding Indian feminist poetic discourse.[16] If, in Hindi, poet's like Champa Vaid, Shakunt Mathur, Amrita Bharati, Jyotsana Milan, Indu Jain, Nirmala Garg, Teji Grover, Gagan Gill, Anamika, etc., find their way into male-dominated new poetic anthologies, in Punjabi, Prabhjot Kaur, Kailshpuri, Mohinder Kaur Gill, Shashi Samundra, Nirupma Dutt, Amar Jyoti, Manjit Tiwana, Vanita, etc., mark their presence on the post-Amrita Pritam poetic scene. In Indian English, from Kamala Das to Eunice de Souza, a flotilla of woman poets radicalizes women's writings in the most fundamental ways. Well-versed in latest theories and movements of woman emancipation in America, France and England, the new crop of young, educated metro-based as well as metro-backed female poets forges ahead with a very bold and confrontationist stance against patriarchy, doing away with the camouflage of spiritualism, nationalism or mysticism which their predecessors had worked under to express their sense of rebellion.

Though the three streams of Indian women's poetry derive their creative metaphors from their respective language-traditions/regions, yet in terms of temperament, there is an increasing congruence on the issue of feminism, suggesting the consolidation of pan-Indian women's poetry in general. Minor differences apart, that too on account of the degree of radicalism, an informal sisterhood of Indian woman poets could be seen in operation. Again for the purposes of focus, three short poems each from three language streams, spread over a period of more than twenty years after the 1970s are discussed in the following sections, mapping the evolution of female assertion.[17] From the 1970s onwards, Indian feminism and women's poetry in different languages evince varying degrees of female awareness within the broad trajectory of radical feminism to a positive assertion of femaleness.

i

Indian English women's poetry of the post-1970s departs significantly from the Toru Dutt–Sarojini Naidu brand of 'sentimental pastiche' (de Souza 1997: 1) as it politicizes the issue of gender on the basis of lived experience rather than on the scriptural sanskritic elevation of the woman as devi, goddess or mother. Of course, it gains insights from radical western feminist discourse, for which at times it is criticized by the native critics as well. Combining the lived, the native and the international is always a challenge for Indian English poetry as a whole; in Indian English women's poetry the challenge becomes an enterprise, for 'gender' is such a hugely contested terrain that it threatens to subsume poetry as much as it sustains it. It is indeed difficult to decide whether it is poetry as (gender) politics or (gender) politics as poetry, but the fact remains that despite different levels of maturity, Indian English women's poetry foregrounds the issue of gender in terms that are difficult to be slotted singularly in the categories of either native, national or international. Self-experience, however, remains the bottom-line even when the expression tends to be derivative.

(a)

Inaugurating a phase of radical feminism in Indian English women's poetry, Kamala Das arrives on the poetic scene 'with a frankness and openness unusual in the Indian context' (Parthasarthy 1976a: 22). In her poem, 'The Sunshine Cat', for instance, she exposes the politics of conjugal relationship—a relationship hitherto transcendentalized beyond bodily union—in her characteristic style of confessional intimacy. Her stance is not just unorthodox; it is sacrilegious and profane by the standards of conservative patriarchy. The poem dares to bring into light the prostitutionalization of the 'wife' as she is reduced into a plaything to be sexually exploited by the 'husband' and his 'men'. The so-called nationalist 'home' stands subverted into a brothel with the husband as its legitimized pimp.

The husband, valourized as a chivalrous protector in conventional wisdom, turns out to be 'selfish/And a coward'. He is 'a ruthless watcher' as he offers his 'wife' to other men. The husband 'neither love[s] her/nor Use[s] her', though the 'wife' loves him; other men also wash their hands off: 'To forget, oh, to forget . . . and they said each of/Them I do not love, I cannot love, it is not/In my nature to love' (ibid.: 25). The woman, meanwhile, is driven to a state of madness, struggling to keep herself intact: 'They let her slide from pegs of sanity into/A Bed made soft with tears, and she lay there weeping' (ibid.). The sexual abuse is violence both to body and mind.

The woman in Das's poetry is driven to create her own secluded world with tears as her wall: 'I shall build walls with tears,/She said, wall to shut me in . . .' (ibid.). During the day time as she is locked inside a room, 'a streak of sunshine lying near the door' provides her company. This sunshine in her secluded agony takes the form of a 'sunshine cat'. The image of the cat has sexual connotations in the Indian context; the cat is 'the steed (and an aspect) of the *yogini* Vidali' (Chevalier and Gheerbrant 1996: 162).[18] The 'sunshine', though transient in terms of its span and season, is also a potent image of positive energy, fire and passion. As winter sets in, along with the receding sunshine, the sexuality of the woman-protagonist also withers away: 'Winter came and one day while locking her in, he/Noticed that the cat of sunshine was only a/ Line, a hair-thin line, . . .' (ibid.). Without the sunshine, the woman is 'half-dead', 'now of no use at all to men' (ibid.).

Though it might be alleged that 'In Das, the sexuality is often so completely self-absorbed, so navel-gazing as to become both narrowly personal and problematically sensationalized and voyeuristic' (Katrak 1996: 288), yet the way the poet politicizes her intimate private speaks of her larger more radical feminist concerns.[19] Also, more than the imported theory, as is often presumed in the case of a radical feminist outburst by an Indian woman, it is the self-experience of the poet that comes into play. The poet does away with the subtle spiritualist obfuscations of medieval women Bhakti poets from Meera to Akkamahadevi for she clearly knows that God is no substitute for a lover.

(b)

During the 1980s or early 1990s Indian women's poetry in English tends to take a rather belligerent stance, which is another extreme of sentimentalism. Most of the poems written during this phase are perhaps more radical than what Kamala Das could ever write, yet they end up generating more hysteria than a discourse of saner mediation. The poetry is relegated to a surcharged statement; the intellectual activist takes over the poet. The woman poets employ vocabulary of the battlefield and guerilla attacks, with no room for negotiation; there are decisive defeats and equally decisive victories. Fathers, husbands and even mothers are adversaries in the battlefield to be literally killed.[20] Instead of rupturing, the gender-binaries are consolidated, for these women poets refuse to enter into any relationship with their Other (male).

In a very terse poem of seven lines Charmayne D'Souza reduces the male–female hierarchy in a series of alliterated phrases or punch lines:

> Woo men
> Womb men
> Woe men
> Whim men
> Warm men
> Who men?
> No, Women. (1990: 1)

In terms of its sound effects, the poem does dazzle the reader, especially a male-reader. The poet unearths not only the semantics of the signifier 'women' but also, through a deft play of acoustics, the politics of pronunciation which foregrounds 'men' more than 'women'. In the process, 'woman' stands erased in a series of acts that she is expected to do towards 'men'.

This formulaic engendering of the complex relationships only suggests stubbornness of stance, and smacks of unrelenting finitude. Poetry is not just a compact arrangement between verb and noun, the role of qualifiers, modifiers and even of adjectives and adverbs in measuring, calibrating and even deciphering situations is very significant for the poetic impulse to hover around or zero in on. The fluidity of experience, with all its conflicts, moments of stalemate and impasse, needs to be as much arrested as it should be unleashed in the poetic text. Charmayne D'Souza's verbal staccatos do not open up the poetic field, rather they pre-empt the poetic argument right at the moment of its take-off. Each line of the poem, as Adil Jussawala puts it, comes as a 'sharp karate stroke[s]' that puts down 'those who bother her [the poet]' (1992: 48). The poet bobs up 'buoyantly after the put down, rather like a Karate-fighter who walks away from the scene of battle least concerned about the condition of her assailant' (ibid.).While attempting a spelling guide for women, Charmayne D'Souza virtually ends up re-writing a polemical primer for the neo-literate urban feminist.

(c)

In the late 1990s, Indian women's poetry in English undergoes almost a generational shift as it longs for those suppressed strands of hermaphrodite awareness, which due to patriarchal politics of heterodox sexuality remain unrealized and unexplored. Invoking the legendary Greek poet, Sappho, as her arch-ideal of inter-sexuality, Rukmini Bhaya Nair, in her poem 'Hermaphrodite Longings', aspires for a self which is 'soft as woman's silk/Rough as the knuckles of a man' (1992: 135). Instead of male–female duality, the poet seeks an organic complementary relationship between the two genders within her single body: 'A man in love must become a woman/before he is done with loving' (ibid.: 133). While defining feminine sexuality, Rukmini, in her critical intervention on the poem, comments that it is not all about 'an exploration of the female body and the female psyche' (2001: 193). The poet is against the division of the human species into 'male and female compartments' (ibid.).

Once the gender division is removed, lesbianism no longer remains a purely a woman-to-woman relationship, it becomes more a relationship of the man in a woman, with the woman in a man. The champions of heterodox sex are too straight for the poet to be part of her love-landscape: 'The fathers and the patrons, the heterosexual/ Saints . . . These stand outside the gates of love' (1992: 135). The transgender personas including transvestites, lesbians, eunuchs and other 'queer' characters hold special attraction for the poet:

> How it is the territory of eunuchs and gays
> Of the women of Lesbos, transvestites
> Slaves, hermaphrodites, the poxy
> Apple-cheeked seventeenth-century brats
> Playing Artemis and Diana, of the specialist

> Men of Indica, sinuous *narivesham* dancers
> Performing only as women, of housewives
> Bargirls, of every damned woman . . . (ibid.)

The 'territory' is not an exclusive absolute zone of gender; it is rather the intermediate zone of sexuality, the erogenous site of 'homosexual love, incest, macho maleness, eunuch bravado or adolescent transsexuality' (2001: 194). These zones of sexuality are tabooed by the homophobic nationalist patriarchy to maintain 'purity' of the nation-state along convenient gender lines.[21]

To the poet, the eunuch is not a sexless being, bereft of desires and longings; rather she/he is one of the manifestations of half-male, half-female. This is how she recounts her one very intimate encounter with a eunuch:

> A man snatched at me this afternoon
> He was a woman, his eyes rimmed with
> Kohl, the veins red with memory, I could not
> Look at him. My eyes fell . . .
>
> Because it was your face. (1992: 134)

The damaged sex of the eunuch reminds one of the distraught Sappho. Rather than going forward in time, the poet regresses in time and discovers the archetype of her queer love in Greek antiquity.

> But I see now why you wore
> The face of a eunuch this afternoon, held me
> Captive with your street smart tongue, straining
> Under a shameless lift of skirts, that sequinned
> Body to reveal your damaged sex (ibid.: 137)

The touch of the hijra is difficult to ignore, rather it allures the poet.[22] She extends the poetics of confession so characteristic of women's poetry in general, that without any fear of backlash from conservative patriarchy, she would declare defiantly:

> In the mutilated body, in the coarse
> Horsewhip tactics of that hijra, scintillating oils
> Jasmine, the blouse a gaudy trap, her hand
> Across me, a sinewy band of teak . . . I could not
> Pass . . . I had to face (ibid.: 134)

The experience leads to an intense hermaphrodite awareness of being: 'Every man has memories of being a woman/and women know that they have been gods' (ibid.).

In her 'queer' love-longings, Rukmini crosses frontiers of cultures and discovers an indigenous version of the Greek Sappho in Indica: 'You *were* him . . . *Ardhanarishwara,* enticingly chaste/Lover of lovers, you were that divided god . . ./ Peerless hermaphrodite, . . .' (italics not mine, ibid.: 134–35).[23] Love knows no boundaries: 'That was love at work,/It jumped the petty fences . . ./Crossed the sea of Indica and Attica' (ibid.: 136). In a cultural cross-over, the poet takes on the position of Sappho's unmarried daughter Kleis: 'You crossed black Acheron, Sappho, to rob me of my vanity/Klies in Indica, distracted by bright ribbons/Sappho does not spare her daughters wherever they are' (ibid.: 137).

History, hitherto defined in patriarchal terms of war, bloodshed and cruelty stands redefined in terms of the love of a woman: 'True histories are histories of women in love' (ibid.: 133). Politics as well as poetry needs women for their persistence: 'And every poet, Catullus included/Enters history through the body of a woman' (ibid.). The very gender of history is that of a woman in love with another woman for 'it is woman/[who] Knows best the rounded feel of a woman's buttocks/How to rub with scented violet, cassia and myrrh . . .' (ibid.). All history is 'a rage of longing, a storm of enduring' (ibid.) and 'bawdy boys' as emperors only know how to overpower.

In Indian English women's poetry, the configurations of feminist poetics are thus varied but not without a definite direction. From self-experience, it gets mired in binaries before it finally transcends gender divisions. The poetry of the 1990s seeks resolution, not in terms of some metaphysical oneness of experience, but through an open acceptance of multiple sexualities. Animated equally by local protest movements right from the Bhakti poetry of woman saint poets and western feminist discourse, it is multi-local as well as multi-vocal. If, in the case of Kamala Das, it could be said that the local matrilineal society of Kerala lends her confidence to assert her female voice, in the case of Charmayne D'Souza, a semi-westernized Goa provides combative energies to her. Rukmini Bhaya Nair draws heavily upon her knowledge of Sanskrit and other classical languages and traditions.

ii

In Hindi poetry, the trajectory of feminism is slightly different from that of Indian English women's poetry. Hindi being the native language, the anxieties of nationalism in it are far more pronounced than they are in Indian English which is inseminated by a host of alien sources as well. During the 1970s, Hindi woman poets struggle to wriggle themselves out of the mysticism of the Meera-Mahadevi complex as they come into contact with western feminist writings and the endeavour is to barge into the external domain. But due to the pressures of tradition, Hindi woman poets transgress the prescribed zone of safety in a rather graduated manner. Therefore, in terms of radicalism, Hindi women's poetry vis-à-vis Indian English women's poetry is much more diffident and the issue of gender remains subservient to poetry. The biological dimensions of feminism are not as much expressed as the poetics of space, language and role-allocation takes precedence.

(a)

Amrita Bharati, a reclusive poet of the 1970s, in her 'Ek Chal Rahi Bhoomika' (2003: 157–59), while playing her role of 'Agony' on the world-stage, yearns to reach out to the people, beyond the scope of a prescribed role: '[T]hat I wasn't acting my role/like a role/but trying to come out of it' (ibid.: 157).[24] There is a definite clamouring for transgression:

> I wanted to go into the audience
> And beyond
> To open the theatre door
> And go out
> Into the street
> I wanted to touch a leper's hand
> Like a lover's . . . (ibid.)

The very desire to exceed the constricted limits of theatre constitutes a contravention of the conventional space allocated to women. Theatre spins an illusion of reality, and the poet seeks to cut loose from the tyranny of this illusion as she outstretches her hands towards a leper in the street. The binary of theatre versus street, actor versus audience creates dissensions in her expansive imagination. Theatre is no more a site of happening; it has become too stylized and stilted to allow even enlightened deviance.

Though Bharati is not as belligerent as Kamala Das, yet as she gets into the role, and begins to play 'the real character', she causes quite a stir; everything around breaks free from the text of the play:

> And with me
> All the props
> The crown of silken thorns, the cross and the nails,
> The water in the chalice of poison, . . .
> And all the people
> —the judge, the jury, the townsfolk and the spies
> Each in their role—come out
> of the play (ibid.: 158)

Real 'Agony' is difficult to bear for the player as well as the audience. The more it is internalized, the more ripples it causes in the outer world. The poet realizes that her rebellion would not suffice for a gender revolution; the people, the agencies of state and arbiters of morality and social decorum will also have to rise above their assigned roles.

In the stride of her role, as the poet comes out on the road challenging gender stereotypes, even as gods withdraw, men as law-makers takeover:

> . . . that there was no backstage anymore
> God
> Had entrusted himself to the law of man
> And I
> Was crying in the middle of the street
> My head placed on a stone (ibid.)

The desire to journey from the constricted and constructed world of theatre to the street amounts to challenging even (male-)gods. Even 'Gods, bent under the burden of sin/[turn] speechless' (ibid.: 159). Of course, as the drama of life is enacted, and the defined roles are defied, a violence of a kind on the stage is performed; the theatre-door however remains unopened: '. . . . that my hand couldn't find the stage door/And all around me' (ibid.). The shackles of theatre remain un-broken, but the poet, even in her moments of failure is able to expose the politics of space/role-allocation. The problem with Bharati's poetry is that instead of situating the question of gender in the social context, she tends to philosophize it. The outward move-ment leads to greater inwardness, though of a turbulent and rebel-lious kind.

(b)

As Hindi women's poetry advances, it attains boldness, even explicitness in its deployment of the female body/sexuality towards an emphatic assertion of women's identity. Indu Jain, a prolific poet of Hindi, in her frenzy of 'Freedom' (1998: 159) reverses the role of the sexes in the sexual act:

> I am a jet of air
> you—the launching pad.
> I was deep in you
> standing erect.
> Now I am ablaze
> steam and fire. (ibid.)

Instead of being with the male, the penetrating power is with the woman as she takes over the role of an active partner. The missionary positions are overturned as it is the woman who stands 'erect'. Instead of romanticized and feminine, 'a gentle breeze' or 'a flowing curvilinear river', the woman in the poem is an overtly phallocentric 'jet of air' that exerts upward thrust. The male aggression is usurped as 'he' is reduced to a passive launching pad. The woman of Hindi poetry acquires the confidence to express her sexuality in 'steamy' terms.

Female sexuality, expressed hitherto in muted terms, suddenly seeks liberation from male bondage: 'However hard you may try/the cords of my hair/shall slip out of your grasp' (ibid.). Once unleashed, it frees itself from male control. The confines of the backyard as well the memory of the lover/husband seem to suffocate the poet:

> I watch the clean light of the stars
> the confines of the backyard repel me
> straight in my flight
> your memory—
> a vow to further distance from you. (ibid.)

Female sexuality comes in the open with a defiance that is self-annihilating. In moments of her sexual realization, the poet seeks to de-memorize the male, for it is the act and not 'him' that matters. The memory of the male is an impediment towards female freedom.

Though the male is not altogether absented, under some exclusive feminist streak, he is denied any agency. The celebration of female sexuality is unequivocal and inhibition-free:

> The day you gathered me in your arms
> Atoms started flying outwards
> Igniting fireworks
> Is giving birth to flame flowers . . . (ibid.)

Though Indu Jain manages to reverse the much-debated Freudian binary of male activism versus female passivism, yet by choosing elongated objects as symbols of female sexuality, she seems to buttress the Freudian thesis of penis envy as the sole basis of gender consciousness.

(c)

Hindi women's poetry of the 1990s largely focuses on the poetics and politics of space; however, its woman protagonist now begins to celebrate her exile and homelessness. She has realized the bondages of her context, and therefore, as a loose free-floating text, she would prefer to remain de-contextualized, un-interpreted. Erstwhile interpretations have undone her. In her poem, 'Bejagah', Anamika refers to a series of arbitrary male interpretations and contexts that she had to suffer right through her school days. She recounts how once a very arbitrary explanation of a *sloka* given by her Sanskrit teacher intimidated her: 'Once fallen from their given position nail/hair and women, are condemned to nowhere' (2003: 152). The entire brahmanical learning stands challenged in the masterly inter-texual interpolation.

The grammar lessons teach language less, and consolidate gender stereotypes more. Anamika enlists some of the 'innocuous' sentences that teachers hammered into her ears right from her first class onwards:

> 'Ram, go to school!
> Radha, cook the food!
> Ram, come eat sweets!
> Radha, hold the broom!
> Brother would sleep now,
> Go and lay his bed! . . .' (ibid.: 152)

These primary utterances gather momentum and as the education progresses they take shape of a well-defined gender division. When the girl-child asks for her 'room', she is told: 'girls are wind, sunshine, the good earth / they don't have a home of their own' (ibid.).

Abandoned from her home, the poet refuses to be interpreted and thus anchored in some male bastion all over again. She does not want to appear as a puzzle to be cracked by some students of B.A. pass course. She begins to tap her homelessness to her advantage. Like Mahadevi Verma she, as an unattached being, too roams in the free sky, but there is no streak of self-annihilation. She rather celebrates her hard-earned exile:

> Beyond all contexts,
> At long last I've gotten here
> Let me be sung
> like
> an unfinished poem
> [of Tukaram]. (ibid.: 153).

De-contextualization thus becomes the trope of empowerment. Exile, ironically, is a space of un-fixated belonging. Anamika harnesses contemporary post-structuralist vocabulary, particularly of French feminists, to articulate her freedom beyond addresses and locations.[25]

iii

While on the one hand, along with the traditional local archetypes of Heer, Loona, Sohni, Sundara, etc., the mythical woman characters of Sita and Savitri continue to enamour Punjabi female imagination, on the other, feminism as a conscious ideology also begins to influence it.[26] Young Punjabi woman poets—mostly college/university teachers and journalists—are acutely aware of the changing contours of feminist theory in the West, and as they negotiate the question of female participation, they seem to establish an over-arching relationship between the lovelorn and vagrant female protagonists of Sufi *kissas* and rather aggressive and firm feminists of the West. The post-Amrita Pritam generation of poets from Manjit Tiwana to Shashi Samundra would go to the extent of even challenging Amrita's legacy with a flamboyance which it ironically inherits from her only: 'Such are the constraints of/poets of Amrita Pritam's age,/ a cigarette is their only solace!' (Dutt, see www.india.poetryinternationalweb.org).[27]

(a)

Amrita Pritam remains one of the formidable feminist voices in Punjabi poetry, and the later woman poets or even her contemporaries derive their poetic energies from the path charted by her. One latter-day Punjabi poet, Manjit Tiwana, furthering the legacy of young pre-partition Amrita Pritam, challenges the politics of the domestication of the woman as housekeeper in her poem, 'Chanan de Talwar'. Though the poem tends to idealize woman as the very brilliance of moonlight which is too dazzling to be contained in the four walls of a house, yet in its poetic build-up it does suggest exile as a better option than home. By choosing 'exile' as her preferred destiny, the poet overturns the patriarchal expectations of woman as an insular repository of the nationalist essence.

The poet, exiled from her home right from her childhood is never allowed to settle. The patriarchal order takes different forms and each time 'snatching my [her] home from me [her]' alleges "see how wanton she is/never does she come to the house" (1995: 62). Being thrown on the crossroads of life, she is an object of gaze. One bystander suggests:

> 'In my being there are many rooms
> and the door of one
> does not open in other
> you can live in one of these rooms' (ibid.)

As the poet stares back at the promiscuous male, another one intervenes: 'spending some moments with someone/is not sufficient for the rest of life' (ibid.). She spurns overt male advances.

The female bystanders question the capacity of the exiled poet in negotiating her homelessness:

> 'There is a golden label
> on the false relationships of home
> How will you enlighten the false labels
> with the flame of your forehead?' (ibid.: 62–63)

Another female passer-by forewarns her against the rather licentious nature of males: 'everyman by hook or crook/runs away from his home/what will you do of that deserted home?' (ibid.: 63). Before the poet is overtaken by the worry of homelessness, another female voice butts in: 'Wind, birds and pure thought/are never in want of home' (ibid.). The images are stereotypically feminine and as such tend to simplify the complexity of woman's homelessness.

A whole range of rebellious female poets—'Sappho, Sylvia/Emily, Rabiya/Sara and Amrita'—from across the languages in their tense voices beacon the exiled poet in moments of despair:

> What walls are you talking about?
> For souls like you
> even the markers of time
> are too narrow (ibid.)

The entire tradition of female poetry engenders confidence in the beleaguered poet: 'and the kind of thought/which your sword of moonlight unleashes/how can anyone stand/its strike' (ibid.). The sword of moonlight is a metaphor both for woman and her poetry. It is interesting to observe that like Indu Jain's 'jet of air', Manjit Tiwana's 'sword of moonlight' is too phallic to suggest the arrival of an alternative female idiom. Also, the way she combines woman poets of different cultures and eras in one poetic sweep, suggests that she tends to take an essentialized view of women's poetry.

(b)

Punjabi women's poetry also gravitates towards an androgynous point of view as Shashi Samundra expresses her admiration, if not love, towards the eunuchs. In her poem, 'Khusre', the poet approaches eunuchs as secular, ideology-free, credo-neutral beings who transcend all man-made divisions:

> I like eunuchs.
> Eunuchs
> dance in every house—
> be it of a Hindu, Sikh, Muslim or a Communist (1992: 36)

There is no sense of shame that these eunuchs suffer from. They actually clap aloud on matters of shame/shamelessness.

The gaze of the eunuchs, according to the poet, is sacred and non-vulgar for it does not look upon women as mere sensual/sexual objects:

> Even when the eunuch's eye is on your body
> It is pure and holy.
> A eunuch cannot be made to suffer
> the burden of vulgarity (ibid.)

Of course, unlike Rukmini Bhaya Nair, Shashi denies the eunuch sex appeal as well as desire, and in this sense stops short of espousing a radical hermaphrodite sex-life. Instead of humanizing the eunuchs, Shashi Samundra tends to spiritualize them. She redeems them but desists from having a sexual encounter with them. Bisexuality is approached more in terms of the effacement of desire than in setting up an erotic universe within.[28]

The poet tends to portray eunuchs as a distinct social category beyond religions and castes. The half-male, half-female biological make-up of the body of the eunuchs remains rather under-expressed. Their zest for life is acknowledged:

> They are not good singers
> Nor good dancers
> But when with self-pride they do all this
> How natural and beautiful they look (ibid.: 37)

But the issue of their sensuality is deliberately circumvented. The fact that these eunuchs enamour the poet is an indication of her love for them at the sexual level, yet she chooses to be reticent and tongue-tied, or is not ready for this kind of radical and bold admission. By way of comparison, Indian English women's poetry of the late-1990s articulates rather freely the possibilities of sex outside the normative heterosexual order.

(c)

In 'Feminism' (2005: 201–2), a poem by a relatively lesser known young poet Jatinder Kaur, Punjabi women's poetry seems to take a possible turn towards post-feminism.[29] The poem is not a routine nativist backlash against the imported credo of feminism; in terms of its critical tenor it is a self-reflexive and ironical re-visiting of the radicalized feminist self. The poem opens on a note of dissent against the feminist poetics of rupture:

> This is a strange quarrel
> This is 'mine', and that is 'yours'
> There is nothing between me and you
> You are you, and me is me, and this is it
> I multiply your and my
> self by two.

Instead of arriving at a negotiated harmony, feminism seems to promote an irrevocable distinctness of genders. The image of radicalism precedes the female self, and thus causes violence within. Instead of creating channels of communications, the rhetoric of feminism has only consolidated the gender divide.

Feminism creates a mirage, a constructed image of the female self, an illusion of freedom that pre-empts any encounter with the real self: 'Standing in front of the mirror, like a sparrow/I quarrel with my image'. The poet wants to peel off the silver paint of the mirror planted on the wall so that it does not spawn false images:[30]

> If I peel off layer from the mirror
> a door would come up in the wall
> Instead of image, the mirror will show
> a clear passage.

But before she could do so, the gods (goddesses) of feminism intervene and obstruct attempts of negotiation with the Otherified male. The gap between the real and the reflected, the actual and the ideologized, the essential and the constructed postpones even a working relationship between genders. As the poet seeks a passage across the divide, the broken splinters of glass threaten to pierce through her tired legs. The images that feminism perpetuates of woman do not let the poetess experience the clear light of the day. Not only does the male order construct images of gender, even radical feminism ends up doing the same. The poet seeks to go beyond gender-constructionism to experience essential femaleness.

Being aware of the limitations of ever meeting her real self in the mirror, the poetess struggles to hold onto the 'firefly in hand' than to chase the ever-elusive sun:

> Right now I am a dwarf
> and the door of sun is far away
> and the firefly I am holding in my fist
> I fear, might die away

If the firefly slips out of her hand, she shall have to reach out to the sun, which is beyond her reach. Though feminism spins its own images of womanhood around, yet the poet dreads to relinquish them altogether, for the journey without images is too arduous: 'It is difficult to look across the mirror/by wiping off the images that prop on it'.

The poet succumbs to the propaganda of feminism but not without an ironical sting: 'well, this is an age of feminism/this is an age of feminism'. Both 'mirror' and 'firefly' in hand stand for the limited potential of feminism; the former suggests its non-participatory, reflective and illusory nature, the latter its ephemeral pettiness. The passage through the mirror-wall and the sun are symbols of vision beyond the gender divide.

Thus, Indian women's poetry from the 1970s onwards does come out of the nationalist mould as it refuses to be the voice of the imagined insular essence; rather it turns inside out the 'home', with women no longer as its granted custodians. Though it stops short of being a separatist subaltern discourse, it does expose the operation of patriarchy and its nationalist ideals of sacrificial motherhood. After the initial crescendo, the pitch of radicalism that women's poetry in all the three language streams slows down and settles for a negotiated feminism, which retains values of femaleness beyond gender roles and stereotyping. Western feminism—both American and French—could be seen making visible inroads into the native female consciousness, yet as the women poets evolve they grow beyond theoretical frames, both imported and indigenous, towards a poetry of personal experience. The regional differences or linguistic peculiarities do not come in the way of the consolidation of a general feminist poetic discourse.

III

As Indian woman poets clamour for the totality of being—beyond sexist divisions and demarcations—they are confronted with large-scale violence in the public sphere that threatens to push them back again into the narrow confines of *ghar*, the stereotypical sphere of feminine silence. As governments in the name of national sovereignty and communities in the name of religious purity tend to adopt militant measures to curb feminist movements, there is suddenly a grounds-well of protest against the increasing re-masculinization of national and international space. While the earlier generation of woman poets exposes the violence within the domestic fold to their gender and sex, the poets of the 1990s address the issue of violence in the outer sphere, where again women are the prime targets. If in English, Rukmini Bhaya Nair, Imtiaz Dharker, Seeme Qasim, Meena Alexandar raise a battle-cry against renewed attempts of intimidation and victimization of the woman in the name of larger national or civilizational goals, in Hindi, Katyayni, Anamika, Gagan Gill, Archana Verma and others dare to write in/against aggressively patriarchal times. In Punjabi, young new voices—from Pal Kaur to Sukhvider Amrit—respond to the growing terrorization of the native as well as global politics with feminist vehemence. Contemporary Indian women's poetry, while retaining its feminist edge, participates and even confronts on fundamental issues—of increasing communalization of national and international politics, commodification of culture, state excesses and the silencing of the subaltern—that loom large on humanity as a whole. Again, for purposes of containment, the next section undertakes a very brief discussion of three woman poets from each language stream.

i

(a)

Indian English woman poets of the 1990s venture to write on political events that otherwise tend to siege and benumb the poetic imagination itself. Adorno's poignant pronouncement, 'To write poetry after Auschwitz is barbaric. And this corrodes even the knowledge of why it has become impossible to write poetry today' (1981: 34), haunts in the background as one reads the poems of these women poets, who refuse to be intimidated in the face of the gravest threat to their body, art and speech. In her *The Ayodhya Cantos*, Rukmini Bhaya Nair devotes a full section of poems entitled *Via Ayodhya* written in response to 'the destruction of the sixteenth century monument known as Babri Masjid at Ayodhya on 6 December, 1992' (1992: 1). The poems, divided into three *kandas*—*The Hanuman Kanda, The Sita Kanda* and *The Vishnu Kanda*—constitute a 'comi-tragedy' (ibid.: 2) involving the three characters, who are portrayed in mixed terms, somberly mythical as well as humorously human, to underline the absurdity of the tragedy at Ayodhya. Two sets of choric voices— one incantatory and the other mundane—belonging to priests and the people interlace the main narrative.

Vishnu, Hanuman and Sita in Nair's rather topical poetic/political allegory are easily identifiable with the key actors of the Ayodhya tragedy. While Vishnu is Lal Krishna Advani, the volatile leader of the *rath yatra*, Hanuman is a local *bhakta* who runs 'a small chai-paan shop at the crossroads of Ayodhya' (ibid.), Sita is a young Muslim girl Sitara, selling marigold garlands for the temples. Hanuman feels betrayed by the fluttery tricks of Vishnu and his promise of Ramrajya: 'He does not know if Vishnu can be trusted any more' ('Ramrajya', ibid.: 21). Sufficiently historicized in the poem, Hanuman is in de-sperate search of a god so much so that 'A Bajrang-Dal stray would do, muttering the Hanuman Chalisa,/ Misquoting the Gita. Someone to talk to, Someone more ignorant/Than himself, some elemental lumpen' (ibid.: 23). Taking the innocence of characters like Hanuman for granted, Vishnu fiddles with history through myth. The poet in her laconic voice reminds: 'In history everything costs. Myth is free' (ibid.: 26). She intervenes in the poetic-narrative through the chorus of the people. In one such chorus, the tone is accusatory:

> Why did Vishnu push his rath yatra
> Into the calm obscurity of Ayodhya?
> Listen, Bhavani, we're sick of politics
> Ayodhya lacks basic civil amenities
> The sacred Sarayu flows just nearby
> But drinking water's in short supply. (ibid.: 26)

As it is the voice of the people, the language of the chorus tends to be direct, prosaic and this-worldly. As politicians meddle with history, they unleash forces beyond control: 'Vishnu stirred up trouble just for fun,/ And when things got hot, he cut and run!' (ibid.: 27).

The second section of the poetic allegory, centred as it is on Sita, brings into foreground the travails of women in general during the male-carnival of communal frenzy. Undergoing the pangs of multiple partitions, Sita/Sitara is molested everyday in the holy city of Ayodhya, while god 'Rudra, Vishnu, bringer of tears, watches Sita's plight': 'The peanuts spill from her helpless grip. Chunni pulled/ Away. Hair in mess, breast squeezed in a wild caress. She is parted/ . . .' (ibid.: 29). As Sita/Sitara literally runs for her life from Faizabad to Ayodhya, it is Hanuman who acts as her helpless rescuer. In their exhausted sleep, Sitara and her friends Ira, Naina, Deena, Indu, Asiya are overtaken by history on the 'cunning highway'; the 'Locks on Babri Masjid come unstuck again' (ibid.: 32). The poet, invoking goddess Bhavani, sums up the ironic situation: 'O Bhavani, what in the/World did they know, cowering in Vaidehi's shrine where a hundred/Sita's glow, their voices hushed and their flowers crushed in dread' (ibid.: 32).

Comparing the Ayodhya events with a B-grade movie, produced by Vishnu, the poet underlines the nasty masculinity of *kar-sevaks*: 'Big stuff/This! No more pussyfoot talkies at Faizabad, saving pigtailed brats/From wanton striplings. There is a man's work to attend to' (ibid.: 34). While highlighting the role of 'Groovy, Man!' (ibid.: 38) in the orgiastic climax of the action-thriller, the role of sadhvis is brought into perspective: 'sadhvis lift their frenzied/Eyes heavenwards, ecstatic' (ibid.: 38). The slogans that these sadhvis raise are not only sexual, they are patriarchal too: '*Ek dhakka aur do! Babri Masjid ko tor do!*' (ibid.: 33). The feminine principle of *shakti* stands caricaturized and distorted for sadhvis only end up internalizing the traditional binary of male reason versus female unreason.[31] Babri Masjid stands gendered as a female which 'Rama enters', while 'prattling Sitara falls below' (ibid.: 34). In the face of this gross display of rabid masculinity, the poet believes that only Sita/Sitara can redeem secular India:

> Who shall atone for December 6
> 1992? Well, there is one major player—
> Call her Hindu or Muslim, Sita or Sitara
> She holds a marigold garland in her hands
> And black headscarf tied firm, she stands
> For our terrors, and all our memories . . . (ibid.: 34)

In women's poetry, the 'fallen' female who bears the brunt of religious fundamentalism, becomes the chosen agent of atonement.

(b)

9/11 unleashed such a reactionary rage and ushered in such a per- spectival watershed that everything civilizational—from poetry to feminism—was dismissed as phony, unreal and irrelevant by the votaries of retaliation.[32] As masculinity mounts pressure to put on hold the women's agenda, and to marginalize women's participation in the public sphere, Meena Alexander ventures to write lyric poetry in her unmistakably female voice, registering her protest against the brutalization of the human landscape. As against fiction, she prefers 'the sharp fragility of the lyric'; she says, 'The lyric poem allows me [her] much better to catch the edginess of things, the sharp nervosity, the flaming, falling buildings' (2002b: 31). Instead of lapsing into her autobiographical past, the poet feels the pressure of writing beyond the enclosed world: 'Though sometimes I feel I just want to write about childhood, I sense now I cannot afford the luxury of writing about a world enclosed' (ibid.: 33). Writing poetry for Meena Alexander is as much an act of personal cleansing as it is a medium of confronting history. Poetry is her 'short incantation/my[her] long way home' ('Blue Lotus', 2004: 44).

The poet approaches 9/11 in a broader context, much beyond narrow jingoistic rhetoric, as the very condition of fearful fragmentation, of 'not knowing what strike next, fire, racial profiling, pestilence—that bitty white powder filled with anthrax spores. . . . And on the other side of the globe in Afghanistan, the terrible bombardment, stones ground down, children starving, women in *burkhas* fleeing. Both are real, disjoined in space, they coexist in time, in a molten time' (2002b: 32–33). In the aftermath of 9/11, she discovers the entire landscape maimed, blood-blotted and monstrous: 'But its leaves are filled with insects/With wings the color of dry blood' ('Aftermath', 2004: 9). At times, imagery turns almost gothic: 'Two or more hand/in hand leapt off the tightrope of ash' ('Hard Rowing', ibid.: 11). On the debris of the twin-towers, 'An eye, a lip and a cut hand blooms/Sweet and bitter smoke stains the sky.' And to accentuate violence, she would add: 'Even the verb *stains* has a thread torn' ('Invisible City', ibid.: 10). Instead of a sky, what she encounters is a 'scrap of what was once called sky', in the falling of the towers, she finds 'A blood seam of sense drops free' (ibid.).

On 'a knot of the rubble' (ibid.), Alexander hears 'a bird cry' which is the voice of the dismantled women and the poet as well. The body of the bird is all 'flesh in fiery pieces' with each piece a 'mute sediment of love' ('Pitfire', ibid.: 11). The poet wonders whether such a body can ever find its essence: 'Shall a soul visit her mutilated parts?/ How much shall a body be a home?' (ibid.). The tragedy of 9/11 is thus seen in terms of the perpetual fragmentation of the woman, and her permanent state of exile and wilderness. And as the poet hears the bird cry, a news flash comes: 'We've even struck the bird's throat' (ibid.), suggesting the total silencing of women in the post-9/11 masculine backlash. In Alexander's poetry, the bird symbolizes the desires of the woman.[33]

Lending an Indian dimension to 9/11, Meena Alexander compares it with another 9/11 that happened in 1893, with Vivekananda as its protagonist.

> A dark rose on its stalk
> Chicago is in the Midwest of course—
> Sisters and brothers of America, he began,
>
> And there was thunderous applause.
> ('Gandhi's Bicycle [My Muse Comes to Me]'),
> 2004: 83)

By way of contrast between the two 9/11s the poet foregrounds civilizational degeneration, when she asks: 'How many would dare say that [brothers and sisters] now?' (ibid.). Instead of creating paradigms of civilizational clash, the poet would like a dialogue among them: 'But we need to say that you and I/even the teeth of war. Come closer now' (ibid.).

As a global citizen, Meena Alexander is as much a victim of 9/11 as of the communal riots of Gujarat in 2002. As gory details of the riots travel all over the world, poignant lyricism that marked the poetry on 9/11 gives way to poetry of anger and disgust. If the poet could hear 'a bird cry' on the rubble of the WTC towers, in Gujarat, 'Even the sparrows/by the temple gate/swallowed their song' ('In Naroda Patiya', ibid.: 75). The doves that the poet sets on her writing fingers simply fly off, and 'From way beyond/hyenas howl' as 'There is too much riveted into death' ('Lyric with Doves', ibid.: 77).

The Gujarat riots batter the very interiority of the female self so much that Meena's poetry, from a soulful requiem, turns into poetry of open combat and confrontation, of uneasy interrogations and accusations. What affronts the female sensibility of the poet most is the way the womb and private parts of pregnant women are torn asunder by the male marauders: 'Out they plucked/a tiny heart/beating with her [mother's] own' ('In Naroda Patiya', ibid.: 75). The spectacle of 'Torn bodies/clattering/in ox-driven cart' (ibid.: 77) triggers off so many questions, which the poet shoots at Gandhi, the saint of Sabarmati: 'Is it [ahimsa] just for the birds and the bees?'; 'What lips,/ what soles/swarmed across the river?/ Is it hot on the other side?' ('Slow Dancing', ibid.: 78). The other side is 'The kingdom of heaven' as 'tiny as a mustard seed', where Gandhi has 'crawled in'.

Along with 9/11 and the Gujarat riots, all other such 'man'-made disasters from partition to the bombing of Hiroshima, flash across the inward eye of the poet reminding her of the bloodthirsty present she is condemned to pass on to her children. Quite a number of the poems in *Raw Silk* are child-centric, in which the poetess as mother is apprehensive about the future of her teenaged daughter in troubled times such as hers. In 'Green Parasol', the mother would like her daughter to 'strip off the worn silk' and 'set fire to old straw' (ibid.: 32), and then:

> light up the broken avenues of desire
> Then be a girl like any other
> at the rim of stone gates

> raise a green parasol
> under a green tree. (ibid.: 32–33)

She would like her daughter to be intensely womanly in the face of vulgar masculine backlash. To Meena Alexander, poetry and womanhood together constitute a civilized alternative to present-day violence.

(c)

Imtiaz Dharker is consciously a poet of commitment and politics. Her very location, and subject position, implicates her inevitably in the cultural politics of the subcontinent.[34] Right in her first collection, *Purdah* (1989) she unfolds the multiple resonances of the women behind the veil; there is an ambivalent acceptance of 'Purdah' as 'a kind of safety' ('Purdah 1', 1989: 3). Love and attack, freedom and bondage, friendship and hostility are nothing more than shifting moods of lovers:

> These two countries lie
> hunched against each other,
> distrustful lovers
> who have fought bitterly
> and turned their backs;
> but in sleep, drifted slowly
> in, moulding themselves
> around the cracks
> to fit together,
> whole again; at peace.
>
> Forgetful of hostilities
> until, in the quiet dawn,
> the next attack.
> ('Battleline', ibid.: 47)

This is a womanly reaction that clamours for the meeting of the lovers as against the rhetoric of partition. The stakes of the poet in the troubled zone of Indo-Pak relations are very high. In their unconscious, both India and Pakistan are one, and it is this unconscious that the poet seeks to invoke.

In her next collection, *I Speak for the Devil* (2003), Imtiaz Dharker, writing against the primitive practice of honour killings, decides to step out of her 'black veil of faith' that 'gave my [her] god a devil's face/and muffled my [her] own voice' ('Honour Killing', ibid.: 5). 'High on the rush of daily displacement' ('Front Door', ibid.: 18), the poet crosses over to forbidden zones, to alien landscapes and to proscribed codes of modesty and morality. This is how she announces the arrival of the new century to her daughter Ayesha:

> So Ayesha,
> Let us put our faith elsewhere.
> The new century is silvered with those girls like you.
> Let's paint our mouths and eyes
> with opal, and splash
> iridescence on our breasts and thighs
>
> There is potential in goodbyes.
> This may not be freedom,
> but it feels like wine.
> ('Announcing the Arrival . . .', ibid.: 23)

In Indian women's poetry, the poet-as-mother is always in dialogue either with her daughter or with her own childhood as a young girl. Such dialogues not only suggest the irrevocability of the feminist movement within the structure of the family, but also map out its progressive shifts from one generation to another. The new mother-daughter combine constitutes an alignment that subverts patriarchy in its very hub.

Postcards from God (1994) focuses primarily on the Babri demolition and its aftermath in terms of a tragedy essentially of the female. In a section entitled 'Bombay: The Name of God', the poet, in a poem exclusively written on December 6, 1992, experiences a sudden transparency of vision which is ironically enough, rather too brittle and transient:

> This morning I woke
> and found my eyelids
> turned to glass.
> Through closed lids
> I saw the whole world
> changed to glass
> Glass door, glass lock,
> glass gods in makeshift shrines.
>
> When I blink,
> glass eyelashes crack.
> ('6 December 1992', 1994: 79)

The shattering glass is as much the shattering of vision as it is the shattering of the secular fabric of the nation. The glass allows the poet to see through the dark designs of leaders: 'Glass leaders laugh/and the whole world can see/right through their faces/into their black tongues' (ibid.). The poetic tension is realized through the metaphor of glass which is transparent, yet very fragile too.

The communal riots that follow the Babri demolition hit the women the most. Dharker zeroes in on one of the half-burnt bodies of a woman:

> And this is left:
> blackened saris, trousers, petticoats,
> the shell of a television set,
> a tin box of bangles
> and face cream,
> a blistered cupboard
> like a looted face
> that opened its mouth
>
> in a scream
> that never found an end.
> ('8 January, 1993', ibid.: 81)

The religion, caste or creed does not matter, what matters is the gender of the body that is charred in communal bonfire. The endless scream of the dead body lends a rare kinesis to the image; it seems to break free from the stillness of the printed page. The lines, as the poet, conjectures 'may scratch their way/into your head—through all the chatter of community' ('Minority', ibid.: 103).

As it happens with other woman poets also, in times of siege Imtiaz Dharker prefers plain-speaking; her poetic propensities simply take a backseat. The following images lack the indirectness usually associated with sophisticated poetry:

> The ugly face is in these days,
> crusted with hate and prejudice.
> Power has come to roost
> in grasping hands.
>
> Monsters stand patiently at our doors,
> ringing our bells,
> waiting to visit us in our homes.
> ('1993', ibid.: 82)

It is unobtrusively poetry of commitment and politics in which the battle-lines are clearly drawn and the enemies are unmasked without fear of backlash. Somehow, despite being an outgoing poet, Dharker tends to fall back on 'home', its assumed security and sanctimoniousness.

In her latest collection, *The Terrorist at My Table* (2006), Dharker deals with the so-called phenomenon of Islamic terrorism post-9/11 from the vantage point of a Muslim mother/woman. In her poem, 'The Right Word', the poet probes into the semantics of the word 'terrorist'. She tries many phrases—'a freedom-fighter', 'a hostile militant', 'a guerilla warrior', 'a martyr'—for the shadow lurking 'Outside the door' (2006: 25) until, as a mother, she discovers in that shadow, an image of 'a child who looks like mine [hers]' (ibid.). For the poet more than anybody else the so-called terrorist is a son to a mother, therefore:

> I open the door.
> Come in, I say.
> Come in and eat with us.
>
> The child steps in
> and carefully, at my door
> takes off his shoes. (ibid.: 26)

Dharker as a woman thus cherishes values of love and affection; she would like to approach human beings without any preconceived political or communal vocabulary. Once again 'home' tends to retain its insularity. But in some poems of the collection, there is a discernible change in dialectics, the inner-outer polarity collapses into a continuum: 'People are running/through my body now/calling out, laughing . . .' ('Open', ibid.: 50).

ii

(a)

If Hindi woman poets of the 1970s and 1980s expose discords and discontents within the discourse of domesticity, the poets of the 1990s break into the zone of the terror-induced stillness of the outer world by way of articulating their dissent in situations that show little tolerance to the poetics of dialogue. And as they speak, there is no camouflage of English; they venture to speak in the tongue of the victim and the oppressor both, risking backlash, physical as well as intellectual. It is remarkable that when major players of the Punjabi literary world chose to remain silent or evasive during the days of terrorism in the border-state, Gagan Gill, a Sikh woman writing in Hindi chooses to herald 'the return of the girl' in the midst of violence through her collection, *Ek Din Lautegi Ladki* (1989). She asks uneasy questions on behalf of those who are hung upside down on the trees for mass-murder:

> The noise of twenty-four voices
> The lamenting of twenty-four desires
> The dread on the face of twenty-four souls
> Knocks every door
> Country-village
> Brothers-friends
>
> *Is there anyone?*
>
> ('Koi Hai', ibid.: 77–78).

The baffling silence as well as surrender of the people of Punjab pro-vokes the poet into a poetry of intervention. The overwhelming question unsettles the conscience of not just a village, but the entire civilization and its masculinist bravado.

Gagan Gill not only pleads on their behalf for mercy, she begins to imagine their last-ditch private prayers/desires as though she is one among those who are lined up for killing. The intensity of her poetic gaze and womanly sensibilities comes into play:

> It is possible that he might have thought of
> some dear face
> or some unfinished job?
> It is possible he might have thought of
> some last unsaid thing
> or the face of his little child?
>
> ('Punjab ki Ek Bus Mein', ibid.: 79)

As the media and state machinery indulge in head counts of those who are killed in the terrorist violence, the poet takes a peep into their vulnerable human selves. She wonders whether there was any last-minute rejection of religion/god: 'knows not, whether, he could/ spit at the word "religion"' (ibid.: 80).

As a daughter of Punjab, the poet cannot shy away from its violent predicament. She, almost like a woman possessed, would run wild beseeching:

> Don't
> kill Longowal.
> Don't.
> Leave him.
> I implore you by our sleepy Guru Granth Sahib
> I implore you by your faith
>   ('Kahan Lagi Thi Goli?', ibid.: 83)

The compassionate involvement stems from the inner conscience of a woman who seeks peace, love and harmony in her Punjab. Gill writes poetry of plunge that demands participation in life, and not just an empathetic observation of a bystander. Poetry becomes an act of ontological transformations, more so when it enters into poetics of involvement with 'deadly' situations.

(b)

Katyayni is another major Hindi poet-activist who stands firm against the revivalist masculinity as it re-surfaces with vengeance in the name of nationalism, statism and religion in the late 1990s. Her activism, instead of postponing her poetry, instills in it a rare urgency, raising it beyond passive intellectual response and sophisticated aesthetic cover-up. In a poem written on the Gujarat riots of 2002, amidst 'the smoke, ash and burnt, half-burnt bodies/and raped women-girls, and torn apart wombs, and infant-bodies cut into pieces' (2002b: 4), the poet hears the curse of Kabir: '*sadho, yah moordon ka desh*' ('Saints, it is the country of the dead'). Meena Alexander too hears the philosophical voice of Kabir post-9/11, but Katyayni's Kabir is more an activist, and not as much a mere brooder who propels the poet into exhorting fellow armchair comrades to rise above their symbolic protests: 'By mere lighting candles, arranging peace marches/by returning after a protest sit-in/we shall only express our helplessness/and cowardice and clever heartlessness too . . .' (ibid.: 5).[35] In Hindi women's poetry, the protest goes beyond mere ironies, convoluted allegories and sardonic understatements; the poetry tends to be a desperate call for action, an eventful intervention. The poet would remind fellow comrades of their inaction: 'Even now most of us/are busy in symbolic gestures, analyses,/carrying guilt in our hearts/like our daily rituals of prayer' (ibid.: 5).

Writing in response to an incident in which a girl-activist is paraded naked in Andhra Pradesh by the state's police, the poet underlines the urgency of writing direct poetry:

> In situations such as these
> No poem happens
> Neither any story takes its form
> Everything becomes mere a statement
> There is only a tension of
> frenzied fingers clenched and
> thrust in palms
> and on the distant horizon
> there is a frozen brightness of the burning eye . . .
> ('. . . Ve Apna Mritulekh Likhte Hain', 2002a: 154).

Unlike her contemporary woman poets, Katyayni's poetry has the passion and fire of radical poetry which forbids any postponement or dilution of anger in the name of aesthetic flair and finesse. It goes to her credit that even when she is most direct, she is able to retain poetic expression. The self-denying directness has its own poetic potential that Katyayni harnesses to the maximum.

In her collection, *Is Paurushpooran Samay Mein* (1999), Katyayni's canvas becomes international as she seeks to talk hard and straight on tragedies reported from Somalia to Peru:

> Today, I want to speak out
> without mincing words on
> the starving children in
> Somalia and Sarguza
> Let us discuss American bombing of Iraq
> and riots in Los Angles . . . (ibid.: 108)

Un-minced protest characterizes Katyayni's poetic enterprise. Poetry, in her case, is not the art of indirection or of symbolic circumlocution, nor it is an imprecise meandering of imagination; it is an act of hard-hitting involvement with an unapologetic insolence.

Katyayni brands the post-1990s as blatantly patriarchal in which poetry itself runs the risk of survival. In women's poetry, the genre of poetry is invariably gendered as female; and the threat to poetry is seen as a threat to the female species as a whole. The poet asks:

> Agitated against aversion to religion
> and burning in the fire of sacred anger
> supremely-holy nuns, amidst their frenzied speeches
> and those redeemers of the pride of past
> who from retailers go on to become the flag-bearer of religion

> pushing great religious luminaries in the background
> should we postpone poetry?
>
> ('Kya Sthgit Kar Dein Kavita?', ibid.: 115)

Of course, the poet refuses to oblige, but the very question points towards the inherent danger to the very future of not only just arts and literature in the late 1990s, but of women as well. In this collection, as many as thirty-four times the word 'poem/poetry' occurs in the titles of the poems themselves revealing Katyayni's utmost concern towards the future of poetry in the new civilizational order. While poets like Meena Alexander and Gagan Gill seek to counter violence through womanly compassion, Katyayni's tone is a tone of belligerence, of unsheathed anger and confrontation.

(c)

Anamika too extends her horizons, as she devotes a section—entitled 'Musalman Kya Hote Hain, Amma?'—of her collection *Khurdari Hatheliyan* (2005) to challenge the emerging cult of communal violence in the public sphere. In her poem, 'Bomb', the poet describes how women are violated and desecrated in the making of the bomb itself. Besides containing 'glass splinters of the bottles of medicine', the bomb also consists of splinters of 'the mirror of the new *bahu*' (wife, daughter-in-law) and 'the heels [of her sandal]' (ibid.: 121). The aspirations of the young new bride are thus shattered much before the bomb explodes. The *laddu*-like innocent-looking bomb is wrapped in newspaper-cuttings which show the news of famine on its one side, and 'one worried woman/in her one fourth clothes/ stretching her body at 45 degrees' (ibid.) on the other. The bomb thus feeds even the voyeuristic male gaze. Most ironically, the bomb is held together by threads which in terms of their appearance look like the colourful threads of *rakhi*, which sisters tie on the wrists of their brothers for sustained family bonding. The very making of the bomb thus causes violence to the woman's mind, body and soul.

In 'Dunge aur Karmkaand', the poet discovers that prayers have lost meaning for 'the smoke of bomb seems/continuous with that of the incense stick' (ibid.: 123). As hands are raised heavenwards and the forehead is bowed earthwards, there is a serious self-doubt on the whole exercise of offering *namaaz*. All religious rites appear vulgar. Yet old habits die hard; the poet still asks for god's grace. Even in the face of lurking threat, the poet, like a mother, holds her cradle of prayers:

> Prayers are like an old cradle—
> knows the sparrow
> whose small nest
> is swinging
> three feet above the ant-hill. (ibid.)

The image of the sparrow, her nest and cradle suggest the irrepressible motherly urge of the poet in times of utter dread. The image of the sparrow, working fastidiously and rearing her chicks with all her small but genuine might, continues to hold hope for the beleaguered female poetic imagination.

The most stirring poem of the section is 'Patta-Patta, Boota-Boota', in which the poet extends Premchand's famous story, 'Idgah', by way of posing questions on the well-being and safety of both grown-up Hamid and his old grandmother in times of communal hatred. The children of the poet ask:

> The violence that we have seen—
> Where must have his grandmother gone?
> Where must have gone his tongs?
> Has Hamid grown old and big—
> this big or even bigger?
> His height more than mine or equal to me?
> Would he be able to save the grandmother? (ibid.: 127)

The fear and fascination that operate simultaneously in the poem lend poignancy to the poetic re-visiting of the old classic tale. Also, like prayers, tales told in her childhood continue to shape the female sensibility of the poet. The innocent children advise her mother not to grow old for they have 'seen very old women/are not able to run in the stampede' (ibid.: 127). They recount the oft-shown images of women in the communal riots: 'that day I had seen on TV—/rioters first tear the clothes of women,/ then stomach' (ibid.: 127). The gap between tale and TV is probably the gap between female and male forms of representation. While the TV camera is ruthlessly male, the tale has motherly warmth.

After a volley of inquisitive questions and apprehensions, the poet, through her children shoots the most unsettling question: 'What do you mean by "Muslims", Amma?' (ibid.: 128). After 9/11, the way Muslims are contradistinguished from other communities as in-nately militant fanatics, the question gathers utmost relevance. The children then go on to provide their own list of Muslims they have known, experienced and seen:

> Who do you mean by 'Muslims', Amma?
> That Jumman Mian of 'Panch Parmeshvar' and his aunt,
> Hakim uncle and his noodles?
> That sweet-sour, warm language-speaking
> literate, sophisticated people of
> the serial called 'Neem ke Ped'?
> Eggsellers? Tailors? Or Tangewale?
> Zakir Hussain and tabla and Taj Mahal
> Shah Rukh Khan and that . . . (ibid.: 128)

Muslims come across as normal people *sans* any streak of fanaticism or religious intolerance. For the children, more than a Muslim emperor, Humanyun is a subject of fun who chose, of all the places, a library to die after an accidental fall from its stairs. It is this fun and innocence that the poet cherishes so as to avoid communalizing communities. Anamika excavates memories and impressions of childhood for her poetic metaphors to juxtapose them with her latter-day adult experiences.

iii

(a)

Post-Green Revolution and post–Operation Bluestar, Punjab unleashes a very distinct socio-political landscape to which Punjabi woman poets respond with an interventionist concern. A number of demographic aberrations have rocked the inner as well as outer domains of Punjabi life as a whole. Illegal immigration of Punjabis abroad (known in popular Punjabi lingo as *kabutarbazi*), the disconcerting proportion of female foeticide, and the dwindling ratio of women in the state, the suicide by farmers, increasing presence of migrant labour and caste-riots are some of the pressing problems of the post-1990s Punjab which implicate its women directly as well as indirectly in its vicious predicament. Sukhvinder Amrit, in her collection, 'Dhup dee Chunni', refers to the plight of innocent Punjabi brides who are married to rich NRIs who are either too old or already married abroad. Referring to some 'Bholi of Vancouver', a favourite destination of *parvasi* Sikhs, the poet highlights her exploitation from all sides:

> Her parent
> tied around her neck
> a long rope
> whose one end was given to
> his aged husband
> and to the another end
> the entire family clung on
> poor creature
> she dies neither live nor die
> in her dreams Pooran comes
> in her eyes Loona weeps . . .
>   ('Supna . . .', 2006: 32)

The tragic echoes of *kissa* Pooran Bhagat thus continue to bedevil contemporary Punjab, with the difference that now Loona stands redeemed as a new woman who asserts her sexuality. In the same poem, another woman, Taro waits for her husband who probably has become a victim of *kabutarbazi*: 'in the hope of his return/she has spent the sunshine of her youth/in the shadows of her sighs' (ibid.: 31). Another dalit woman labourer, Kartaro, becomes a rape-victim of an upper-caste landlord: 'She had gone to cut grass in the day/has come back with a load full of darkness/neither does she speak/nor hear' (ibid.: 32). Such representations not only unsettle the progressive claims of Punjab, they expose its poor gender profile as well.

In another poem, Sukhvinder Amrit virtually writes an elegy on what was once her refulgent Punjab. Her concerns become wider and go beyond the questions of gender. She wonders what would happen to her poetry 'When instead of crops/in the fields suicides begin to grow' ('Antika', ibid.: 95); 'when to restless souls/the tablets of sulphas/begin to appear the most effective medicine' (ibid.: 96). She expects poetry not to ditch in her such trying moments:

> Yes, O poetry!
> Even then you remain around my life
>
> By being
> a shelter
> hope
> resolve and
> moonlight . . . (ibid.).

In Punjabi poetry, moonlight continues to fascinate female imagination; if, to Amar Jyoti, the woman is a 'patch of moonlight'

('Chanan dee Kaatar', 1988: 9), to Manjit Tiwana she is a 'machete of moonlight' ('Chanan dee Talwar', 1995: 62).[36] Poetry, woman and moonlight form a symbiotic association which shines through the darkest hour of life.

In the face of rampant female foeticide in her state, Sukhvinder Amrit suggests her own way of seeking fulfilment through her poetry. In her other collection, *Kanian*, she asks: 'Who says that/ I could not give birth to/my desired foetus?' ('Kaun Kahinda Hai', 2000: 60). Her reply to the question reveals the value she assigns to her poetic output:

> See here
> the features of my poem
> match completely
> with voice immersed in love
> co-mingling which
> it has come about.
>
> > (ibid.)

For Indian woman poets, poetry is an encounter as well as escape, engagement as well as withdrawal; it is a medium of self-assertion as well as self-denial, of effusive articulation as well as restrained expression. Its poetics is, therefore, that of a slogan as well as of a lyric. It is a genre of raising questions and seeking answers too.

(b)

The Babri demolition does not go un-protested in Punjabi women's poetry. In fact, it brings back memories of the partition and the communal violence that came in its wake into the poetic play. Pal Kaur is a prolific woman poet in Punjabi who in one of her poems, 'Saryu Nadi', bewails the loss of the structure in terms of the vandalization of her childhood pastime of making sandy homes on the banks of the river Saryu. The narrative poem begins as the poet recounts her congenial past of an innocent girl-child who used to play on the banks of the river Saryu:

> We used to play 'home-home'
> Sometimes it used to be your foot
> and my hands which made sandy homes on it—
> Sometimes it was my foot
> and your hands—

> Sometimes we used to make homes adjacent to each other
> with our feet touching each other
> through the sands.
>
> ('Saryu Nadi', 2007: 116)

As 'feet' attain adulthood, tensions begin to surface. One day the male partner, on some provocation, plucks out his feet from the sand, and thus breaks the sandy structure in a violent rush. The poet, as the female partner, bemoans this change of heart:

> Instigated by some hot wind
> you started waving
> your fingers in it.
> Then you came gushing forth
> and brought down the structure. (ibid.: 117)

Pondering over the debris, the poet is confronted with a host of questions dispersed on the sandy banks of Saryu: 'who are you/who am I?' (ibid.). The pristine and placid past is pitted against the violent patriarchal present. Such a contrast, even contrived as it is, enables the woman poet to foreground the violent backlash of the communal male.

The way the male partner changes his stance every now and then baffles the female poet: 'As the wind changed its direction/your entire outlook changed/your flag changed again' (ibid.: 118). The poet cautions her boy-friend of the devious ways of those whose flag he holds aloft now: 'you are waving a flag/whose colours you don't recognize' (ibid.). According to the poet, the demolition of the disputed structure signifies total bankruptcy of the male-order:

> The river inside so dried in you
> that now even your eyes do not moisten.
> The home inside you has crumbled
> and you just carry its debris in your body. (ibid.)

The crisis is thus approached in terms of gender, according to which the male continues to be the ruthless, emotion-less aggressor, and home continues to be the possessive sanctuary of the woman.

The poem ends on a note of desolation of childhood dreams. The river bemoans its tragic destiny:

> Every particle soaked in blood
> of the sandy bank of the river asks:

> Who will gather questions dispersed in the sand
> who will hear the laments
> of the waters of river
> from where should I bring feet
> to play 'home-home'! (ibid.)

The river's lament is not very different from the laments of Amrita's or Waris Shah's Heer. In a way, Pal Kaur's poem is as much a re-writing of Amrita's 'Akhaan Waris Shah Noo', as the Babri demolition is a re-enactment of the partition on a smaller scale. Such an inter-textual connection within Punjabi women's poetry indicates the continuous presence of the womanly voice in times of violence.

(c)

It is evident that neither Hindi nor Punjabi women's poetry is pro-vincial in its approach and scope. The co-ordinates of *ghar* continually expand till they finally lapse into those of *bahir*. Young emerging woman poets in Punjabi dare to think beyond the native ghettoes. In a short poem, Deep Shikha Brar, disturbed by the fake encounter killings of Sikh youth during the days of militancy, expresses her resentment against the nation-state's rather blind system of justice dispensation:

> The message for the rest of the world is
> trigger genocides
> and then emerge scot-free.
> Punishment for what
> to who and why!
>
> (Untitled 2005: 52)

In the culture of killings—both by the state and the militants—the goddess of justice holds on to her blindness. The poet observes that as people resigned to their fate begin to live without their dear ones who become victims of violence, the goddess of justice seems to sink into slumber.

From the local scene of bloodshed, the woman poet shifts her attention to the violent history of the entire subcontinent. The local is never forsaken; it, in fact, provides a necessary springboard to look beyond. The poet wonders: 'God knows how many Pakistans we shall have/How many times the carnival of blood would be staged in Delhi' (ibid.). The image of the partition continuously haunts the Punjabi imagination. Each act of genocide, anywhere in the country or in the world, brings back the bloody saga of partition into active memory. The metaphor of Pakistan is the metaphor of secession, disintegration within, an indigenous trope of Balkanization. Urvashi Butalia, a Punjabi woman-historian, is inspired to retrieve the history of women, implicated as they were in the partition, after suffering first hand in the anti- Sikh riots of 1984.[37]

In a teleological swoop, Deep Shikha includes the fall of the twin World Trade Center towers to complete her image of a violent world: 'God Knows today how many trade towers would be blown up!' (ibid.). The poet steers clear of gendering the violence for her concerns include the entire humanity, and not just women. This marks a new level of confidence in the post-1990s' women's poetry in Punjabi and other languages as well. Of late, most of the woman poets react against their being branded as 'woman poets' for now they speak for the entire 'mankind' across the divisions of gender. There is hardly any visible marker of womanly presence in the poem, though of course at a subterranean level, one can hear the echoes of a sensitive and hurt female.

The poem concludes on a note of subdued anger against the helplessness of the goddess of justice:

> when shall the blind-fold on the eyes
> of this powerless icon of justice untie itself
> an icon which claims to dispense justice
> but right now it appears blindfolded holding balance
> alone, ashamed and silent. (ibid.)

Deep Shikha does not grant much concession to the goddess on account of her gender, except that her helplessness is slightly redeemed by her sense of shame. The woman poets of the post-1990s are iconoclasts in the sense that they refuse to be seduced by images or other constructed gospels even if they are engendered in female terms. The female gender of the goddess of justice is no consolation if it does not deliver justice to the deprived and the needy. Aesthetically speaking, the poem may not be very mature, yet it points towards the higher stakes of the woman in 'human' affairs.

IV

From a co-opted discourse of protest, Indian women's poetry finally attains visibility to pose a challenge to the hegemonic patriarchal structures in terms of its own self-invented gender-specific idiom, forms, metaphors and style. From the conventional forms of prayer, ode, elegy and lyric, Indian women's poetry turns increasingly subversive and ironical, interrogative and dialogic. Instead of moving from complexity to rhetoric, as is normally the case with protest literature, it moves from rhetoric to complexity. Except for a period around the late 1970s, when radical feminist tendencies held some sway, there are no slogans, no easy accusations, not even pronounced name-calling in much of the latter-day Indian women's poetry. There is an earnest desire to negotiate a transitional as well as a transactional poetics of space between *ghar* and *bahir* so that binaries do not simplify the process of the redefining of the gender.

Notes

1. A. K. Ramanujan, the poet-translator, entitles his anthology of love poems from classical Tamil as *The Interior Landscape*. This landscape pertains to the domain of *akam* as against *puram*—two domains of poetry of the classical Sangam period. *Akam* poems 'are love poems; *puram* poems are all other kinds of poems, usually about good and evil, action, community, kingdom; it is the "public" poetry of the ancient Tamils, celebrating the ferocity and glory of kings, lamenting the death of heroes, the poverty of poets. Elegies, panegyrics, invectives, poems on wars and tragic events are *puram* poems' (Ramanujan 1967: 101). One anthology of eighteen short stories by Indian women writers edited by Lakshmi Holmstrom (1990) takes the title *Inner Courtyard* which is suggestive of the preferred spatial matrices of Indian female imagination.

2. The dialectics of *ghar-bahir* gained currency in critical idiom following Partha Chatterjee's use of it in his reading of Bengali woman autobiographies written during the freedom struggle. This is how he explains the dynamics of *ghar* and *bahir*: 'The world is external, the domain of the material; the home represents one's inner spiritual self, one's true identity. The world is a treacherous terrain of the pursuit of material interests, where practical considerations reign supreme. It is typically the domain of the male. The home in essence must remain unaffected by the profane activities of the material world—and woman is its representation' (1993: 120).

3. In the 'Preface' to their very famous *Woman Writing in India: 600 B.C. to the Present*, Susie Tharu and K. Lalita point out how the multifaceted genius of Toru Dutt and Sarojini Naidu remains under-stated in the nationalist accounts: 'Even the celebrated Indo-Anglican poet Toru Dutt, whose work invariably found place in syllabuses, was usually presented as a brilliant, but protected upper-class child-poet, who died early of consumption. Rarely did students learn that, like her uncle Romesh Chunder Dutt, she was a

nationalist and a passionate republican; that she was widely read in history and literature of the French Revolution; or that she had translated speeches made in the French Chamber of Deputies around the time of the Revolution for Indian nationalist journals. Hardly ever is it mentioned, in the context of the literature classroom, that Sarojini Naidu was called the Nightingale of India as much for the rhythm and modulation of the speeches she made during the Independence movement as for her delicate verse' (1995: xviii). Mahadevi Verma was also not an ordinary conventional Hindu woman. David Rubin informs: 'Her marriage, officially dated from 1913, became the source of a continuing scandal, for when she came of age she refused to live with her husband, although on various occasions she paid formal visits to her inlaws' home. She tried unsuccessfully to persuade her husband to remarry, as he was free to do so, even though divorce was impossible for her unless she changed her religion (Buddhism being the only possible alternative for her). Only after several years did her husband and both families cease their attempts to live in the conventional Hindu wedded state' (1998: 150–51).

4.   Khushwant Singh, in his 'Editorial' to Amrita Pritam's *Selected Poems* informs: 'Amrita was given in marriage to a son of a prosperous trading family, the Kwatras, who owned a popular general merchandise store in Lahore's Anarkali Bazar. It was as a mark of respect for husband, Pritam Singh that Amrita replaced suffix Kaur by Pritam to become Amrita Pritam. The couple had two children, a boy and a girl. Thereafter the husband and wife drifted apart; he to revive his business which had been ruined by the partition of the Punjab, she to continue her career as a poet and writer of fiction' (1982: v). Amarjit Chandan, another famous Punjabi diaspora writer, in an obituary published in *Guardian* (U.K.), gives us more information about the persona of Amrita: 'Though Amrita Pritam's father was a mystic, devout Sikh, she did not practise the religion, and her relationship with that community always remained uneasy. She had love affairs with Punjabi Muslim poets—the well-known Sahir Ludhianvi among them—cut her hair, drank alcohol and smoked in public, all sacrilegious acts for a Sikh woman' (quoted in Massey 2005: 1).

5.   In the entire patriarchal discourse, right from the Vedic era onwards, the nation is projected as 'mother'. The Sanskrit popular adage—*janani janambhumishch swargadapi greeyasi* (mother and motherland are more exalted than even heaven) continues to enamour the patriarchal nationalist imagination.

6.   The poets of the Dwivedi period and *chhayavad* tend to personify India as *Bharat Mata*/Mother India. Invariably, the image is of a crowned and beautiful woman in 'shackles' shedding 'tears of blood', or of the same woman holding aloft a trident and leading her countless sons and daughters to battle. Sumitranandan Pant, in his poem 'Bharatmata Gramvasini', depicts India as a very poor backward mother who evinces dignity in times of crisis: 'Golden crops trampled by alien feet/frustrated, yet tolerant as the earth;/ lips quivering with sobs:/silent and smiling/a joyous autumn moon/ eclipsed'(2002: 141).

7. The deployment of a female body-part is exceptional for it underlines the generative capacity of women, hitherto denied through the paternal privileging of the pen-penis analogy. American feminist Showalter, while underlining the seminal role of the female body in female writing, observes that 'the process of literary creation is much more similar to gestation, labor, and delivery than it is to insemination' (1989: 463).

8. Pandita Ramabai (1858–1922), was a radical Maharashtrian woman reformer. In 1887 she published a prose tract, 'The High-Caste Hindu Woman', which is reckoned as one of earliest Indian feminist statements. She had the audacity to expose the politics of dumping women in the backyard: 'The woman's court is situated at the back of the home, where darkness reign perpetually. There the child-bride is brought to be forever confined. She does not enter the husband's house to be the head of a new home. But rather enters the house of the father-in-law to become the lowest of its members, and to occupy the humblest position in the family' (2000: 148).

9. At best, Mahadevi's lyrical poetry offers an apt example of 'intermediate orality' which, as Kumkum Sanghari puts it, 'continuously interacts with print or moves back and forth between print and oral transmission' (2002: 39). It stops short of inaugurating a highly literate feminism.

10. Mahadevi entitles one of her collections *Deep Shikha* (Verma 1962), which was published in 1942. Even otherwise, the image of the flickering lamp is all pervasive in her poetry. One lyric opens thus: 'Like wax my body's melted, my heart burned out now like a lamp' (Rubin 1998: 185).

11. Nirala, in his 'Badal Raag'—a set of six poems—portrays the 'cloud' in robust patriarchal and imperial terms. A part of the poem reads:

> Blind-dark-impenetrable-licentious—cloud!
> O free self-willed! —
> Slow-volatile-unrestrained on the wind chariot
> O sublime!
> Being of shoreless desires
> obstacle-free vast!
> Flood of rebel!
> season of rain in the awesome sky
> O emperor! ('Badal Raag-2', 1956: 177)

12. This is the opening poem of Amrita Pritam's collection *Lummiyan Vatan* (1949) published by an Amritsar and Delhi-based publisher, Sikh Publishing House Ltd.

13. It must, however, be remembered that the first *Heer* in Punjabi was written by a poet called Damodar who had not given it a tragic ending. Even Maqbul, the early eighteenth-century Punjabi poet followed Damodar who sent the united lovers Heer and Ranjha to a Haj pilgrimage to Mecca. It is only Waris Shah who gave the epic a tragic ending. Since tragedy appeals more to the human mind, the epic became not merely popular but immortal.

14. Urvashi Butalia, in her significant study of the partition, *The Other Side of Silence* informs: 'As always there was widespread sexual savagery; about 75,000 women are thought to have been abducted and raped by men of religion different from their own (and indeed sometimes by men of their own religion)' (1998: 3). The history or official records of governments—of both India and Pakistan—are silent about the travails of these women. The 'generality of Partition' (ibid.) as it exists in history books simply erases women from the scene of the huge tragedy.

15. It would be sweeping to assume that 'sex' remains absolutely unarticulated in pre-independence Indian women's writing. Its assertion comes from a quarter which, ironically, is dubbed as the most retrogressive one, namely that of the veiled world of the Muslim woman. The reference is to Ismat Chugtai's Urdu short story 'Lihaaf' (2001a), which brought into the open the issue of lesbianism within the family-fold. None of the three female poets discussed in the chapter come anywhere near to Chugtai's degree of radicalism.

16. The first attempt to organize women's trade unions had been made in 1972, when the Self-Employed Women's Association (SEWA), a kind of Gandhian socialist union of women vendors, was formed in Ahmedabad. Not many well-organized women's movements of the type of SEWA came up, yet from the 1970s onwards, local-level women forums raised the banner against rapes, dowry-deaths, stray instances of sati, etc. Some rape cases such as those of Rameeza Bee's in 1978, Maya Tyagi's in 1980 and Guntabehn's in 1986, along with the case of Roop Kanwar's attempt at sati in 1987, and Shah Bano's case of seeking maintenance after divorce did generate widespread resentment. Local-level women organizations—Nari Mukti Sangharsh Sammelan in Patna in 1988, Chingari in Gujarat in 1986, Mahila Dakshata Samiti in Delhi in 1978, Mahila Utpidan Virodhi Manch in Ranchi in 1985, etc.—did emerge along with the women wings of national political parties. Of late, right-wing parties have floated a number of organizations such as Mahila Agadhi, Durga Vahini, Matri Mandal, etc., to galvanize their women cadres. The information is culled from Radha Kumar's essay 'Contemporary Indian Feminism' (1989: 20–29) and Urvashi Butalia's essay 'Confrontation and Negotiation: The Women's Movement's Responses to Violence Against Women' (2005: 325–55).

    At the international level, particularly in the U.S., the movements for women's liberation start around the mid-1960s. In 1961 John F. Kennedy instituted a 'Commission of the Status of Women'; unhappy with its progress, some formed the 'Civil Rights Organization' and then 'National Organization for Women' in 1966. From the 1970s onwards, the youth left wing and then Black Movements collaborated in the enterprise of women's emancipation.

17. The poems chosen for this section are short and are not necessarily well-known, for the purpose here is not as much the discussion of mile-stones as it is to map out the trajectory of feminist concerns within the poetry of different language streams.

18. The cat is a symbol of femininity and independence. A woman always imagines herself as such a mysterious, graceful, languorous, downy and slightly predatory cat. A cat is the alter ego of an owner; so if one dislikes a cat, he also dislikes her owner. Ladies who combine advantages of both sexes harmoniously, usually take cats. Such women are beautiful and intelligent, feminine and efficient, sweet and persistent in gaining their goal. Spinster replaces her non-existent baby by a cat. The cat also needs care and tenderness' it's playful and naughty, like a child. A lonely woman with a cat treats men distrustfully, and enters into intimate relationships unwillingly (see www.womanspassions.com/articles).

19. Rosemary Marangoly George, while rereading 'My Story', calls Kamala Das 'queer' (2000: 731–63). The poem under discussion also expresses distrust towards heterosex, and the comfort level of the woman-protagonist with her cat suggests her leanings towards, what is perceived by canonical patriarchy as, deviant sex.

20. Tara Patel questions her mother for her complicity with the patriarchal order:

> I cannot live like you, mother,
> Maintain the status quo.
> I've moved out of the square one
> I cannot be a dutiful daughter.
> With what unquestioning righteousness
> You bore your cross, mother?
>> ('Mother', 1991: 35)

In her poem, 'Coffee or Me', Charmayne D'Souza thinks of even killing her father on the issue of taking subject options for a course. The cold-bloodedness is rather too candid:

> If I take economics
> I will die
> If I take history,
> He will, he says.
> May be, I can kill him
> With the Law of Diminishing Returns.
>> (1990: 65–66)

21. During the ancient or medieval period, homosexuality is not much a crime, it is during the modern period with the development of the nation-state and the Euro-American ascendancy in the modern world that 'the drive to impose uniformity in sexual matters acquired a new force and urgency. . . . Indian nationalists today, both right wing and left wing, are often virulently homophobic, viewing homosexuality as a foreign disease, a capitalist perversion from which nation's purity must be preserved' (Vanita 2005: 13–16).

22. Hijras, in the case of another Indian woman poet in English, Anna Sujatha Mathai, are treated more as objects of sympathy than desire; they are like 'stone, can neither wound/nor arouse'. They are a 'crude parody of the female/ their tears are hidden and silent' ('The Riddle of Eunuchs', 2005: 27).

23. Ardhnarishvara is an Indian image of 'the lord who is half woman'. The 'lord' here is Shiva and 'nari' is Parvati. However, there are all kinds of interpretations and even versions of the myth of Ardhanarishvara. From an advaitic perspective, it represents the fusion of 'The feminine and the masculine . . . partial attainment, *en route* to transcendence' (Goldberg 2002: 3); from the perspective of Sankhya *darshan* it is the unity of *purush-prakriti*, and from a Buddhist angle it represents the resolution of the duality of *samsara-niravna*. From the viewpoint of western feminism, while first-wave feminism seeks liberation from the prison of gender through the image of Ardhanarishvara, third-wave feminism rejects it, for it sublimates feminine subjectivity and difference into a male-favoured unity.

24. The last two lines of a brief sketch of Amrita Bharati given by Lucy Rosenstein towards the end of her translations of her 'Eighteen Poems' suggest the drift of the woman poet: 'She published six collections of poems, a volume of prose, and translations of yoga treatises and Sri Aurobindo's verses. Single-mindedly devoted to spiritual practice she lives in Sri Aurobindo's ashram in Pondicherry' (2002: 77)

25. An important message of 'French feminism is that women should celebrate the fact that they are marginalized. This may seem strange especially if considered from a liberal Anglo-American tradition of equal rights and equal opportunities, but for Irigaray, female exclusion is inevitable within a male-oriented world-view, and so women should instead exploit their disruptive, anarchistic position on the margins. By refusing to be assimilated into the mainstream (male) ideology, women become subversives or saboteurs' (Tolan 2006: 336).

26. The characters of Sita and Savitri are reckoned in the patriarchal discourse as benchmarks of woman's purity. Punjabi woman poets re-inscribe feminist meanings into the stereotypes. Amar Jyoti, in a title poem to her collection 'Mannun Sita Na Kaho', writes: 'Do not brand me Sita/Before I am asked to/ undergo fire-ordeal/I would like to argue/with my co-traveler' (1998: 24). A woman poet of the 1970s, Santosh Sahni asks: 'If a divine incarnation like Ram/ was not satisfied with you/even after your ordeal by fire/what to talk of ordinary men?' (1972: 29). Manjit Tiwana writes a long poem, *Savitri*, in 1989.

27. In one of her later poems published in her Sahitya Akademi award–winning poetry collection, *Kagaz te Canvas*, Amrita Pritam defines herself thus: 'a pain which I smoked like a cigarette/and some poems/which I have dropped like the ash of the cigarette' (1970: 60).

28. Cixous, while positing bisexuality as an alternative to the destructive masculine hegemony, distinguishes between two types of bisexuality. One bisexuality is 'a fantasy of a complete being, which replaces the fear of castration, and veils sexual difference. . . . Two within one hole, and even two wholes', and bisexuality 'is the location within oneself of the presence of both sexes, evident and insistent in different ways according to the individual . . .' (1994: 41). While Shashi Samundra seems to endorse the first form of bisexuality, Rukmini Bhaya Nair comes nearer to the second one.

29. Like 'feminism', 'post-feminism' is also not a well-defined ideology. In fact, those who use this term always tend to put it in inverted quotes. For example, Tania Modleski's book, *Feminism Without Borders: Culture and Criticism in 'Post-Feminism'* (1991) and Imelda Whelehan's *Feminist Thought: From the Second-Wave to 'Post-Feminism'* (1995) barricade the term in inverted commas. The term gained currency in the West around the mid-1980s, following the realization of the excesses of second-wave feminism which disrupted family, the value of maternity and even sex. In a very loose yet functional sense, post-feminism would mean a type of negotiated feminism, i.e., it is not radically anti-male; it, as Sarah Gamble puts it, 'tends to be implicitly heterosexist in orientation, postfeminists seek to develop an agenda which can find a place for a men as lovers, husbands and fathers as well as friends' (2001: 36). Imelda Whelehan would define post-feminism as a credo 'in which the worst excesses of second-wave feminism can be discarded in favour of a political healing process in which family can be once again made whole—freed from the indecent assaults of sexual politics' (1995: 196).

30. The metaphor of the mirror that Jatinder Kaur employs in the poem reminds one every bit of Sandra Gilbert and Susan Gubar's use of the same image in their *The Madwoman in the Attic*: 'Before the woman writer can journey through the looking glass toward literary autonomy . . . she must come to terms with the images on the surface of the glass with, that is, those mythic masks male artists have fastened over the human face both to lessen their dread of her "inconsistency" and by identifying her with the "eternal types" they have themselves invented to possess her more thoroughly' (2001: 596). The poet, however, re-contextualizes the metaphor in the context of feminist excesses and its radical and divisive constructions of gender.

31. Malini Bhattacharya explains the cultural politics of the Rithambara myth: 'Invoked by feminists to counter the traditional view of women as victims, it is taken over by Hindutva to give a feminine face to the supreme and triumphant unreason of history. It is on one hand a concession to "modernity", a deliberate demonstration that Hindutva is not incompatible with women's pre-eminence; on the other hand, this pre-eminence is on the basis of a very traditional binary construction in which "male" is associated with "reason" and "female" with "intuition" and "emotion" as opposed to it. In fact, can we deny that certain brands of feminism in our country tend to internalize this reason/emotion opposition, which is nothing but the projection of the "other" by dominant ideology, in this case, patriarchal ideology? Can we deny that in doing so they are not only internalizing patriarchal values, but they also get dangerously close to the ideological trap of historical irrationalism set by Hindutva, a position undermining the concept of equality and social justice, which is basic to the struggle for women's rights?' (1994: 6–7).

32. Post-9/11, women go missing from the public sphere. Laura Zimmerman asks 'Where are the Women?' as she discovers that in the U.S. media, women are constantly marginalized. She quotes a journalist: 'As we witnessed at the time of 9/11 and later during the wars in Afghanistan and Iraq, national

emergencies push women even further to the sidelines. "To feel voiceless in a democracy in so difficult a time," prize-winning journalist Geneva Overholser said on National Public Radio in November 2001, "is very close to feeling disenfranchised"' (2003: 5). In another intervention, Zillah R. Eisenstein finds an all-pervasive 'gender apartheid and sexual terrorism' after 9/11. She provides a feminist explanation of 9/11: 'September 11 must also be viewed in relation to the way that male patriarchal privilege orchestrates its hierarchical system of domination. The age-old fear and hatred of women's sexuality and their forced domestication into womanly and wifely roles informs all economies. Global capitalism unsettles the preexisting sexual hierarchical order and tries to mould women's lives to its newest needs across the East/West divide. Differing factions within the Taliban are fully aware of the stakes involved here, which is, in part, why they root their war strategy in the active subordination of women' (2002: 81).

33. In Meena Alexander's poetry, the bird-poet identification is complete. In 'Ghalib's Ghost', it comes to the fore very graphically:

> I was partridge, the one with speckled wings
> Poking here and there with her beak, gobbling stones.
>
> One afternoon, the roof blew off our house.
> Roofs blew off many houses, courtyards filled with clouds.
>
> I fell from our upper room into a circus.
> Petals paraded through hot skies, veiling sun and moon.
>
> (2004: 15).

34. This is how Dharker defines herself on her own website: 'Imtiaz Dharker (sometimes credited as Dharkar) calls herself a Scottish Muslim Calvinist, brought up in a Lahori household in Glasgow, working in Bombay. She is a poet, artist and documentary film-maker and all her books, *Purdah, Postcards from god, I speak for the devil* and *The terrorist at my table*, include her own drawings. She now lives between India, London and Wales' (see www.imtiazdharker.com). From spellings, to her religion to her location, there is fluidity in her being that becomes a fit subject for a body-snatching game.

35. Meena Alexander's Kabir believes that terror cannot be wrapped in clothes any longer, and that it needs to be confronted collectively. This is how Meena Alexander concludes her poem on 9/11, masquerading as the new Kabir: 'Kabir, the weaver sings/ *O men and dogs/ in times of grief/ our rolling earth/grows small*' ('Kabir Sings in a City of Burning Towers', 2004: 14).

36. For Julia Kristeva, a champion of feminine difference, 'femininity is exactly this lunar form, in the way that the moon is the inverse of the sun of our identity' (1996: 45).

37. In her *The Other Side of Silence*, Butalia's mother, while giving her personal account of the partition speaks thus: '… it took 1984 to make me understand how ever-present Partition was in our lives too, to recognize that it could not be easily put away inside the covers of history books' (1998: 5).

Bibliography

Primary Sources:

(English)

Alexander, Meena. *Illiterate Heart*. Evanston: Triquarterly Books, North Western Press, 2002a.

———. *Raw Silk*. Evanston: Triquarterly Books, North Western Press, 2004.

Ali, Agha Shahid. *The Country Without a Post Office: Poems 1991–1995*. Delhi: Ravidayal, 2000. Indian edn.

———. *Rooms are Never Finished*. Delhi: Permanent Black, 2002.

———. *The Final Collections: Call Me Ishmael Tonight & Rooms are Never Finished*. Delhi: Permanent Black, 2004.

Bhatt, Sujata. *My Mother's Way of Wearing a Sari*. Delhi: Penguin India, 2000.

D'Souza, Charmayne. *A Spelling Guide to Woman*. Delhi: Disha/Sangam Books, 1990.

Daruwalla, Keki. *Collected Poems: Poems 1970–2005*. Delhi: Penguin India, 2006.

Das, Gurcharan. 'Mira', *Three English Plays*. Delhi: OUP, 2001.

Das, Kamala. 'The Sunshine Cat', in R. Parthasarthy, ed., *Ten Twentieth Century Indian Poets*. Delhi: OUP, 1976.

de Souza, Eunice, ed. *Early Indian Poetry in English: An Anthology 1829–1947*. Delhi: OUP, 2005.

Dharker, Imitiaz. *Purdah and Other Poems*. Delhi: OUP, 1989.

———. *Postcards from God*. Delhi: Viking, 1994.

———. *I Speak for the Devil*. Delhi: Penguin India, 2003.

———. *The Terrorist at My Table*. Delhi: Penguin India, 2007.

———. www.imtiazdharker.com.

Ezekiel, Nissim. *Collected Poems 1952–1988*. New Delhi: OUP, 1989.

Gandhi, Leela. *Measures of Home*. Delhi: Ravidayal, 2000.

Gandhi, Mahatma. *Bapu's Letters to Mira*. Ahmedabad: Navjivan Publishing House, 1949.

Hoskote, Ranjit, ed. *Reasons of Belonging*. Delhi: Penguin India, 2002.

———. *Vanishing Acts: New and Selected Poems 1985–2005*. Delhi: Penguin India, 2006.

Kakkar, Sudhir. *Mira and the Mahatma*. Delhi: Penguin, 2004.

Khair, Tabish. *Where Parallel Lines Meet*. Delhi: Penguin India, 2000.

Kolatkar, Arun. *Jejuri*. Bombay: Pras Prakashan, 2001. 6th edn.

———. *Kala Ghoda Poems*. Mumbai: Pras Prakashan, 2004a.

Mahapatra, Jayanta. *A Rain of Rites*. Athens: University of Georgia, 1976.

———. *Waiting*. Delhi: Samkaleen Prakashan, 1979.

———. *Relationship*. New York: Greenfield Review Press, 1980a.

Mahapatra, Jayanta. *Selected Poems.* Delhi: OUP, 1987.

———. *A Whiteness of Bone.* Delhi: Viking, 1992.

Mathur, Anurag. *A Life Lived Later.* Delhi: Penguin India, 2005.

Mehrotra, Arvind. *Middle Earth.* Delhi: OUP, 1984.

———, ed. *The Oxford Anthology of Twelve Indian Poets.* Delhi: OUP, 1992. 6th edn.

———. *The Transfiguring Places.* Delhi: Ravidayal, 1998.

Moraes, Dom. *Collected Poems: 1954–2004.* Delhi: Penguin India, 2004.

Naidu, Sarojini. *The Sceptred Flute.* Allahabad: Kitabistan, 1943.

———. *The Feather of the Dawn.* Bombay: Asia Publishing House, 1961.

Nair, Anita. *Malabar Mind.* Calicut: Yeti Books, 2003.

Nair, Rukmini Bhaya. *The Ayodhya Cantos.* Delhi: Penguin India, 1992.

———. *Yellow Hibiscus: New and Selected Poems.* Delhi: Penguin India, 2004.

Nambisam, Vijay. 'The Deserted Temple'. www.openspaceindia.org/7_vijay.htm. Accessed April 12, 2008.

Namjoshi, Suniti. *Sycorax: New Fables and Poems.* Delhi: Penguin India, 2006.

Padhi, Bibhu. *Painting the House: Poems.* Hyderabad: Disha Books, 1999.

Parthasarthy, R., ed. *Ten Twentieth Century Indian Poets.* Delhi: OUP, 1976a.

———. *Rough Passage.* New Delhi: OUP, 1977.

Ramanujan, A. K. trans. *Speaking of Shiva.* Delhi: Penguin Books, 1973.

———. *Relations.* London: OUP, 1977.

———, trans. *Hymns for the Drowning.* Princeton: Princeton University Press, 1991.

———. *The Collected Poems of A. K. Ramanujan.* Delhi: OUP, 1995.

———. *Uncollected Poems and Prose.* Delhi: OUP, 2001.

Sahni, Archna. *First Fire.* Calicut: Yeti Books, 2005.

Sen, Sudeep. *Postmarked India: New & Selected Poems.* Delhi: Harper Collins Publishers India, 1997.

———. *Distracted Geographies: An Archipelago of Intent.* Delhi: Indialog, 2004.

Seth, Vikram. *The Poems 1981–1994.* Delhi: Penguin India, 1999a.

———. *All You Who Sleep Tonight, The Collected Poems.* Delhi: Penguin India, 1999b.

Tagore, R. *One Hundred Poems of Kabir.* London: Macmillan, 1961.

Thayil, Jeet. *English: Poems.* Delhi: Penguin India, 2003.

(Hindi)

Agney. *Loutata Hoon Us Tak.* Panchkula: Aadhar, 1998.

Alokdhanva. *Duniya Roz Banati Hai.* Delhi: Rajkamal, 1998.

Ambuj, Kumar. *Atikraman.* Delhi: Radhakrishan, 2002.

Anamika. 'Bejagah', in Anamika, ed., *Kahti Hain Auraten.* Allahabad: Itihas Bodh and Sahitya Upkrama, 2003.

———. *Khurdari Hatheliyan.* Delhi: Radhakrishan, 2005.

Atm-Bodh: An Anthology. Ujjain: Madhyapradesh Dalit Sahitya Akademi, 1995.

Bharati, Amrita. 'Ek Chal Rahi Bhoomika', in Lucy Rosenstein, ed. and trans., *New Poetry in Hindi (Nai Kavita): An Anthology.* Delhi: Permanent Black, 2003.

Bharati, Dharamveer. *Andha Yug*. Alok Bhalla, trans. Delhi: OUP, 2005.

Bharati, Kanwal. *Dr. Ambedkar kee Kavitayei. Multiple Marginalities: An Anthology of Identified Dalit Writings*. Badri Narayan and A. R. Misra, eds. Delhi: Manohar, 2004.

Boddhisatav. *Hum Jo Nadiyon Ka Sangay Hain*. Delhi: Radhakrishan, 2000.

Changosiya, Rameshchandra. *Ujala*. Ujjain: Madhyapradesh Dalit Sahitya Akademi, 1995.

Chaturvedi, Pankaj. *Ek Sampoornta Ke Liye*. Panchkula: Aadhar, 1998.

Chaturvedi, Sanjay. *Prakashvarsh*. Panchkula: Aadhar, 1993.

Chauhan, Subhadra Kumari. 'Jhansi ki Rani', www.manaskriti.com/kaavyaalaya/jhansi. Accessed August 11, 2007.

Dabral, Manglesh. *Hum Jo Dekhte Hain*. Delhi: Radhakrishan, 1995.

Bharati, Kanwal, ed. *Dalit: Nirvachit Kavitain* Faridabad (Haryana): Sahitya Upkram, 2006.

Dalit Sahitya (2004 & 2005) Varshiki. Jayprakash Kardam, ed. Vol. 6, No. 6 and 7.

Dangwal, Viren. *Dooshchakra Mien Strashta*. Delhi: Rajkamal, 2002.

Dhoomil, Sudama Pandey. 'Mochiram', *Sansad se Sadak Tak*. Delhi: Rajkamal Prakashan, 1980. 3rd edn.

Dinkar, Ramdhari Singh. *Rashmirathi*. Patna: Udyachal, 1960.

Garg, Nirmala. *Kabari Ka Tarazoo*. Delhi: Radhakrishan, 2002.

Gill, Gagan. *Ek Din Lautegi Ladki*. Delhi: Rajkamal, 1989.

Gupt, Maithilisharan. *Bharat Bharati*. Chirgaon: Saket Prakashan, 1989. 3rd edn.

Gupta, Ramnika, ed. *Dalit Chetna: Kavita*. Hazaribagh (Bihar): Navlekhan Prakashan, 1996.

Harishchandra, Bhartendu. *Bharat Durdasha* in Brijratandas, ed., *Bhartendu Granthawali*. Kashi: Nagri Pracharini Sabha, 1951a.

Jagudi, Leeladhar. *Ishwar ki Adhyakshta Mein*. Delhi and Patna: Rajkamal, 1999.

Jain, Indu. 'Freedom', in Kailash Vajpeyi, ed., *An Anthology of Modern Hindi Poetry*. Delhi: Rupa, 1998.

Jha, Krishan Mohan. *Samay Ko Cheerkar*. Panchkula: Aadhar, 1998.

Joshi, Rajesh. *Nepathya Mein Hansi*. Delhi and Patna: Rajkamal, 1994.

———. *Do Panktiyon ke Beech*. New Delhi and Patna: Rajkamal, 2000.

———. *Dhoop Ghari*. New Delhi and Patna: Rajkamal, 2002.

Kabir. *The Bijak of Kabir*. Ahmad Shah, trans. Delhi: Asian Publication Services, 1977. 1st edn. 1917.

———. *The Bijak of Kabir*. Linda Hess and Shukdeo Singh, trans. Delhi: OUP, 2002.

———. *Kabir: The Weaver's Songs*. Vinay Dharwadkar, trans. Delhi: Penguin Books, 2003.

Kamal, Arun. *Saboot*. New Delhi: Vani, 1989.

Kamal, Arun. *Dhoop Ghari*. New Delhi and Patna: Rajakamal, 2002.

———. *Naye Illake Mein*. Delhi: Vani, 1999. 2nd edn.

Katyayni. *Es Paurushpoorn Samay Mein*. Delhi: Vani, 1999.

———. *Jadoo Nahin Kavita*. Delhi: Vani, 2002a.

———. 'Ah Mere Logo! O Mere Logo!', *Udbhavana Pustika: Gujarat par Kavi*. Delhi: Udbhavana, November 2002b.

Kukrati, Hamant. *Naya Basta*. Delhi: Vani, 2002.

Kumar, Vijay, ed. *Sadi Ke Ant Mein Kavita*. Delhi: Radhakrishan, 1998.

Malay. *Likhne Ka Nakshtra*. Delhi and Patna: Radhakrishan, 2002.

Mandloi, Leeladhar. *Raat Biraat*. Panchkula: Aadhar, 1995.

Meera. *Songs of Meera: In the Dark of the Heart*. Shama Futehally, trans. Delhi: HarperCollins Publishers, 1997. 2nd edn.

Mirabai. *Devotional Poems of Mirabai*. A. J. Alston, trans. Delhi: Motilal Banarsidass, 1980.

Muktibodh, Gajananmadhav. 'Andhere Mein', *Pratinidhi Kavitain*. Delhi: Rajkamal Prakashan, 1991. 4th paperback edn.

Narayan, Badri and A. R. Misra, eds. *Multiple Marginalities: An Anthology of Identified Dalit Writings*. Delhi: Manohar, 2004.

Nirala, Suryakant Tripathi. 'Ram ki Shakti Pooja', *Anamika*. Allahabad: Bharati Bhandar, 1988a. 8th edn.

Prakash, Uday. *Raat Mein Harmonium*. Delhi: Vani, 1998.

Rosenstein, Lucy, ed. and trans. *New Poetry in Hindi (Nai Kavita): An Anthology*. Delhi: Permanent Black, 2003.

Rubin, David, trans. *The Return of Sarasvati: Four Hindi Poets*. Delhi: OUP, 1998.

Saxena, Naresh. *Samudra Par Ho Rahi Hai Barish*. Delhi: Rajkamal, 2001.

Shukla, Dinesh Kumar. *Kabhi Ton Khulein Kapaat*. Allahabad: Anamika, 1999.

Shukla, Prayag. *Beete Kitne Baras*. Delhi: Vani, 1992.

Srivastava, Aikant. *Ann Hain Mere Shabd*. Panchkula: Aadhar, 1994.

Srivastava, Mithilesh. *Kisi Ummeed Ki Tarah*. Panchkula: Aadhar, 1999.

Sumanakshar, Dr. Sohanpal. *Sindhu Ghati Bol Uthi*. Delhi: Rashtriya Prakashan Samiti, 1990.

———, ed. *Ambedkar Shatak*. Delhi: Bhartiya Dalit Sahitya Akademi, 1992.

Vajpeyi, Ashok. *Samay ke Aas Pass*. Delhi and Patna: Rajkamal, 2000.

Vajpeyi, Kailash, ed. *An Anthology of Modern Hindi Poetry*. Delhi: Rupa, 1998.

Valmiki, Omprakash. *Buss! Bahut Ho Chuka*, Delhi: Vani, 1997.

Verma, Mahadevi. 'Main Neer Bhari Dhookh ke Badli', *Mahadevi Sahitya*. Jhansi: Setu Prakashan, 1970.

(Punjabi)

Amrit, Sukhwinder. *Kanian*. Ludhiana: Lahore Book Shop, 2000.

———. *Dhup dee Chunni*. Chandigarh: Lokgeet Prakashan, 2006.

Atamjit. *Pooran*. Amritsar: Jaideep Prakashan, 1991.

Aulukh, Ajmer Singh. *Salwan*. Chandigarh: Lokgeet Prakashan, 1997.

Batalavi, Shiv Kumar. *Luna*. Sant Singh Sakhon, trans. *Bharati Journal of Comparative Literature*, Vol. 1, No. 1. 1985.

Brar, Deep Shikha. Untitled Poem, *Trishunku*. Poetry Special Issue, No. 31–32, July–October, 2005.

Dard, Hira Singh. *Chonwin Dard Sunehe*. Jallandhar: Punjabi Brothers Educational Publishers, 1944.

Dheer, Santokh Singh. *Aaun Wala Sooraj*. Delhi: Navyug Publishers, 1985.

'Dil', Lal Singh. *Naglok*. Jallandhur: Lakeer Prakashan, 1997.

Gharu, Iqbal. *Jai Bhim, Jai Bharat*. Amritsar: Naveen Prakashan, 2002.

Hundal, Harbhajan Singh. *Kale Din*. Amritsar: New Age Book Centre, 1978.

Kallarmajri, Gurmeet. *Nadiyo Vapis Parat Aao*. Jallandhar: Shiv Prakashan, 2002.

Kallarmajri, Gurmeet and Singh, Sarabjeet, eds. Agaj. Bhadson (Patiala): Foreman Yaadgari Prakashan, 2002.

Kaur, Jatinder. 'Feminism', in Vanita, ed., *Punjabi Nari Kavi*. Delhi: National Book Trust, 2005.

Kaur, Pal. *Peengh*. Ludhiana: Chetna, 2007.

Kesar, Kesar Singh, ed. *Ghadar Lahar de Kavita*. Patiala: Punjabi University Publication Bureau, 1995.

Madhopuri, Balbir. *Bhakhda Pataal*. Delhi: Arsi Publishers, 1998.

Musafir, Gurmukh Singh. *Musafirian* and *Toote Khand* in *Musafir de Kavita*. Kartar Singh Duggal, ed. Chandigarh: Musafir Trust, 1999.

Nadeem, Shahid. *Dukh Dariya*. VCD, Lahore: Ajoka Theatre, 2005.

Pash. *Reckoning with Dark Times: 75 Poems of Pash*. Tejwant Singh Gill, trans. Delhi: Sahitya Akademi, 1999.

Pritam, Amrita. *Lummiyan Vatan*. Amritsar and Delhi: Sikh Publishing House Ltd., 1949.

———. 'To Waris Shah', in Khushwant Singh, ed. and trans., *Selected Poems*. Delhi: Bharatiya Jnanpith Publication, 1982.

———. *Kagaz te Canvas*. Delhi: Navyug, 1993.

Ramoowalia, Iqbal. *Palang Panghura*. Delhi: Ajanta Books International, 2000.

Samundra, Shashi. *Bougainvillea de Vastar*. Delhi: Navyug, 1992.

Shabad: Special Issue on Dalit Literature. Vol. 10, July–December 2007.

Shudarak, Sadhu Singh. *Nav Manthan*. Jallandhar: Shiv Prakashan, 2002.

Singh, Pooran. 'Pooran Nath Jogi', *Pooran Singh: Jeevani te Kavita*. Mahinder Singh Randhawa, ed. Delhi: Sahitya Akademi, 1976. 3rd edn.

Tiwana, Manjit. *Dargha*. Delhi: Navyug, 1995.

'Udasi', Sant Ram. *Jeewani Ate Smuchee Rachna*. Rajinder Rahi, ed. Chandigarh: Balraj Sahni Yaadgar Prakashan, 1996.

'Udasi', Sant Ram. *Chonveen Kavita*. Rajinder Rahi, ed. Chandigarh: Lokgeet Prakashan, 2004.

Vanita, ed. *Punjabi Nari Kavi*. Delhi: National Book Trust, 2005.

Veera, Madan. *Bhakhiya*. Jallandhar: Koknoos Prakashan, 2001.

Virdi, M.L. Advocate, ed. *Dalit Peera*, Phagwara: Dalit Panther Punjab Parkashan, 1994.

(Gujarati)

Bhatt, Bindu. *Meera Yagik ki Diary*. Virendra Narayan Singh, trans. Delhi: Rajkamal, 2006.

(Marathi)

Dangle, Arjun, ed. *Poisoned Bread: Translations from Modern Marathi Dalit Literature*. Hyderabad: Orient Longman, 1994 rpt.

Dhasal, Namdeo. 'So That My Mother May Be Convinced. . .', in Gail Omvedt, trans., *We Shall Smash This Prison*. Delhi and London: Longman, 1980.

———. *Namdeo Dhasal: Poet of the Underworld (Poems 1972–2006)*. Dilip Chitre, ed. and trans. Chennai: Navayana, 2007.

Indian Literature: Accent on Marathi Poetry (176). November–December 1996, Vol. 39, No. 6.

Paswan, Dr. Sanjay and Dr. Pramanshi Jaideva, eds. 'Select Pieces of Dalit Poetry', *Encyclopaedia of Dalits in India: Literature*, Vol. 11. Delhi: Kalpaz Publications, 2002.

(Urdu)

Miraji. *Beveled Glass: Selected Translations*, in Geeta Patel, trans. *Lyrical Moments, Historical Hauntings*. Delhi: Manohar, 2005.

Secondary Sources

Adorno, Theodor W. *Prisms*. Samuel Weber, trans. Cambridge: MIT Press, 1981.

———. 'Cultural Criticism and Society', in Brian O'Connor, ed., *Adorno Reader*. Oxford and Malden: Blackwell, 2000.

Ajneya, Satchchidananda Vatsyayan. *Sadanira: Sampoorna Kavitain*. Vol. 1 and 2. Delhi: National Publishing House, 1986.

———. 'Raag-sambandhon ki Prishtha-bhoomi', in Pushpa Bharati, ed., *Dharmvir Bharati ki Sahitya-sadhana*. Delhi: Bhartiya Jnanpith, 2001.

Alexander, Meena. 'The Poet in the Public Sphere': Meena Alexander in Conversation with Lopamudra Basu. *Social Text*, Vol. 20, No. 3, January 2002b.

Ali, Agha Shahid. *The Half Inch Himalayas*. Middletown, Conn.: Wesleyan University Press, 1987.

———. *A Nostalgist's Map of America*. New York and London: Norton, 1991.

Ambedkar, B. R. 'State and Minorities', *Dr. Babasaheb Ambedkar: Writings and Speeches*. Vol. 1. Delhi: Education Department, Government of Maharashtra, 1979a.

———. 'The Buddha and his Dhamma'. *Dr. Babasaheb Ambedkar: Writings and Speeches*. Vol. 11. Delhi: Education Department, Government of Maharashtra, 1979b.

Anderson, Benedict. *Imagined Communities: Reflections on the Origin and Spread of Nationalism*. London and New York: Verso, 1996. 7th Impression.

Appadurai, Arjun. *Modernity at Large: Cultural Dimensions of Globalization*. Delhi: OUP, 1997.

Arendt, Hannah. 'What is Freedom?' *Between Past and Future: Six Exercises in Political Thought*. New York: Penguin Classics, 1961.

Arnold, Matthew. 'Dover Beach', in Charles and Hallam Tennyson, eds., *Victorian Poetry 1830–1890*. London: Ginn & Co., 1971.

Ashcroft, Bill, Gareth Griffiths and Helen Tiffin. *Key Concepts in Post-Colonial Studies*. New York and London: Routledge, 2004. 1st Indian rpt.

Assmann, John. 'Translating Gods: Religion as a Factor of Cultural (Un) translatability', in Sanford Budick and Wolfgong Iser, eds., *The Translatability of Cultures: Figurations of the Space Between.* Stanford: Stanford University Press, 1996.

Bakhtin, Mikhail. *The Dialogic Imagination: Four Essays.* Caryl Emerson and Michael Holquist, trans. Austin: University of Texas Press, 1998. 11th rpt.

Bal, Gian Singh. *Bhagti Paramapara: Santa de Smajik Sarokar.* Chandigarh: Lokgeet Prakashan, 2007.

Ballard, Roger. 'Panth, Kismet, Dharm te Kaum: Continuity and Change in Four Dimensions of Punjabi Region', in Pritam Singh and Shinder Singh Thandi, eds., *Punjabi Identity in a Global Context.* Delhi: OUP, 1999.

Bama. *Karukki.* Lakshmi Holmstrom, trans. Chennai: MacMillan, 2000.

Baral, K. C. 'Protocols of Poetry: A Study of Vikram Seth's *All You Who Sleep Tonight*', in G. J. V. Prasad, ed., *Vikram Seth: An Anthology of Recent Criticism.* Delhi Pencraft, 2004.

Barthes, Roland. *The Pleasure of Text.* Richard Miller, trans. New York: Hill and Wang, 1976.

———'Myth Today', in Susan Sontag, ed., *A Barthes Reader.* New York: Hill and Wang, 1998. 11th printing.

Bassnett, Susan. *Translation Studies.* London and New York: Routledge, 1991.

Batalavi, Shiv Kumar. 'Pooran Bhagat', in Haribhajan Singh, ed., *Kissa Punjab.* Delhi: NBT, 1974.

———. *Shiv Kumar: Sampooran Kavi-Sangra.* Ludhiana: Lahore Book Shop, 1999.

'Bechain', Shyroj Singh. 'Aghoshit Pabnadiyon ke Beech Satta Vimarsh aur Dalit', *Hans,* Special Issue on Dalit Writings, August 2004.

Benjamin, Walter. 'The Task of the Translator', in Marcus Bullock and Michael Jennings, eds., *Walter Benjamin: Selected Writings*, Vol. 1, 1913–1926. Cambridge, Massachusetts, London: The Belknap Press of Harvard University, 1996, 254–55.

Benonana, Gurbaksh Singh, ed. *Kavita Ghadar Lahar ki.* Jallandhar: Desh Bhagat Yaadgar Committee, 2001.

Bentham, Jeremy. *The Panopticon Writings.* Miran Bozovic, ed. London and New York: Verso, 1995.

Benvenuto, Christine. 'Conversation with Agha Shahid Ali', *The Massachusetts Review,* Vol. 43, No. 2, Summer 2002, www. massreview.org/07.

Beston, John B. 'An Interview with Nissim Ezekiel', *World Literature Written in English,* Vol. 16, No. 1, April 1977. University of Texas at Arlington, U.S.

Bhabha, Homi, ed. *Nation and Narration.* London and New York: Routledge, 1990.

———. 'Of Mimicry and Man: The Ambivalence of Colonial Discourse', *The Location of Culture.* New York and London: Routledge, 1994.

Bhagal, Pyara Singh. 'Punjabi ki Upakeshit par Chamatkari Ghadar Kavita', in Gurbaksh Singh Benonana, ed., *Kavita Ghadar Lahar ki.* Jallandhar: Desh Bhagat Yaadgar Committee, 2001.

Bhalla, Alok, trans. 'Introduction' to *Andha Yug*. Delhi: OUP, 2005.

Bharati, Dharamveer. *Kanupriya*. Delhi: Bhartiya Jnanpeeth, 1996. 8th edn.

Bharati, Kanwal. 'Dalit Kavita: Pratikranti ke Swar', in Jayprakash Kardam, ed., *Dalit Sahitya (Varshiki)*, 2005.

———. *Dalit Sahitya ki Avdharana*. Rampur: Boddhisatav Prakashan, 2006.

Bhattacharya, Malini. 'Women in Dark Times: Gender, Culture and Politics', *Social Scientist*, Vol. 22, No. 3/4, March–April, 1994.

Butalia, Urvashi. *The Other Side of Silence: Voices from the Partition of India*. Delhi: Viking, 1998.

———. 'Confrontation and Negotiation: The Women's Movement's Responses to Violence Against Women', in Mala Khullar, ed., *Writing the Women's Movement: A Reader*. Delhi: Zubaan, 2005.

Bihari. *The Satsai*. Krishna P. Bahadur, trans. Delhi: Penguin/UNESCO, 1990.

Birije-Patil, J. 'The Interior Cadences: The Poetry of Nissim Ezekiel', *The Literary Criterion*, Vol. 12, No. 2 and 3, 1976.

Bloom, Harold. *The Anxiety of Influence*. New York: OUP, 1973.

Brodsky, Joseph. *On Grief and Reason: Essays*. London: Penguin, 1995.

Callewaert, Winand M. *The Millennium Kabir Vani*. Delhi: Manohar, 2000.

Chacko, P. M. 'Ezekiel's Family Poems', *Indian Journal of Writings in English*, Vol. 14, No. 2, July 1986.

Chain, Chain Singh, ed. *Ghadar Lahar de Kahani: Ghadari Babian de Jubani*. Jallandhar: Desh Bhagat Yadgar Committee, 2002.

Chandan, Amarjit. 'Sampadaki' to *Bahut Sare Suraj* by Lal Singh 'Dil'. Chandigarh: Lokayat Prakshan, 1992.

———. *Being Here: Ten Poems and a Statement*. Amarjit Chandan, Amim Mughal and John Welch, trans. London: The Many Press, 1993.

Chari, V. K. 'Bhakti and Image Worship', *The Adyar Library Bulletin*, Vol. 59, 1995.

Chatterjee, Partha. *The Nation and Its Fragments: Colonial and Postcolonial Histories*. Princeton: Princeton University Press, 1993.

———. *Nationalist Thought and the Colonial World. The Partha Chatterjee Omnibus*. Delhi: OUP, 2005 (1986). 4th Impression.

Chaturvedi, Jagdish, ed. *Nishedh*. Delhi: Jnan Bharati, 1972.

Chaturvedi, Ramswarup. 'Andha Yug', *Nai Kavita: Ek Sakshya*. Allahabad: Lokbharati, 1973.

Chaudhuri, Sukanta. *Translation and Understanding*. Delhi: OUP, 1999.

Chelliah, J. V., trans. *Pattupattu: The Tamil Idylls*. Tanjavur: Tamil University, 1985.

Chevalier, Jean and Alain Gheerbrant, *Dictionary of Symbols*. John Buchanan-Brown, trans. Harmondsworth: Penguin, 1996.

Chugtai, Ismat. 'Lihaaf' (Quilt), in M. Asaduddin, ed. and trans., *Lifting the Veil: Selected Writings of Ismat Chugtai*. Delhi: Penguin India, 2001a.

———. 'Roots', in M. Asaduddin, ed. and trans., *Lifting the Veil: Selected Writings of Ismat Chugtai*. Delhi: Penguin Books, 2001b.

Cixous, Helene. 'The Newly Born Woman', in Susan Sellers ed., *The Helene Cixous Reader*. New York and London: Routledge, 1994.

Cohn, Bernard C. 'Representing Authority in Victorian India', in Eric Hobsbawm and Terence Ranger, eds., *The Invention of Tradition*. Cambridge: Cambridge University Press, 1992. Canto edn.

Coomaraswamy Ananda. *Essays in National Idealism*. Delhi: Munshiram Manoharlal, 1981. 1st Indian edn.

Dalmia, Vasudha. *The Nationalization of Hindu Traditions: Bhartendu Harishchandra and Nineteenth Century Banaras*. Delhi: OUP, 1997.

Dard, Hira Singh. 'Punjabi Kavi-Itihas vich Ghadar Gunj da Sthan', *Punjabi Duniya*, Vol. 11, No. 2–7, February–July, 1960.

Das, B. K. 'The Self in Nissim Ezekiel's Poetry', in R. S. Pathak, ed., *Quest for Identity in Indian English Writing-II*. New Delhi: Bahri Publications, 1992.

———. 'Ramanujan, the Poet: An Overview', *Indian Literature* (162), Vol. 37, No. 4, July–August, 1994.

Das, Gurcharan. *The Elephant Paradigm: India Wrestles with Change*. Delhi: Penguin Books, 2002.

Derozio, Henry Vivian. 'To India—My Native Land', in Eunice de Souza, ed., *Early Indian Poetry in English: An Anthology 1829–1947*. Delhi: OUP, 2005.

de Souza, Eunice. 'Interviews with Four Indian English Poets', *The Bombay Review*, No. 1, 1989.

———. 'Introduction' to *Nine Indian Women Poets*. Delhi: OUP, 1997.

———. *Talking Poems: Conversations with Poets*. Delhi: OUP, 1999.

Devy, G. N. 'Alienation as a Means of Self-exploration; A Study of A. K. Ramanujan's Poetry', *Chandrabhaga*, No. 6, Winter, 1981.

———. *After Amnesia: Tradition and Change in Indian Literary Criticism*. Bombay: Orient Longman, 1993.

———. *In Another Tongue*. Madras: Macmillan, 1995.

Dharmvir, Dr. *Kabir: Baj Bhi, Kapot Bhi, Papeeha Bhi*. Delhi: Vani, 2000.

Dharwadkar, Vinay. 'Dalit Poetry in Marathi', *World Literature Today*, Vol. 68, No. 2, Spring, 1994.

———. 'Introduction' to *The Weaver's Songs*. Delhi: Penguin Books, 2003.

'Dinkar', Ramdhari Singh. *Kurukshetra*. Patan: Udyachal, 1946. First published in 1943.

Dirks, Nicholas B. *Castes of Mind: Colonialism and the Making of Modern India*. Delhi: Permanent Black, 2002.

Donadio, Rachel. 'The Irascible Prophet: V. S. Naipaul at Home', *The New York Times*. August 7, 2005. http://query.nytimes.com. Accessed February 11, 2008.

Dowson, John. *Classical Dictionary of Hindu Mythology and Religion, Geography, History and Literature*. Whitefish: Kessinger Publishing, 2003. First published in 1888 as a part of Trubner's Oriental Series, London.

Dube, Saurabh. 'Colonial Registers of a Vernacular Christianity', *Economic and Political Weekly*, Vol. 39, No. 2, January 10–16, 2004, 161–71.

Dutt, Nirupama. 'Caste in His Own Image', *The Little Magazine*, Vol. 1, No. 5, November–December 2000.

———. 'Hasdi Udasi', *Ik Nadi Sanwali Jahi*, www.india.poetryinternationalweb.org. Accessed December 19, 2007.

Eisenstein, Zillah. 'Feminisms in the Aftermath of September 11', *Social Text*, Vol. 20, No. 3, 2002.

Eliot, T. S. *The Waste Land*. Frank Kermode, ed. New York: Penguin Classics, 1998.

Ezekiel, Nissim. 'Naipaul's India and Mine', *Journal of South Asian Literature*, Vol. 11, No. 3–4, Spring–Summer, 1976.

Faiz, Ahmed Faiz. *The Rebel Silhouette*. Agha Shahid Ali, trans. Delhi: OUP, 1991.

———. *100 Poems of Faiz Ahmad Faiz*. Sarvat Rahman, trans. Delhi: Abhinav, 2002.

Fanon, Frantz. *The Wretched of the Earth*. London: Penguin Books, 1990 rpt.

Fave, Kelly Le. 'Ghazal', in Agha Shahid Ali, ed., *Ravishing Disunities: Real Ghazals in English*. Delhi: Ravidayal and Permanent Black, 2002.

Figuira, Dorothy Matilda. *Translating the Orient*. Albany: State University of New York Press, 1991.

Fitter, Chris. *Poetry, Space, Landscape: Towards a New Theory*. Cambridge: Cambridge University Press, 1995.

Foucault, Michel. 'Panopticism', *Discipline and Punish*. Harmondsworth: Penguin, 1985.

Fukuyama, Francis. *The End of History and The Last Man*. Harmondsworth: Penguin Books, 1992.

Gaeffke, Peter. 'Kabir in Literature by and for Muslims', in Monika Horstmann, ed., *Images of Kabir*. Delhi: Manohar, 2002.

Gandhi, Leela. *Postcolonial Theory: A Critical Introduction*. Delhi: OUP, 1999.

———. 'Preface' to *Nissim Ezekiel's Collected Poems*. Delhi: OUP, 2005. 2nd edn.

Gandhi, M. K. *Collected Works of Mahatma Gandhi*. Vol. 32. New Delhi: Publications Division, 1958–84.

———. *Hind Swaraj and Other Writings*. Anthony J. Parel, ed. Cambridge: Cambridge University Press, 1997.

———. 'Notes 103', *Collected Works of Mahatma Gandhi*. Vol. 22. Delhi: Publications Division, 1996.

Ganguly, Debjani. 'Can the Dalit Speak: Caste, Postcoloniality and the New Humanities?', *South Asia*, Vol 23, Special Issue, 2000.

Gamble, Sarah. 'Postfeminism', in Sarah Gamble, ed., *The Routledge Companion to Feminism and Postfeminism*. London and New York, 2001.

Gaur, Ramesh. 'Pita ke Naam Ek Patra', in Jagdish Chaturvedi, ed., *Nishedh*. Delhi: Jnanbharati, 1972.

Geertz, Clifford. *Interpretation of Cultures: Selected Essays*. New York: Basic Books, a Division of Harper Collins, 1973.

George, Rosemary Marangoly. 'Calling Kamala Das Queer: Rereading "My Story"', *Feminist Studies*, Vol. 26. No. 3, Points of Departure: Indian and the South Asian Diaspora, Autumn 2000.

Ghosh, Amitav. 'The Ghat of the Only World', *The Imam and The Indian*. Delhi: Ravidayal & Permanent Black, 2002a.

———. 'The Diaspora in Indian Culture', *The Imam and The Indian*. Delhi: Ravidayal & Permanent Black, 2002b.

Giddens, Anthony. *The Nation-State and Violence*. Berkeley: University of California Press, 1987.

Gilbert, Sandra and Susan Gubar. 'The Madwoman in the Attic (1980)', in Julie Rivkin and Michael Ryan, eds., *Literary Theory: An Anthology*. Massachusetts and Oxford: Blackwell, 2001.

Gill, H. S. 'The Human Condition in Puran Bhagat: An Essay in Existential Anthropology of a Punjabi Legend', *Contributions to Indian Sociology*, Vol. 19, No. 1, 1985, Sage Publications, New Delhi/Beverly Hills/London.

Gill, Tejawant Singh. 'Nexus of Myth and Reality in *Luna*', *Bharati Journal of Comparative Literature*, GNDU Amritsar, Vol. 1, No. 1, 1985.

———. 'Painters at the Sikh Court', *Summerhill IIAS Review,* Vol. 7, No. 1 & 2, Summer–Winter, 2001.

Gioia, Dana. 'Disappearing Ink: Poetry at the End of Print Culture', *The Hudson Review*, Vol. 56, No. 1, Spring, 2003.

Goldberg, Ellen. *The Lord Who is Half Woman: Ardhanarisvara in Indian and Feminist Perspective*. New York: SUNY, 2002.

Greenblatt Stephen. 'Culture', in Frank Lentricchia and Thomas McLuaghlin, eds., *Critical Terms for Literary Study*. Chicago and London: The University of Chicago, 1995. 2nd edn.

Guha, Ranajit. 'On Some Aspects of the Historiography of Colonial India', in Ranajit Guha ed., *Subaltern Studies: Writings on South Asian History and Society*, Vol. 1. Delhi: OUP, 1982.

Guha-Thakurta, Tapati. 'The Endangered Yakshi: Careers of an Ancient Art Object in Modern India', in Partha Chatterjee and Anjan Ghosh, eds., *History and the Present*. Delhi: Permanent Black, 2002.

Gupt, Jagdish. *Shambook*. Allahabad: Lokbharati, 1977.

Gupt, Maithilisharan. *Saket*. Chirgaon (Jhansi): Sahitya Sadan, 1974. First published in 1929.

Gurtu, Shachirani, ed., *Mahadevi Varma: Kavya-kala and Jeevan Darshan*. Delhi: Atmaram & Sons, 1951.

Guru, Gopal. 'The Interface Between Ambedkar and the Dalit Cultural Movement in Maharashtra', in Ghanshyam Shah, ed., *Dalit Identity and Politics*. Delhi: Sage, 2001.

'Hariaudh', Ayodhyasingh Upadhyay. *Priyapravas*. Banaras: Hindi Sahitya Kutir, 1947. First published in 1914.

Harishchandra, Bhartendu. 'Hindi ki Unnati par Vyakhyan' in Brijratandas, ed., *Bhartendu Granthavali*. Vol. 2. Kashi: Nagri Pracharini Sabha, 1951b.

'Harit', Biharilal. *Bhimayana*. Delhi: Harit Prakashan, 1973.

Harrex, S. C. 'Small-Scale Reflections on Indian English-Language Poetry', *The Journal of Indian Writings in English*. Vol. 8, No. 1–2, January–February, 1980.

Hasan, Zoya, ed. *Politics and the State in India*. Delhi: Sage, 2000.

Hasrat, Sukhpalveer Singh. 'Loona da Yatharath', *Sooraj di Dosti*. Chandigarh: Raghbir Rachna Prakashan, 1984.

Hawley, John Stratton. *Three Bhakti Voices: Mirabai, Surdas and Kabir in Their Times and Ours*. Delhi: OUP, 2005.

Hitchcock, Peter. 'The Genre of Postcoloniality', *New Literary History*, Vol. 34, No. 2, Spring 2003.

Hobsbawm, Eric. *Nations and Nationalisms Since 1780: Programme, Myth Reality*. Cambridge: Cambridge University Press, 1990.

Hollander, John. 'Ghazal on Ghazals', in Agha Shahid Ali, ed., *Ravishing Disunities: Real Ghazals in English*. Delhi: Ravidayal and Permanent Black, 2002.

Holmstrom, Lakshmi. *Inner Courtyard*. London: Virago, 1990.

Huntington, Samuel. *The Clash of Civilizations and the Remaking of the World Order*. New Delhi: Penguin India, 1997.

Illaiah, Kancha. 'Towards the Dalitization of the Nation', in Partha Chatterjee, ed., *Wages of Freedom: Fifty Years of Indian Nation-State*. Delhi: OUP, 1998.

———. *God as Political Philosopher: Buddha's Challenge to Brahminism*. Kolkata: Samya, 2001.

Ivekovic, Rada and Mostov Julie, eds. 'Introduction' to *From Gender to Nation*. Delhi: Zubaan, 2003.

Jaaware, Aniket. 'Eating, and Eating with, the Dalit: A Re-consideration Touching Upon Marathi Poetry', in K. Satchidanandan, ed., *Indian Poetry: Modernity and After*. Delhi: Sahitya Akademi, 1998.

Jaffrelot, Christophe. *Dr. Ambedkar and Untouchability*. Delhi: Permanent Black, 2004.

Jaidev's *The Culture of Pastiche*. Shimla: IIAS, 1993.

Jain, Naresh. 'Patriarchal Distortions in Folklore'. *Summer Hill IIAS Review*, Vol. 7, No. 1 and 2, Summer–Winter, 2001.

Jameson, Fredric. 'Third-world Literature in the Era of Multinational Capitalism', in Michael Hardt and Kathi Weeks, eds., *Jameson Reader*. Malden and Oxford: Blackwell, 2000a.

———. 'On Interpretation: Literature as a Socially Symbolic Act', in Michael Hardt and Kathi Weeks, eds., *Jameson Reader*. Malden and Oxford: Blackwell, 2000b.

Jas, Dr. Jaswant Singh. *Desh Bhagat Babe*. Jallandhar: New Book Company, 1975.

Jayadeva. *Gitagovinda: Love Song of the Dark Lord*. Barbara Stoler Miller, trans. Delhi: Motilal Banarsidas, 1977.

Joshi, Prabhash. 'Narmada ke Barmaan Ghaat par Inki Jhonpadi', in Suresh Chandra Tyagi, ed., *Bhavani Prasad Mishra*. New Delhi: Asir Prakashan, 1988.

Jussawala, Adil. 'New Poetry: Taking a Line', *Indian Review of Books*, Vol. 1, No. 6, March 1992.

Jyoti, Amar. *Mannu Sita Na Kaho*. Amritsar: Ravi Sahit Prakashan, 1988.

Kallarmajri, Gurmeet. 'Dalit Punjabi Sahit Adhunik Pripekh', *Shabad*. July–December, 2007.

Kamble, Baby. *Jina Amucha* (The Prisons We Broke). Maya Pandit, trans. Chennai: Orient Longman, 2008.

Kamble, Shantabai. *Mhasya Jalmachi Chittaskatha* (Marathi). Pune: Sugava Prakashan, 1998. 3rd edn.

Kapoor, Narinder Singh. 'Ghadar Lahar aur Uski Kavita', in Gurbaksh Singh Benonana, ed., *Kavita Ghadar Lahar ki*. Jallandhar: Desh Bhagat Yaadgar Committee, 2001.

Katrak, Ketu. 'Post-Colonial Women's Colonised States: Mothering and M-othering in Bessie Head's *A Question of Power* and Kamala Das's *My Story*', *Journal of Gender Studies*, Vol. 5, No. 3, 1996.

Kaul, Suvir. *Poems of Nation, Anthems of Empire: English Verse in the Long Eighteenth Century*. Delhi: OUP, 2000.

Keats, John. 'Ode to the Nightingale', in Miriam Allott, ed., *The Poems of John Keats*. London: Longman, 1970.

Keay, F. E. *Kabir and His Followers*. Delhi: Mittal Publications, 1995 rpt. 1st edn. 1931.

Kennedy, Alan. 'The Written Rites', in Madhusudan Prasad, ed., *The Poetry of Jayanta Mahapatra*. New Delhi: Sterling, 1986.

Khare, Sharad Narayan. 'Kshudha-2', *Dalit Sahitya*, 2004.

Khilnani, Sunil. *The Idea of India*. London: Hamish Hamilton, 1997.

Khullar, Ajit. 'Old Psalms for New Times', *Indian Literature*, No. 103, September–October 1984.

King, Bruce. *Three Indian Poets*. Delhi: OUP, 1991.

———. *Modern Indian Poetry in English*. Delhi: OUP, 2001. Revised edn.

Kolatkar, Arun. 'Interview with Four Indian English Poets'. Eunice de Souza, ed. *The Bombay Review*, No. 1, 1989.

———. *Sarpa Satra*. Mumbai: Pras, 2004b.

Kristeva, Julia. 'Stabat Mater', in Robert Con Davis and Ronald Schleifer, eds., *Contemporary Literary Criticism*. New York and London: Longman, 1989.

———. *Julia Kristeva Interviews*. Ross Guberman, ed. New York: Columbia University Press, 1996.

Kumar, Radha. 'Contemporary Indian Feminism', *Feminist Review*. No. 33, Autumn, 1989.

Kumar, Shiv K. 'Poster Prayers of Nissim Ezekiel', *Journal of South Asian Literature*, Vol. 11, No. 3–4, Spring–Summer, 1976.

Kurup, P. K. J. *Contemporary Indian Poetry in English*. Delhi: Atlantic, 1991.

Lacoue-Labarthe, Philippe. *Poetry as Experience*. Andrea Tarnowski, trans. Stanford, California: Stanford University Press, 1999.

Lal, P., ed. *Modern Indian Poetry in English: An Anthology and Credo*. Calcutta: Writers Workshop, 1969.

Lal, Vinay. *Of Cricket, Guinness and Gandhi: Essays on Indian History and Culture*. Calcutta: Penguin India and Seagull Books, 2005.

Lasch, Christopher. *The Minimal Self: Psychic Survival in Troubled Times*. London: Pan Books, 1985.

Li, Victor. 'The Premodern Condition: Neo-Primitivism in Baudrillard and Lyotard', in Tilottama Rajan and Michael J. O'Driscoll, eds., *After Postmodernism: Writing the Intellectual History of Theory*. London, Toronto, Buffalo: University of Toronto Press, 2002.

Limbale, Sharankumar. *Akkarmashi* (Outcaste). Santosh Bhoomkar, trans. Delhi: OUP, 2003.

———. *Towards an Aesthetic of Dalit Literature: History, Controversies and Considerations*. Alok Mukherjee, trans. Hyderabad: Orient Longman, 2004.

Lorenzen, David. 'Who Invented Hinduism?', *Comparative Studies in Society and History*, Vol. 4, No. 41, 1999.

———. 'Marco Della Tomba and the Kabir-Panth', in Monika Horstmann, ed., *Images of Kabir*. Delhi: Manohar, 2002.

Lovesey, Oliver. 'The Place of the Journey in Randolph Stow's "To the Islands" and Sheila Watson's "The Double Hook"', *ARIEL*, Vol. 27, No. 3, July 1996.

Lukacs. *The Theory of the Novel: A Historico-Philosophical Essay on the Forms of Great Epic Literature*. Anna Bostock, trans. Cambridge and Massachusetts: The MIT Press, 1971. First published by P. Cassirer, Berlin, 1920.

Macauliffe, Max Arthur, trans. *The Sikh Religion: Its Gurus, Sacred Writings and Authors*. Vol. 1–10. Oxford: Clarendon Press, 1909.

Madhopuri, Balbir. *Chhangia Rukh*. Chandigarh: Lokgeet Prakashan, 2004.

Mahapatra, Jayanta. 'The Inaudible Resonance in English Poetry in India', *The Literary Criterion*, Vol. 15, No. 1, 1980b.

Mann Tejwant. *Daulat Ram Rachit Panjabi Kissa Kavi: Ek Adhiyan*. Amritsar: Literature House, 1991.

Massey, Reginald. 'A Poet Passionate about the Suffering of Her Punjabi People', Friday, November 4, 2005, *The Guardian*, www.guardian.co.uk/obituaries/story. Accessed January 8, 2008.

Mathai, Anna Sujatha. *Life on My Side of the Street*. Delhi: Sahitya Akademi, 2005.

'Meenu', Rajat Rani. *Navein Dashak ki Hindi Dalit Kavita*. Delhi: Dalit Sahitya Prakashak Sanstha, 1996.

Mehrotra, Arvind. 'The Emperor Has No Clothes', in Amit Chaudhuri, ed., *The Picador Book of Modern Indian Literature*. London: Picador, 2001.

Mehta, Naresh. *Utsava*. Allahabad: Lokbharati Prakashan, 1979.

———. *Mahaprasthan*. Allahabad: Lokbharati Prakashan, 1983.

Menon, Ritu. 'Do Women Have a Country?', in Rada Iveleovic and Julie Mostov, eds., *From Gender to Nation*. Delhi: Zubaan, 2002.

Mies, M. and Vandana Shiva. *Ecofeminism*. London: Zed Books, 1994.

Mishra, Jyotiprasad Nirmal. *Stri-kavi-kaumudi: Hindi mein Striyon ke Kavya-sahitya ka Vistrit Vivechan*. Allahabad: Gandhi Hindi Pustak Bhandar, 1931.

Mishra, Vijay. 'The Diasporic Imaginary: Theorizing the Indian Diaspora', *Textual Practice*, Vol. 10, No. 3, 1996.

———. *Devotional Poetics and the Indian Sublime*. Albany: State University of New York Press, 1998.

———. 'Diaspora and the Art of Impossible Mourning', in Makarand Paranjape, ed., *In Diaspora: Theories, Histories, Texts*. Delhi: Indialog Publications Pvt. Ltd., 2001.

Modleski, Tania. *Feminism Without Borders: Culture and Criticism in 'Post-Feminism'*. London and New York: Routledge, 1991.

Mohan, K. 'Gender Identities in Colonial Punjab', in Pritam Singh and Shinder Singh Thandi, eds., *Punjabi Identity in a Global Context*. Delhi: OUP, 1999.

Mohanty, Chandra Talpade. *Feminism without Borders: Decolonizing Theory, Practicing Solidarity*. Delhi: Zubaan, 2003.

Mohanty, Manoranjan. 'Ideology and Strategy of Communist Movement in India', in Thomas Pantham and Kenneth L. Deutsch, eds., *Political Thought in India*. New Delhi: Sage, 1986.

Mohanty, Niranjan. 'Chicago and AKR', *Indian Literature* (162), Vol. 37, No. 4, July–August, 1994.

Mohanty, Satya P. 'Identity, Multiculturalism, Justice', *Literary Theory and The Claims of History*. Delhi: OUP, 1998.

Moraru, Christian. *Rewriting: Postmodern and Cultural Critique in the Age of Cloning*. New York: State University of New York Press, 2001.

Murugkar, Lata. 'Dalit Panthers Manifesto', *Dalit Panthers Movement in Maharashtra: A Sociological Appraisal*. Bombay: Popular Prakashan, 1991.

Musafir, Gurmukh Singh. *Musafir Diya Kahaniyan-2*. Kartar Singh Duggal, ed. Chandigarh: Musafir Trust, 1999.

Naik, M. K. 'Echo and Voice in Indian Poetry in English', in Chirantan Kulshrestha, ed., *Contemporary Indian English Verse: An Evaluation*. Delhi: Arnold Heinemann, 1980.

Naipaul, V. S. *India: Million Mutinies Now*. London: Minerva, 1997.

———. 'The Testament of the Tenth Muse', in K. Satchidanandan, ed., *Indian Poetry: Modernism and After*. Delhi: Sahitya Akademi, 2001.

Nandy, Ashis. *The Intimate Enemy: Loss and Recovery of Self Under Colonialism*. New Delhi: OUP, 1993 rpt.

Nehru, Jawaharlal. *An Autobiography*. London: Beadley Head, 1936.

———, Joginder. *Punjabi Canadian Sahit*. Chandigarh: Lokayat Prakashan, 1998.

Nemade, Bhalchandra. 'Nativism in Literature', in Makarand Paranjape, ed., *Nativism: Essays in Criticism*. Delhi: Sahitya Akademi, 1997.

Nilsson, Usha S. *Mira Bai*. Delhi: Sahitya Akademi, 1977. 2nd edn.

Nimesh, Ramdas. *Bhimkathamritam*. Delhi: Galaxy Publication Council, 1990.

Nirala, Suryakant Tripathi. *Tulsidas*. Allahabad: Bharati Bhandar, 1938.

———. *Parimal*. Lucknow: Ganga Granthagar, 1949a.

———. 'Panchvati-Prasang' and 'Shivaji ka Patra', *Parimal*, Lucknow: Ganga Granthagar, 1949b. First published in 1930.

———. 'Badal Raag', *Parimal*. Lucknow: Ganga Granthagar, 1956. 7th edn.

———. 'Jago Phir Ek Bar I & II', *Rag-Virag*. Ramvilas Sharma, ed. Allahabad: Lokbharati Prakashan, 1980a. 6th edn.

———. 'Kukurmutta', in Ramvilas Sharma, ed., *Raag-Viraag: Nirala ki Sarvashreshtha Kavitayein*. Allahabad: Lokbharati, 1980b. 6th edn.

———. 'Todti Patthar', *Anamika*. Allahabad: Bharati Bhandar, 1988b. 8th edn.

Olds, Mason. 'Religious Humanism', *Utah Humanist*, Autumn, 1995, http:/www.humanistsofutah.org/1996. Accessed February 15, 2008.

Omvedt, Gail. *We Shall Smash This Prison!* Delhi, London: Orient Longman, 1980.

———. 'Ambedkar and After: The Dalit Movement in India', in Ghanshyam Shah, ed., *Dalit Identity and Politics*. Delhi: Sage, 2001.

———. *Buddhism in India: Challenging Brahmanism and Caste*. Delhi: Sage, 2003.

Orsini, Francesca. *The Hindi Public Sphere 1920–1940: Language and Literature in the Age of Nationalism*. Delhi: OUP, 2002.

Pai, Sudha, 'From Harijan to Dalits: Identity Formation, Political Consciousness and Electoral Mobilization of Scheduled Castes in Uttar Pradesh', in Ghanshyam Shah, ed., *Dalit Identity and Politics*. New Delhi, Thousand Oaks and London: Sage, 2001.

———. *Dalit Assertion and the Unfinished Democratic Revolution: The Bahujan Samaj Party in Uttar Pradesh*. Delhi: Sage, 2002.

Pant, Sumitranandan. 'Bharatmata Gramvasini', David Rubin, trans. *The Return of Sarasvati*. Delhi: OUP, 2002. Paperback.

Paranjape, Makarand. 'Introduction' to *Sarojini Naidu: Selected Poetry and Prose*. Delhi: Indus, 1993.

———. 'Reflections on the Changing Identity of Indian English Verse', in K. Satchidanandan, ed., *Indian Poetry: Modernism and After*. Delhi: Sahitya Akademi, 2001.

Partharsthy, R. 'How it Strikes a Contemporary: The Poetry of A. K. Ramanujan', *The Literary Criterion*, Vol. 12, No. 2 and 3, 1976b.

———. 'The Exile as Writer: On Being an Indian Writer in English', *The Journal of Commonwealth Literature*, Vol. 24, No. 1, 1989.

Pash. *Ud de Baajan Magar*. Amritsar: Balraj Sahni Yaadgar Gherelu Pustakmala, 1974.

Patel, Geeta. *Lyrical Moments, Historical Hauntings: On Gender, Colonialism, and Desire in Miraji's Urdu Poetry*. Delhi: Manohar, 2005.

Patel, Tara. *Single Woman*. Delhi: Rupa, 1991.

Patke, Rajeev S. *Postcolonial Poetry in English*. New York: OUP, 2006.

Pawade, Kumud. *Antasphota* (Marathi). Aurangabad: Anand Prakashan, 1995. 2nd edn.

Perry, John Oliver. 'Determinations of Poetry', in Madhusudan Prasad, ed., *The Poetry of Jayanta Mahapatra*. New Delhi: Sterling, 1986.

———. *Absent Authority: Issues in Contemporary Indian English Criticism*. New Delhi: Sterling, 1992.

Plato. *The Republic*. Benjamin Jowett, trans. http://classics.mit.edu/Plato/republic. Accessed April 12, 2008.

Poetry Review, Vol. 83, No. 1, Spring 1993.

Prasad, Jayashankar. *Kamayani*. Varanasi: Prasad Prakashan, 1936.

Prasad, Mata. *Hindi Kavya mien Dalit Kavyadhara*. Varanasi: Vishvavidyalay Prakashan, 1993.

Radhakrishanan, R. *Diasporic Mediations: Between Home and Location*. University of Minnesota Press: Minneapolis and London, 1996.

———. 'The Use and Abuse of Multiculturalism', *Theory in an Uneven World*. Malden and Oxford: Blackwell, 2003. Indian rpt. 2004.

Rahman, Anisur. 'On Translating a Form: The Possible/Impossible Ghazal in English', in Anisur Rahman, ed., *Translation: Poetics and Practice*. Delhi: Creative Books, 2002.

Rai, Alok. *Hindi Nationalism*. Delhi: Orient Longman, 2001.

Ram, Ronki. 'Untouchability in India with a Difference; Ad Dharm, Dalit Asssertion and Caste Conflicts in Punjab'. *Asian Survey*, Vol. 44, No. 6, November/December, 2004.

Ramabai, Pandita. 'The High-Caste Hindu Woman', in Meera Koshambi, ed., *Pandita Ramabai Through Her Own Words: Selected Works*. Delhi: OUP, 2000.

Ramakrishnan, E. V. *Making It New*. Shimla: IIAS, 1995.

Ramanujan, A. K. *The Interior Landscape: Love Poems from a Classical Tamil Anthology*. Bloomington: Indiana University Press, 1967. Later Published by OUP, Delhi in 1994.

Ramanujan, A. K. trans. *Poems of Love and War: From the Eight Anthologies and the Ten Long Poems of Classical Tamil*. Delhi: OUP, 1996. First published in 1985 by Columbia University Press, New York.

———. 'The Indian Oedipus', in T. G. Vaidyanathan and Jeffery J. Kirpal, eds., *Vishnu on Freud's Desk: A Reader in Psychoanalysis and Hinduism*. Delhi: OUP, 1999.

Ramazani, Jahan. *The Hybrid Muse: Postcolonial Poetry in English*. Chicago and London: The University of Chicago Press, 2001.

Rao, Raja. *The Meaning of India*. Delhi: Vision Books, 1996.

Rao, R. Raj. *Nissim Ezekiel: An Authorized Biography*. New Delhi: Viking, 2000.

Rg Veda Samhita: Hymns from the Rg Veda. Jean Le Mee, trans. New York: Alfred A. Knopf, Inc., 1975.

Rode, Ajmer and Bharati Navtej. *Leela*. Vancouver: Rainbird Press, 1999.

Rosenstein, Lucy. 'Eighteen Poems', *Hindi: Language, Discourse, Writing*. Vol. 2, No. 4, January–March 2002.

Rushdie, Salman. *Imaginary Homelands: Essays and Criticism 1981–1991*. London: Granta Books, 1991.

———. *Midnight's Children*. London: Vintage, 1995.

———. 'In Defence of the Novel, Yet Again', *Step Across This Line: Collected Non-Fiction 1992–2002*. London: Jonathan Cape, 2002.

Sahni, Santosh. *Thhor Kamlani*. Delhi: Navyug, 1972.

Said, Edward. *Culture and Imperialism*. London: Chatto & Windus, 1993.

———. *Reflections on Exile and other Literary and Cultural Essays*. Delhi: Penguin India, 2001.

———. 'On Mahmoud Darwish', www.grandstreet.com/gsissues/gs48. Accessed March 10, 2008.

'Sainik', Naresh Chandra Saxena. *Amar Balidani Jhalkaribai*. Allahabad: Sahitya Sangam, 2002.

Sangari, Kumkum. 'Feminist Criticism and Indian Literary History', *Hindi: Language, Discourse, Writing*, A Journal of Mahatama Gandhi International Hindi University, Vol. 2, No. 4, January–March 2002.

Sara, Har Iqbal Singh. 'The Scythian Origins of the Sikh Jat', *Panjab Past and Present*. Ganda Singh, ed. Vol. 11, Part 2, Serial No. 22, 1977, 247–69.

Sarkar, Tanika. *Hindu Wife, Hindu Nation: Community, Religion and Cultural Nationalism*. Delhi: Permanent Black, 2001.

Sarvagoda, Mukta. *Mitaleli Kavade* (Marathi). Pune: Cetasri Prakasana, 1983.

Saxena, Sarveshwar Dayal. *Sampoorna Gadhya Rachnain*, Vol. 4. New Delhi: Kitab Ghar, 1992.

Schomer, Karine. *Mahadevi Varma and the Chhayavad Age of Modern Hindi Poetry*. Berkeley: University of California Press, 1983.

Shah, Ramesh Chandra. 'Bhakti-Poetry in Hindi: Its Response to Challenges', in C. D. Narasimhaiah and C. N. Srinath, eds., *Bhakti in Literature*. Mysore: Dhavayaloka, 1989.

Shahane, Vasante A. 'The Religious-Philosophical Strain in Nissim Ezekiel's Poetry', *Journal of South Asian Literature*, Vol. 11, No. 3–4, Spring–Summer, 1976.

Shankaranand, Swami and Ayodhyanath Brahmchari. *Shankranand Bhajanavali*. Ganeshpura (Mainpuri): Padam Singh Bookseller, 1945.

Sharma, Ramvilas. *Bhartenduyug aur Hindi Bhasha ki Vikas Parampara*. Delhi: Rajakamal, 1975. Rev. edn.

Sher-Gil, Amrita. 'Indian Art Today', in Vivan Sundaram, *Amrita Sher-Gil*. Bombay: Marg Publications, 1972.

Shiva, Vandana. *The Violence of Green Revolution: Third World Agriculture, Ecology and Politics*. Goa: The Other India Press, 1991.

Showalter, Elaine. 'Feminist Criticism in Wilderness', in Robert Con Davis and Ronald Schliefer, eds., *Contemporary Literary Criticism*. New York and London: Longman, 1989.

Sidhu, Sewa Singh. *Giani Hira Singh Dard: Jeewan te Rachna*, Patiala: Punjabi University, Publication Bureau, 1982.

Singh, Doodhnath. *Nirala: Atmahanta Aastha*. Allahabad: Neelabh Prakashan, 1972.

Singh, Gulwant. *Kadaryar: Jeevan te Rachana*. Patiala: Punjabi University, 1980.

Singh, Gurbhagat. 'Difference and Discourse', *Indian Literature* (150), Vol. 35, No. 4, July–August, 1992.

Singh, Gurcharan, ed. *Babbar-Kav Sangreh*. Patiala: Publication Bureau, Punjabi University, 1988.

Singh, Dr. Gurcharan. *Studies in Punjab History and Culture*. New Delhi: Enkay Publishers, 1990.

Singh Gurharpal, Parekh, Bhikhu and Vertovec Steven, eds. *Culture and Economy in the Indian Diaspora*. London and New York: Routledge, 2003.

Singh, Dr. Guriqbal. *Naxali Punjabi Kavita: Alochnatmak Adhiyan*. Ludhiana: Chetna Prakashan, 1999.

Singh, Guru Gobind. 'Bachitra Natak', in Dr. Sewa Singh, ed., *Dasam Granth de Chonvi Baan*. Delhi: NBT, 1998.

Singh, Dr. Jodh. 'Thematic Study of Bachtra Natak', in S. S. Bhatia and Anand Spencer, eds., *The Sikh: Tradition and A Continuing Reality: Essays in History and Religion*. Patiala: Publication Bureau, Punjabi University, 1999.

Singh, Mohan. 'Mukh Band' (Preface) to *Musafirian*, in Kartar Singh Duggal, ed., *Musafir de Kavita*. Chandigarh: Musafir Trust, 1999.

Singh, Namvar. *Namvar Sanchiyata*. Nand Kishor Naval, ed. New Delhi and Patna: Rajkamal, 2003.

Singh, Pankaj. *Re-presenting Woman: Tradition, Legend and Punjabi Drama.* Shimla: IIAS, 2000.

Singh, Pooran. *On Paths of Life.* Delhi: Uttar Chand Kapoor and Sons, n.d.

———. *The Spirit of the Sikh.* Patiala: Punjabi University, 1981.

Singh, Pritam. *Punjab Economy: The Emerging Pattern.* New Delhi: Enkay Publishers, 1995.

Singh, Raghbir. 'Andeman te Bharati Jailan Vich', *Kale Pannian de Dastan.* Jallandhar: Virsa Prakashan, Desh Bhagat Yadgar Committee, 2002.

Singh, Dr. Sarabjit. *Parampara te Pravah.* Chetna Prakashan: Ludhiana, 2002.

Singh, Satyanarain. 'Journey into Self: Nissim Ezekiel's Recent Poetry' in Vasant A. Shahane and M. Shivaramakrishna, eds., *Indian Poetry in English: A Critical Assessment.* Bombay: Macmillan, 1980.

Singh, Ujjwal Kumar. *Political Prisoners in India.* Delhi: OUP, 1998.

Skinner, Quentin. 'Introduction', *The Return of Grand Theory in the Human Sciences.* Cambridge: Cambridge University Press, 2000 rpt., Canto Paperbacks.

Spivak, Gayatri Chakravorty. 'Discussion: An Afterword on the New Subaltern', in Partha Chatterjee and Pradeep Jeganathan, eds., *Subaltern Studies*, Vol. 11. Delhi: Permanent Black and Ravidayal Publishers, 2000.

Sri Guru Granth Sahib. 'Shalok 99', *Shaloks of Baba Farid.* Dr. Gopal Singh, trans. Vol. 4. Delhi, London, New York: World Sikh Centre, 1984.

Sridhar, M. 'Caste, Religion and Gender: Forms of Oppression in Telugu Dalit Women's Poetry', in Malashri Lal, Shromishtha Panja and Sumanyu Satpathy, eds., *Signifying the Self: Women and Literature.* Delhi: Macmillan India, 2004.

Srinivas, M. N. *Social Change in Modern India.* New Delhi: Orient Longman, 1998 rpt.

Stevens, Wallace. 'Thirteen Different Ways of Looking at a Blackbird', *The Collected Poems of Wallace Stevens.* New York: Vintage Books, 2000.

Sudhakar, Lakshminarayan. *Bhimsagar.* Delhi: Harit Prakashan, 1985.

Tagore, Rabindranath. *Gitanjali.* London: MacMillan, 1952.

———. *Rabindranath Tagore: Selected Writings on Literature and Language.* Sisir Kumar Das and Sukanta Chaudhuri, eds. Delhi: OUP, 2001a.

———. 'Baul Songs: A Review of the Book *Sangit Sangraha: Bauler Gatha*', in Sisir Kumar Das and Sukanta Chaudhuri, eds., *Rabindranath Tagore: Selected Writings on Literature and Language.* Delhi: OUP, 2001b.

Tahir, M. Athir. 'A Coat of Many Colours: The Problematics in Qadiryar', in Pritam Singh and Shinder Singh Thandi, eds., *Punjabi Identity in a Global Context.* Delhi: OUP, 1999.

Thapar, Romila. *Cultural Transaction and Early India.* Delhi: OUP, 1987.

Tharoor, Shashi. *The Great Indian Novel.* Delhi: Penguin India: 1993.

———. *India: From Midnight to the Millennium.* Delhi: Penguin Books India, 1998.

Tharu, Susie and K. Lalita, eds. *Woman Writing in India: 600 B.C. to the Present.* Vol. 1. Delhi: OUP, 1995.

The Holy Bible: The Old Testament. Vol. 2. New York: Thomas Nelson & Sons, 1952.

The Longman Dictionary of Poetic Terms. Jack Myers and Michael Simms, eds. New York: Longman, 1989.

The Shorter Oxford English Dictionary. Vol. 1. William Little, H. W. Fowler and Jessie Coulson, eds. Oxford: Clarendon Press, 1973.

Tiwana, Dalip Kaur. *Katha Kaho Urvashi.* New Delhi: Navyug Publishers, 1999.

Tiwana, Manjit. *Savitri.* Delhi: Navyug, 1989.

Tolan, Fiona. 'Feminisms', in Patricia Waugh, ed., *Literary Theory and Criticism: An Oxford Guide.* Delhi: OUP, 2006. 1st Indian edn.

Trivedi, Harish. 'Progress of Hindi: Part 2', in Sheldon Pollock, ed., *Literary Cultures in History: Reconstructions from South Asia.* Delhi: OUP, 2004.

Trumpp, E., trans. *The Adi Granth or The Holy Scriptures of the Sikhs.* Delhi: Munshiram Manoharlal Publishers Pvt. Ltd., 1978. 3rd edn.

Valmiki, Omprakash. 'Premchand: Dalit Sahitya Ke Sandharbha Mein', *Dalit Sahitya,* 2005.

Vanita, Ruth. 'Introduction' to *Love's Rite: Same-Sex Marriage in Indian and the West.* Delhi: Penguin India, 2005.

Vaudeville, Charlotte. *Kabir.* Vol. 1. Oxford: Clarendon Press, 1974.

———, trans. *A Weaver Named Kabir.* Delhi: OUP, 1993. 2nd Impression, 2001.

Verma, Archana. 'Mahadevi: Saseem se Aseem Ki Aor', *Vak,* No. 2, April–June 2007.

Verma, Mahadevi. *Deep Shikha.* Allahabad: Bharati Bhandar, 1962a.

———. *Rashmi.* Allahabad: Sahitya Bhavan, 1962b. 6th edn. First edn. 1932.

———. *Nihar.* Allahabad: Sahitya Bhavan, 1971. 7th edn. First edn. 1930.

Verma, Dr. Ramkumar. *Eklavya.* Allahabad: Lokbharati, 1973. 2nd edn.

Vertovec, Steven. 'Three Meanings of Diaspora', *The Hindu Diaspora: Comparative Patterns.* London and New York: Routledge, 2000.

Vidyapati. 'Two Poems', in K. Ayyappa Paniker, ed., *Medieval India Literature: An Anthology.* Vol. 2. J. P. Srivastav, trans. Delhi: Sahitya Akademi, 1999.

Vimal, Kumar. 'Bharati ki Kanupriya', in Pushpa Bharati, ed., *Dharmvir Bharati ke Sahitya-sadhana.* Delhi: Bhartiya Jnanpith, 2001.

Vinay. 'Mukhbir', in Jagdish Chaturvedi, ed., *Nishedh.* Delhi: Jnan Bharati, 1972.

Viramma, Josiane Racine and Jean-Luc Racine. *Viramma.* New York and London: Verso, 1998.

Walcott, Derek. *Sea Grapes.* London: Jonathan Cape Ltd., 1976.

———. *Midsummer.* London and Boston: Faber and Faber, 1984 edn.

Westcott, Rev. G. H. *Kabir and the Kabir Panth.* Delhi: Munshiram Manoharlal Publishers Pvt. Ltd, 1986. 2nd Revised edn. First published by Christ Church Mission Press, Cawnpore, 1907.

Weyer, Robert Van de. 'Introduction' to *The Harper Collins Book of Prayers.* New Jersey: Castle Bridge, 1997.

Whelehan, Imelda. *Feminist Thought: From the Second-Wave to 'Post-Feminism'.* Edinburgh: Edinburgh University Press, 1995.

White, Hayden. *Tropics of Discourse: Essays in Cultural Criticism.* Baltimore and London: The Johns Hopkins University Press, 1985.

Whitman, Walt. *Leaves of Grass.* Sculley Bradley and Harold W. Blodgett, eds. New York: A Nortan Critical Edition, 1973.

Williams, Raymond. *Keywords: A Vocabulary of Culture and Society*. London: Fontana Press, 1976.

———. 'Base and Superstructure in Marxist Cultural Theory', in Jon Higgins, ed., The Raymond Williams Reader. Oxford and Malden: Blackwell, 2001.

Wilson, H. H. *A Sketch of the Religious Sects of the Hindus*. Delhi: Cosmo Publications, 1977. 1st edn. 1861.

Yeats, W. B. *The Variorum Edition of the Poems of W. B. Yeats*. Peter Allt and Russell K. Alspach, eds. New York: The Macmillan Company, 1957.

Zelliot, E. *From Untouchable to Dalit: Essays on Ambedkar Movement*. New Delhi: Manohar, 1992.

———. 'Stri Dalit Sahitya: The New Voices of Woman Poets', in Anne Feldhaus, ed., *Images of Woman in Maharashtrian Literature and Religion*. Albany NY: SUNY, 1996.

———. 'Of Dalit and Culture', http://frontierweekly.googlepages.com/dalits-38–49.pdf. Accessed November 17, 2007.

Zimmerman, Laura. 'Where Are the Women?: The Strange Case of the Missing Feminists. When Was the Last Time You Saw One on TV?', *The Women's Review of Books*, Vol. 21, No. 1, October, 2003.

Index

For Product Safety Concerns and Information please contact our EU
representative GPSR@taylorandfrancis.com
Taylor & Francis Verlag GmbH, Kaufingerstraße 24, 80331 München, Germany